THE FOREVER BOX

THE FOREVER BOX

The
FOREVER
BOX

Kristin Clark Taylor

B

BERKLEY BOOKS, NEW YORK

A BERKLEY BOOK
Published by the Penguin Group
Penguin Group (USA) Inc.
375 Hudson Street, New York, New York 10014, USA
Penguin Group (Canada), 90 Eglinton Avenue East, Suite 700, Toronto, Ontario M4P 2Y3, Canada
(a division of Pearson Penguin Canada Inc.)
Penguin Books Ltd., 80 Strand, London WC2R 0RL, England
Penguin Group Ireland, 25 St. Stephen's Green, Dublin 2, Ireland (a division of Penguin Books Ltd.)
Penguin Group (Australia), 250 Camberwell Road, Camberwell, Victoria 3124, Australia
(a division of Pearson Australia Group Pty. Ltd.)
Penguin Books India Pvt. Ltd., 11 Community Centre, Panchsheel Park, New Delhi—110 017, India
Penguin Group (NZ), 67 Apollo Drive, Rosedale, Auckland 0632, New Zealand
(a division of Pearson New Zealand Ltd.)
Penguin Books (South Africa) (Pty.) Ltd., 24 Sturdee Avenue, Rosebank, Johannesburg 2196, South Africa

Penguin Books Ltd., Registered Offices: 80 Strand, London WC2R 0RL, England

First edition: April 2011

Library of Congress Cataloging-in-Publication Data

Taylor, Kristin Clark.
    The forever box / Kristin Clark Taylor.
        p.   cm.
    ISBN 978-0-425-24196-7 (hardback)
    1. Taylor, Kristin Clark—Childhood and youth.   2. African American women—Washington (DC)—
Biography.   3. Presidents—United States—Staff—Biography.   4. Public relations personnel—Washington
(DC)—Biography.   I. Title.
    E840.8.T39A3   2011
    973.928'092—dc22[B]   2010054244

PRINTED IN THE UNITED STATES OF AMERICA

10   9   8   7   6   5   4   3   2   1

This book describes the real experiences of real people. The author has disguised the identities of some,
and in some instances created composite characters, but none of these changes has affected the truthful-
ness and accuracy of her story. Penguin is committed to publishing works of quality and integrity. In that
spirit, we are proud to offer this book to our readers; however, the story, the experiences, and the words
are the author's alone.

For my sister
Noelle

ACKNOWLEDGMENTS

Always, first and foremost, my prayer of gratitude to my heavenly Father for guiding my pen as I wrote and for speaking directly to my heart. It is through Him that all of my words flow; I am mightily fortified by His constant presence.

Profound thanks also to my six older siblings, Joann, Ingrid, Noelle, Donald, Tanya, and Nikki, for their boisterous love and for nurturing my spirit even as a young child. Mother and Daddy are smiling down on each of us, patting us gently on our heads because we've made them so very proud. How blessed I am to be "the baby" of this bunch, the happy little caboose at the end of our long familial train. Thank you for your shared memories, and for loving me as I wrote. My gratitude to each of you for creating the magic that was my childhood.

There are many miracles within the Berkley Publishing Group and I am grateful for having worked with several of them. My profound thanks to my editor, Denise Silvestro, for coaxing my words onto paper and for so gently pulling my childhood stories from the cobwebbed corners of my mind, straight into the bright and brilliant light of day. I know, beyond the shadow of a doubt, that our union was divinely inspired. My heart is so glad to have finally found you.

Also within the Berkley family, special thanks to Meredith Giordan, for assuring an orderly transition from manuscript to book, and to the two greatest publicists I know, Rosanne Romanello and Julia Fleischaker. To Leslie Gelbman, publisher of Berkley, as well as to the special folks within the larger publishing family of Penguin, my gratitude for providing the creative outlet I needed to share my stories.

To my wise and wonderful agent, Diane Freed: Can you feel the gratitude that's pouring from my heart? Thank you for your faith in me, and for guiding this book toward its true home. Thank you for folding me so lovingly into your literary embrace and for preserving the spirit of this project as it evolved. In you, I've found *two* blessings: an agent extraordinaire and a true friend as well.

The idea of one day writing about my Forever Box has been brewing in my soul for a bit. My longtime friend and fellow writer Laura Randolph was the first to nudge me forward with this project. Thank you, lovely Laura, for sprinkling your magic over my manuscript and for renewing my interest in *finally* giving birth to this little literary baby. You are extraordinary.

The Taylor family showered me, collectively and individually, with constant support and sustenance as I wrote. Thank you for rallying close. Special thanks to Steaven Coates Sr., the superb photographer, for handling the tiny treasures in my box with such admirable tenderness as he photographed them for this book, and for his keen and caring eye.

Of all the Taylor family, however, it is Lonnie Taylor who has molded and shaped my life in immeasurable ways. More than anyone, you have helped me evolve into the person I am today. Thank you for your support as I wrote and, from a larger perspective, for helping to create the biggest miracle of all: our two children, for without you they would not be.

How blessed I am to have so many wise and wonderful sister-friends in my life who kept me buoyant as I wrote. To my oldest friend in the world, Novellia "Cookie" Pounds, I thank you for the cherished childhood memories of playing Mother-May-I, making mud pies, and for the magical summer evenings we spent whispering together until the streetlights came on. I love you for always walking by faith and not by sight. Our late-night, long-distance prayer sessions kept me focused as I wrote. You are a miraculous and wondrous Woman of God.

My heart is happy and my spirit is glad to have been steered toward so many other special people who showered me with support as I wrote: Claud, Joann, Paige, Brant, and Claire Anderson; Fred and Bryna Berman; Marga Bushara; Donald, Anthony, and Michelle Clark; Valerie Cooley-Elliot; Kathleen Farrell; Kianna Ferguson; Susan Friedman; Karen Gaddis; Carlos and Linda Jones; Andre Latham; LaRita Lynch; Charlie Miles; Elena Motaynep; Vickie West; and everyone at Elite. Tender kisses also to my special, quiet friends who never judge but always love; thank you for accepting me simply for who I am.

Finally, and most important, it is my two children, Lonnie Paul and Mary Elizabeth, who stoke the fire in my heart. That you both came *through me* on your way into this world is a miracle of such magnitude that it takes my breath away. It fills my soul with comfort and gladness to know that, long after I leave this earthly place, the two of you will step forward to become the careful keepers of our familial flame. You'll carry the torch and light the light. Because you exist, I am certain that my life has not been lived in vain. Because you exist, I am certain that our legacy will live on . . . which is about as close to the comforting, concentric concept of *forever* as I really need to get.

CONTENTS

INTRODUCTION

———— ↶↷ ————

C EDAR.

The sharp, pungent smell of its woody fragrance makes my soul smile. When I inhale deeply, I can actually feel the weight of its dusky scent lingering lightly in the recesses of my memory. Its aroma brings back the blustery feel of a crisp winter day; barren oak trees standing tall, their branches stretching like old, arthritic fingers, reaching higher and higher to scrape the sky.

The smell of cedar steers me directly toward countless age-old mental snapshots from my past—memories and mementos that are now carefully stored away within the depths of a handsome, heavy cedar repository, which I call my Forever Box. In my box are precious, tangible pieces of my past that can be touched and turned around in my own hands whenever I please: a yellowed newspaper article about a family member now long gone, the tiny clay elephant my daughter made for me when she was a mere toddler, love notes and ribbons and many things magical—all of them steeped in the pleasing and powerful scent of cedar.

A quick whiff will magically re-create an isolated memory from my childhood. Suddenly, I am transported to a golden, sun-splashed fall afternoon, twirling, twirling in our back-yard, my thin brown arms outstretched and my face turned upwards toward the sky.

Other cedar-scented memories abound. The earliest is not even one of my own, but was told to me by my brother and five sisters. Early in my infancy, so it was said, my mother would swaddle me in my Cinderella pink baby blanket and carry me downstairs so that the two of us could stay close while she wrote. Since we couldn't afford the luxury of an upstairs crib *and* a downstairs crib, Mother simply impro-vised and made do with what she had—an instinctive, pro-tective, universal skill shared by mothers everywhere.

Removing a wide, cedar-lined drawer from their bedroom bureau, Daddy would dutifully carry the drawer downstairs and place it in a corner in our living room. Mother, holding me in a squirming bundle, would lean over to gently, lov-ingly, place me inside. There I'd lie while she wrote, her baby girl (the youngest of seven), swaddled and secure inside the cedar drawer, joyous beyond belief from simply listening to the happy, hollowed-out *tap-tap-tapping* sounds of Mother working away on her Underwood typewriter. So perhaps it is as early as then, when I was weeks old, that the smell of cedar first permeated my soul.

Today, the pungent aroma of cedar helps solidify my own sense of stability and continuity. It reminds me of that vision from my infancy, as told to me by my siblings, of Mother sitting primly at our olive-green card table in the corner of the living room, typing furiously, leaning down into my makeshift cedar "crib-drawer" every now and then to kiss me on my forehead while I napped. (Mother's old Underwood typewriter, still bulky and beautiful, sits in my home library today, shrouded in her heavenly presence, many of its keys well-worn from the constant pressure of her slender fingers so many decades ago.)

There are other memories, too, which surface the second I open the lid of my Forever Box and touch one of the treasures inside. My imagination might pick me up and swing me straight back to my first day of kindergarten. I remember with startling clarity the smell of Elmer's Glue swimming around my head and the Dance of the Butterflies fluttering deep down in the pit of my stomach, and how my heart yearned so desperately for Mother to come and whisk me back to the safety of our home.

The beauty of positive, pleasing memories is that *every one* of us can call them up, at will. But it takes time. Practice. Discipline. Who among us, for instance, can ever forget their first day of school—what we wore, where we sat, how we felt? With very little effort and a great deal of joy, I am back there again, at the first day. The open, sunny classroom. The biting, brilliant feeling of excitement that showered over my little shoulders as I sat with my classmates at the hexagonal-shaped art table. The mild nervousness that moved around in my little spirit as I sat at that table, preparing to embark on my first art project. Yes, I can remember quite clearly how each one of us sat ramrod-straight, intent and focused on the art assignment we'd just received from our teacher (which involved drawing various shapes onto colored construction paper). And if I sit still long enough, I can even conjure up my teacher's essence; her rosebud mouth (which reminded me of a knot in a balloon), her sensible brown lace-up shoes, and the way her bracelets tinkled softly when she passed around more construction paper or put out more glue.

I recall the details. Sitting at that art table all decked out in my finest first-day-of-school red plaid jumper, passionately praying that the flaxen-haired beauty sitting beside me wouldn't reach right over and snatch the last red crayon before I could swipe it for myself. How in the world was I to draw an apple for Mother if all the red crayons had already been taken?

And in the end, it hadn't really mattered that I'd had to use a purple crayon to draw my apple (alas, all the red crayons had been taken). Nor did it matter that my coloring skills were untidy and more than a little wild—or that some of my strokes were so hard they tore clean through the paper.

What *did* matter way, way back then (and still counts for so much today) is that Mother loved my purple apple simply because I'd made it with my own hands—and because I'd made it for *her.* She loved it so much she taped it to our kitchen wall for all to admire—and eventually, she carefully packed her precious piece of art into her own Forever Box, for successive generations to admire and appreciate.

Today, decades after her death, I still have that purple apple, and it sits nestled safely in the lower-left-hand corner of my Forever Box. Why? Because Mother had the presence of mind, even back then, to save it so that I would have it for *today*. She purposefully preserved that piece of our past—which I, in turn, have preserved for my own children, and which they will eventually share with their own progeny.

Decades later, my drawing remains perfectly intact. Most of the paste still adheres. My name is still clearly scrawled in that careful, kindergarten penmanship, along the lower-right-hand corner of the paper. And at any time of the day or night, when my adult son or daughter pulls open the heavy lid of my Forever Box, they can feel for themselves the wild, waxy crayon tracks that their mother drew all those many years ago. (I'd drawn Daddy a similar picture during my first day in nursery school, but at least *that* time I'd been lucky enough to get to the red crayon first!)

It fills my soul with gladness that my children are so easily able to return with me to those precious memories from the past.

Memories of their mother in her brand-new jumper on the first day of school.

Memories of the powerful, pungent smell of cedar on a crisp, wintry day.

Memories of yesterday, today, and forever.

ॐ

THE magic that occurs whenever I open my Forever Box is mesmerizing; almost miraculous. When I reach down into its depths to withdraw a precious trinket, I am transported to a past that is rich in color and pulsating with the power of yesterday.

Throughout most of this book, I am seven years old again, growing up in Detroit during the 1960s, a powerful, pent-up time when Motown crackled with culture, color, and finger-snapping energy.

Yes, indeed, my childhood was wondrous. I was happy. Safe. Surrounded by love and laughter. A skinny-legged, little golden-brown girl with fuzzy pigtails and a penchant for making friends who were decades older than me.

These elderly women are also "the special ones" I celebrate within the pages of my book, along with the principles they instilled in my spirit and the life lessons they passed along, which will live on, quite literally, forever. I celebrate their collective stories, and the extraordinary tales of their own youth, as well as the trinkets they so generously shared with me (which are now safely preserved in my Forever Box) before they departed this earth. I celebrate the friendships we forged and the love that bounced between and within us every time we were together—infinite, otherworldly, everlasting love, which neither the passage of time nor the inevitability of death can erase.

❧

In the crafting of this book, I also hope to offer a precious peek at some of the treasures so carefully stored inside my Forever Box. Every photo shown within these pages is a piece that actually lives within the cedar box's darkened recesses: antique lace and crocheted doilies, beaded bags, and favorite

childhood books. A heartbreakingly beautiful teacup and saucer set, given to me when I was a child, by an elderly neighbor-friend one rainy, summer afternoon, just after we'd finished praying together in her parlor. The christening gown worn by myself and all six of my siblings at different times during our infancy, on that special day when each of us took our first spiritual steps toward our living, loving God.

But it is not solely the *stuff* in my Forever Box that I celebrate.

Far from it.

This is a clamorous, clanging celebration of what can happen when we—all of us—actively, mindfully, decide to preserve the most positive pieces of our past and pass them down to the generations who will follow in our footsteps long after we've taken our last breath.

I am a memory-maker, a keeper of keepsakes. And within these pages, I issue to you a personal invitation: Learn how to mindfully appreciate the power of preservation. Experience the magic that begins the moment you begin preserving the special trinkets and treasures from your personal past. Become a memory-maker in your own right.

Plucking from the past deepens my spirit and connects me more directly to the wondrous, fast-moving world around me. Whether it's my mason jar filled with antique buttons or, more elaborately, a few of the dried red roses preserved from the day of my mother's funeral, in those final moments before I uttered to her my last good-bye, I've learned to come as close to forever as I can get. How? By rustling up yesterday's sounds and images so they can become a comfortable, conscious part of my daily life.

Long after our own ashes have been scattered to the wind and our bones have turned to dust, it is entirely possible for whole pieces of ourselves—our histories and the depth of our own unique existence—to remain behind for our surviving loved ones to pore over and to ponder. It is these lasting remnants—the ones we purposefully decide to preserve— that offer the generations who will come after us tangible evidence that we even existed at all, and that our years on this earth counted for something positive and pleasing.

I hope that my stories—real-life, childhood vignettes that unfold over the course of several rain-soaked summer days—will slow you down and lift you up. In a few instances, my childhood recollections may be a bit murky, the mental images shadowed and cobwebbed. But what remains as clear as a summer day is the laughter and love that permeated my soul on those four magical days. I hope that before we begin our journey you'll close your laptops and disconnect all things electronic so that we can travel back to those slow, languid days of yesterday—to the stories that spring from the purest parts of my past.

The first story is about Mother, an elegant, golden wisp of a woman whose lingering spirit will cover me, always, in gladness, glory, and eternal love.

Sweet Mother, resplendent in her elegant church hat.

Kristin Clark Taylor

Church Hat

—— ❧ ——

I WATCHED HER CLOSELY as she slept.

As far as I could tell, her breathing was normal, but still, I was worried. I leaned in closer, peering for additional proof that my sweet mother was alive, beyond the shadow of a doubt. The rise and fall of her chest was simply not enough to convince me, 171 percent, that she was still with me in the land of the living. So, as gently as I possibly could, I reached over toward her slender, bronze-brown wrist and felt for a pulse. How much could a seven-year-old girl actually know about the normalcy of her mother's pulse? Yet still, I tried, just like I'd seen it done on *Dr. Kildare*. After a second or two, I felt a soft throbbing. She was alive for sure. Mother hadn't left me alone on this earth after all. She was only enjoying a rare and much-deserved afternoon nap on our living room sofa.

Mother and Daddy were decidedly, deliciously, devoted to

raising their seven children in the bright light of love, laughter, and spiritual solidity. There was nothing more important to the two of them than bringing us up to know that we were loved—and boy, did we know it. They also taught us to cling to several beliefs that remain, to this day, ingrained in our spirits. The first, we were to worship our heavenly Father with all our hearts, minds, and souls because we were His children, and He was our gentle Savior. The second, we were to treat others as we ourselves expected to be treated; that is, with unconditional love, kindness, compassion, and respect. And the third, we were to always, *always* be mindful of the fact that both of them loved us with a fiery, ferocious intensity. These powerful beliefs and principles bounced and swirled happily around us when we were all growing up. Yes indeed, all seven of us—my brother, my five sisters, and I—knew, with startling clarity, that we were well loved. Such comforting knowledge allowed us to walk with a certain swagger that would bounce us up to the tips of our toes. It instilled in us a powerful spunk and verve, as well as a conscious bond with and awareness of God Himself. We knew, sure as shooting, that God was good—because Anybody who would put two people like Mother and Daddy on His good, green earth must be hugely and heavenly Supreme.

On this particular afternoon, though—even at the tender age of seven-going-on-eight—I was still keenly aware that I shouldn't have been nitpicking at Mother while she rested. So why did my fingers keep brushing her cheek and why was I trying so valiantly, what with the pulse-taking and all, to assure myself that she was still alive? *Because I simply couldn't help myself. I wanted her awake.* I wanted her eyes to flutter open, find their focus, and rest their gentle gaze directly and solely on me. I needed to feel the pounding of her heart strongly enough through her pretty polka-dot sundress so that I could match it with my own heart rhythms. I adored my mama in great, gulping doses—so much so that I actually missed her while she slept.

This particular afternoon, as summer thunder rumbled far off in the distance, Mother's nap seemed to have transported her to another place entirely. As I continued to study her, it gradually occurred to me that she was in the midst of a delicious dream. She smiled softly, eyes still closed. I wanted to kick myself or maybe bite my own tongue because I was so frustrated over our separation. I was powerless. Her smile told me she was in the clutches of pleasant slumber—maybe she was lying on a white, sandy beach with palm trees swaying in a balmy breeze; or dreaming my favorite fantasy: lying suspended in midair, on top of a billowing, fast-moving cloud. Suffering succotash! I was growing madder by the minute— not at her, but at myself for not being able to reach her, wherever she was. I thought of doing something naughty—spitting on our living room carpet or ripping the "Do Not Remove" label from one of the sofa cushions—as a cheap tactic to finally wake her up and get her attention. But I didn't. I couldn't. And still she slept. Out like a light. Her left cheek lay flat against the knobby arm of the sofa and her legs stretched out gracefully, like two golden parentheses, along the sofa's length.

Finally, I turned to God Himself.

Lifting my face upward toward the ceiling, I prayed a

hopeful prayer: *Please wake Mother up soon, God, so that we can laugh and talk and laugh some more. And if You can, while you're at it, please wake her up before anyone else gets home so that we can have precious personal minutes to ourselves.*

Nothing.

But then, all of a sudden, I got another idea about how best to wake Mother up. The eyelid-blowing test! Why in the world hadn't I thought of that before? The eyelid-blowing test, in my mind, was the final litmus test that could really, truly gauge if someone was either alive (and just sleeping) or dead as a doornail. So I leaned in close yet again and blew gently onto her closed eyelids. Her eyelashes fluttered slightly, but she quickly seemed to settle back into her dream world. Propelled by something I couldn't identify—something deep inside me, which I now realize was the powerful pull of "Mother-love"— I blew yet *again*. This time, I used much more sudden, forceful puffs, just to make sure I'd finally gotten her attention. I needed my heart to get on the same page as my head. I needed to make sure my mama was alive.

It worked! Sort of.

Mother sighed softly, murmuring something about raisin oatmeal and tigers in the attic, then she shifted her position slightly more toward me; that beautiful, brown face of hers now partially shadowed by the late afternoon sun-and-cloud combination of that strange-weather day.

I had her now. It was time to rock and roll.

"Ma? You awake?" I whispered hotly into her ear.

The sound of my voice was so close it must have felt moist. I was being completely irrational. How could she be awake when I was watching her *sleep*? As I spoke, I could hear my own seven-year-old voice cracking in quiet desperation. I wanted my mama.

Instinctively, her right arm reached out for me and encircled my tiny waist, drawing me in closer. She was waking slowly, swimming back up toward the surface of consciousness, but still being cuddled in the arms of a pleasant summer-afternoon thunderstorm dream.

Her touch touched me directly. I dropped my small face straight down into the graceful, soapy-smelling curve of her neck. Safe. Secure. Even my waist was elated, because Mother was touching it. At that moment, I knew exactly where I needed to be. *Not* outside jumping double Dutch between the raindrops with my friends, or splashing around in my red rubber rain boots out back. No sirree. I was with Mother. Nowhere else and no one else existed in the world.

"Ma? I have to ask you something *important*," I whispered urgently, lying through my little white Chiclet teeth.

Her beautiful skin shone reddish-brown, the color of a shiny copper penny. I noticed the startling highlights in her complexion, so beautiful I could have scooped them up with my hands, like golden nuggets. What on earth was I going to ask her when she fully came to? When the raisin oatmeal or tigers in the attic or whatever else she was dreaming about finally fluttered away and I was left standing there, looking expectant and immature and demanding? I knew full well I had no specific question on—or in—my mind. All I wanted her to do was come back from her dream and send her brilliant, sun-splashed smile bouncing directly toward me.

"Yes, baby?" she hummed. "What's going on in that little head of yours? What question do you have for your mama that is just so important?"

I could feel her willfully trying to pull herself out of sleep, bless her dutiful heart. She was the best of mothers to her children *even while she slept.* She hadn't gotten mad or even a little bit salty when I'd blown on her eyelids or pulled at her wrist. (If someone had bothered me like that while I slept, I probably would have pinched the soft flesh under their arm.)

But not Mother. Somehow, she knew I needed her.

I don't know much, but I do know this: *All* mothers can sense, in the deepest part of their souls, the precise moment when their child needs them. They just can. Mother knew I needed her then. I still need her today.

"What's on your mind, Beauty?" she asked again, more alert this time. A slow smile danced a lazy samba across her face as she finally found and met my gaze. She sat up and reached for me again, drawing me to her, leaning over toward me to plant a sweet, brown Hershey-chocolate mother-kiss smack in the middle of my forehead. I loved her as much as I loved God and Jesus and peanut M&M's; a strong, strange love that is not of this world at all, but from some other place I've never seen, visited, or even read about in our Encyclopedia Brittanica.

She was the most beautiful, brilliant woman I'd ever seen. Skin the color of soft caramel candy. High cheekbones shaped like little mountains. Eyelashes of mink. Hands small and birdlike, prominently veined like my grandmother's, and like mine. A laugh that tinkled like fine crystal; her laughter never guffawed or banged around the room like a noisy brass band.

By anybody's standards (not just my own), Mother was breathtaking. Her physical beauty attracted attention. In her younger days, as a way to offset the cost of her college tuition, she'd worked once in a while as a professional model, so her image popped up in public from time to time. Newspapers published photos of her with captions underneath describing her as a rare jewel of unparalleled beauty. I'm sure such attention embarrassed my humble mother. To her, vanity was a bad habit; unseemly and off-putting. She and Daddy never tolerated it from any of their children.

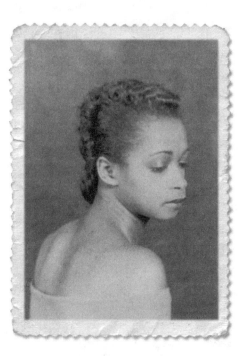

Mary Elizabeth Clark
COURTESY OF THE AUTHOR

The *Pittsburgh Courier* ran a front-page article about her, with a banner headline reading, "Brown Venus Is Carnegie Tech Model," and then the subhead, "Has Posed at Yale, Harvard." The article itself showered Mother with praise and affection, and when I actually read it for myself a few years later, I was actually taken aback, knocked slightly off balance. The accompanying photo revealed a profile that was unmistakable, the posture intimately familiar. There she stood, probably in her late teens or early twenties, gloriously draped in a dark velvet sheath that flowed off her bare shoulders and rested in a graceful pool at her feet. Seeing this "other" side of Mother stirred my spirit in a new and intense way; it was the first time I'd seen her as anything other than a devoted wife, the loving mother of seven children, and a professional career woman we were all proud of. Heck; that she even *had* a life before us—and a thriving, exciting, fairly glamorous life at that—seemed incongruous and illogical. Gazing at the newspaper and magazine articles, my heart raced. Was this woman really Mother—or just some wise guy trying to pull a prank on me? How was it that she had not only existed but thrived in a world without us? How was it possible that someone had dubbed her "Brown Venus" before even I had dubbed her "Mother?"

It almost didn't fit. But this much was clear: Whoever wrote that headline had been right on target: Mother was, indeed, a "Brown Venus." Both the article and the photos were mesmerizing.

There she stood in a graceful, languid pose, small, perfect hands held as delicately as a china doll's. Surrounding her in a small circle were a handful of serious artists, all sitting on stools with their canvases and easels in front of them, all obviously concentrating very hard on trying to capture her beauty for all time.

There were other articles as well. "Sepia Siren," one newspaper called her. "The world's most perfect face and figure." (It is said that a sculpture still stands of her today in one of the exclusive private boarding schools in Michigan.) She was absolutely captivating. That this wonderful, wise woman *belonged to me* was a gift that simply took my breath away.

On this particular afternoon, though, I wasn't thinking about modeling or magazines or art students sitting on stools. I was trying to figure out how I was going to fully engage her attention, now that she seemed to be awake. Part of me felt guilty for having pestered her so relentlessly. But mostly I felt happy because that very same pestering had finally paid off: She was awake and she was reaching out to pull me closer and—for the moment, anyway—she belonged exclusively to me!

Rare as it was, the house was almost empty. The only ones home were my older sister Noelle, who was upstairs studying in her bedroom; and our cat, Kaboodle, who slink-slithered around the legs of our living room table.

I still had to come up with a question, though. Nothing came to me.

"What *is* it, sweetheart?" Mother asked, beginning to sense, incorrectly, that I might be sick or in need of a fever check (the cool flat of her hand against my forehead used to make me happy to be sick).

"Is something bothering my Beauty?" (She called me this often, but I noticed she used it mostly when we were by ourselves. Why? Because I am certain, even way back then, that she was sending me a private message. At least twice a week, she'd read to me from Anna Sewell's heartbreaking but endearing novel, *Black Beauty*; a story of how this beautiful black horse suffered through many trials and travails, yet still emerged victorious—"on the *good* side of bad," as Mother used to like to say. In her own way, especially during those racially charged years of the mid-'60s, she was instilling in me the wonderfully immutable fact that I was indeed *black* and I was indeed *beautiful*—a message every black child needed to hear, especially growing up during those tumultuous years. By selecting this particular book, and reading it to me regularly, Mother was purposefully and gracefully showering me with a sense of racial pride and heightened self-esteem. Sure, the book was about a horse. But its underlying message—and even its title—cemented within me a powerful place of contentment and a more stabilized sense of self-awareness.

She was fully awake now and looking expectant. After a minute or two, she sat up.

My stomach felt rumbly. Worry and guilt rose up into my throat like bile. One thing Mother didn't abide by in any of her seven children was lying. And lying was exactly what I'd done when I told her I had an "important" question to ask. My longing for her attention at any cost was beginning to backfire and trip all over itself with frightening speed, and even worse, I think it was beginning to dawn on her, too. Her youngest child, her baby girl, her Black Beauty, had simply been fibbing to get a little attention.

I eased down onto the sofa and stretched out my short body so that my head was smack dab in the middle of her warm lap. We fit together on our sofa perfectly. A summer breeze blew, causing the metal blinds to clatter lightly at the open window above us. From my lying-down position, I gazed up through the open blinds and spied a piece of the sky; clouds hanging low with moisture and growing darker by the minute. I inhaled deeply, pulling in her magnificent mother-smells and the heavy, newly wet earth smells from outside, and I thought to myself, *This must be what heaven is like.* My stomach was still a-rumbling with worry, though. And the fact that Mother was now fully awake and catching on to my fib made me temporarily redefine my notion of heaven—because there was no way in the world heaven would have opened its Pearly Gates to let in lying, manipulative seven-year-old girls. Of this I was certain.

Suddenly, I had an idea. God and Jesus and Captain Kangaroo dropped it straight into my brain as a little gift. I had it! A legitimate reason for having awakened Mother!

"Tell me about the time you went downtown to buy yourself that hat for church," I demanded as demurely as I could.

I wanted to hear her voice, to feel the warmth of her body and the rhythm of her chest as she spoke. I needed the drama of her long-ago, real-life story to wrap itself around my narrow shoulders like a sheer summer garment, and Mother was the only one to satisfy that need. It was a story I'd heard at least a hundred times before, but somehow it never grew old. Even Kaboodle stopped slinking around and adopted a dignified-looking, sphinx-like position under the table, ears perked up ramrod straight, ready to actually listen—rare, indeed, given the finicky nature of the feline. Thunder rumbled again, this time closer. The metal blinds continued their clattering, and upstairs, a sudden breeze slammed the bathroom door shut. Mother touched my cheek lightly with the back of her hand. My soul smiled.

"You're sure you're not tired of this story by now, sweet-heart?" she asked in mock amazement.

She knew in her heart that I would never tire of it, and I knew in my own that she never *wanted* me to. It was an experience that we simply could not let breathe its last breath, even if Mother herself would—and did—breathe hers.

"I'll never be tired of the church hat story, Ma. *Never.*"

I wasn't lying then. Only the truth stirred around in my heart.

"Okay, then, you got it," she said in agreement. Absently, she stroked my bare arms. *Thankyouthankyouthankyou,* every hair follicle and skin cell on my forearms whispered softly, silently up into her face. *Thank you for your touch.*

"You know how Mommy likes to dress up real nice and pretty for church, right?" she asked, setting the story up.

I nodded yes before she could even finish the question, for we both knew it was rhetorical. It was *always* the question she started with. I nodded again, blinded by the protective power of her proximity. She did indeed get all gussied up and fancy for church. She was right about that part. Every

Sunday, she and Daddy would take charge of the spiritual assembly line of preparing six girls, one boy, and themselves for the eleven o'clock service. Because there were nine of us altogether, plentiful supplies were required, which is why we had a huge cardboard box that was filled to the brim with a variety of Sunday-go-to-meeting paraphernalia. Although somewhat jumbled, the box always seemed to hold whatever we needed: White church gloves in various sizes. Velvet headbands. Knee socks and half-slips. Lacy anklets. Patent leather pocketbooks. And what wasn't in the box could usually be found on our bathroom counter (which was usually neat but always cluttered): a barrage of bobby pins, barrettes, Dixie Peach hair oil, Dippity-do hair gel, AquaNet Hairspray, VO5, pink sponge curlers and, for the eldest sisters, tubes and tubes of Maybelline mascara. (My brother and father always seemed a bit more organized; there were only so many belts, ties, and crisply-starched handkerchiefs two men could actually need.)

When it was time for church, our collective excitement and expectation ricocheted off every wall. A current of spiritual electricity hummed through the house.

A big day in the Clark household, Sundays. People got pretty and God stepped in close.

We all looked good, the nine of us, and we filled up our very own pew (second from the front, on the left side of the church if you're facing the pulpit).

But Mother looked the best.

"Well, long before you were born, Beauty, I took the bus downtown to buy myself a new church hat. Lord knows I needed a new one, and I'd had my eye on a pretty sharp one for quite some time. I'd saved a little extra money, and I was determined to get that hat! If it was the last thing I did, your mother was going to buy that charming church hat."

Silence. I was already lost in her loving, literary presence. I could barely speak or even breathe. Every image Mother painted as she spoke sprang to life, jumping out from behind the darkened nooks and crannies of my little mind like miniature, friendly-faced ghosts.

As I lay there looking up at her face, I visualized Mother, for the thousandth time, as a much younger woman, standing patiently at the corner bus stop in the searing heat, picking delicately through her small, beaded change purse for the exact bus fare. Although she never said that it was the law back then for black people to sit at the back of the bus—even a glorious, gold-dusted woman like Mother simply on her way downtown to buy a church hat—I already sensed as much. I also vaguely wondered why Daddy hadn't just driven her downtown. (In Detroit, the venerable Motor City, every family owned a car, and for this reason, Mother drove only rarely. Daddy did all the driving. I finally concluded that, on this particular day, Daddy must have been at work.)

She continued, still stroking my happy arms.

"It was a Saturday afternoon, and my, was that bus crowded!" Mother remembered, a hint of sadness in her smile.

I visualized the perspiring passengers and the oppressive heaviness of heat and maybe even hatred rolling outward from their bodies like waves. There'd be a blond-haired, middle-aged man seated in the front of the bus, maybe on his way to the racetrack, hoping and praying his lucky horse would come in. Or the red-haired, freckled-faced housewife riding in from Farmington Hills, eager to make it downtown, too, to nab that set of butcher-block knives she'd heard were only on sale until Monday—but in my imagination, both of *them* sat at the front of the bus.

I even visualized the bus driver, with his wide, bountiful butt melting miserably over the sides of his raised platform driver seat, his hardened, beady eyes like tiny raisins looking impatiently at the beautiful bronze woman who was my mother. I could almost feel the bus driver's impatience toward Mother as she made her way up the bus steps. And there, standing like tall but wilting ears of corn in a choked cluster at the back, stood the black people. Hot. Silent. Stoic.

Because of Mother's amazing grace and gentle humility, it was always difficult for me to visualize exactly where or how she herself fit into that crowded cornfield, but I knew she must have made her way to the back of that bus, simply because it was expected—and I bet you dollars to doughnuts she probably did it without rancor, resentment, or riled-up feelings of white-hot hatred. She was on a mission. She was going to board that bus and get downtown to buy that hat if it was the last thing she did.

"What happened when you finally got there, Ma?" I asked, trance-like.

We were dancing a dance together, Ma and me. She was leading, and I was blissfully following her every step.

"Well, I pulled that cord hard, because I was coming to my stop. It seemed as though that entire bus wanted to get off at that stop with me!" *But the black folks had to get off last. You had to wait, Ma, for all the other ladies—and even all the other men—to get off before you. And even then, you probably had to exit through the back. All that indignity just for a pretty church hat.*

"Let me tell you, Beauty; that store was as crowded as I've ever seen it!" she exclaimed softly, shaking her head at the very memory. Her long, slender fingers picked a fleck of lint from my dress, and then patted my arm gently.

"But I knew exactly where I was going, believe me when I tell you I did, Krissy baby. Nothing could have stopped me that day. Plus, I'd called several days ahead and spoken to a very nice saleslady. Each time I called to check on whether my hat was still there, the saleslady smiled through her voice and promised me that it was."

Pushing her voice up an octave and expertly adopting the voice of a somewhat snooty saleslady, Mother imitated the clerk:

"'Yes, ma'am, it's here, all right. I'm looking right at it!'"

Mother was great when it came to imitating people. She was on a roll and continued imitating the saleslady.

Mother threw her head back gently and laughed, the sound tinkling like the wind chimes hanging under our porch in the backyard.

(I loved our backyard, with my swing set back near the tomato plants and the small patch of lily of the valley near our wire fence. I even had a playhouse, which sat on a small patch of grass just beside our back porch, strong and real and sturdy as a poplar—and oh, what a playhouse it was! It wasn't plastic like Barbie's and it was much, *much* bigger than the houses you could make with Lincoln Logs or LEGOs. This was a *life-size* house—big enough for me and my best friend, Cookie, to actually stand up in!)

But here's the real reason my house was as precious to me as a boxful of Sugar Daddys and cinnamon sticks: Daddy built it just for me, with his own two hands. Granted, it was a tad ramshackle, and it did lean a tiny bit to the right, but he'd made it for *me*—and I loved him for it. Cookie and I even managed to squeeze in a tiny table and a couple of rickety three-legged stools, which afforded us countless imaginary tea parties, with real-life mud pies that we'd make with our own hands—mixing dirt and water, then pouring the concoction into one or two of my mother's aluminum pie tins.

Sure, Daddy built my house using worn, irregular pieces of warped wood, which I think came from the alley, but my humble abode had a real window with curtains and a real door with a real doorknob and, coolest of all, *real shingles on the roof!*

Beyond the shadow of a doubt, Daddy was the prince of my little life. He loved each of his seven children in huge-but-equal doses, and we knew for a fact that he'd move heaven and earth to please and protect us. I'm telling you the truth: The man loved me so much, he even pretended to eat my yucky, dripping mud pies. He once spilled an entire pie in his lap, and we both laughed until our stomachs hurt.)

Mama continued with her story, building steam like a quiet locomotive.

"The saleslady on the phone even asked for my name and I told her proudly, 'Mrs. James W. Clark,'—she even promised to hold it for me in the back until I could get there, which I thought was quite kind."

My mind painted the picture of Mother, legs crossed, sitting at the small telephone table in the little nook between the kitchen and the front hallway, patiently looking up the phone number for the store in our thick Yellow Pages, then dialing the number on our heavy-as-a-load-of-bricks black rotary telephone. I'm sure she smiled inside when the saleslady so graciously offered to put the hat on hold for her until she arrived. Mother always did appreciate good service. Imagining Mother smiling made me smile, too, if only by way of that magical mother-child osmosis.

I pushed, eager. "Then what happened, Ma? What happened when you got there?"

My heart was pounding as though I was hearing the story for the first time. That's how it was with Mother. Everything she touched was forever fresh. Startlingly alive. Crackling with color, energy, and truth.

"Well, honey, I cleared a path through that crowd of shopping women like Moses parting the Red Sea. I was moving through that store like there was no tomorrow. I was on a *mission*, baby. A hat-buying mission."

Silence from me. Breath-holding. I swear. I was pretty dramatic for a seven-year-old.

"Even as I made my way through all those pushy women and cackling hens, I kept praying that the saleslady had remembered to keep my hat on hold. I'd just finished making a navy blue A-line dress with a white-ribbon collar that would match it perfectly. In fact, I picked the fabric for my dress especially for this hat I was about to buy. I just *knew* they would look perfect together."

Mother was an expert seamstress, sewing many of our dresses, lined jumpers, and sometimes even our winter coats. She was darned proud of it, too. I wanted her to feel her own pride, so I made her describe the hat and dress again for me, so she could hear the words in her own ears.

"Oh, that dress fit my body like a glove, Beauty. I didn't even use a pattern for that one. I just went by sight, feel, and pure desire."

"And the hat, Ma. Describe the hat in the store."

"A sharp-looking little navy blue pillbox, dainty and as ladylike as could be. It was one fine hat, Beauty, let me tell you . . . But you know that already now, don't you?" she asked, smiling down into my face.

I had the distinct feeling, at that moment, that if I'd sat up and looked at her square in the face, I'd have seen her eyes glistening. Maybe with sad tears. Maybe with the immediacy and urgency of the memory she was describing, still obviously fresh in her mind. At this point in the story, the hairs at the nape of my neck always stood up at full attention. It was definitely the most compelling part of the plot, but also the most painful and unpleasant. Even for my seven-year-old heart.

The sound and smell of fat raindrops on hot asphalt wafted into our living room, but neither of us made a move to get up and close the living room window. Wet-earth smells blew in. Another rumble of thunder, closer now, as the sky prepared to crack open and pour. I snuggled in closer to her and hung on tightly, her clingy, cloying papoose. I could hear the sound of softly creaking floorboards upstairs as my sister padded from one room to the next, continuing to pull the bedroom windows closed against the rain.

"What happened when you got there, Ma? When you asked Mrs. Crenshaw if you could try on the hat just once before you bought it?"

After hearing the story so many times, I already knew the saleslady's name—as well as what happened next. A slow simmer began at the fringes of my soul, along with a downright thunderous rumble in the pit of my stomach—not the place that rumbles when you're hungry, but when you're angry.

Or worried.

Or scared.

A pause. Heavy, leaden silence. Mother gazed down at me and tugged gently on one of my pigtails, all fuzzy from the thick summer humidity.

"Mrs. Crenshaw just stood there staring at me like she'd lost her ever-loving mind—as if she'd just seen a three-headed Martian with polka-dot arms and two hundred little legs do a backward somersault in the middle of the hat department," Mother said, making a weak attempt at humorous imagery to distract me from what was to come next.

But there would be no distractions. I was having none of that. Mother continued, in her high-pitched, saleslady voice:

" 'You're the lady who's been calling on the phone about the pillbox?' " She was right-on with her imitations, my mother.

The air around us grew thicker. I blinked rapidly.

"What'd you say then, Ma? How'd you answer?"

"First, I looked her steady in her eyes. And then I answered nice and slowly, just in case she didn't understand," Mother said, the slightest tone of condescension splashing around in the currents of her voice. I envisioned her standing there eye to eye with Mrs. Crenshaw, slowly, carefully enunciating every word in slow-motion dignity.

" 'Yes, that would be me.' "

She was a riot, my mom; perfect in her elocution and razor-sharp with her wit. *That would be me.* Who even speaks like that in normal conversations?

She continued recounting her conversation with Mrs. Crenshaw.

" 'You and I have spoken on the telephone several times about the hat—and you *are* Mrs. Crenshaw, correct?' " Mother asked.

I always thought it was slightly weird that Mother would have asked the saleslady her name since back then all salesladies were required to clearly display their employee badges on their lapels. This saleslady, I imagined, wore hers proudly and as big as day so that it would be hard to miss, perfectly pinned to the right lapel of her fancy-shmancy suit. But Mother never did anything without a reason. There was definitely a reason she'd asked the salesclerk to repeat her name.

"Well, Krissy," Mother continued, smiling sadly now while fingering another fuzzy, flyaway tendril of my hair, "you know your mother never did get that hat."

"Why, Ma? Tell me again why."

"Because Mrs. Crenshaw told me she hadn't realized when she'd spoken to me all those times on the phone that"—and here, a pursing of her lips so slight it was almost imperceptible— "the store management had suddenly changed their policy and they were no longer able to put merchandise on hold, especially hats."

We sat quietly together as the sky finally cracked wide open and the rain fell down in sheets.

"What happened when you asked if you could at least try the hat on?" I asked, my heart leaping and lurching forward inside my chest like the Little Engine That Could.

"She told me I couldn't *even try the hat on* . . . that if I tried it on, I'd have to buy it. And if I got home and decided I didn't like it, 'returning it was not an option.'"

Outside on our street, I could hear bicycle tires swishing along the rain-soaked pavement—either mucho-macho Curtis proving to everybody that he didn't care whether his bike rusted or not, or show-offy Sheila, who used to be my friend until the week before, when she'd called me a skinny-legged beanpole. (Sheila was my friend, but she'd become a little show-offy since she'd just gotten a brand-new banana bike. Jeez. I had a banana bike, too—but did anyone ever hear *me* constantly flapping my gums about how great I thought it was? No sirree. My parents taught me better than that. Bragging was forbidden, under any circumstances.)

Mother, wide awake now and more alert that ever, forged ahead with her story.

" 'Well, I'd say that sounds mighty strange, wouldn't you agree, Miss Crenshaw? All of these sudden changes in store policy only just going into effect *the minute* I walk into the store and you see my face?' "

Mrs. Crenshaw, by then, must have been a real nervous Nellie. Mother imitated her again:

"'I cannot speak to whether or not you regard our store policies as "strange," ma'am,'" the old battle-ax said to my mother, "'but I would certainly hope you'd appreciate the fact that we can't just have *everybody* parading in here wanting to try on hats before they buy them, and begging for them to be put on hold. From a business standpoint, trying on the hats discourages the other women—prospective buyers, I might add—from trying on and purchasing the same merchandise afterward. It's simply a *hygienic* issue, ma'am, not a personal one. I'm sure you can appreciate that.'"

"'Well if I can't even try on the hat, Mrs. Crenshaw, then I certainly won't be purchasing it.'"

"'Whatever you choose,'" Mrs. Crenshaw retorted. "'Now good day to you.'"

Then she turned her back on my mother to help another customer.

She turned her back on my mother.

Hatred was a sentiment I did not know well, not at that young age, because we were taught not to familiarize ourselves with its demonic intensity. Mother and Daddy dedicated their lives to teaching us that hatred only destroys. But this much I knew: I didn't *like* Mrs. Crenshaw one bit. She sounded stupid. Dumb. Ignorant. Mean. Most of all, she'd denied Mother something that she'd wanted very badly, and she'd snatched at Mother's dignity, trying—unsuccessfully— to rip it all to shreds. Still, the devil in my heart won over the God in my soul, so I said it:

"I *hate* Mrs. Crenshaw and I hope she's dead now," I said flatly and without apology.

The minute I said that, Mother leaned way over in shock and anger—rather painful and viselike for me, what with my head being in her lap and all.

"Kristin Kay Clark, don't you *ever* let me hear you say you hate anyone! You know better. We do not hate."

She was pretty angry at me for saying it, but I didn't care. I *did* hate Mrs. Crenshaw, and I did hope that she had died. I'd already visualized her as old as dirt even back then. Certainly she'd be dead all these years later. Of *something*, I hoped. Heart attack, maybe. Or a car accident. Or maybe by getting one of her fancy high-heel pumps caught in a sidewalk grate and being run over by a bus.

"I'm sorry, Ma. I didn't mean it." Or maybe slipping in the bathtub and hitting her face on the faucet, then bleeding to death in her own bathroom.

"I should hope you *would* be sorry, young lady," Mother said in a hot but not white-hot whisper. She was cooling down a little but she was still pretty mad. I prayed she wouldn't tell Daddy when he came home from work. He'd give me one of his disapproving sidelong glances and involuntarily squint his eyes.

I wondered, then, whether Mother had ever really shared the full story, in all its detail, with any of my other siblings. It wasn't spoken of in our home. Maybe, I thought, it existed as a shared secret between the two of us. I kind of hoped it was.

"Keep going with the story, Ma. Let's just forget I ever said the 'hate' part. It's just that that part of the story always makes me mad. They should have let you buy that hat. They didn't even let you *try it on!*"

I think I used the word *hate* on that afternoon because it was the most venomous, vicious word I could muster up from my somewhat limited vocabulary. But even in my own seven-year-old soul, I realized that actual *hate*—particularly toward an entire race of people—did not exist in my heart. In fact, most of my childhood schooldays—the first ten years, in fact—were spent in a predominately all-white world. Since kindergarten, I'd attended the Roeper School, a lushly landscaped private school located in Bloomfield Hills, an affluent suburb of Detroit. In the first few years of my attendance, there were only a few black students in the entire class, maybe three at the most. It was a sprawling campus that felt more like college than kindergarten. Roeper students were gentle, loving, and completely accepting of my brown skin. I had many close friends. Mother called it a "progressive" school, and she loved its unique, creative approach to educating the *whole* child—body, mind, and soul.

We called our teachers by their first names and often held classes outside. The campus sat on acres and acres of rolling hills, with swimming pools (two, I think) and sunny, private glens where you could cuddle up with your favorite book. I wrote my first poem in a tree house near what was then a wide, open field used for baseball games, raucous games of Red Rover, and fun-filled field-day activities. The main building of the campus was a refurbished mansion that sat majestically atop a high hill. We held our assemblies and ate our daily meals in what was once the great room of someone's home. The master bedrooms and suites were our comfortable classrooms; what had once been a wealthy family's attic had been charmingly, magically transformed into the art department. I'd never known anything like it.

Very beautifully, and with a sense of enlightened power and self-determination, my ten years at Roeper taught me how to nurture and maintain my spiritual and emotional equilibrium. The school seemed to have a spirit and a pulse. I was bountifully blessed to be within its protective embrace as I developed spiritually.

Not only the school but the *environment* within it proved a vital support system for me, a black child growing up in the turbulent '60s. Sure, spending every weekday and most early evenings completely surrounded by children of a different race sometimes felt a bit schizophrenic. There were many times when I felt like a high-wire artist trying to balance between two starkly different realities. I didn't realize until much later that my beloved Roeper School actually provided a strong, sturdy bridge between those two distinctly different worlds. Along with my close-knit family, Roeper filled my youthful heart with love and happiness. And throughout my childhood, the promise of inclusion and pure, human compassion were rare and wonderful life principles. My parents had been wise indeed to work so diligently to get me into that special school. My life had been—and still is, to this day—immeasurably strengthened because of the Roeper experience.

In fact, it was Mother and Daddy who sacrificed in order to ensure that my years at Roeper were fruitful and fascinating. The tuition was steep, and additional money was often required for extracurricular activities. And it was also the generosity of my older siblings—who contributed what they could toward my tuition, in addition to nurturing me emotionally and physically—that helped spur me forward.

As sad as my soul felt when it happened, my siblings eventually began to fly away from our safe little nest, launching out to begin their own exciting new lives. They were beginning to earn their own incomes, and they shared much of what they earned with Mother and Daddy, just because they knew it was the right thing to do and because their collective sense of familial responsibility was centered, generous, and selfless.

Their enduring commitment to "family first" and their unrelenting dedication to the notion—and practice—of one-helping-another enriched my life deeply. So even at age seven, they'd already showered me with such constant, unconditional love that I knew of nothing else. I grew up believing—*knowing*, with absolute clarity of mind—that to give and receive love, in its purest form, was effortless and all-encompassing, as were the principles of kindness, respect, and spiritual generosity. From the moment I was born and ever since, it has been my family who has imprinted these values deep into my heart. It is part of who I am.

Despite all that, though, I remained resentful and angry about what had happened to my mother when she'd tried to buy that precious church hat all those years ago, long, long before she'd even brought me into this world. Each time I listened to her church hat story, it made me want to stick out my tongue or look cross-eyed at the first person I saw.

But on that afternoon, all I wanted was for her to keep talking.

"What happened next?" I asked, though I already knew.

Stretching, catlike, she rose and turned toward the open window and closed it. Through the window screen, the rain sprayed a fine mist on her forearms. I thanked God for the mist. For her arms. For the raindrops that had finally found their way into our comfortable house and home. She was focused again, and answered my question quickly.

"Well, I turned around, walked right out of that store, crossed the street, and caught the bus back home. Out of the corner of my eye, I could see Ms. Crenshaw already helping another customer. And guess what she was doing, Beauty?" she asked.

I knew the answer, but it was too painful to say aloud.

"She was helping that other woman try on *my* hat," Mother answered for me.

My heart told me that the woman who was trying on Mother's hat had to have been white, even though Mother never specified. She didn't have to mention the color of the other customer's skin or the saleslady's bigoted behavior; not at that moment, anyway. It would have been rude and unseemly, which Mother was not.

A sudden crash of thunder made me jump. Kaboodle, no longer statue-like under the table, dashed like a furry bolt of lightning into the kitchen through the louvered living room door. The thunderclap seemed to shift the ions in the room, and the newly arranged energy helped steer us gently toward the happy, redemptive conclusion of the story.

"That very next Saturday, I went down to the fabric store. By the end of that day, I want you to know that I had myself a beautiful hat that I'd made with my own hands. You know the very hat, honey, because it's still sitting upstairs in that flowered hat box in the attic—right next to my Forever Box. I'm keeping it fresh, so that you can remember this story, and maybe even tell it to your own children one day, decades from now—long, long after I'm gone."

The very idea of Mother leaving me—whether it was to go to work, run an errand, or even just to answer the phone—was unsettling enough. The notion of her *dying* was, to me, simply unfathomable. (Heavens to Betsy! I didn't even like it when she took an afternoon *nap*, simply because it took her away from me for those precious few moments!) No sirree. I was having absolutely none of that "when-I'm-gone" nonsense. Not from Mother.

The other thing she'd said that unsettled my nerves was all that stuff about one day having children of my own. Those words caused an immediate and severe burning sensation deep in my chest, in that hard-to-reach place behind my rib cage and my spine. I wondered and worried, in my own little head, *Wait a ham-sandwich minute! What in the world was she talking about—having my own children one day?*

Absurd.

Hogwash.

Malarkey.

At seven going on eight, I didn't even want to spend one ounce of emotional energy trying to visualize myself with my own children, if only because I was still one myself. In fact, I didn't want to spend one ounce of energy focusing on anything else besides the softness of Mother's skin and how happy I was—at that precise moment—to be able to inhale her magical Mother smells.

❧

I REMEMBER the shooting pangs of pride I felt toward Mother on that stormy summer afternoon, not only for having faced the indignity of racial prejudice with such grace, but for pushing so powerfully through such a dark moment in order to "make it to the other side of bad"—to that place that was positive and solution-driven.

Mother had been mistreated, denied, and turned away, but that had not deterred her. If anything, it served to spur her forward, catapulting her toward her own creativity and resourcefulness. She'd crafted a solution within her own mind about reasonable alternatives—and the by-product was something more beautiful than even she could have imagined. That it happened to unfold from a simple, unfortunate church hat experience was fortuitous indeed. In one simple story, she'd taught me how to leapfrog over some of the ugliness in world around us.

The fact that she was asking me to keep her church hat so that I could one day share it with my own children was lost on me at that young age. Today, I recognize the rationale behind her request: She wanted me to show her hat to my children so that they, in turn, could absorb important life lessons about pride, resourcefulness, and self-respect.

Needless to say, today, Mother's hat sits perfectly preserved in its original hatbox. My prayer today is that my children will be wise enough to preserve both the hat *and* the story behind it, passing it along to successive generations so that it never ever dies. And if they, in turn, teach their own children the same lessons, this comforting, cyclical pattern will continue—and Mother's lessons about life and love will live on, quite literally, forever.

However, on that rainy summer afternoon, the only thing I needed was Mother. I knew nothing of cyclical patterns or life lessons or the preservation of principles. What I *did* know was that Mother was now fully awake and close, and I was content. I never wanted this moment in time to come to an end.

So what did I do? First, I completely dismissed her preposterous prediction that one day she'd be gone. I totally forced it out of my seven-year-old mind. Second, I reached up from my spot on the sofa and pulled her back down toward me, laying my little head in her warm, inviting lap.

Eventually, Mother and I both fell asleep to the rolling, rumbling sounds of that magical summer thunderstorm.

I'm certain that I dreamed about her church hat as we napped that afternoon.

How do I know?

Because it was the first time I think I ever smiled in my sleep.

ᕲᕤ

TODAY, I know precisely what Mother's pillbox hat looks like because I keep it carefully stored in its original hatbox, painstakingly wrapped in layers and layers of tissue paper, bubble wrap, and clear cellophane. And anytime the spirit moves me, I can reach into my hatbox, hold the hat tenderly in my hands,

and allow the memories of
that magical afternoon with
Mother to seep directly into
my soul. Not only the hat—
but the story behind it—help
sustain Mother's legacy, and
before I leave this earth I will
pass it along to my own two
children, who will pass it on
to theirs.

No, Mother's hat cannot fit
comfortably within the dim
confines of my mahogany,
cedar-lined Forever Box—but that's just fine with me. I know
where it is when I need it—and, like Mother said that summer afternoon, it is, indeed, "one fine hat!"

What *does* fit comfortably into my box? The original copy
of *Black Beauty*, the one Mother used to read to me regularly
as a child. Many of the pages are dog-eared from use and yellowed with age, but the memories still burn brightly, as will
Mother's sweet, sweet spirit.

A Forever Box can take many different forms, whether
it's a hatbox, a hope chest, or even something as simple as a
wicker basket. Creating a repository in which to house and
hold the most pleasing and positive parts of our past is the
most important element of memory-making.

It's also vital to keep in mind that the power of preservation lies not only in collecting tangible trinkets and beautiful
baubles, but in the ability to pass down from one generation

to the next the family values and principles that were once held so dear by our ancestors. It is possible for an entire belief system to remain intact, not just for days but for decades—into perpetuity, in fact—if we're purposeful about precisely how and what we want to preserve for our children and our children's children.

Principles and life lessons about kindness, compassion, faith, and friendship can all live forever if we work hard to pass them down with care and caution to those newly born and yet-to-be born. What a comfort it is to know that our vision and values can burn on as brightly as the North Star—but only for as long as we fan their flames.

And how long is that?

Forever.

If we do it right.

SCRATCH BISCUITS

⸻ ☙ ⸻

THE NEXT MORNING, it was still raining. I know this because I heard the *ffflliitt, ffflliitt* sound of bicycle tires swishing past our house. My bedroom window was open slightly, and a few fat raindrops made their way through the screen, landing on my windowsill then bouncing down onto the crown of my nose. The rider seemed to be circling continuously and directly below my window. I knew it was Sheila, a girl in my neighborhood who'd just gotten a brand-new banana bike—and she wanted everyone to know it, too! Show-off to the nth degree.

I decided to put her out of my mind and to put jealousy out of my heart—at least for the time being. I had something important planned for the morning, and nothing was going to get in my way. I rose and stretched, then lowered myself to my knees for my morning prayer. *Thank you, God, for letting me rise to see a bright new day. Please watch over me and my family throughout the day, and take care of the people who are sad or sick, like Mr. Grassley down the street, who has the gout in his left foot; and poor Miss Beulah, who fell clean through her back porch when she stepped on that piece of rotted wood. I love you, Lord. And I know that You love me. Please keep everybody safe and don't let Kaboodle get hit by a car since you already know how he loves trying to catch those sparrows that are always hopping near the curb.*

After washing up quickly in our upstairs bathroom, I heard Daddy's whistle. He was an excellent whistler, my father. I loved the way he'd wet his lips, quick like a snake, then let out his short, staccato-like chirp; Father Bird sending out the signal for his baby chicks to gather close around him.

From the sound of his whistle, I could tell he was standing at the bottom of the stairs, calling us all down to breakfast. That's kind of how Daddy communicated. By whistling. Or sidelong glances. Or maybe a slow smile that would make its way across his face when he was simply happy to be close to us. He was indeed a man of few words, yet he managed to get his point across more effectively than just about anybody I knew. Go figure.

Because there were so many of us—and because he used words so sparingly—Daddy devised his own unique way of communicating with us, and we all understood him instinctively and completely. His whistling was an excellent (and entertaining) way of getting our immediate and collective attention—whether we were at a picnic in the park or scattered in different rooms throughout our house.

I spent long summer nights with Cookie, who lived right next door. We'd whisper and giggle and sometimes play tag with our father's flashlights (as long as they didn't notice, because both men were kind of fussy about their flashlights. They'd get all salty about our running the batteries down, so we didn't play flashlight tag all that often. It just wasn't worth it, especially since there were so many other fun things for the two of us to get into on warm summer nights.).

Cookie's father, too, had his own unique whistle, a beckoning call for his youngest daughter to drop everything and come a-running. When Mr. Pounds, a tall, elegant man who loved his wife and three daughters with that same father-passion as Daddy, came out onto his porch and let out his smooth-sounding warble, we both knew it was time to end our evening. We'd hug each other good-bye, then make mad dashes toward the safety of our homes, each pulled like little moths toward the brightened porch lights that beckoned us back to our families.

On this particular gray and stormy morning, breakfast was warm and waiting (the whistle told us as much), so we all trampled downstairs and grabbed our seats at the kitchen table. Time for more prayer. Before each and every meal, we always said the Blessing of the Food in unison—all nine of us. *Gracious Father, we truly thank You for the food we're about to receive, for the nourishment of our bodies, in Christ's sake. Amen.*

I was always so *excited* to be sitting at the kitchen table with my parents and siblings, my short legs dangling and swinging happily under a table crowded with sixteen other knees, legs, and feet. I also think I might have been the praying-est

seven-year-old on the block; two prayers within the first fifteen minutes of the day! Praying seemed to settle down my
small spirit. And whenever I spoke to God, I was certain that
He was listening closely (even though I always imagined Him
performing about thirty million other tasks at the same time,
like making sure all the airplanes in the sky didn't go crashing into one another and making sure the sun wasn't shining
in Nairobi and Nantucket at the same time. He had quite a lot
to do—this much I knew for sure—but I also knew that he
always had time to listen to my prayers).

When it came to praying, I'd also devised this secret trick,
which I haven't shared with anyone else until now: If you
squeeze your eyes shut real tight while you pray, I'm pretty
sure God can hear you better. And for really important
prayers, squeeze your eyes shut as tightly as you can, cross
your fingers on both hands and scrunch up the toes on your
left foot all at the same time. (Toe-scrunching is pretty hard,
especially when you're wearing sneakers or rubber rain boots,
but trust me, it can be done in emergencies.) Daddy probably
wouldn't have liked it, and I could already hear his quiet but
stern disapproval: "You don't need to perform any tricks or
engage in any high jinks to communicate with the Lord, Buttercup. He's always with us—leading us, guiding us—and
He always hears our prayers. Quiet, private prayer, without a
lot of banging around, is the best way to still your soul—and
even seven-year-old girls with fuzzy pigtails and pretty smiles
need stillness and peace in their lives. So talk to Him more
often, Buttercup . . . And don't let me catch you crossing your
fingers or scrunching your toes while you're doing it!"

Yes, indeed. My father was a man's man; a doting daddy with many hidden talents. Besides whistling, he was also an excellent fisherman. Preparing for a fishing excursion with Daddy was just about as much fun as the excursion itself. The night before, we'd water our front lawn for about fifty thousand hours (I often worried that we'd flood the house), then we'd wait. Later that same night, when everyone else was sleeping, and the water had had a chance to soak into the soil real good, we'd grab two flashlights and our Maxwell House coffee tin, which was already filled with dark, rich soil. Stooped at the waist, trying like all get-out to spy a bloodworm or two rising to the surface of the grass, my father and I would speak in whispered tones. I always yelped with excitement whenever I spied one of the squiggly things.

"Quiet, Buttercup! You'll scare them back into the ground!" Daddy would say, a half-smile passing over his shadowed silhouette. With great care and concentration, I'd squat down and pull the heartiest worms ever so gently from their soil. There was a certain way you had to catch those slippery guys, too—and you had to be quick as lightning. Surprisingly, they could squirm back into the warm, wet earth real fast, and many times they'd wiggle away before I could get a good enough grip to pull them from the earth. Daddy taught me to plunge my fingers into the soil quickly, with a sudden thrust, then pull the worm out as gently as possible. Sure, one reason he wanted us to be gentle with those worms was because they could tear in half if we pulled too hard. (I know. Gross.) But the most important reason, I still believe to this day, was because he simply didn't want those worms to suffer. That's the way Daddy was—as gentle as a cool breeze and as kind as a grandmother or maybe even a nun.

After we collected about thirty of the squirming things, we covered the top of the coffee tin with aluminum foil. Daddy would let me use the sharp knife to poke holes in the foil so the worms could breathe a little (it was the only time I was allowed to handle kitchen knives, so for me, it felt adventurous and daring). Then we'd get upstairs and fall fast asleep.

Only minutes after my head hit the pillow (or so it seemed), Daddy was kneeling beside me, gently shaking me awake. "Wake up, Buttercup!" he'd say in an excited whisper. "It's time to shake a leg! If we don't move now, all the fish will swim to the other side of the river and all we'll catch is tin cans and old rubber boots!" A warning such as this always made me leap right up and shimmy straight out of my warm bed into the peaceful (and somewhat frightening) predawn morning.

It was always dark outside when we began our fishing expeditions. Those quiet morning moments with Daddy, moving around silently in the kitchen, trying to pack our cheese sandwiches with only the night-light to guide us, were some of the most precious in my life. I loved the feel of our spacious, creaking house during those magical moments as the sky turned from midnight black to a deep, cobalt blue. It somehow felt like our house was sleeping (or at least breathing) all by itself.

Moving carefully down the darkened steps into the basement, we'd continue our father-daughter, getting-ready-to-go-fishing routine. Just at the bottom of the stairs, Daddy would pick me up so that I could reach the string that hung from the ceiling. One quick tug on that string—*click*—and soft, yellow light immediately illuminated everything around us. (Thank goodness. Our basement was scary, and I was never a huge fan of the dark. I know, I know, I was Scared Susie. Kind of a wimp. But of this I was fairly certain: There were mean little snaggle-toothed monsters that lived under our basement stairs, and they only came out when Daddy and I were moving around down there in the dark.)

We knew just what to do, my father and I, and usually we did it in complete silence. In the basement, it was my job to pull out the fishing rods and position them carefully at the bottom of the stairs. Daddy carried up the rods and his heavy, metal tackle box. My job was to bring up the Maxwell House can of worms and our woven fishing basket. (I always started to feel a little sad for those unsuspecting worms, though. They were so comfortable and happy in their rich, dark soil; so completely unsuspecting of the terrible fate that was soon to befall them . . . It was bad enough to get skewered with a hook—but to get gobbled up by a hungry perch, too? Just plain cruel. I wasn't sure God liked such cruelty. But I figured if Daddy didn't think it was cruel, then it couldn't be cruel; so I'd trip happily up the steps behind him, excited as all get-out.)

Loading the station wagon usually required two trips. It was my responsibility to bring along the bagged lunches: usually two cheese sandwiches, a couple of apples, a few extra slices of bread, and a big bag of Cracker Jack (of course Daddy always let me keep the prize inside). The extra bread, Daddy always said, was "for the fish, just in case they're in the mood to eat it."

The very last task I always performed before we headed out was to check the tackle box for an extremely important item: In one of the small compartments, Daddy always kept an old, tiny copper bell, which he'd hang at the very tip of my pole as soon as we got to the pier. I loved that old bell. Whenever we were fishing and I'd hear its soft tinkle, I'd just about faint from excitement—because it meant a fish was on the other end of my line! An actual *fish*—with gills and fins and a tail that was still flopping around, even after we'd reeled him in! (Immediately after unhooking the fish from our line, we'd drop it into our reed basket and submerge the basket in water so that the poor thing wouldn't suffocate.) Yes, indeed, catching a fish with Daddy was more adventurous than climbing to the top of Mount Everest. More exhilarating than stepping off the edge of the world. Even more fun than riding the Tilt-a-Whirl and the Zipper at the state fair.

Once we set off down the road, we'd usually drive to Belle Isle because they had the best piers. Many times we'd even go to Canada, since it was just across the river. (What other seven-year-old could boast that she'd fished with her father in two different countries within the short span of only one summer?)

Whenever I caught a fish, Daddy made it seem like I was the only person on the face of the earth, and like I had just performed a modern-day miracle. After I reeled it in (he'd always let me reel in my own catch), he'd inspect the fish really closely, then give me this serious-but-silly-looking salute. Then he'd gently hook his strong arms under my armpits and twirl me around and around in happy, happy circles. We could be at the pier at Belle Isle, or the lake at Palmer Park or even on the other side of the bridge in Canada, and he'd *still* twirl me around and around. Shoot, there could be a hundred other people around. No matter. Daddy and I danced our Just-Caught-a-Fish dance no matter where we were or who else was watching. I could not have been more loved.

Although Daddy has long since left this earth, the tiny copper bell he gave me an entire lifetime ago remains with me. It's tucked away in a corner of my Forever Box, and when you shake it gently, it still tinkles. And every time I look at it today—every time I shake it gently to hear its soft tinkle—I think of Daddy. Now, on a regular basis, I share with my two children those famous fishing stories of long ago. Stories about worm hunts and fishing poles. Of copper bells and Cracker Jack. Of moving around in those quiet, predawn hours and the Maxwell House coffee tin that lasted throughout my entire childhood.

I consider it a heavenly privilege and a Divine honor that God allowed the passage of time to overlap onto itself so that my own children, when they were very small, had the opportunity to go fishing with my father, too. And fish they did. I only wish I could have witnessed it more clearly the first time Daddy took them out, but my vision was blurred by the tears of happiness that were stinging my eyes. There it was, right before me: a real-life vision of not only two but *three* generations of fishing happiness. (And yes, Daddy would take my kids to a spot on Belle Isle that was very near the same spot we'd enjoyed a lifetime earlier.)

Both the three-generational fishing memories *and* my precious copper bell will exist long after I leave this place. And what will also exist, because I have shared these fishing stories with my children, are the memories of those early morning excursions and how brave I felt bustling around so busily in those dark, predawn hours, doing the Just-Caught-a-Fish dance with my father.

COURTESY OF THE AUTHOR

And although this obviously cannot fit into my Forever Box simply because it's not an actual bauble or trinket, here's something else that can be passed along from one generation to the next, which Daddy helped instill in my spirit: the power of unconditional love. It doesn't have to be a loud, clanging love; it can be completely silent. Daddy taught me that feeling love is important, of course—but *showing* it is equally vital, and such a demonstration need not always be dripping with syrupy words and sentimental sayings. Such huge, gulping doses of love can involve slippery worms, soggy cheese sandwiches, and even sharp-toothed hairy monsters that live under the basement stairs.

⚭

AFTER breakfast that morning, we all fell into the familiar, collective rhythm of cleaning up our bright yellow kitchen. Each person had a task. Usually (but not always), I'd wipe the table clean and dry the plates, while another sibling returned the forks and knives to the silverware drawer beside the stove. (I'd always yearned for the task of wiping down our white enamel teapot, which always sat on the left rear burner of the stove, but Mother wouldn't allow it until I was taller.)

But on *this* morning, I snuck away from my kitchen chores early because I needed to check on something important. I opened our screen door and stepped out onto the front porch. The rain fell hard and heavy, and one upward glance revealed a low-hanging sky of gray gossamer. Fat, blood-red worms wiggled this way and that on the asphalt, happy to be out from underneath the dark earth. But the worms weren't what I was focusing on at that moment. I had a mission to accomplish.

Peering across the street, I saw exactly what I was looking for. Even through the rain, I could see her: my friend Mrs. Luella Rae Simpson, sitting on her front porch. Her lowered head told me she was either praying, reading her Bible, or was fast asleep. Whatever the case, I knew that her mere presence on the porch was a signal to me, an unspoken invitation to let me know that it was fine for me to come over for a visit.

I tried to run between the raindrops to avoid getting thoroughly soaked as I dashed across to her house. Even as I ran, I whispered quick, shooting prayers for the unsuspecting worms in the street because, sure as shooting, they were about to get squashed by the tires of passing cars. *Just wait till Mr. Fisher swings his shiny blue Rambler into his driveway when his shift lets off at Ford. Squish! Splat! Keep these little worms safe, Lord. Tell them to go back down into the grass before it's too late.* Those poor smashed worms wouldn't even be suitable bait for our fishing days.

The moment she saw me running toward her, ol' Mrs. Simpson leaned forward in her rocking chair and started hollering.

"Look both ways before you cross that street, missy!" she yelled loudly. I swear, the woman was always screaming. And even as I ran, I could just *feel* the passionate prayers she was shooting in my direction, asking God to get me safely to the other side of the street. I could tell—by the sheer decibel level of her voice—that she was genuinely concerned about the possibility of my getting flattened by a passing car, just like Mr. Fisher was about to flatten all those worms.

I was running like the wind, raindrops pelting my hair, hands and arms. But even in the corner of my mind, I could feel myself worrying about whether nosy Sheila was peeking out of her window, spying on me. Of course, in my effort to avoid as many raindrops as possible, I ran zigzag all the way there, so it took me a little more time than usual to get to Mrs. Simpson's house.

As much as I loved my friend, I sure wished she'd quiet down. And although I hated to admit it, even as I was hoofing it across the street, I could feel the hot flames of embarrassment beginning to burn my brown cheeks. *Why'd she absolutely insist on doing all that hootin' and hollering? What if she fell out of her rocker or something like that?* Show-off Sheila would never have let me hear the end of it. I imagined the sound of Sheila's voice; a tense, teasing whisper directly into my ear: "Why are you best friends with a hundred-year-old woman anyway?" I could hear her asking me with disdain.

Just as quickly, God came in close and slapped all that embarrassment right off my slender shoulders. He reminded me that Mrs. Simpson was my *friend*—and a good one, too. She was as excited to see me as I was to see her. We were bosom buddies.

But her barking continued, sounding a little like a seal.

"Watch out! I *know* you see that car coming down from Oakland Street, don't you?" she yelled again, leaning even farther out of her rocker now. I was beginning to think that all the excitement with the rainstorm and the approaching car and my upcoming visit might have been too much for her. It might give her a heart attack or something. But Luella Rae

Simpson was as strong as an ox; always was, from what I could remember. When her husband was alive (I don't remember him well; I was very young when he died), I watched her one day from our hallway window as she lifted up the back of their car while he scrambled underneath to rattle around near the rear axle, fiddling around with something that required a wrench. Or at least I *think* she lifted that car up by herself. (If there was a jack involved, I definitely didn't see it.) Plus, when her husband scrambled out from underneath the car, she let the car down nice and easy-like, snapped at her house dress with her dish rag, then calmly walked back inside to finish boiling her collards. No joke. When I tell you, you'd better believe it: She was strong as an ox. There would be no heart attacks today.

"Just wait till that car passes, baby, then come on across!" she continued in her loud, flat voice.

"Did you hear me, girl? I'm telling you to *wait* a ham-sandwich minute!"

Now she was gesturing wildly, making all kinds of warning signs with her hands. I did listen. And I did see the car, too. It was a full block away. I could have easily made it— even with my strategic, zigzag pattern—but, out of deference to Mrs. Simpson, I stopped at the curb and waited for the car to pass. It was an candy-apple-red T-Bird going much too fast, and as it passed by, dirty rainwater splashed all over me, all the way up to my neck. Jumping jackrabbits! Mother had just washed my cotton jumper that morning.

Mrs. Simpson saw the whole thing

"Shouldna' been standing so close to the curb, missy!" she

chided as soon as I'd climbed safely up the front stairs of her porch. "You might not have gotten your little narrow backside splashed from head to toe if you hadn't been standing so close to the street. Didn't you *hear* me hollering at you to wait?" she asked through a gentle smile, smacking her gums, which told me she didn't have her teeth in. Still, bless her heart, she had her handy dish towel ready the moment I arrived. For some strange reason she kept that dish towel with her everywhere she went, even if she was moving from the living room to the kitchen—but *this* time it actually came in handy. She reached in close to dry my rain-sprayed face in gentle plucks and pats, smacking softly and shaking her head in mock disgust.

"Chil', you're soaked to the bone," she muttered, leaning even farther forward to wipe down my skinny arms and large potato-shaped knees. *Don't let her topple over, God. Let her keep her balance and pleasepleaseplease protect her from falling out of her rocking chair.*

"Plus, you just keep growing like a weed!"

I could tell she was genuinely thrilled to see me. Really, truly happy.

She kept on: "You were just over here a few days ago, and I do declare you look a good half-inch taller since then. I should toss you out back with the rest of the beautiful weeds in my garden," she said, pulling me in close for a hug.

Mrs. Simpson smelled like mothballs, boiled chicken, and Vicks VapoRub. Not a bad or unpleasant kind of smell, just an **old-people's** smell, like when you sniff the inside of an overcrowded closet or maybe when you crawl up into your attic on a hot summer day. She also kind of cackled when she laughed, and she walked a little stooped over, because of her age and all.

She was pretty old, all right—and I really, truly loved the fact that she was so old! Why? Because she had loads of rich and wonderful real-life stories to share with me every time I visited, which is precisely why I spent time with her just about every other day (especially in the summers when school was out). I think I remember her telling me (but I can't confirm with 182 percent accuracy, since it happened so long go) that her parents had been sharecroppers, and her great-grandparents had been slaves. It was like being best friends with a walking, talking history book, except with a soft lap, a tender touch, and a loving heart. Yes, indeed. The two of us would spend hours rocking together on her front porch in the searing summer heat or retreating, finally, into the dimly lit rooms of her home (which somehow always remained cool, even though she didn't have air-conditioning).

A comfortable moment of silence stood between us. Finally, she spoke.

"You say your prayers this morning?" she asked matter-of-factly, studying my face carefully for an honest answer.

"In a way," I answered as honestly as I could. After all, I reasoned with myself, I *had* said my morning prayer as soon as I'd awakened, but it was shorter than usual, so I wasn't sure if it still counted. Plus, I'd prayed for the worms in the street, *and* we'd all said the blessing before breakfast, but I still didn't know if these were fervent and passionate enough for Mrs. Simpson's standards. Mrs. Simpson was one powerfully praying woman, by golly.

"Either you did or you didn't," she answered crisply, but without rancor or sarcasm.

"Well, then, yes, ma'am, I talked to God on my way over here," I replied halfheartedly, relieved that I hadn't had to lie. It was true, I *had* talked to Him—briefly. Never mind that my prayer to Him had been about the bloodworms, or that my morning prayer had lasted only a few brief seconds. Something deep within me assured me, right then and there, as I was standing on her porch, that God doesn't discriminate or pass judgment on which prayer is more important than another. He listens to them all. Of *that*, I was sure, even if— but not just because—I scrunch up my toes.

"Always make time to pray, baby, no matter how busy you are. Jesus gave His entire life for us. The least we can do is give a moment of our own back to Him."

As usual, she was correct.

I made a mental note to put prayer in the center of my life—or try to, anyway. Mother and Daddy always seemed to keep God close around them, and I knew I had a responsibility to communicate with Him on a pure and fundamental level. Even though I was only seven, I knew that everything was in God's hands, and that His hands were guiding everything.

The only problem was that I didn't always have the *time* to pray. My playhouse out back always beckoned. There were fireflies to be caught in the dark of night. There was the magnetic pull of Mother's lilting voice that distracted me from my prayer time as well, especially on the nights when we'd sit together reading *Black Beauty*. Then there was the ice-cream man in his slow-moving truck, the Pied Piper of our entire neighborhood who made every child in a five-block radius drop whatever they were doing to come a-running.

Of all the things that could have—and did—distract me from whatever I was doing (even *praying*—sorry, God), I think the ice-cream man was the most powerful. The far-off, melodic tinkling sound of his truck was enough to make *any* child rise up from their knees mid-prayer. Mrs. Simpson would have been so, so disappointed. No doubt, the ice-cream man had more power and pull in our neighborhood than Martin Luther King Jr. himself. (No disrespect meant to Dr. King, but it's true. Or at least put it this way: If any child on my block saw two people walking down the street toward them, one being Martin Luther King Jr. and the other being the ice-cream man, I'm pretty sure they'd run like the wind toward the ice-cream man, nickels and pennies in hand. It's just how the kids in my neighborhood were.)

Our *parents*, however, were an entirely different story. Inside just about every neat, well-kept home on our block were what I called the FEOs—the Four Essential Objects. The first: a framed color photograph of Martin Luther King Jr. The second: an aged and yellowed palm frond from the most recent Palm Sunday service (usually tucked or taped behind the King photo), a family Bible, and the latest issue of *Ebony* magazine displayed on the living room table. I saw these as important indicators of the abiding faith and pride that existed within our close community. (To this day, I still have my grandmother's palm frond from a Palm Sunday service she attended probably long before I was even born.)

So no, our parents weren't anywhere near as excited about the ice-cream man as us kids.

But in our eyes, the ice-cream man was *magic*.

The very sound of that scratchy, repetitive little melody coming out of the speaker on top of his truck would stop kids in their tracks. If you were praying, you stopped (but not before promising God that you'd be back in five minutes). If you were in the middle of an argument with your best friend, you'd freeze first (to make sure that what you were hearing was, indeed, the sound of his truck), then you'd go a-running, promising to pick up the argument where you left off as soon as you finished your Nutty Buddy. Shoot, even if you were in the bathroom, for goodness' sake, you'd finish up at break-neck speed!

Kids scrambled wildly to get to their parents for spare change, hopping up and down like little jumping beans and crying, "Hurry *up*, Daddy! Find that quarter! The truck is driving away! He's *leaving*! Come *on*!" Then finally, the mad dash to catch the truck, because oftentimes he *had* turned the corner, to everyone's disbelief and disappointment. (And I know personally that there's *nothing worse* than missing the ice-cream man—whether it was because you were a dime or a nickel short, or because your prehistoric parents were embarrassingly slow at pulling their wallets out of their pockets, there's not really too much else that could be worse in a child's life.)

As if reading my mind, Mrs. Simpson continued:

"A long time ago, a saint of a man named Francis de Sales instructed people to commune with the Lord, no matter how busy they were," she said. "In fact, and let me see if I can remember this right"—she muttered almost to herself, pulling absently at the fraying hem of her housedress—"he said something like, 'We should all pray for at least fifteen minutes a day.'"

She sat still for a minute in heavy concentration, then continued, as if remembering the punch line to a joke. "'*Except* if we're too busy . . . then, we should pray for *thirty* minutes!'"

She really tickled herself with that one, laughing and wheezing and laughing some more at St. Francis's urgent plea for all of us to make time to pray more, no matter what else is on our busy agendas.

A sudden loud crack of thunder sent me straight into Mrs. Simpson's ample lap. I landed right on top of her Bible, hoping at that very moment that I hadn't committed some blasphemous sin by ripping the pages, which were as delicate as the skin of an onion—definitely not designed to withstand the sudden weight of a seven-year-old girl (even a skinny-legged beanpole like me). But she received me graciously, encircling me with both arms. As she hugged me, she let out another loud, whooping laugh (that cackle again), and she leaned over to place her heavy bible (the King James large-print version) on the floor so she could kiss me on top of my head.

"Think you can still fit that growing body of yours into my lap?" she asked with humor humming in her heart. All I knew was that I was content where I was—in her lap—even though her wrinkled skin (unlike Mother's) smelled slightly of mentholatum and old-people medicine. We sat together on her front porch rocking silently, happy to be together. Even as we rocked, though, I kept a keen eye out for Sheila, who'd never let me hear the end of it if she saw me being a big baby for sitting on the lap of a hundred-and-fifty-year-old lady.

After a few minutes, Mrs. Simpson stood up and settled me in the rocking chair while she shuffled back inside her house. The rain was still coming down in sure, steady sheets. From across the street, I watched our house. One of my siblings—I couldn't tell precisely which one because her face was obscured behind the screen—opened our front door to let Kaboodle out onto the porch. Our cat crouched at the edge of the top step, wary and reluctant to be outside, so close to the rain. I smiled when, only a moment later, a thin, golden female arm opened the door again, and Kaboodle dashed back into the warm safety of our house.

Minutes passed.

What in the Sam Hill was Mrs. Simpson *doing* inside her house for such a long time? Why would she leave me outside all by myself when we were supposed to be enjoying each other's company? Should I go check on her, just in case she'd tripped on the throw rug in her hallway or had a heart attack in the bathroom or gotten electrocuted by a faulty wire in her kitchen? A moment later, all of these questions were answered as the mouthwatering aroma of her homemade scratch biscuits came wafting through an open window. My heart danced a happy jig, and my little soul sent up a prayer of gratitude

What touched me most deeply, though, was something far beyond her merely preparing those delicious biscuits. It tugged at my little heart to know that this sweet, Bible-reading, bent-over woman had actually taken the time to prepare for my arrival, all so that I could have a special treat. Her famous scratch biscuits aren't easy to make, either; there's the dough that needs to be prepared, then refrigerated for a time, followed by the time-consuming task of kneading the darned stuff. To say nothing of pulling out the wooden rolling pin and spreading that dough flat-as-a-pancake on the counter, then using a mason jar to cut out the circular shapes that transform the dough into beautiful round biscuits. You better know it, making scratch biscuits is more than a notion, and I felt honored that she'd gone to such trouble. I visualized her arthritic hands kneading the dough, and I really hoped it hadn't caused her any pain. I imagined her moving around in her kitchen, slowly pulling out eggs from her refrigerator, large enamel bowls from her cupboards, and then rooting through her pantry for the shortening. She'd made a huge effort on that rainy afternoon, and it certainly touched me deeply.

So I continued sitting there on the porch, pulling in the smell of Mrs. Simpson's baking, smiling like a Cheshire cat the whole time, my skinny legs dangling happily from her white wicker rocker. *Lord knows you should have lotioned those legs before you ran out of this house,* I heard Mother whispering to my imagination. *Not even a two-hundred-year-old woman, sweet as she is, wants to look at a pair of rusty, ashy knees, much less on a dreary day like this, Beauty! Pay more attention to your appearance!*

In that moment, I also began to worry a little that my body weight was probably becoming too much for Mrs. Simpson during our regular visits. Sure, she was miraculously robust and strong as an ox, but she was still as old as Methuselah. I decided I'd better sit in my own porch chair the next time I came over to visit. Goodness! The woman had about five chairs on her front porch! Why did I always insist on sitting in her *lap*? The last thing I wanted to do was harm her. She baked scratch biscuits and crocheted beautiful table doilies. She read to me from her Bible. She cared deeply about whether or not I'd be squished by a car as I crossed the street. She was one of my best friends.

Finally, I got up and walked into her house. I found her in the kitchen, leaning almost into the oven, checking on her biscuits. Because she was so old, I worried about her something terrible. As soon as she saw me, she straightened up to a standing position and nodded toward the kitchen table— which meant she wanted us to sit down and talk.

Uh-oh. Her head nodding worried me a little. *Was I in trouble?*

We sat together for a spell in comfortable but complete silence. I tried to look at her out of the corner of my eye to see if she'd fallen asleep (old people always seem to fall asleep in the middle of their sentences or while they're reading the Bible), but I was a little startled to see that she was staring directly at me, as alert as if she'd just had five or six cups of Maxwell House coffee. I cleared my throat. We listened to the wall clock tick-tocking away. Finally, I turned to watch her watching me. Her face looked thoughtful, maybe even a little worried. *Something's up*, I thought to myself. *She's got something on her mind.*

Sure enough, she started in:

"Just because you're in summer recess doesn't mean you

stop studying your lessons, you know," she said, finally getting around to the point. It was too sweet. She was worried about her little friend, concerned that my brain would get rusty and slow-moving if I slacked on my summer homework.

"You been studying your lessons?"

Goodness me. Here it comes: The old "you-better-be-doing-your-homework" lecture. Jeez.

"Yes, ma'am," I lied handily and instinctively. Here I go again, on my way straight to hell for lying to Mother yesterday and Mrs. Simpson today. And more likely than not, Mrs. Simpson will leave this earth before I will because she's about a thousand years old, and I'm only seven. Drat it all! I won't even get to meet her in heaven, 'cause I will surely be in hell for lying.

But that didn't make me want her biscuits any less.

I knew for a fact that she couldn't eat her own scratch biscuits anymore. Although I'm not certain, I think I remember overhearing Mother talking quietly with my sisters one day, in hushed, worried tones, about Mrs. Simpson's "high blood pressure" and her "sugar dia-blee-teez." How was a seven-year-old to recognize the word *diabetes*? Somehow, these medical terms translated into the fact that poor Mrs. Simpson couldn't even enjoy her own baking! (Selfish to say, but I found myself smiling a little at this thought, because it meant *more for me!*)

"We'll get back to the subject of your lessons later," she said, still eyeing me suspiciously as though she just *knew* I hadn't cracked open my black-and-white marble notebook since school had let out a few weeks earlier. (Her instincts were right. I hadn't.) Despite myself, I was becoming a little impatient for those biscuits to be done. *How much longer? They're not burning, are they? You didn't forget about them, did you? Are you sure you even remembered to turn the oven on?*

She'd spooned some boiled cabbage from a pan on the stove into a large pink bowl, and she said a quick blessing before she began to eat. (She knew I had absolutely *zero* interest in cabbage—and that my sole reason for living was to scarf down her delicious biscuits the second they came out of the oven.) We continued sitting at the table together in comfortable silence—she gumming at that crazy cabbage, me sitting pensively, waiting for those darned biscuits to finish baking.

After about five or six minutes, I felt as if I *had* to get something off my chest: this ongoing, delicate matter of my being called a skinny-legged, potato-kneed beanpole, which hurt my feelings immensely. (I swear, my self-esteem swayed back and forth with as much regularity as the pendulum of my Aunt Lilly's grandfather clock.) I couldn't resist telling Mrs. Simpson—right there as we sat at her red-speckled kitchen table with shiny chrome legs and matching red vinyl chairs—about this nasty old name. I mean, really. A *skinny-legged beanpole?* Come on . . . and were my knees really, truly shaped like potatoes? I launched in, telling her exactly how I felt and explaining how much it had hurt my feelings.

Mrs. Simpson kept gumming away at her cabbage, though, not saying a word, but I could tell she was listening carefully as I blew off steam. She just kept chewing and looking at some invisible spot on her table and chewing some more. Shoving it in. I kind of wished she'd put in her teeth. Mother would have died a thousand deaths before sitting at anybody's table gumming away at food, much less without a tooth in her mouth. But Mrs. Simpson wasn't Mother. She was my friend. My toothless, cabbage-eating, biscuit-baking friend. And I loved her more than life itself.

Finally, she spoke.

"Let me get this straight. If someone calls you a three-legged horny toad, you just all of a sudden *become* a three-legged horny toad? Is that what I'm hearing from you, chil'?"

No sympathy from *her*, by golly. Not one bit. Not even an ounce.

She finally stopped chewing, though, and was studying me carefully. In the next second, she reached over to pull my chair closer to hers. I swear she was strong as an ox, that woman. She leaned in close to my face, the flat palms of both of her hands on either side of my cheeks. We were eye to eye. Even though her breath smelled kind of cabbagey, I listened attentively as she spoke.

"Your parents raised you to know that you are deeply loved by everyone around you—by both of them, of course, by your siblings, by your good friends, and—most important— by the sweet Lord Jesus Himself. You're a little brown queen, honey—and don't you ever let anybody tell you different. You understand?"

I nodded, feeling better already. Even my knees felt like they were shrinking down to their regular size, from over-sized Idaho russet potatoes to, say, two medium-sized door-knobs. *Why did I allow self-doubt to cloud my thinking and knock me so off-center?*

Mrs. Simpson continued, newly fortified by my head nodding. "And you've got to learn that anybody who calls another person a mean name doesn't think very highly of herself, so what you've got to do is pray for them, honey. Be kind to her."

I gazed down at my feet, trying to make sense of Mrs. Simpson's instructions to be nice to everybody. I mean, I'd heard of turning the other cheek and all, but this was ridiculous. *Pray* for the person who'd likened my knees to a food that grows underneath the *dirt* and say nice things to the very person who may as well have called me a scatterbrained scarecrow? Come *on*.

But Mrs. Simpson meant business.

"It's unhealthy to let negative thinking and mean words float around in the universe. By fretting about those words, you're giving them way too much power. They're like little mean-spirited needles . . . trying to prick little holes into this beautiful balloon of ours that is God's loving universe."

I stopped breathing momentarily, disappointed. I wasn't quite sure what she meant about the universe and the pricked balloon and all, but I did understand the part about having to be kind, no matter what. I tried to replay Mrs. Simpson's words in my head.

Mrs. Simpson sat up straighter. The spirit of divine goodness and grace was moving in around her, fast and furious. I could feel it. "Always, always pray for those who hurt you, baby, no matter how hard it is," she said simply. "Be kind to her, not mean. Patient, not bitter."

She was on a spiritual roll now, and going to town on that cabbage: "I've always believed that kind deeds are like little prayers. And Lord knows we don't have enough of either in this world we live in today—kind deeds *or* little prayers." *Kind deeds are like little prayers.* I made a mental note to remember that phrase for when I got older. I liked the way it sounded. And then, as if in afterthought, she added: "And since when did you let somebody's name-calling get you all riled up and feeling poorly about yourself?" she asked, getting loud now, just like she had on the porch.

I didn't have an answer.

Then, with a saucy smile and a brightness of eye, she added, "And as fast as you're putting on weight, a 'beanpole' isn't what she should have called you at all. Maybe 'pudge' or a 'piglet,' but definitely not a beanpole. You're growing way too fast for that. Sounds to me like she might need glasses, 'cause she sure isn't seeing straight if she thinks you look like a beanpole. A *beanpole*? Ha!"

Mrs. Simpson was trying to be funny for my sake. She wanted to comfort her friend, to reassure her biscuit-eating buddy. It was so sweet I could have cried right then and there. I had an advocate. A protector. A best friend who boiled chicken and held my hand. I resisted the urge to ask her how she thought those biscuits were coming along; I was still a little worried she'd forgotten about them. And I knew Mrs. Simpson well enough to know that once she got started on subjects like the Lord or making the universe around us a healthier, happier place to live, there was really no stopping her.

I tried mightily to come up with a diversionary tactic. I mean, I love the Lord too, and I believe in universal peace as much as the next person—but I thought I smelled the biscuits burning. I considered walking over to the sink to get a glass of water and then, by sheer coincidence and just because I happened to be standing next to the oven, I could take a peek inside.

But nothing doing.

Before I could even rise from the table to try out my diversionary, water-drinking tactic, she reached over, gently plucked my forearm, and gave me a cheerful wink.

"Come on, let's go get comfortable. Let's have some tea and read a little more. Our biscuits still have a few more minutes."

Thank you, Lord, for letting her remember about those biscuits. And if it's not too much trouble, pleasepleaseplease remind her to take them out of the oven before they burn.

I loved reading the Bible with Mrs. Simpson—and I loved the feeling of being led by the hand into her dimly lit parlor. After settling me into my favorite chair, she ambled slowly but surely toward the china cabinet. A few seconds later, she was shuffling back, deftly carrying two delicate teacups and matching saucers. She set them down gently, each of them on their own fancy doily. Raindrops spattered against the windows. We were settling in to read.

Her parlor was sheer glory. In my seven-year-old mind at least, I remember lace coverlets on every chair. Handmade doilies on each table, most crocheted by Mrs. Simpson herself (some of them were even made by her grandmother, about a thousand years ago). In the far corner, a walnut-stained curio cabinet filled with antique trinkets and crystal baubles. As we sipped on our Lipton tea, she read to me from the book of Psalms. It was funny, the way it always happened: somehow, the woman seemed to know precisely which biblical passages to read at precisely the right time, and she always centered them around whatever seemed to be moving in my heart or troubling my mind. She was trying to send me a message that day, as we sat together in her parlor: to be patient with Sheila, and to rely on God for an answer on how to deal with the conflict between us. I tried hard to concentrate on her words, which, at that moment, were from Psalms 27:14 ("Wait on the Lord: be of good courage, and He shall strengthen thine heart: wait, I say, on the Lord.")—but the smell of the biscuits took over my mind, my heart, and my nose. I knew they'd be ready soon. Either that, or burned to a sad and sorrowful crisp.

After a time, we got up and, hand in hand, slowly made our way back to the kitchen. She leaned down to check the oven, smiling to herself. Her smile revealed great news:

It must be eating time!

I watched, mesmerized, as she spread both butter and her homemade peach preserves over each piping-hot biscuit. Before she could even bring the plate over to the table, I was reaching for them. Simultaneously, I heard Mother's inner voice whispering in my ear: *"Don't be rude, Beauty. Take your time when you eat—and always, always leave a little something on your plate when you're finished with your meal. Don't ever become a member of the Clean Plate Club! It's not ladylike to gobble up every crumb. Gobble, gobble. You're not a turkey!"*

I want to tell you that those biscuits melted in my mouth—and I ate about seven of them. I could feel the beginnings of nausea rumbling around in my lower stomach, but I convinced myself it was because I was troubled about Sheila.

Mother would have stuck needles in her eyes if she'd known her baby girl was across the street digging into that plate of biscuits with the force of a John Deere bulldozer. But Mother didn't have to know, now, did she?

Suddenly, I was up on Mrs. Simpson's lap again. I couldn't contain myself. My arms had to hug her. My heart had to thank her. My words had to reassure her: "I love you so much, Mrs. Simpson. The biscuits were heavenly. Thank you so very, very much for going through all that trouble to make them especially for me." I felt better after I'd said it, but she looked a little taken aback.

Then, as if it were an afterthought, I remembered this:

"And I know you always pray for me, Mrs. Simpson. I want to tell you how much I appreciate that, and I want you to know that I pray for you, too. I ask God to take care of you, 'cause I worry about your falling down the steps or choking on your boiled chicken or maybe getting stuck in your bathtub or something. That's why I pray for God to protect you. I don't want anything to happen to you." *Drat! I was suddenly near tears. Wimp!*

She blinked rapidly for a second or two, then quickly licked her top lip; a sure sign that what I'd just said went straight to her heart.

"Well now, you just come here, child," she said in a whisper.

I moved again into her outstretched arms, happy beyond belief to be in her arms.

"It makes me so happy that you keep me in your prayers," she said softly. "And it makes me happier even still that you pray on a regular basis."

I smiled softly, eyes downcast. My jumper was almost dry, I noticed. I wondered whether the dirty rainwater from the street (from when the car splashed me) would leave a stain. Mrs. Simpson wanted to say something else, so I turned my mind away from my jumper and toward my beautiful friend.

"Remember this, too, sweetie: Although I am so deeply touched that you pray for me—and I don't want you to stop!— remember also that prayer is not just about asking for what you want so much as it is silencing your small voice to listen to the Supreme Voice that dwells inside and all around every one of us."

I was pretty sure I understood what she'd just said about not just asking God for what we want when we pray (Mother and Daddy had taught me this, too), but I was more than a little puzzled when she said the part about "silencing my small voice." Was she trying to tell me—in a way that wouldn't hurt my feelings—that I yammered a little too much and that people were starting to get sick and tired of my incessant chatter? Is that what she'd meant by "silencing my own voice"? I didn't learn until years later that by "creating silence" she meant just that: the intentional, sustained effort to silence one's soul for quiet contemplation and to listen for—and actually *hear*—the voice of God when He speaks to us.

She kissed the top of my head and nodded briskly toward the parlor. "Now come on. Let's get back to our reading. We've kept the good Lord waiting long enough, what with the biscuit making and all. It's His time now."

As we were making our way back into the parlor, one big

fat biscuit crumb fell from my plate onto the kitchen floor. Thank goodness she was walking in front of me, snapping her dishrag as we moved through the hallway. Faster than a jumping jackrabbit, I picked up the crumb from the floor, kissed it up to God, then popped the buttery morsel into my mouth. I wasn't worried about catching the cooties because (1) I'd kissed it up to God and (2) Mrs. Simpson had the cleanest, shiniest kitchen floor I'd ever seen in my life—skittering dust bunnies and all.

In the parlor again, we repositioned ourselves, automatically selecting our favorite chairs: hers, an overstuffed green arm chair with handmade lace arm covers crocheted by her grandmother; and mine, a deep, wine-colored wing chair that surrounded my little head like a protective friend. I felt safe in the chair. I loved its musty old smell. There was a television in the room, but we rarely watched it when we were together. Once I watched *The Wizard of Oz* on it because I could see it "in color." Well, by "color" I mean that her husband, before he died, had attached one of those red, green, and yellow pieces of plastic over the screen, which meant, by definition, that they were the proud owners of a color TV.

She was as focused as a laser beam. All she wanted to do was read to me from the Bible.

She cleared her throat and began to read aloud in her strong, throaty voice, from Romans 8:38–39. Every word she spoke reminded me that, no matter how bad things got or how mean people became, nothing—but *nothing*—could get in the way of the infinite and everlasting love that God and

I had between us. And Mrs. Simpson was right about what she'd said earlier: I *should* be praying for Sheila instead of sending her nasty thoughts.

Slowly, I rose and went over to kneel at her lap. I knew she wanted to pray, and I knew I wanted to as well. We clasped hands and lowered our heads. This time, she lowered her voice to a whisper, as if God himself were standing there right beside us. I lowered my head, too, and clamped my eyes so tightly shut I could have made myself go blind. (I resisted the urge to cross my fingers and scrunch my toes, just in case God didn't believe in all that silliness.)

This was indeed an important prayer: Even though she'd been mean, she was still my friend—and I wanted my friend back. No matter how pigheaded and obstinate we'd both been, I didn't want to be angry anymore. I missed Sheila, and I didn't like it that we were mad at each over a silly banana bike and cruel name-calling.

"Father God," Mrs. Simpson petitioned, "we praise You and uplift Your holy name. I ask You right now, Father, to let Miss Kriss know that she was made in your image, and that she is a wonderful girl with a good, strong brain and a pure, loving heart. Remove those shadows of self-doubt that sometimes surround her, Lord, and guide the two girls back toward the light of friendship and forgiveness. Lead them and guide them toward the truth. Toward Your truth—which is the only Truth there is."

My eyes were clamped tight, of course, but I sure was tempted to open them for a quick peek at Mrs. Simpson, just to see what she was doing with her face and all. I wanted to see her expression, 'cause her voice was beginning to sound kind of like she was about to cry. She finished with a flourish, raising her hands toward the ceiling.

"Amen!" she whispered, hands still uplifted above her.

"Amen," I repeated softly, lifting my hands in the air as well (even though it felt awkward because I didn't know what to do with them up there like that).

"Amen!" we finished in unison.

I felt better already. Less bony. A tad more graceful.

She studied me for a moment, trying to make sure I was listening. After a minute more, she spoke: "I hope you don't go thinking that the amount of friends you have makes you the person who are—cause if you do, you're just dead *wrong*, honey!"

I must have looked confused, because she continued on: "What I'm trying to say, baby, is that you don't need a certain number of friends—only a number of friends you can be certain of!" I liked that one, too, and vowed to memorize it and pull it out when I was older. *You don't need a certain number of friends; only a number of friends you can be certain of.* Good stuff, indeed.

On that rainy afternoon, with my full stomach and renewed spirit, it was Mrs. Simpson who'd shown me the clear path. The path without the bumps or the anger or the jealousy—and let's face it, I had been a little envious of Sheila's new bike, pure and simple. Plus, I was angry at the name she'd called me, but already I felt that anger melting away like butter on a piping-hot scratch biscuit. I felt renewed. Hopeful. And infinitely thankful to my friend Mrs. Luella Rae Simpson.

Taking a final sip of tea, she wiped both of the cups and the dainty saucers clean with her ever-present dish towel, then she handed them over to me in a neatly stacked, precarious little pile. Because she was trembling slightly, the dishes made little rattling sounds as she held them in her outstretched hand.

"These are for you," she said without fanfare or ceremony. "You know I don't even take them out unless you come over, so I figured you'd probably get more use out of them than me—you know, for when you're older and start attending fancy tea parties and Garden Club meetings." *What in the world is a "Garden Club meeting"? I know that Aunt Bee sits on the Board of Directors of hers—along with Clara and all the other Fine Ladies of Mayberry—but how does this pertain to me? What do the Garden Club Ladies actually do in Detroit (as opposed to Mayberry)? Are they glorious Lipton tea–drinking ladies who sit cross-legged in their pretty gardens, laughing and talking among the neat rows of collard greens and tomatoes?*

Hot tears sprang to my eyes before I could stop them. She might have been old, but she had eyes like a hawk. Even in her shadowy parlor, she saw the shine of my tears immediately.

"Don't go getting all fussy on me now, chil'. It's just a couple of old cups and a few saucers. Not even a full set. Just put them away for safekeeping till you're ready to use them. And when you finally do use them, think of me."

Right then and there, I pledged to take good care of her beautiful teacups—maybe I could even save them long enough until I became a real woman with a real family, when we would sip on tea every Sunday afternoon after church.

After some time, she patted the arm of her chair, indicating it was time for her to rise. She said she had to "fetch something" from upstairs. About two thousand hours later, she came back downstairs, dish towel in her left hand, a carefully folded, yellowed piece of paper in another. Reaching the bottom of the stairs and slightly winded, she handed me the piece of paper.

"My mother gave me this a long, long time ago, after I'd had a disagreement with a girl, Billie Jean Watkins, who lived on the property next to ours."

She watched me watching her.

"Go ahead; unfold it. Read it, nice and loud so I can hear it again," she instructed, still standing there with her dish towel. "My mama gave it to me, and I'm asking you to read it out loud, 'cause it sounds like you need to hear it. Now *read!*"

The woman could certainly be bossy when she wanted to.

I carefully unfolded the note, studying the writer's neat penmanship.

"Think about your friend Sheila when you read it," was her last instruction.

I cleared my throat, ready to obey and perform for my friend:

If I knew you and you knew me,
And each of us could clearly see,
By that inner life divine,
The meaning of your heart and mine;

I'm sure that we would differ less
And clasp our hands in friendliness,
If you knew me, and I knew you.

I looked up at her, worried that I'd mispronounced most of the words (at the time I still wasn't a proficient reader), but she was already shuffling toward the sunroom, rummaging around for something else. A busybody, she was. Finally, she pulled out a small brown paper bag, offering it to me with kind, tired eyes. Realizing that she was offering the bag for me to take home my teacups in, I made a mad dash into her kitchen and swiped the nearest hand towel I could find. I whizzed back into the sunroom.

"I'll bring your towel back, Mrs. Simpson. I promise I will," I mumbled as I wrapped the china safely inside the towel's folds. Before I knew it, my brown bag was full of treats.

My very own china.

And about seven or eight scratch biscuits Mrs. Simpson had wrapped earlier for me to take back to my family. (I could still feel their warmth though the aluminum foil.)

It had been a wonderful visit.

As I crossed the street on my way back home, Mrs. Simpson stood on her front porch and hollered out one last Holy reminder. As usual, she'd hollered out precisely what I needed to hear, precisely when I needed to hear it:

"Remember what it says in Proverbs 17:17, sweetness!"

Did that mean I'd have to look it up in our Bible when I got home? Shoot! Cookie and I were going to catch bumblebees in Miss Marla's backyard garden! And I knew it because I could see the mason jars already lined up on the top step of her porch, with holes punched into the lid of each jar so the bees could breathe.

As if reading my mind, Mrs. Simpson recited the verse while she was standing on her porch. I have to admit, it was the first time in my life I'd ever heard Scripture being hollered by a hundred-and-fifty-year-old woman.

"It says, 'A friend loveth at all times!'"

Now, *that* was a good one. *A friend loveth at all times?* Just hearing the words calmed my soul and softened my heart.

At that moment, the rain stopped. The sun didn't suddenly start shining and the birds didn't suddenly begin chirping or anything that dramatic, but the rain did stop, which I took to be a divine miracle or a spiritual sign or something.

Turns out it was.

In that next moment, I heard the unmistakable swish of her bicycle tires before I saw the shine of her face. Sheila rode past me, colored streamers flying from her handlebars.

"I like your new bike. It's sure pretty," I said simply.

She slowed down and glanced back at me, surprised and pleased. And then, the six magic words that made me feel all right with God and Mrs. Simpson and everybody in the whole wide world: "You wanna ride it some time?"

Sheila was offering me a ride on her fancy bike! I guessed we were friends again. I felt like clapping and hopping up and down in relief, but that wouldn't have been cool. Instead, I just smiled and reached out to hold her hand.

After a brief moment, I looked straight into her eyes and spoke quietly, calling her by her nickname out of pure habit. "I'm sorry, She-She. I don't know exactly what happened to make us so mad at each other, but I sure would like it if we could be friends again."

I waited, holding my breath, praying that she wouldn't reject my apology. If something wicked or cruel-hearted had come out of her mouth at that point, when I was at my most vulnerable, I'd have probably smacked the taste out of her mouth. Or knocked her into next week. Or snatched her baldheaded.

But she didn't.

"What're *you* sorry for, girl?" Her face told me she was sincere; she honestly couldn't figure it out. "Shoot, *I'm* the one who called you a 'skinny-legged beanpole'!" She kicked her front tire in disgust. "I should be apologizing to *you!*"

Another brief moment of silence, then she spoke again.

"Girl, you *know* you're not a beanpole, right?" she asked with only a hint of a grin on her face.

"Of *course* I know that, She-She," I answered, fighting the urge to pull at my fuzzy pigtail. "I figured you were just in a bad mood about something else." *Why was I minimizing all of this, when it had been weighing on my mind for days on end? What a coward.*

"You know why I called you that?" she asked, casting a furtive glance up and the down the street, as though she was worried that someone else might be listening.

She'd piqued my curiosity. In the back of my mind, I wondered if Mrs. Simpson was still standing on her porch, watching us become friends again. If she was, I knew she'd be smiling and praising God and thanking Him for answering her prayers. But I dared not turn around to look. This time belonged to me and Sheila.

She answered her own question.

"Because my sister called me that same name the day Mama and Daddy gave me this here new bike," she said, tapping the handlebars lightly. "I mean, she really screamed it, too. I'm surprised you didn't hear her big mouth."

I might have been mean at times, but I was never ever *cruel*—and to call your own sister a skinny-legged beanpole was just plain mean. It was sinful and downright cruel. In all of my seven long years of living, not one of my six siblings had ever said anything mean or bad to me. All I *ever* received from them was love—pure, unconditional, uncomplicated love. I felt tears stinging my eyes; tears for poor Sheila, who had a sister mean as a junkyard dog. (I'd heard tell that she used to pull the legs off spiders and fry ants on the hot asphalt with a magnifying glass.)

I tried to comfort my friend.

"She's just jealous 'cause you got a new bike." (Never mind that it was *me* who'd been secretly jealous, too!) She's just mad 'cause her own bike is about five thousand years old and has about two hundred spokes missing, so she can barely ride that old ugly thing."

I could see the beginnings of a smile on Sheila's face, so I continued, praying that my humor would help her hurting heart.

"Her handlebars are so rusty, I wouldn't ride that old bike if she *paid* me!"

Heartened by her grin, I forged ahead.

"Shoot," I said even louder, "my mama might have to take me to the doctor for a tetanoose shot if she found out

I'd even *touched* her rusty old, beat-up bike!" (I hadn't mastered the pronunciation of "tetanus" just yet, but my effort was well-intentioned.)

Finally, Sheila laughed. A loud, long laugh that made her double over and clap her hands in glee. I had to reach out to steady her body *and* her bike so that she wouldn't topple over. In that instant, while Sheila was distracted, I took a lightning-fast glimpse toward Mrs. Simpson's house. There she was, standing at the top step of her porch. She'd seen the entire scene, and I prayed her vision was good enough to see that Sheila—at that precise moment—was actually *doubled over in laughter!*

Mrs. Simpson waved a pleasant, happy wave to me from across the street. I could tell by her body language that she was pleased as punch that the two of us had finally made up. I also knew that she was thanking the Lord above for answering her prayers about renewing our friendship. *Whatever you do, Mrs. Simpson, pleasepleaseplease don't start hollering and yelling from across the street. Not in front of Sheila. I'll die a thousand deaths.*

But Mrs. Simpson didn't yell. She just kept waving, more than likely thanking God for reuniting two little girls in friendship. *I* was thanking God, too, while I steadied Sheila as she laughed against her bike that day. And my mind was whirring. How is it that God knows exactly what we need, exactly when we need it? How is it that He answers each and every one of our prayers so faithfully? And how in the Sam Hill is it that, no matter what challenges we face, He never turns His back on us?

After a minute, our laughs turned into happy whimpers, and we straightened up to wipe the tears from our eyes. She looked at me again, forcibly trying to repress another gale of laughter.

"Her handlebars sure are rusty, aren't they?" Sheila asked through happy tears.

"Rustier than her rusty old knees when she forgets to put on the Jergens after her bath!" I answered, on a roll now.

And with that, both of us doubled over into laughter yet again, letting Sheila's fancy new banana bike drop gently onto the grass in front of my house. The more she laughed, the harder I laughed.

Not only was our laughter contagious, but our friendship was contagious, too, because about two or three minutes later, good ol' Cookie came bounding off her porch to join us in the fun. She didn't even know what we were laughing at—and we couldn't even explain it to her because we were laughing so hard—but by sheer virtue of the fact that the three of us were fast friends, she assumed it must have been hilarious. So there we sat on my front lawn, the three of us laughing like hyenas—then laughing even harder once we stood up to discover that our backsides were soaked to the bone. (We'd all forgotten that the grass was still wet from the rain.)

A minute later, though, a familiar sound stunned all of us into sudden silence. We froze in our positions; listening. Attentive.

There it was again!

Instinctively, and without uttering so much as a word, we each sprinted off in different directions, running like the wind toward our own homes. Seconds later, we came together again, armed with the coins we needed. And as fast as three jumping jackrabbits, we tore down the street to catch that ol' ice-cream man before he turned the corner.

ᔔ

NEEDLESS to say, the treasures that Mrs. Simpson gave me that day are still dear to me. My friend had shared with me a piece of her past that she deemed precious and perhaps even irreplaceable. Two beautiful teacups, each filled with the memories of the countless warm, shining summer afternoons that Mrs. Simpson and I spent together. Whether it was reading from the Good Book, rocking together on her front porch, or sipping hot Lipton tea in her parlor, it was really our love that sustained us.

So thank you, Mrs. Simpson, as I magnify your memory. Thank you for nudging me toward the joy and relief and freedom that comes from leading a spiritual life. Thank you for helping me become God-centered and filled with faith—not with fear—and for showering me with the powerful reminder that *none* of us is perfect; and for that reason, we are not free to judge others. We must only show compassion and forgiveness. At all times.

And today, sweet friend of mine, your precious teacups remain perfectly intact—generations later. Not a mark or a scratch or a chip. And I know that, even now, as you look down on me today, you're shaking your head in quiet pride—pride that your fine, fuzzy-haired, seven-year-old friend grew into a memory-maker who's able to sidestep the constraints of time and place, and travel way, way back to those golden, sun-splashed days of her childhood.

A Forever Box holds sweet, sentimental trinkets and interesting baubles, of course, but it also exists as a way to remind us to hold fast to the friendships of our past as well. If handled with care, our loving relationships with those long since departed can live forever. The powerful joy that comes with pure friendship can live on indefinitely. And when we preserve and pass down those beautiful trinkets and treasures from a special friendship, we help validate the fact that that person made a lasting, significant difference on this earth, and it reminds us that their earthly presence counted for something big and bold and beautiful.

Today, Mrs. Simpson is gone. My father is no longer alive, either. But fortunately for me, the love I have for both of them is boundless and unforgettable. And whenever I hold the teacups that Mrs. Simpson gave me on that wonderfully rainy afternoon, I am reminded of God's infinite wisdom, his glorious grace, and his tender loving kindness. I am reminded that, if we are to hear the voice of our Higher Power, then we must still our bodies and silence our minds. I am reminded that we are here to love, not to judge. To show compassion, not cruelty.

Without a doubt, it was Mrs. Luella Rae Simpson (along with my parents) who helped teach me about the enduring, everlasting power of prayer. The simple act of holding one of her teacups in my hand reminds me all over again that our prayers are heard, they are answered, and they provide us a direct, sustained way to communicate with our Creator— whatever Creator it is that we choose to worship.

When I look at my china, I think of you, Mrs. Simpson, and the warm memories we will always share.

My heart is filled with gladness.

And every time I remember our summer days, kind friend, these Biblical words come to mind: *My cup runneth over.*

IN PRAISE OF PUMPS

———— ⌗ ————

B Y THE FOLLOWING morning, it was raining cats and dogs again, making this the third day of steady downpour. The neighbors stood outside on their porches, peeking up at the sky and chattering to one another about the "Forty Days and Forty Nights" Bible story of nonstop rain, but I wasn't really worried. A quick peek out the front door told me that the gutters on our street were not yet clogged, and the rainwater hadn't yet risen above the curb—which it did sometimes during heavy storms. So I figured if ol' Noah could survive, then we could, too.

This summer day, I was embarking on yet another mission, and I had every intention of accomplishing it before the sun went down. But for *this* particular mission, I was going to have to enlist a little bit of Mother's help. I wanted to get down the street to see Miss Miriam, because we hadn't visited in more than two weeks and I was just a little worried about her, what with the nasty weather and all.

There were a couple of challenges to this mission: Unlike Mrs. Simpson, who lived across the street, Miss Miriam lived farther down the block. I was no scaredy-cat, mind you, but from my seven-year-old perspective, her large, looming house looked a little spooky. There might be monsters. Plus, it was a rare thing for me to walk so far from home by myself. I wasn't being a little-girlie-baby, by any means. It's just that I generally stayed within very, very close proximity to our house. I felt uncomfortable straying too far. But friendship called, and something deep inside told me that Miss Miriam really wanted me to visit.

So I sidled up to Mother, who was busy unpacking groceries and arranging the canned green beans "just so" in our cupboard.

"I'm worried about Miss Miriam," I told her in an urgent whisper. "I sure would like to go down to her house for a visit, but it's raining too hard and you know I lost my Bozo the Clown umbrella last week, so I can't really walk by myself." *Hint, hint.*

Mother stopped momentarily, grimacing at a dented can of Green Giant sweet peas. (She *hated* dented vegetable cans because she thought they gave off salmonella or cooties or some kind of lethal, liquid poison that seeps into the vegetables from the inside of the can.)

Finally, she looked down at me, rolling the dented can of peas around and around in her hand. I could tell she was considering taking the can back to A&P to see if she could either get a refund or a new, non-dented can. Sweet Mother. She could get quite salty when it came to protecting her children. Our health and well-being were her top priorities, and she'd do anything to keep us away from danger—in this particular case, away from potentially spoiled food that might kill us or make us sick. Finally, she focused on me.

"I guess I could walk you over," she said slowly, her eyebrows furrowed as she studied the can again. (She was *really* worried about that dented can of peas.)

"Run, get your rain boots from the hall and I'll meet you on the porch. We'll take Daddy's big umbrella. I'll call Miss Miriam on our way out the door to let her know you're coming."

I loved Daddy's big black umbrella. I felt so safe underneath, and I never ever got wet when we used it. That thing was huge, with about a thousand spokes underneath to hold it up nice and wide, and it had a thick wooden handle shaped like a J. Only an adult could carry it. Only an adult would want to. It was like a magic shield; the best umbrella I'd ever seen.

On the way to Miss Miriam's, I resisted the urge to stomp through every puddle we passed. Mother wouldn't have liked it one bit, and I didn't want to splash dirty water on her pretty little rain boots. (Mother always wore pretty things, and these rain boots were among my favorites. They were gray, with a black patent leather heel and four black buttons that looked like shiny raisins going up one side and a fancy gray zipper going up the other side. I always thought it was utterly cool that the color of the zipper was gray, to match the boot fabric. Every other zipper I'd ever seen was the ugly, steel-looking color that turned kind of rusty brown after it had been used for a while.)

No, I didn't want to mess up her fancy rain boots. Plus, it would have been kind of rude to walk into Miss Miriam's beautiful home with sopping-wet feet, dripping water and maybe mud all over her shiny, highly polished hardwood floors.

Mother and I arrived at the curb where I would cross the street. Butterflies danced a silly jig in the pit of my stomach. What a girlie-girl. The thought of leaving Mother's side—even for a few minutes—made my stomach hurt. Big baby. I turned and waved a weak and pitiful good-bye, so close to tears that I couldn't speak.

"Call when you're finished, sweetheart, and one of us will come back to this very spot to pick you up!" Mother said, pointing to the curb. "And tell Miss Miriam we all said hello. Send her our best, Beauty."

I hitched up my overalls and turned to look at my mother again. I ignored the ridiculous lump rising in my throat. I just *hated* seeing Mother walk away from me, under any circumstance. But I was on a mission; on my way to visit my beautiful friend. It was time to cross the street.

"Look both ways!" Mother warned as I splashed my way to the other side. I could feel her presence there behind me— standing, watching, making sure I made it safely, probably smiling to herself as she watched her youngest child running zigzag between the raindrops. The moment Mother heard Miss Miriam's squeaky screen door open and slam shut, she knew I was safe. I could imagine her standing there for a moment, then turning to walk back home, mentally preparing to tackle another of a hundred waiting tasks in the busy Clark household.

Once inside, I always hightailed it straight up to Miss Miriam's bedroom, taking two steps at a time. I arrived just outside her bedroom door slightly winded, my heart pounding like crazy. I swear I was a nervous child and quite the worrier, too, for a seven-year-old. I thought I was going into cardiac arrest—or at least feeling the first few, tight wheezes of an oncoming asthma attack. No doubt about it: I was just a tad dramatic.

The moment I entered Miss Miriam's world of sterling-silver hair combs and colored perfume bottles, I was instantly transported to a world of finery and fashion, satin wraps and sequined hats. My name wasn't Kristin anymore. It was Dorothy Dandridge, maybe. Or Lena Horne. Fancy women who shimmied when they walked.

To this day, I still don't know why Miss Miriam spent so much time in her bedroom. Maybe she was sick and elegantly immobile and I was just too young to realize it. I don't even remember who else lived in the house with her, because she was always in her bedroom. Maybe she was a boarder. I simply didn't know. But I *do* know this: I learned to walk in my first pair of high heels when I was seven—and they were *her* heels, bright yellow satin pumps.

She was sitting primly in her vanity chair, studying her cheekbones in the mirror when I entered her room. She didn't exactly smile when she saw me, but I could tell she was happy to see me because her eyes were very bright, and it looked like they were dancing all around. She accepted my hug graciously, even elegantly. By that I mean she didn't even budge from her sitting position when I moved in close to hug her. She just kept sitting there on her little tufted chair, waiting for me to figure out the best way to embrace her—physically, rather awkward, especially if you're trying to give someone a big bear hug. After about thirty seconds, though, she lifted her face ever so slightly and turned her right cheek toward me so that I could kiss it. Kind of like how the movie stars do it. Or Queen Elizabeth. She was the classiest woman I knew, and I felt lucky to be her friend.

"So what are we going to do today?" she asked through a thin smile, holding her left hand up close so she could inspect her fingernails. Needless to say, her nails were always immaculate and her "cuticle beds"—as she called them—were never torn or ragged. Miss Miriam was definitely not a nail-biter. She was way too classy for such nonsense. She once told me that the secret to keeping healthy, neat-looking nails was to massage the cuticles gently, immediately after you've washed your hands, while the skin is still soft. Unfortunately I could never remember to do this because my hands were just always so *busy*. Who had time for proper cuticle care? I'd rather be using my hands to draw giant *X*'s on the sidewalk in front of our house with a piece of thick, white chalk so that Cookie and I could play hopscotch or Mother-May-I until the streetlights came on. Or making mud pies—sloppy, dripping pies, sometimes with pebbles in them—that we'd let "bake" simply by leaving them in the hot sun all day, in neat little rows along the bottom step of Cookie's back porch. No sirree, at that young age, my hands were busy doing other things that were much more fun than cuticle massage. I did promise myself, though, to either remember the manicure tip for when I grew up, or to pass this wisdom along to my older sisters. (I ended up doing both.)

But on this day, I had an idea. I'd been thinking about it for a little while, and if anybody on God's green earth could do it, it would certainly be Miss Miriam. For some reason, I felt embarrassed about blurting it out, but she *had* asked what I wanted to do that day, so I thought I may as well spill the beans.

"I'd sure like to learn to walk in high-heel shoes one of these old days," I said as demurely—and evasively—as possible. I didn't want it to seem like I was *demanding* to learn at that precise moment. I was trying to make it sound almost like an afterthought, rather than a plea. She saw right through it immediately.

"So is the direct answer to my direct question that you'd like for me to *teach* you to walk in high-heel shoes?"

Heavens to Betsy! My elderly friends were the loves of my life, but they didn't believe in pussyfooting around when it came to communicating. Maybe they sensed that they didn't have much longer on this earth anyway, and for that reason alone they might as well just get straight to the point in every conversation. They certainly must have realized that their body clocks were tick-tick-ticking. Shoot, if I was a hundred years old, I probably wouldn't waste any time getting straight to the point, either—especially if I knew it could literally be a day or even a minute before I had to leave this earth to go and meet my Maker. No, I couldn't blame her one bit for her directness—but it did make her seem kind of brash and intimidating. (It dawned on me, later in my life, that Miss Miriam probably wasn't quite as prehistoric as I'd originally thought . . . but at the time, it felt to me like she was old enough to have walked through the Garden of Eden right alongside Adam and Eve and the serpent and all.)

"Well, yes, I would like to learn," I answered, feeling a little silly. I wondered if another fuzzy tendril of my hair had popped free. Miss Miriam was the queen of propriety and fashion, and it wouldn't have sat well with her if my hair had been popping out all over the place. I patted my head self-consciously, trying to adjust my two pigtails. She observed this, of course, and just *had* to comment.

"Your pigtails are absolutely adorable, sweet thing." (She used words like *absolutely adorable* because of her classiness, I think. If anyone else had said it, it would have sounded stilted and fake and too over-the-top. But coming from Miss Miriam, it was a super-supreme compliment, and I felt my self-confidence inflate just the tiniest bit.)

So I forged ahead, newly confident.

"Thank you, Miss Miriam. And yes, I would very much like you to teach me to walk in high-heeled shoes. But only if you feel up to it."

She eyed me carefully, the hint of a smile on her face.

"Well, it's about *time* you asked! I was actually beginning to worry. Here you are, seven going on eight, and you still can't navigate in a pair of heels. You know you can't splash around in those horrid plastic rain boots and your scuffed

Keds for the rest of your life, Chipper. Now let's get this show on the road!"

Wow! What an uncharacteristic outburst of enthusiasm—especially from prim-and-proper Miss Miriam! But her comment was kind of a backhanded insult, too. I didn't know whether to feel offended by her comment about my "horrid" rain boots and "scuffed" Keds or not. Somehow, because I knew her so well, I just had to assume that she hadn't meant to bruise my tender little ego. She simply wanted me to join her in her fine, fine world of fashion. And I was happy to be recruited.

She stood up and walked toward a huge armoire. (I think I remember it being even taller than she was.) She opened its doors to reveal a column of shoe boxes, each box label-side-out and stacked neatly atop one another. It might have been my overactive imagination, but I'm pretty sure I spied several fancy dresses in there. Some sequined gowns. I thought I even saw a feathered boa toward the back, but I didn't want to gawk.

Peering into the armoire, Miss Miriam carefully inspected her inventory. After a few seconds, she selected one special shoe box and yanked it out crisply, as expertly as any shoe saleslady.

"These will do for now," she said with what I could hear was mounting excitement in her voice. Classy or not, *this* lady was getting all revved up about our upcoming Fashion Extravaganza.

She opened the box with a bit of ceremony, removing two magnificent satin pumps. Thrusting them in my direction, she directed me to go sit on the bed to remove my Keds. (My "horrid" Keds, as she'd called them.) In those days, most children wore shoes inside their rain boots just because it was practical, but it always felt a little ungainly to me. Still, Mother insisted, so that was the way it had to be. I had to wear both the shoe *and* the boot.

Feeling slightly self-conscious and praying to Jesus that my damp feet wouldn't stink up her bedroom to high heaven, I sat on the edge of her bed and set my feet free. I sat completely still for a moment, just to see if I could smell my own feet stinking up the room. I would have died a thousand deaths. Miss Miriam liked the smell of *French perfume* and *scented talcum powder*—not the neighbor girl's smelly, rain-soaked feet.

But if she smelled anything, she didn't let on. She was just excited. And then, before I knew it, her pumps were on my feet!

"Now stand up, Krissy. Stand up and take your first steps!"

Her voice had grown slightly louder, which told me she was happy to be so fully engaged in this fashion fiesta.

I wiggled this way and wobbled that way as I walked, but Miss Miriam's bejeweled hands held my skinny arms steady as she patiently, urgently whispered instructions into the perfumed air around us with ladylike finesse:

"You're not charging the Red Brigade in those shoes, honey pie! You have to take teeny-tiny steps. Don't ever rush yourself when you're all dressed up—even if your feet are killing you. *Don't ever rush.* Remember that! Ladies don't hurry. Go slow; take your sweet time. And when you're wearing high heels, learn to balance yourself from inside the tips of your toes, not on the balls of your feet."

Inside the tips of my toes? What in the devil does that mean? Where can one actually locate the "inside" of the tip of a toe?

I didn't dare ask.

After a few minutes of teetering around, we both sat back down on her bed. I felt luxurious. I think I even tipped my nose up into the air slightly, like a famous movie star. I'd walked in my first pair of heels! Go tell it on the mountain! I was now, officially, a little lady.

I gently removed her pumps from my feet, proud as a peacock and feeling very grown-up, taking special care to return both shoes back to their tissue-papered box. I resisted the urge to rub my aching toes. Dorothy or Lena would never have done that. Instead, I tied my Keds back up and walked over to her vanity table as gracefully as I could manage.

"My ma says to tell you hello," I said, fingering one of her ornate, sterling-silver hair combs on her table. What did the women of yesterday do with their hair to avoid flyaway frizzies, especially in the rain and humidity? I tugged self-consciously at my own fuzzy tendrils.

"Your mother is an angel," said Miss Miriam definitively, moving back to her vanity table and gently pushing me off her chair so that she could sit down. "And she's as smart as the dickens—all of you Clark women are. Tell her I send my love, too, honey. That woman is a jewel; smart as a whip, prettier than a bushel of golden apples, and, even after seven children, she's kept her trim figure. It comes as no surprise that she modeled in her younger days, with a figure and a face like that!" *How in the Sam Hill did Miss Miriam know about Mother's modeling days when I only just found out about them myself? Why was I always the last person on earth to find out all the good stuff?*

She continued her praise of Mother.

"When God made her, He threw in all of the right ingredients: brains, beauty, grace, compassion, and humility."

My goodness! Miss Miriam wasn't big on compliments, so I was a bit taken aback by her observations. Pulling me close in so that I stood directly beside her, she picked up a silver hand mirror and held it up so that I could see my face. Then, she picked up one of her antique hair combs and carefully inserted it into my hair. I looked at my reflection, cocking my head ever so slightly, trying to suppress a smile. Until that point in my young life, I'd never worn anything in my hair except for the occasional ribbon or plain bow—and even then it was usually for something like picture day at school or maybe to church on Easter Sunday. An antique comb was a very special thing. I was feeling prouder by the minute.

Holding the mirror closer up to my face, she said to me, "Just look at that beautiful brown face of yours, honey pie."

I looked.

It *was* brown; that much was certain—but I didn't necessarily see beauty in the face that stared back at me. Feeling I needed to respond, I simply smiled weakly and nodded my head. My two pigtails were sticking out so far, the mirror couldn't even capture their entire image.

"There is no greater beauty than a woman who has confidence in herself, who is beautiful from the inside out, and who is comfortable in her own skin," Miss Miriam said. "Too many of us get caught up in the snares of self-pity, powerless-ness, and superficial beauty."

What in the world? I thought a "snare" was the contraption with the sharp teeth that would clamp around a bear's paw or a human's foot if they accidentally stepped on it during a walk in the forest. But I guess I'm wrong. Drat. I'll have to look up that word, too! Mel's Bells. I'm gonna spend half my summer with my head stuck in the dictionary.

Miss Miriam prattled on about the glorious strengths—and weaknesses—of today's woman. I could tell that the things she was saying were probably right on target, but she had kind of a bad habit of using words that were too big; too big for a seven-year-old, that's for sure.

"And although I'm far too old to do it, little women like you will one day soon evolve into full-fledged adults, and *that's* when you can do your part to help nudge your sisters—*all* of them, black and white, young and old—nudge them toward a place where they're treated with respect, paid as much at their jobs as the men they work with, and looked upon as equals in this unequal society of ours."

It sounded like a lot of work.

Miss Miriam's words didn't really resonate with me until years later, after I'd transitioned into what she called "a full-fledged adult." Without a doubt, she was a woman ahead of her time. She was the modern-day Gloria Steinem—with a slightly better sense of fashion.

"Did you get your cookies on your way up?" Miss Miriam asked. She was examining her cheekbones in the mirror again, but this time she turned her face sideways in an effort to get a glimpse of her profile, which looked kind of funny, but I dared not laugh.

I didn't have the heart to tell her that I was usually too frightened to stop in her kitchen—especially when thunder was rumbling outside and her glass windows were rattling like madmen all over the place.

"No," I answered, fighting back another lie. "I'm not really hungry, and we're probably going to be eating pretty soon after I get home."

In that moment, I tried to visualize Miss Miriam eating dinner. Did she eat by herself? Did she actually walk down to the kitchen and eat at the kitchen table? Or did she eat in her bedroom? Who cooked? I somehow couldn't imagine my glamorous woman-friend bending down low into the oven to check on her homemade scratch biscuits like Mrs. Simpson did—that kind of thing definitely wouldn't ring her bell. I did hope that she had someone else to eat with, though. I hated the thought of her eating in that big kitchen all by herself.

I also had something else on my mind, and I needed to get it off my chest.

"Miss Miriam?" I asked, wishing God would send me a sign if what I was about to ask was out of order or inappropriate for a seven-year-old to be asking a two-hundred-year-old lady.

"Yes, you sweet thing, what is it?"

"Does thunder scare you?"

I didn't know if it was considered disrespectful to be asking such things of an old and elegant woman, but we were friends—and true friendship knew no borders or boundaries.

It was a legitimate question, about the thunder. I wondered—and worried—about her sleeping alone in that big old bed of hers, probably sitting up at night with her sheets held up to her chin, her teeth chattering and all, frightened of the nighttime noises outside. I loved Miss Miriam, and I definitely didn't want her to be scared—of thunder or anything else.

She smiled, smoothing her red velvet robe. I thought of Miss Simpson and the faded old dish towel she carried around with her constantly, and of me and Mother sitting on the sofa talking about racial dignity and the power of pride. How lucky I was to have these three miraculous ladies in my life! My heart grew so large with love for all of them that I thought it might open up and burst. Each of these women were so different, yet so much the same. And each of them loved me more than pancakes or the color pink. More than waffle cones or water fights with Cookie. Even more than candy apples or Captain Kangaroo!

But my question about thunder still lingered between us. For some reason, it was important to me that I know she wasn't scared.

She took her time answering. (As I knew from my high-heel-walking lesson, she was *not* a woman to be rushed.) Her eyes looked a little dreamy.

"Sometimes at night, when the thunder gives a great clap like it did last night, I sit bolt upright in bed and look all around, like something's going to jump right out of my closet. Last night, a tree branch scraped against my window and I just about had a heart attack.

"'Who on God's green earth is prowling around in my

backyard?' I actually said out loud. Thank the Lord above that
no one actually *answered* me, little one, or I really would have
fainted dead away. Oh yes, child. I was scared. That ol' storm
was loud enough to rattle my windows, and I was praying to
the dickens that all that wind and rain wouldn't rip out my
hydrangeas."

So typical of her. Selfless. Classy. Unaffected. Praying for
the safety of her hydrangeas more urgently than praying for
her own personal safety. I loved her in large, gulping doses.

"Why do you ask, baby? Did last night's storm scare you?"

"Yes, ma'am, it scared me pretty bad. I heard that same
thunderclap you did, and it scared me so bad I . . . I . . ." And
here I hesitated because what I was about to say was definitely, well, unladylike. *Indelicate.*

"That you *what*, child?" she prodded, sounding a little impatient. "Speak your piece. You know you don't have to hold your
tongue with me."

". . . that I peed the bed," I answered honestly, feeling a great
burden lifted from my shoulders. (She'd *asked*, hadn't she?)

Mother hadn't even been angry when it happened, either.
All she'd done was fish around in the upstairs linen closet for
some fresh sheets, had my sister Noelle wipe me down with a
warm, soapy washcloth in our green bathtub, and asked my
other sister Nikki to put the new sheets on the bed. I loved
my older siblings with a furious force—and they loved me
right back, surrounding me with light and laughter from the
moment I was born, and ever since. I felt blessed and smiled
upon that we were such a close-knit group. They, along with
Mother and Daddy and God, were the center of my life.

Still, there was the matter of the little *accident* with my overactive bladder. I tried not to feel embarrassed, and I deeply regretted having used the word *peed* in my conversation with Miss Miriam. Even Mother scowled at words like that because she considered them crude.

But Miss Miriam only nodded sympathetically. "You're certainly not the first child to"—and here, she cleared her throat and pursed her lips slightly as though she'd just sucked on a slice of a bitter lemon—"*wet* the bed during the night, and you certainly won't be the last. Don't give it another thought. For a child your age, I'm afraid you might just worry yourself a little too much. There'll be enough of life to live—and worry about—later, once you're good and grown. For now, play hide-and-seek. Eat ice cream cones. Pull the dandelions out of Mr. Dewey's front lawn and give them to your mother as a beautiful bouquet. Enjoy your life, because before you know it, you'll be my age!"

Two hundred years old? Will I still have my banana bike?

She continued, "Yes, yes, enjoy life while you're still young, so that when you *do* eventually grow old like me, you won't have any regrets—because by then, honey, it'll be too late."

She continued giving me advice about the future and the world around us. Everything she said sounded wise—but I couldn't quite absorb all the larger life lessons she was talking about, using all those big words. So I just nodded and hoped that I *looked like* I understood.

"As you grow into a young lady, honey pie, hold fast to the indisputable truth that it's us women who hold the keys to unlocking the secrets of this world around us. The men are the hunters and the gatherers—which is important, of course—but *we* are the nurturers. The protectors! The ones who watch, and listen and learn. We are the ones who create that universal magnetic field, to which everyone is instinctively drawn. Yes sirree, Bob. We still have a lot of work to do—but who in the Sam Hill says we can't be beautiful and well-dressed while we're doing it?" (She laughed a little when she said that last part; I think she thought it was kind of clever.)

I kept listening, getting the gist of her message about how women are so powerful and all, but I was still a little confused. *Did the word* nurturer *have anything to do with loving nature? If that's the case, I could be counted as a "woman," too, 'cause I liked camping out and walking in the woods at Belle Isle and canoeing at Palmer Park as much as the next woman did! Hot diggity! Miss Miriam must think that I'm a woman, too!*

I smiled as she spoke, glowing and newly confident in my new womanhood. She continued:

"Today's women—women of the '60s—have both power *and* beauty. We've come a long way, sweetie. Not all that long ago, women couldn't even vote. Why, I wouldn't even be surprised if one day—certainly not in my lifetime and probably not in yours—the people of this country even elected a female president! Why honey, if you let your imagination *really* run all over Robin's red barn, this world may one day even see a black man in the White House! What we have to do is have *faith*, honey! Faith in God, and in the uncompromising belief that He knows what we *want*—but he gives us what we *need*!"

She was really getting excited now. I kind of hoped she hadn't forgotten about our high-heel-walking lesson.

Miss Miriam's predictions about a female or a black man as president, though, had really started me thinking. I thought about her words. Could I imagine a woman or a black man in the White House? It was a difficult question for a seven-year-old growing up in the mid-'60s. Still, my answer was a resounding *yep*. For just a quick flash of a minute, sitting there in Miss Miriam's spacious bedroom, I let my imagination run a few gallops ahead of my mind. Who could I see in the White House besides . . . well . . . a white male? I could certainly picture someone as dignified as, say, Martin Luther King Jr., sitting behind his big fancy desk in the Oval Office, signing important papers and maybe lowering himself to his knees every once in a while, to pray for his country and the world and all. (And was the Oval Office really oval?) I'd always pictured the White House as tall as a skyscraper, with black iron gates all around, and white, frilly curtains in each window that were probably handmade by the First Lady. Yes, indeed. Martin Luther King would have fit quite comfortably.

Who else?

I could also have imagined someone like George Washington Carver being president, just because he was so brilliant and all (and we'd just finished studying him in school). I could visualize him building his own lab down in the White House basement so he could do his experiments any time he wanted. Sure, he'd probably fly all over the world doing important things and helping the sick, poor, and suffering people—but he would probably have a *huge* plot of land out back where he could grow as many peanuts as he'd like, and he could even experiment on them in his secret lab in the White House basement.

I could have imagined *Daddy* as president in a red-hot minute, too. He'd be fair and kind to everybody, and the first two things he would have done as president would be to stop all the wars around the world, then tear down that horrid department store that wouldn't sell his beautiful wife the hat she'd wanted so badly for church. The only really elaborate thing he'd probably request is for somebody to dig him a big fishing hole out back (but not show-offy big) so he could go fishing whenever he wanted. (Did the White House even have a backyard?)

Another few ideas popped into my mind, too: James Earl Jones would have been a good president, what with his booming voice and barrel chest and all. His mere presence alone would signal to the world that we were a strong country, and all of our enemies would be frightened. Sidney Poitier might have worked well, too—especially since Mother and all my older sisters worshipped the ground he walked on. (Even though I'd never seen one of his movies all the way through, I loved his diction and his dignity, and the way he set people straight so *handily* whenever they tried to insult him.)

Miss Miriam's question about a lady president had me stumped, though. Then, Eureka! Gadzooks! I had it! How about Shirley Temple? I remember hearing my parents talking about the fact that she was even thinking about running for Congress that following year—so that qualified her as a politician, didn't it? Plus, she'd probably invite children from all over the country to the White House, to come and see her great movies, like *Little Princess. Curly Top. Bright Eyes.* Maybe she'd have something like a lottery, where every kid in America got to pick a number, and if their number was selected, they got to fly to Washington, DC, and watch *Heidi* and maybe pop popcorn with President Shirley Temple herself. Pretty cool stuff.

ↇↄ

MY "political" predictions, all those many years ago, were laughable. Sophomoric and silly-sounding. But they were also based on something tangible and touchable; they were based on hope, faith, and the promise of a bright new future.

These were the powerful beliefs that Miss Miriam had instilled in my little hopeful heart—the promise that we, as a nation (particularly women), were moving into uncharted territory, facing a world filled with promise and possibility. A world with no limits.

And as I stood with Miss Miriam that afternoon, fingering all of her finery, who knew that there'd actually come a day when this little pig-tailed, skinny-legged girl would work in the White House and sit in the Oval Office with the president of the United States? (And yes, the Oval Office is, indeed, oval—but considerably smaller than it appears on television.) Who knew that this little potato-kneed girl from Motown would one day walk her own son through the Rose Garden or speed through the city in the president's motorcade, or introduce him to Mother and Daddy before they left this earthly world? It seemed like a fantastic, faraway fantasy an Alice-through-the-looking-glass dream—that yes, one day, this little pigtail-wearing girl would walk proudly through the *front entrance* of the West Wing, where black people were at one time expressly forbidden, and yes, she'd live to see the historic day where a black man could be elected to the highest office in the land. *Who knew?*

Miss Miriam did.

Miss Miriam and God.

❧

EVEN through my daydreaming about George Washington Carver and Shirley Temple being in the White House, I could still hear Miss Miriam going on and on about how much progress black people and women have made. Boy, was she revved up!

I didn't quite understand why she was suddenly launching into all this talk about the power of women, but I certainly liked the way it sounded. I was feeling proud about my gender. I AM WOMAN! A proud, independent, forward-thinking *woman*! Why, one day soon, I'd be able to bring home the bacon and burp the baby *at the same time*! And maybe one day, I'd even be brave enough to burn my bra (once I started *wearing* one, that is . . . but let's not put the cart before the horse).

At least not just yet.

For now, mastering the art of walking in high heels was enough of a task.

She reached over and took my hand.

"You are absolutely beautiful, little friend of mine. Don't you ever, *ever* let anyone tell you any different."

I blushed at the compliment. Sometimes I didn't feel beautiful at all. I was, at times, ashamed of the color of my skin and my flyaway, frizzy hair. Virtually all magazine and television ads I ever saw pictured sultry, flaxen-haired, red-lipped women with tiny waists and creamy, milky-white complexions. Although I was aware on a cognizant, intellectual level, that there was certainly more to the world than pale complexions (heck, my own mother had been a *model*, for pete's sake!), Miss Miriam's compliment that afternoon stirred my pride and bolstered my self-esteem. I also said a silent prayer of gratitude for magazines like *Ebony* and *Jet*, because they lifted me out of my insular little seven-year-old world on the East Side of Detroit and showed me an exciting, sophisticated outside world filled with black people who were smart, savvy, wise, and worldly.

As long as Miss Miriam was in a generous mood with her compliments, I took the chance of hoping she'd be equally as generous with the magical things hanging in her wardrobe. After all, we *were* on the topic of beauty.

"Can we look at some of your gowns?" I asked tentatively, hopefully.

Even the thought of it seemed to infuse her with more energy. Her spirit sat up straighter, right along with her spine. The pull of—and pride in—her glory days of yesteryear seemed to expand the very walls around us. Before I knew it, she was opening doors again, pulling things out. My ears were hungry for the sound of the *swish, swish, swish* of her sequined finery being pulled from the closet.

"Here's one of your favorites," she said in a whisper, as if it were a big surprise.

She was right.

I loved looking at the long lavender gown. The sound of its movement was as powerful and evocative to me as the sight of its beads and bodice. The sleeves were long and tapered, with tiny clusters of pearls around the neckline. I must have gasped. It didn't even smell like mothballs. Nothing in Miss Miriam's house did. Mothballs were definitely not her style.

The only thing her house smelled like was lilac, lavender, talcum powder, and the tiniest hint of Murphy's Oil soap—but all in just the right doses, nothing overpowering the other.

"What say we get this thing on you?" she asked, scanning her neat column of shoe boxes to select the perfect pair—no digging around in a messy closet, desperately trying to find a stray shoe for Miss Miriam, no way in the world. After a moment, she found the right box, expertly yanked it out, then opened the lid to reveal the most beautiful pair of lavender pumps I'd ever seen. I was running out of breath. *Try it on?* Sure, during other visits I'd seen the dress lying across her bed, and I'd always admired it from afar, but trying it on? What if I popped a pearl or busted a bead?

She glanced over at my expression.

"Stop looking so worried, child! Be happy! Be excited! Get ready to get glamorous!" she entreated. "Every woman should know how to move *correctly* in a full-length gown. You have to know how to move just so to make these beads catch the light in exactly the way you want them to, and you need to know how to make your dress *sound* when you walk! You know . . . that swishing sound I know you love."

My butterflies began their dance.

"You sure about this, Miss Miriam? This gown's way too long for me, and I'm only just getting the hang of the high heels. Maybe I should wait until I'm a little older. I don't want to snag or rip anything."

She actually smirked, maybe in disappointment or mild disgust at my lack of enthusiasm, that I would actually say something so utterly stupid.

"A true lady doesn't wait until the day of the ball to teach herself to move elegantly in her gown," she said crisply, pulling tight the sash around her velvet robe. I think she might have been a little frustrated. "I'll pin it up, of course . . . I don't want you breaking your neck and having your father come down here looking to break *my* neck because I hurt his baby girl! Now get behind that dressing screen, take off those *dungarees* that you're wearing—or whatever you call them— and get into that gown before I change my mind."

The butterflies danced away, floating up into the darkened clouds outside. I was excited, on my way to being Dorothy again—a Dorothy Dandridge with fuzzy pigtails and a beanpole-skinny body. I disappeared behind her Oriental dressing screen, untied my Keds again, and pulled off my T-shirt, careful not to knock over any of her precious things. Even the sudden thunderclap didn't rattle me in the least. I was a little lady on a mission. I was getting ready to get beautiful.

"Wrap that purple silk dressing gown around you—the one that's hanging on the back of that chair—and come on out, for heaven's sake. It's not like you've got that much to hide," she chided me gently. She was excited about the impending fashion show, too. I could tell by her voice.

She was right, again. I didn't have much to wrap, conceal, or cover. My chest was nonexistent ("headlights," one of my aunts called them), and my waist hadn't even developed *into* a waist yet, and I certainly had no hips or backside to speak of at all. Maybe Sheila had been right. Even though we'd made up and become friends again, her description of me as "a skinny-legged beanpole" might have been right on target. But at that same moment—as my self-confidence was beginning to buckle—God nestled Himself straight into my seven-year-old soul: I might be a beanpole—but I bet your bottom dollar that I was about to become the most *elegant* seven-year-old beanpole *this* Motor City had ever seen.

Shyly, slowly, I emerged from behind the dressing screen. Miss Miriam had already retrieved her pincushion (the one shaped like a strawberry), ready to adjust the hem and the sleeves. Her spine-straight posture was another indication to me that she was as excited as all get-out. I listened carefully to her instructions:

"Now when I put this over your head, don't move a muscle. Just hold your head up straight and your arms up in the air even straighter, pointing toward the ceiling. When I tell you to, slip your right arm through the right sleeve, then your left arm through the left, okay?"

It was getting complicated—all these instructions—and I didn't want to mess it up. I did as I was instructed, standing ramrod straight until I was told otherwise.

And then the magic came.

The sound and feel of the thousands of tiny beads showered around my head and shoulders, cool on my skin. But I dared not move a muscle until I heard from Miss Miriam, the boss.

"Good girl," she said, mumbling now through the straight pins pursed between her lips. "Now slowly lift up your head and slip your right arm through. Good. Now your left. Now let me get these old knees of mine working, so that I can kneel down and get you all hemmed up," she mumbled through the pins, leaning over as nimble as a gymnast. "Stay still, girl!"

After a moment or two of her leaning down toward the bottom of the gown, busy putting straight pins into the hem, we were ready.

"Head up high," she said crisply, this First Lady of Fashion.

My head snapped up to full attention. I even had the nerve to lift my chin again ever so slightly. I wasn't even Dorothy now. I was *Nefertiti*. I was a beautiful black swan. My neck felt two feet long, and if I'd had feathers, I would have preened them right then and there. I stood gamely on my tiptoes, try-ing to gain the height required to be womanly. Quick as a flash, Miss Miriam slipped first my right foot then my left into her matching, magical lavender pumps. *Keds, be gone! Thank you, again, God and Jesus, for this precious, gown-giving woman who's teaching me how to walk in heels. Bring on the thunder, and I will not be scared. I'll even confront those sharp-toothed monsters that live underneath our basement stairs the minute I get home! I am woman! I am brave! And I look good, too!*

Miss Miriam sat up straight, regarding me fully and with a great degree of pride, then issued her command: "Now *walk*, little woman, *walk*!"

Obediently and instinctively, I walked gingerly across the

room. My poor toes were jammed together like sardines, but that's just the price you have to pay for wearing a pretty pump. And then, I did it: *I squeezed the inside of my toes—and it worked!*

Miss Miriam sat at the edge of the bed, legs crossed, pincushion in her lap. She was clapping in tiny, quiet, seal-like claps, giddy as a schoolgirl. "Strut your stuff, child! Make it yours!"

I was on the verge of feeling confused and a little disoriented because of all the directions, instructions, and commands she was yelling, but I kept up with her. I did as I was told.

I walked, in her beaded gown and high-heeled shoes, from one end of the room to the other. I even had the nerve to sway my nonexistent hips the tiniest little bit, like I'd seen Lena Horne sway in her movies. Oh buddy, did I walk. Back and forth across her bedroom. I walked.

Without stumbling.

"Slow down when you walk. You're too pretty to rush. *Let them wait!* Negro women have been rushed and herded and pushed this way and that for far too long. It's *our* time now, Chipper! Take tiny steps. You're not playing Mother-May-I, for Lord's sake, so why are you taking such giant steps? No, baby doll, you're strutting at the Savoy now. So make it count."

A full-length mirror stood in one corner of the room. It must have been God himself who led my steps toward that mirror without wobbling. I looked. *Thank you again, God. I actually do look like a Savoy lady! Thank you for Miss Miriam. Thank you for her beauty and elegance.*

I tiny-stepped my way back toward Miss Miriam and ended

up collapsing into her waiting arms. Even in the beaded gown and heels, our embrace was urgent. I hoped and prayed that none of the beads had fallen off while we were hugging, but I didn't really care about that. I was in her arms.

Just that quickly, I surrendered to the sweet pull of my imagination, so I stood up again. I was the most famous actress in the world, preparing for one final sashay down the red carpet. I could even hear the muted, popping sounds of the photographer's lightbulbs flashing, and the drowned-out screams of my adoring fans. I could feel the crush of reporters as they pushed themselves against the wood barriers, shouting out questions about my newest love interest and my upcoming movie. Random pieces of paper were being thrust into my hands—*those pesky autograph seekers!* I turned again toward the mirror.

"Now give me a pivot, baby! *Pivot!*"

My first thought was, *What in heaven's name is a "pivot"? A fancy ballroom dance that adults do?* I'd heard Mother and Daddy talk about the Lindy Hop and the fox-trot, but never ever the pivot. I didn't want to disappoint her, so I stood there, waiting. It was the first time I'd ever heard the word—and every time I hear the word spoken (even today, as an adult) my mind hearkens back to the miraculous Miss Miriam.

In the twinkling of an eye, all the reporters and flashbulbs and screaming fans vaporized into thin air. I was Kristin again—the little girl who didn't even know what the word *pivot* meant.

Miss Miriam saved my hide without even recognizing it.

"*Turn*, baby! Let me see you turn!"

So that's what "pivot" means? To turn?

Still, I vowed to ask Mother to help me look it up in our dog-eared Webster's Dictionary as soon as I got home. I wanted to read the literal definition for myself. (Plus, it pleased Mother to no end when I asked her to help me look up certain words in the dictionary.)

But back to the task at hand, which was considerable: Miss Miriam was asking me to "pivot" in high-heeled shoes *and* a full-length gown that was twice the length of my body! Had she lost her ever-loving mind?

It was at that point that I figured if I was ever going to be a lady's lady, if I was ever going to embrace grace and wrap confidence around my shoulders, now was as good a time to begin as any. So I turned slowly, toes squeezed tight, beaded arms stretched out long and luxuriously at each side.

Miss Miriam clapped again, then put one hand to her mouth. It looked, for a frightening minute, like she was going to cry, but then she smiled a bright smile, opened her arms, and I walked over to her, collapsing into her embrace again. It was time to take off the dress and shoes.

My feet hurt.

As I was changing behind the screen, I could hear Miss Miriam moving around the room, picking up things and straightening up. By the time I'd laced my Keds and emerged from behind the dressing screen, her bedroom was back in order: the pincushion put away, the gown hung up, and the shoes returned to their proper box.

She was on bended knee again, though—this time, carefully sifting through a steamer trunk filled with beautiful, ladylike things. I remember thinking that it very well might have been a magical trunk, packed full of the items that helped make ladies become even more beautiful than they already were. Without turning around, she extended her right arm backward toward me.

"You might as well take this little number for yourself, because I'm not going to be using it anytime soon. Lord knows I've had my share of fun in my younger days, but now it's time to pass that mantle on to someone else."

I didn't even want to look at what was in her hands. I was concerned about her voice. She *really* sounded like there were tears in it now. Plus, she refused to turn around and look at me. She just kept her head bent down toward the contents in the steamer trunk. This wasn't good. Old people weren't supposed to get sad; it didn't seem fair. Eventually, I gazed down at the object in her hand: a beaded evening bag, with strings of tinier beads hanging down from the bottom. It was fairly heavy in my hands, too, and the inside was lined with ivory satin.

The hairs at the nape of my neck were beginning to rise. Hot tears began to pool. My breathing suddenly felt shallow, as if someone were pinching my nose closed. I just couldn't get enough oxygen into my little lungs. The pure power of love was moving through every corner of that room. Its magnetic intensity threatened to carry me away. But her words helped calm me down.

"Take good care of that thing, child. I've had that bag for eons."

And then she paused. "Something tells me," she said very

slowly, all quiet and reflective now, "that my dress-up days are over . . . but yours have not yet even begun."

I knew, then, that her heart was full and her mind was dancing with memories of yesterdays long, long ago. Her voice caught as she spoke. I was beginning to feel bad. I didn't come to visit to make her cry. *Good Lord.*

She refused to move away from that trunk, and her back was still turned toward me, which I thought was rather odd. So I knelt beside her and hugged her from behind. Miss Miriam was my heroine and my friend. Even Sheila wouldn't believe that Miss Miriam's fancy-shmancy evening bag was now mine; she wouldn't believe me even if I swore on the grave of my now-dead goldfish, Chomper. I could barely believe it myself.

But in that same moment, I realized something else: Miss Miriam's steamer trunk held, for her, not only precious baubles, but pleasing memories of her past.

It was her own version of a Forever Box.

I felt bountifully blessed that she'd chosen little old *me* to help preserve such a precious part of her past, and I had every intention of taking my newfound role as memory-maker very, very seriously. These women—these wonderful, wizened women who were my friends—were entrusting me with invaluable, irreplaceable pieces of their past, and even then, I recognized the magnitude of their acts.

Even though they fully recognized—and fully embraced—their own finite mortality, they still wanted me to pass parts of themselves along to future generations. They expected me to carry a tiny piece of their existence with me into the future.

And they were entrusting me to cherish their stories, and to chase away all the cobwebs that threatened to obscure their memories.

And then, before I knew it, Miss Miriam had moved back over to her vanity table. The woman was nimble and quick, I'll tell you that much. She scanned the vanity table, touching each of her perfume bottles lightly with her index finger.

She stopped at one, turning toward me.

"I just must be in a giving mood today, child. You caught me on the right day. Now, take this perfume bottle and keep it for yourself. You can even use it right now—spritz some lightly on your wrist before you go home and I bet you dollars to doughnuts your mother will be pleased."

The bottle was white and delicately fluted, with two colorful butterflies on one side and two lovely tulips on the other. I didn't know what to do.

"Take it!" she whispered urgently. *Well gosh! She's being bossy again, isn't she?*

She said it again, this time with a smile. "You better take this bottle before I change my mind."

Having said those words, I grabbed the bottle (somewhat greedily, I'm sure she probably thought), and thanked her profusely. All of my gift-giving friends were leaving me important parts of themselves, and I felt honored and humbled. They were leaving me things they wanted me to remember them by. And I would cherish each item for the rest of my life, making sure to pass them along to my own children, when I finally had them, so that they, too, could remember Miss Miriam's kind spirit and hear the shared stories.

Miss Miriam had turned thoughtful, sentimental even, and, unfortunately, a little wistful.

"Now when you grow up and wear long gowns, you'll know how to move. What to do. The proper way to walk. Don't ever forget it, my sweet. And if you ever have children—and I pray that you will—teach them grace and humility. Teach your daughters how to walk in long gowns and high heels, smiling all the time—even if their feet are hurting so badly their toes are singing Dixie. Teach them how to smile *into* themselves— that way, when they're at a fancy party, their smile won't be fake or forced because it'll be coming from some very real place deep, down inside their own souls. Don't forget that."

I was a little confused. How can someone "smile into themselves"? And who in the world smiles when they don't really want to? (How innocently naive I was back then. Little did I know that, in today's rough-and-tumble world, *fake* smiles are almost as common as the real ones.)

She continued, tossing out advice left and right: "Rely on your own natural beauty. Don't get me wrong, now: There's nothing wrong with enhancing your beauty—but don't let those enhancements *define* you. Be subtle in everything. When you start wearing lipstick, don't slap it on like you're painting Mr. Sexton's picket fence. Apply it lightly, so people can barely tell you have any on."

Miss Miriam was actually crying now; quiet tears that just about broke my little heart. (I hate to say it, but it's the truth: Lots of people look downright ugly when they cry. But not Miss Miriam. Even her tears were graceful.)

The conversation had shifted slightly. I could tell she was not only talking about simple fashion tips, but about life in general—about what's right and wrong.

"When you grow up, sweetie, *always* remember to treat others with kindness and respect. Even when you're dressed to the nines and all decked out in your Sunday best, remember to treat people with dignity and decorum. Never get too big for your britches. God doesn't like that at all."

She scoffed slightly, wrinkling her nose.

"I've seen these movie stars on TV so taken with themselves that they forget about the other people around them," she said with what sounded to me like disgust.

"I don't care *what* color your skin is—black or white or purple with red polka dots—*all women* should behave with an eye toward kindness, compassion, and universal love. Believe me when I tell you that it doesn't take beads or bangles to make a person pretty—it takes a generous spirit and a gracious disposition."

She was getting louder again. She pointed her finger at me.

"You're as pretty as a picture, Chipper—but never *ever* become so preoccupied with your own beauty that you blind yourself to the people around you. That right there is downright ugly behavior. And, as you've probably already heard, God don't like ugly."

She was on a roll.

"If a woman is pretty on the outside and mean or cruel on the inside, then she's as ugly as a mile of unpaved road. Here are the things you should always remember, particularly as it relates to your growing into a proper young lady: Always be kind to others. Work *hard* to stay pretty—on the inside and well-presented on the outside. When you're speaking with someone, look them straight in the eye. If they say something funny, don't hee-haw like an ol' mule; instead, smile and laugh a light, graceful laugh. Be humble in all things—never brash or arrogant or wild-acting. And remember: Satin pumps don't make the woman; it's the *inner beauty of the woman who makes the satin pumps!*"

She really tickled herself with that last line, because she laughed out loud—a soft, tinkling laugh that sounded like my grandmother's crystal. As for me, I was just glad she'd stopped crying.

I was pretty sure I knew what she was saying, but I hadn't been able to absorb absolutely *everything*. (What did "preoccupied" and "brash" mean again?) All in all, though, I knew she was telling me to always be nice, even if I grew up to be a fancy lady who wore beaded gowns.

She was winding down. She had to have been a little tired, I thought as I watched her straightening the combs and perfume bottles on her vanity. Miss Miriam was ready to rest.

I leaned over and kissed her on her cheek.

"Good-bye, Miss Miriam. Please don't go out in all this rain. If you need something, you *know* my mom will send one of us girls over right away. Just call and one of us will come a-running. I love the bag and the perfume you gave me, and I promise to remember what you said about beauty and being nice and about how great women are. I can't see myself having children any time soon, 'cause I'm still just a kid myself—but if I do, I promise to share these beautiful items with them one day. I love you so, so much. Now get some rest. I'll be back to visit in a couple of days."

After I left her bedroom, I hightailed it down the steps— a wide staircase in the middle of the foyer, if I remember correctly—and sprinted into her kitchen. No longer were the little monsters lurking in the shadows. I sauntered into the room bravely, swaggering like John Wayne in the Wild West.

There was the drawer: a deep, metal bread drawer with a fairly heavy lid. Pulling it open, I grabbed two pinwheel cookies and sat down at her kitchen table to eat them. I didn't like the sliced pecans on top, but I ate them anyway because I didn't want to hurt her feelings.

I was careful not to leave even a crumb behind. When I was finished, I rose from the table and strode with confidence over to the kitchen phone on the wall to call Mother so she could meet me across the street. I wondered, briefly, what Miss Miriam was doing right at that moment, upstairs alone in her bedroom—but most of all I thought about how lucky I was to have a woman like her in my life. At the bottom of the stairs, I yelled up (without *screaming*, mind you): "I'm leaving now, Miss Miriam, but I'll be back in a few days! Thank you again—so very, very much—for the purse and the perfume! I promise to keep them forever!"

"Okay, sweetie pie! You're my little lady now! Take good care of that bottle I gave you! The perfume is from Europe!"

And then, as if in afterthought, she yelled downstairs again.

"You eat your cookies?" (By then, I could tell she was

growing weary of all the yelling back and forth; Lord knows that hollering through her house was definitely not something she did on a regular basis. Tacky and undignified to the extreme.)

"Yes, ma'am. I had two cookies, and they were delicious! Thank you! I love you! I love you! Good-bye!"

"Good-bye, my sweet! I love you, too! Come again and I'll teach you the fox-trot!"

Outside, Mother stood waiting patiently with her black umbrella. Looking both ways, I ran across the street and sought comfort and cover under our wide, safe umbrella; our shield. I showed her the perfume and the purse, and she smiled quietly.

"That Miss Miriam is something else indeed," Mother said with a hint of awe in her voice. "You're lucky to have her as such a good friend."

And then Mother leaned down closer, sniffing the air around me. I smiled, embarrassed.

"You certainly smell good, Beauty!"

I smiled as close to a grown-up smile as I could muster. Pride swam all around my little head like hot air.

"Why thank you, kind miss!" I answered, curtsying in my rain boots.

Mother continued with our jesting. "You absolutely *must* give me the name of your perfume, ma'am," she said, gazing down at me with a knowing smile.

"Of course, of course," I answered back, trying my level best to sound like a haughty, nose-turned-up-in-the-air fancy lady. "I'll even let you spray some on your wrist if you like . . .

but just a little bit, if you don't mind. It's from Europe, and it's very, very precious." *Where was Europe again?*

We continued walking toward home, avoiding the puddles, feeling solid and safe under Daddy's big umbrella.

As we walked, I scrunched my toes up real hard inside my Keds so I could be *just a little* more elegant. When we finally got to our house, my feet hurt so bad they were barking like Chihuahuas. But I had my gifts from Miss Miriam.

When we got to the top of the porch, Mother shook the raindrops off the umbrella, closed it up tightly, then leaned down and spoke to me directly, face to face:

"Take good care of your things. You might want to use them later," she said simply.

She opened our screen door and we walked into the house together. Inside, after I'd kicked off my Keds and rain boots, I bounded upstairs, heading straight to the linen closet in the hallway. I reached in and yanked out a fresh towel, then retreated to the bathroom and locked the door behind me. Carefully, slowly, I wrapped both the purse and the perfume in the towel. Even through the thick towel, I could smell the fragrance of Miss Miriam's fancy European perfume.

Next, I snuck into Mother and Daddy's bedroom and riffled through their closet until I found what I was looking for.

Even though my feet still hurt like the dickens, I carefully placed one foot—then the other—into a pair of Mother's favorite leather pumps. And for the next few minutes, I was transformed again . . . into a glorious, grown-up fancy lady who knew how to walk in shimmering, satin pumps simply by squeezing the insides of her toes.

I felt strong now—invincible. Fearless. Newly matured, and mightily empowered, thanks to my friendship with Miss Miriam.

Pumped up and full of bravado, I began to feel boisterous. It was time to take another big step—literally and figuratively. Approaching the basement door, I yanked it open, peered down the long, dark staircase, then actually took two or three steps down. It was the first time I'd ventured down into our basement alone. But this was something I *had* to do, a mission I just *had* to accomplish. When I got to the bottom, without hesitating, I snuck a peek underneath the stairs, fully prepared to confront those pesky little sharp-toothed monsters face to face. They just didn't scare me anymore. I looked underneath the stairs again. Nothing. Only a few cardboard boxes and my rusted-out tricycle. (I'd *long* since graduated to my two-wheeled banana bike . . . tricycles were for babies.) Those mangy monsters had lost their power!

I ran back up, taking the stairs two at a time. I was proud and puffed up. I felt so in control. And even more than that, I was *finally* free of fear.

☙

TODAY, whenever I entertain guests or attend elaborate events, Miss Miriam is the person who most immediately comes to my mind. Even as I'm rushing about in excited preparation— most often, dashing from closet to bedroom to bathroom—I hear her words of wisdom: "Slow down. Don't rush. Let them wait!" Her words calm my spirit and soothe my soul.

Miss Miriam was a woman's woman; her every movement

and memory epitomized grace, elegance . . . and, most of all, humility. When she passed away, part of her life continued through me. How? Because today, my own adult daughter walks with grace and elegance, but humility is what showers over her soul. Today, I know, as does my own daughter, that physical beauty is fleeting—and that real beauty emerges from the inside out. We both know how important it is to recognize that no amount of makeup, bedazzling jewelry, or even worldwide fame can make a cruel person beautiful.

What defines true beauty?

A kind and compassionate spirit.

Dignified, respectful behavior.

Spiritual generosity, and the enhanced ability to empathize with others.

Today, Miss Miriam's memory still burns on within my spirit—and my goal is to impart her wisdom upon all women who are trying hard to embrace their own intelligence, inherent power, and inner beauty. Miss Miriam's words of wisdom were simple, straightforward, and startlingly honest. This is what she taught me, and this is what I pass along now:

1. Constantly remind yourself of the fact that you are your own unique definition of beautiful—whatever that definition means to you.

2. If you have children (not necessarily your own biological children, but *any* youth in your life), teach them—through your own actions—that *true beauty is an inside job.*

3. Go about your daily duties with grace and confidence.

4. No matter how pretty or powerful you are, you must *always treat others with respect.* Haughtiness is unattractive—not to mention sinful—and the *only* time it's ever acceptable to look down on someone is if you're getting ready to pick them *up.* So whether you're walking the red carpet on your way to your own movie premiere, or walking down the alley, kicking an old, rusty coffee can, treat others as you would want them to treat you. Whether you're air-kissing others at a fancy White House soiree, or pitching horseshoes at a family reunion in the public park, never *ever* stick your nose too far up in the air—because it just might get *stuck up there,* and then where on earth would you be?

5. And as old-fashioned as this may sound, always try to look your best. Take care of yourself, mentally, physically, and spiritually. Don't look sloppy.

Today, my beaded evening bag and fluted perfume bottle are tucked away in my Forever Box. I bring them out often, to transport myself back to that magical afternoon in Miss Miriam's bedroom, where I first learned to walk in high heels and where I learned how to *swish* when I walked. It is the memory of Miss Miriam, and

other women like her, who remind me to love and respect everyone equally—and to celebrate the inherent beauty of all women, everywhere.

Physical beauty is elusive and mercurial.

Genuine beauty comes from within.

And remember this: A sequined gown doesn't make the woman . . . it's the inner beauty of a woman that makes the sequined gown!

Mary Elizabeth Sorsby

VICTORIOUS

I AWOKE THE NEXT morning with a smile in my heart, even though the sky was still smoldering gray. Thunderclouds rolled and roiled in the far distance. Those old clouds did nothing to dampen my enthusiasm, though—because today was the day that belonged to sweet Mama Lilly, my maternal grandmother. Today was the day she would pull me gently to her soft, talcum-powdery bosom and whisper how much she loved me, the youngest grandchild of my mother's seven children. Today was the day Daddy would toss both me and my red plaid overnight bag into the backseat of our station wagon and drive me to her neat little low-lying house on the other side of the city, so that I could actually spend the night with this softly plump, pillowy woman. Such an excursion was, to me anyway, a bright, bold adventure. My excitement knew no bounds. As I nibbled on buttered toast (Wonder Bread, my favorite) and Cream of Wheat for breakfast in the final minutes before our departure, I could barely even breathe.

Good-bye, kitchen chair, I whispered to myself as I rose from the table to carry my dishes to the sink. *I'm so, so sorry you won't be able to come and join me in my adventure.* Almost pulsating with excitement, I plunged my thin brown arms up to my elbows in warm soapy water, scrubbing my Cream of Wheat bowl vigorously. Searching for the dish towel so that I could dry my dishes and place them back in our cupboard, my gaze fell upon our white enamel teapot, sitting, as usual, at the left rear burner of our stove. I actually regarded it with something close to pity, simply because it had to remain stationary in its same old boring place on the stove. No, it wouldn't be joining me on my excellent adventure to Mama Lilly's. I bid it adieu. *Farewell, kitchen teapot. Shine on brightly—and keep boiling your fine, fresh water without me while I'm away.* The remainder of the morning passed much the same way until I heard Daddy yell from upstairs, "You all ready, buttercup? It's time to shake a leg! Kiss everybody good-bye and let's get on the road! I want to beat the traffic."

His words were music to my ears.

Fare thee well, clear windowpane, I said, rapping gently on the delicate glass of our front hall window as I prepared to leave.

Until tomorrow, metal mailbox, I whispered as we walked out onto the front porch and lifted its hinged lid one last time, letting it fall back into place with an unceremonious clap.

Daddy and I made our move.

Now fully outside and truly, unmistakably, *officially* on our way, we walked hand in hand to the car. Coming to the edge of our freshly mowed front lawn, I knelt quickly and plucked a few blades of grass, clasping them neatly in the palm of my small brown fist. These blades of grass were the lucky ones. I opened my fist and smiled. *As for you, tender green blades of grass, you get to come with me!*

Right then, Daddy's strong arms swung my body high up into the air, bringing me down in a wide, smooth arch, and nestling me gently into the backseat. I clasped the grass tightly, tucking the freshly pulled blades into the front pocket of my overnight bag. Never mind the fact that, in plucking the grass, I'd also pulled a great glob of mud from the still-moist earth as well. Who cared? What could one expect after three full days of rain? Yes, it would create a mess, but Mother would surely launder everything as soon as I returned home. I pictured her standing in front of our washing machine in the basement, pulling the mud-stained clothes out of my overnight bag and maybe smiling to herself as she separated the soiled items. *What am I going to do with my Beauty?* she'd think, shaking her head in quiet admiration as she sprinkled in a cupful of Tide. *My baby girl is always trying to pluck and save every little thing in her path to create memories for later. Even blades of grass.*

My father leaned forward in the front seat and turned the key in the ignition. After a few false starts, our station wagon roared to life. Daddy checked his rearview mirror, smiling at me as he backed up. I caught his wink in the mirror—a wink and a smile, directed only toward me! (He was also a wonderful winker, by the way.)

I was in heaven.

Before I knew it, we had arrived.

Hand in hand again, Daddy and I walked up Mama Lilly's front steps together. They were painted a dark, dark green in several thick, shiny coats—to make the porch look more like grass than cement, I guessed.

☙

WITH Daddy gone and me now all alone with Mama Lilly, the ions in the air seemed to change. Every room in her home somehow suddenly felt *emptier*—yet filled to overflowing with adventure and possibility. I didn't want to venture into any room without her—not because I was frightened, but because my sole desire was to be in as close proximity to my grandmother as was physically possible. I wanted and needed to share her same space, to drink in her gentle energy, to allow the molecules of our bodies to commingle and reacquaint themselves all over again, as eagerly as if we were strangers or brand-new friends.

If Mama Lilly moved from the kitchen to the dining room, I followed close behind, her miniaturized shadow. If she wanted to retrieve something from one of the bedrooms—a pillow or a quilt or a shiny trinket to show me—she knew instinctively to wait a minute or two, until I realized she was leaving the room, which gave me time to catch up with her so we could walk *together*, hand in hand.

For some strange reason, the sun *always* seemed to be shining in Mama Lilly's sparkling kitchen. I could never quite figure that out. Even at *night*, the room seemed to brighten, an otherworldly glow. Not a scary, alien-from-another-planet, radioactive glow, but rather, a warmth so powerful it filled the room with spiritual light and love. It sounds hokey, I know, but it's the truth: Not once in my little life had I *ever* been scared to move around in her kitchen. Not even at night. Not even in the dark—and you *know* how I am about the dark.

In her kitchen, every appliance shone as brightly as the North Star. Her refrigerator, a bulky Frigidaire the size of a boat, hummed quietly in a corner beside the screen door. On her kitchen table were a green-and-white-striped napkin holder and a clear bottle of what I always called "zacarin," a clear liquid used for sweetening tea and coffee.

Just inside her pantry, she kept a metal stepstool. I'd always been impressed with how that stepstool was designed: when it wasn't being used, it stood flat against the pantry wall. But when you needed to use it, you simply pulled a little latch on the side and three stair steps magically unfolded, forming a miniature ladder. Quite clever.

There we stood in her sparkling kitchen, rays of sunshine ricocheting off the chrome appliances, the sheer curtains stirring lightly in the breeze. Instinctively, I knew that it was time for her to decide what to make for our dinner. My soul smiled in laughter and in love.

I watched as she opened the heavy-as-a-load-of-bricks refrigerator door and leaned in, her eyebrows furrowed in measured concentration. I prayed a silent prayer: *Pleasepleaseplease, Lord, let it be fried chicken. Please let her pull out chicken from her great, gleaming refrigerator, so I can stand close by and watch as she drops each floured piece into that bubbling, boiling grease—grease so hot it makes you think of heaven and hell at the same time. Fry it up real good, Mama Lilly, till every piece is golden brown and my mouth is watering like a little outdoor spigot.*

And always, she'd enlist my help.

Even before the frying began, I knew exactly what to do—because we'd done it so many times before. I'd drag that wonderful, expandable stepstool over to her cupboard so that I could scramble up to the third shelf, where she kept the spices. Sure as shooting, there I'd find the navy blue cylindrical container—the one that pictured the Umbrella Girl, spilling salt as she walked in the rain, covered by her oversized umbrella. I'd hand the container down to my grandmother ever so carefully and sometimes, if she was in the right mood, she'd even allow me to shake the Morton salt directly onto the chicken as it she was frying it up.

Ours was a carefully choreographed concert. Our kitchen dance was all our own. And on that one special afternoon, after I'd shaken the salt and unfolded the TV tables, we settled ourselves in front of her living room television. (Her TV, a behemoth floor-model RCA that seemed to take up half the room, sported a wire coat hanger on its top—"for clearer reception," according to my grandmother, who'd promptly removed the rabbit-ear antennae as soon as the TV had arrived from the store.)

Positioning ourselves close to each other but a few feet away from the TV, we'd eat an early chicken dinner while watching *Bonanza*.

"I do love that handsome Ben Cartwright," she sighed as the opening credits came onto the screen.

My seven-year-old memory of Mama Lilly, at least as it

related to her beloved *Bonanza*, was that she admired the widowed Ben Cartwright and his three caring, capable sons, Adam, Hoss, and Little Joe. She loved the otherworldly allure of the Cartwright's lush and lovely thousand-acre Ponderosa Ranch—so starkly different from the densely packed neighborhoods of inner-city Detroit where we lived.

That was precisely what I loved most about Mama Lilly—the deliberate, almost dutiful manner in which she transported herself from her beautiful little tidy house in the city to a larger, infinitely more exciting world of foreign interests and borderless boundaries. Yes, she loved her life, her church, and her family with a pure and powerful force—but she also loved the larger, looming universe around her and, unlike many elderly women, she didn't shirk from it at all. She forced herself to explore different worlds; places that would have, under normal circumstances, been strictly off-limits to elderly black women in the mid 1960s.

She'd recently returned from an expedition to Egypt, and she'd come back all revved up about the history of our culture. Even then, I knew it was rare for a woman—black *or* white—to travel so far, especially at such an advanced age. She'd absorbed so much on that particular trip, and she couldn't wait to share her experience with me.

"Traveling to Egypt reminded me all over again that our people are strong and resilient, Krissy Baby. You *do* know that the dawn of civilized society began in Africa, don't you, sweetheart?"

I watched her watching me. She looked so *proud*.

"Our African forefathers created sophisticated societies,

developed commerce and trade, and led the rest of the world into the Age of Enlightenment."

I visualized my grandmother's plane landing in Egypt, rolling right up to the door of a famous pyramid or something. I could just see her, slowly disembarking after the long flight, taking her sweet time stepping down onto the tarmac. Maybe she wiped her forehead with the embroidered handkerchief she always kept close. Very quickly, probably, she adapted to the rhythm of the country and the Continent, making that rhythm all her own. I imagined her purposefully placing her dainty little feet onto the very soil from which her own, not-too-distant forefathers sprang.

Yes, indeed, Mama Lilly was a woman who remained active and vitally engaged until the very end of her life. Staying in only one place and doing only one thing didn't interest her at all. And on this day, she was certainly excited about Egypt.

"Cairo was definitely my favorite spot," she confided.

Immediately, my mind painted a picture of my beautiful, silver-haired grandmother negotiating the busy back streets of Cairo, maybe riding on a donkey cart through a crowded bazaar, or careening through the crowded city streets in a beat-up taxicab. In the distance, she could probably see those stately white mosques or maybe even some more pyramids. (My geography skills weren't exactly great, so I wasn't even sure if the pyramids were anywhere *near* the city of Cairo. But it was a wonderful image, so I decided that they were.)

"What was special about Cairo?" I asked. I really wanted to know.

"For one, it's a city filled with wonderment and honor," she said in a voice filled with respect. Her eyes took on a faraway look.

Wonderment and honor? Who actually used words like that in normal conversation? She was definitely my Mother's mother. Both of them spoke the King's English at all times—even when they were conversing with seven-year-olds like me.

She continued with her list.

"Secondly, I just love the history behind the actual name of the city—'Cairo'—because I've heard it means 'victorious' in Arabic. Did you know that, honey? Well, it's the truth . . . and Lord knows, we are a 'victorious' people, aren't we, baby?"

At that moment, I promised myself to name our next family pet Cairo—whether it was another cat, dog, or even a goldfish. I liked the sound of the word *victorious* (even if I hadn't been completely sure of its definition). To me, the word sounded *strong*, like an army of a thousand men, all riding Arabian horses, carrying shining silver shields and gleaming swords so sharp they could lob off your ear (or your head) in a single stroke. I decided I liked the word as much as she did—because whenever I was with my miraculous grandmother, I felt *victorious* myself.

I felt safe. *Victoriously safe.*

Suddenly, she snapped her fingers, as if she'd just remembered something pretty important. I was holding my breath.

"Mama brought you something special back from Cairo, baby."

I didn't want to appear greedy or overeager (Mother would certainly have disapproved), but boy, was I curious. What on earth had she brought back for me, all the way from Africa?

"Give me a minute to try to remember where I put it."

I sat quietly in my armchair, hoping and praying that God would enlighten her and guide her toward the gift she'd purchased for me. He must have heard my prayers, because seconds later, she was barking out instructions:

"Run to my bedroom and bring Mama that cardboard box in my closet," she instructed. I could feel my fingers beginning to tingle; I was about to receive a gift from my grandmother! I wanted to laugh and shout or maybe dance a little jig, but I also realized that something about that moment called for a certain solemnity. Some serious sharing was about to occur.

I was so excited, I didn't even have time to be scared about going into her bedroom by myself. I knew there weren't monsters, but one can never be completely certain of such things. Still, I ran like the wind to her bedroom. I didn't want to waste one minute—not only because I was eager to see what she'd brought me, but because it was gradually beginning to dawn on me that, yes, I *would* be alone in the bedroom without her. I didn't like it one bit.

As soon as I entered, I bolted straight to her closet, yanking open her closet door with such force that the doorknob fell off. There on the floor was the box, just like she'd promised. The minute I saw it, I realized that I'd seen it many times before, but had never given it so much as a thought. I regarded it warily. It looked kind of heavy. *Did she expect me to lug that big thing all the way back to the living room by myself?*

I didn't realize it at the time, but that was Mama Lilly's version of her own Forever Box. It was corrugated cardboard, a little beat-up and bent at the corners, but filled with thick, dark fabrics of royal blue velvet, chocolate brown brocade, and satin so dark it looked like midnight. My heart told me that what was *inside* the box was quite special long before my brain did. I realized I was handling history. *Her* history. I think I might have shivered.

She yelled from the living room, "Is it too heavy for you to pick up by yourself, baby? If so, just holler and Mama will come help."

Nothing doing. I wasn't about to make my elderly grandmother haul a heavy box even one step.

I'd do it by myself.

Bending over, I picked up the box by its base, staggering a little underneath its weight. I lurched forward, almost tripping over the fallen doorknob on the floor. If I had actually tripped, all her precious stuff would have come tumbling out, and I would have just died a thousand deaths right then and there. Even at seven, I recognized well the importance of handling precious items with reverence and care.

"I'm coming, Mama Lilly!" I yelled, hoisting the box a bit higher so that the lid came just below my nose. "I'll be there in a quick jiffy!"

In the living room, the ions in the air had changed yet again, becoming super-charged, you might say. Mama Lilly must have felt it too. A thin line of perspiration shone on her top lip, and she smiled an excited smile, reaching for the box.

"Set it right down here, baby," she instructed, and I did as told.

"Now open it carefully and reach in."

Time seemed to slow. Part of me felt like I was being

transported to another place. I peeked inside and saw a thick swatch of deep blue velvet the color of royalty. Mama Lilly was leaning in right beside me, pointing down into the box. I held my breath.

"Pull that velvet off the top, very, very carefully," she said.

Using her own two hands, Mama Lilly reached into the box and gently pulled out the package. Turning toward me, she gingerly placed the velvet-covered gift into my hands. I adjusted my little body accordingly so that my lap could create the space I needed to open my present. All of a sudden, everything had become so somber and serious. For goodness' sake—weren't we just humming the opening tune to *Bonanza* together, giggling about Hoss's ridiculously large, ten-gallon hat and whispering about how handsome Little Joe was? But I could feel in my heart that something special was about to happen; some magical moment was about to occur between my grandmother and I.

Out of respect for the moment itself, I placed my gift— very carefully, mind you—on the arm of the chair and walked over to the television to turn down the volume. The moment felt like it deserved to be experienced quietly. Mama Lilly liked that I did that. She smiled a soft smile, her eyes dancing as she watched me sit back down.

"Open it, baby! Unwrap that velvet so you can see what's inside. Don't be such a slowpoke. Mama's going to celebrate another birthday just waiting on you!" She was pretty excited.

I pushed away the velvet. Suddenly, I was holding an object I knew had to be mine. It *felt* like it belonged to me—like it had belonged to me maybe even before I was born. Mama Lilly leaned forward, smiling.

"It's for you. I saw it sitting on a rickety old shelf while I was shopping in Cairo. For some reason, I thought of you the minute I saw it, and I knew I had to get it for you."

I peered closer, my heart pounding about five million times a minute.

There it sat. An off-white leather purse, with leather drawstrings. There were gold-embossed drawings on the purse— images of Egypt that, for me, brought the ancient country to life. At the bottom of the purse, a drawing of three gold camels, marching in a line. Just above the camels, an ancient column (like the kind in Rome). There was also a gold-embossed drawing of a tree (which I assumed must be a special Egyptian tree, because I'd never seen one like it growing in Detroit.)

I sat frozen in my chair.

"That's your special purse from Cairo, now," Mama Lilly said. "You take it to church with you or carry it whenever you want to feel special. If you treat it with care, it will last a long, long time."

I touched it very lightly, worried that the oil on my hand from my fried chicken dinner might stain the precious leather. Already, I cherished my Egyptian purse with such fervor I would have slept with it under my pillow had I not been worried about the weight of my head denting it all up. I loved that purse more than fresh strawberries. More than making snow angels in the backyard. Even more than apple butter in the fall or dancing with Daddy in our kitchen.

Mama Lilly gazed over at me, eyes twinkling with love.

"Thank you, Mama Lilly," I whispered, trying mightily not to cry. *What a baby.* "I love my purse, and I'll keep it forever."

She smiled—kind of sadly, I thought.

"Forever's a mighty long time, child. How about just taking care of it for as long as you're here on this earth?"

I considered what she'd just said. For some reason, it frightened me a little. Worry began nibbling away at my overactive imagination. *For as long as I'm here on this earth? Exactly what did she mean by that? That I was going to fall off the face of the earth one day soon—or maybe that I was going to die or get kidnapped or something?*

I was scaring myself. I decided just to be happy.

"I'll treat it really well," I promised, trying not to visualize myself slipping off the side of the world and falling through space.

I meant it, too. I pledged to myself, right then and there, to keep my Egyptian purse out of harm's way. I wouldn't even bring it in for show-and-tell. There was no way in the world I was going to carry it to church or even take it to school. My class sometimes had peanut butter and jelly for snack, and I'd stick needles in my eyes if one of my friends smudged the precious leather with peanut-butter-covered fingers, even accidentally.

My grandmother reached for the purse and held it in her hands. She looked at it for what felt like a long time. Maybe she was thinking about her trip, about the camels and donkey carts and pyramids and all. Most probably, she was thinking about the power and pull of that continent, about the dawn of civilization and how everything started in Africa. Finally, she spoke.

"Yes, yes, yes," she said, almost speaking to herself. "Mama thought this little number had your name written all over it." (A few weeks after our visit, I took her statement literally— by writing my name on the purse in red ink. I think I did it because I wanted to make sure people knew that this precious purse belonged to me and me alone. By writing my name on it, I didn't think I was defacing it; I was simply making sure that folks knew that my grandmother loved me enough to have brought me back this exotic gift from a foreign land. To this very day, my Egyptian purse lies safely tucked away in my Forever Box, a little bruised and beat up, but *with me* nonetheless. If you look closely, the red ink is still clearly legible. In my second-grade chicken scratch, I'd carefully written my name: *Kristin Clark*.)

Mama Lilly patted the small space beside her; an invitation for me to come sit close. I moved in quickly, eager to smell her talcum-powdery grandmother-smell and lean my head against her shoulder. Her plumpness pleased me to no end. There was nowhere else I wanted to be.

As evening came, we sat together on the front porch, rocking gently on her glider. Purple streaks marked the sky, slowly changing to cobalt blue, then midnight blue, then, finally, to the black of night. We spoke in hushed tones. The power of the past seemed to wrap itself around our shoulders.

Mama Lilly wanted to talk.

And I wanted to listen.

The sounds of nighttime surrounded us. Crickets chirped

loudly in the background. Every now and then a car drove past, its tires making swishing sounds on the wet pavement. Mama Lilly spoke of family history, of how her great-grandmother had been a slave. I imagined a beautiful, utterly charming woman who looked just like Mama Lilly—except shackled in chains or maybe being torn away from her children as they were being sold away to a different master.

She didn't go into much more detail, but I had already learned enough about what my people had had to endure: These brave, beautiful women (and men) had come to America in chains and shackles. I'd seen some pictures and read some of the books in the school library (the ones for kids, like about Harriet Tubman and Frederick Douglass and all). I knew that a lot of my ancestors hadn't even survived the trip; many of them died on the way over. I also knew that they'd been forced to lie down in tight rows at the bottom of the boat, in a space so small it reminded me of the first time I ever saw someone in a coffin—at my Uncle Tommy's funeral (and I had nightmares for months afterward). I remember thinking, as I looked at poor, dead Uncle Tommy lying there, *Why in the world would someone have stuffed him into such a tight box— with a lid on it, no less? Is he supposed to spend the rest of his life being stuck underground, without even any space to move around?* Well, that's about as much room as the slaves had on their voyage—which, essentially, was *no* room at all. No room to roll over or sit up or even reach up to scratch your nose if you felt an itch. The only difference, though, was that the slaves were *alive*. They had to eat and breathe in those tight spaces, for weeks on end. At least Uncle Tommy was dead. The slaves were living and breathing . . . kind of like being forced to lie in your own floating coffin.

My eyes itched. My heart battered around in my chest. My past was mingling with my present, and it made my seven-year-old heart swoon in pain and sadness. I reached over for Mama Lilly's hand. Her warmth warmed me. She squeezed my hand, patting it lightly.

I shook my head vigorously, in an effort to rid myself of those horrible images of my foremothers on the auction block, being ripped from the arms of their screaming children as they were being sold away, or lying in their floating coffins. I didn't hear myself whimper, but Mama Lilly certainly must have, because she scooted me closer to her warm body and placed my head gently onto her bosom.

"There, there, honey pie," she murmured down into the crown of my head. "You mustn't cry."

As she stroked my cheeks, more tears appeared. I cried for the great-great-grandfather I never even knew, who'd been forced to stand really, really still—without screaming or making any little noise at all—while he was being whipped. I cried for the children who were my age who'd been snatched away from their mothers and families, never to lay eyes on them again. I cried because I was slowly but surely coming to realize that the world is not all sweetness and generosity and sparkling light; that there *is* darkness sometimes, and that people can and will be cold and cruel to each other, on purpose! I cried at the realization that, even though my insular, neatly packaged little sugarcoated world might have been filled to the brim with love and laughter, a huge chunk of life was not. Large parts of the outside world were hateful and haunting, with real-life monsters that captured and killed and certainly aimed to hurt. My tears wouldn't stop.

I could feel Mama Lilly reaching for her embroidered handkerchief, trying to pull it from the front pocket of her housecoat. I leaned away from her just a tiny bit, to give her room to get the hankie, but I was still crying pretty hard. Even as I cried, I hoped she wasn't getting worried; after all, she was pretty old and there wasn't much she could do with a blubbering seven-year-old in the dead of night. *Please God, don't let her have a heart attack.* I also prayed that my nose wouldn't start running all over the place, because even though she was my grandmother and I loved her more than applesauce with cinnamon, it still would have been pretty embarrassing if she'd had to wipe it like I was a one-year-old baby. (Thank God she didn't have to.)

After a minute of digging around in her pocket, though, she did find her kerchief (as she called it). As soon as she pulled it out, she leaned in close and started plucking and patting my tearstained face with such tenderness and love that it almost made me start crying all over again. I swear. Life is funny like that. Emotions can definitely get tricky.

This scene on Mama Lilly's porch reminded me very much of the same scene on Mrs. Simpson's porch just two days earlier—the way Mrs. Simpson had so gently and lovingly patted my face dry with her ever-ready dish towel after I had gotten splashed by that speeding Thunderbird as I was crossing the street. The constant tenderness my elderly lady friends displayed toward me was unimaginably comforting.

Their collective closeness buoyed my little spirit. It made me feel safe. Connected. Smiled upon from above. Protected from the evil that lurked in the darkened shadows.

In her sweet, floral-scented effort to calm me down, Mama Lilly clucked quietly for a few minutes and patted my face softly with the palm of her hand. When my breathing had normalized and the sniffling had subsided, she began to speak—so softly I just about had to stop breathing to hear her.

"Mama doesn't want you to be sad, baby," she whispered. "But you *should* be aware of the fact that, unfortunately, there is cruelty in the world. People aren't always nice to each other—whether it's one person calling another person a mean name." Immediately, I thought of what Sheila and I had just been through. "Or an entire race of people trying to wipe out another—it's just the sad fact of the matter: Human beings *can* be cruel. Mighty, mighty cruel. And one of our jobs as responsible, civilized human beings—for as long as we're here on this earth—is to do our part to cancel out as much cruelty as we can. Sitting by and letting it happen is simply not an option."

She looked down at me then, but she kept patting my cheeks softly. I never wanted her to stop. Still, the image of my great-great-grandmother, shackled and standing high up on the auction block, trying her mightiest to twist away from the calloused, groping hands of the slave trader, remained riveted in my mind. Even then, what little I knew about slavery, I hated. And I hated it because I couldn't get a grip on why one race of people would want to *own* another race—in the same way I owned the new bag of marbles my sister Noelle had just given me, or my new pair of patent leather church shoes or even my new plaid Western shirt with the fancy pearl buttons from Sears, Roebuck & Co. None of it made any sense. People were supposed to own *things*—not other people.

I looked up at my grandmother, hoping she'd blow away the poisonous pictures that were forming in my mind.

She looked down at me and smiled her sweet, sweet smile.

"Mama knows your mother and father have already talked to you a little about slavery, honey, 'cause they asked my advice about how much they should say, and when."

My mother, seeking advice from her own mother, about how best to communicate with her baby girl about the ugliness of slavery?

I imagined my parents, sitting at Mama Lilly's kitchen table, concerned looks on their faces, as they probed and prodded about the best way to teach me the life lesson that people were sometimes cruel and hateful and bigoted and ugly; that they sometimes enslaved each other and whipped each other and sold each other away like cattle. And there we were—three generations, all trying to make sense of an historical atrocity that had affected each of us powerfully, personally, and in profoundly different ways.

"Mama already knows you know a little bit about this painful part of our history, and I strongly believe it's better that you learn about it from your family first. I say this, honey, because I know that the history books you'll read—or may have already read—have a strange way of twisting up the real facts into little knots that are sometimes hard for young minds to untangle. What happened to our people is what happened to our own bloodline—it lives and breathes and pulsates within our own veins. Mama's not telling you to ignore the history books, but I *am* telling you—just like your mama and daddy have told you—to feel it within your own spirit. Let it burn into your own mind, and your own memory. And, more than anything, you must *learn* from these horrible lessons."

She rubbed my arm and spoke again.

"Why do you think it's important for us to learn about the atrocities of our past?"

Lord God almighty. She couldn't actually be waiting for me to answer such a question, could she? I knew she considered me to be a smart seven-year-old, but this was bordering on ridiculous.

So I just stayed silent. I just hoped and prayed that she'd answer her own question. How in the world would *I* know the reason we'd want to remember such a poisonous part of our past? I hadn't a clue.

An uncomfortable silence began growing between us, like a stink plant or poison ivy. It didn't feel good at all. *Was she actually waiting for an answer?*

After what felt like about a thousand hours of just sitting there together, she finally did answer her own question—and her voice was no longer a whisper, but a forceful declaration:

"We try to remember it *forever*, so that nothing like it will ever happen again." It was a lesson I'd remember for the rest of my life, in increasingly sophisticated levels of awareness as I grew older. Mama Lilly had been exactly right, on many different levels: The more aware we are of our past mistakes, the less likely it is that we'll repeat them.

I wondered, then, as we sat together on the porch that evening, whether there was a deeper reason behind her bringing that beautiful purse for me, all the way from Egypt. I wondered, as we rocked together, whether she'd wanted to remind me that, although our people were once kings and queens and had actually given birth to civilized society, we'd also faced unimaginable atrocities and indignities—indignities such as slavery that would leave us bent, but not broken. Weakened, but not paralyzed. (Perhaps that's why one of her favorite sayings was always, "It doesn't matter if you stumble and fall; take pride in the fact that you shake yourself off and *get back up!*")

I remembered again what she'd told me the word *Cairo* meant in Arabic: "victorious." And I sensed that "victorious" meant courageous. Brave. A winner, no matter what the circumstance.

That my people have survived such pain and indignity over the course of history, only to grow stronger and wiser as a result, certainly makes me feel *victorious*. And my grandmother's urgings to learn more about not just my own history but the history of the entire world around me helped open up my spirit and widen my spiritual embrace. She helped me realize that, no matter what the color of our skin, we are all connected to each other by simple virtue of the fact that we all inhabit this same planet, we all breathe the same air together, and we all occupy a singularly unique and wonderfully collective space within this one universe.

Shortly after that powerful but somewhat painful evening, I began to pray for increased awareness and understanding about the world around me. I knew full well that what Mama Lilly had taught me that evening—about knowing our history so we can avoid future mistakes—was right on target, but it was still a bit unsettling.

My prayer was this: *Please God, help me understand why some people are mean and hateful. Shower me with knowledge about compassion and universal love and how to move away from hatred. If there are lessons I need to learn, Lord, teach them to me so that I may help bring love and tolerance back into this world— not just for me, but for all races, everywhere. Even though I'm only seven, guide me in a way that helps make this world a better place.*

I believe it was the first prayer I'd ever uttered that actually expanded beyond and leapfrogged over the people in my immediate sphere of influence (my family, Mrs. Simpson, Miss Miriam, and all of my friends at school) and actually included the larger world around us. It was my first spiritual plea for compassion and empathy and for guidance and it signaled to me a maturation of spirit and a deepening of heart. Mama Lilly was the woman who helped nudge me to that spiritual place, and I'll always be grateful to her for teaching me to pray for the wider world around me. Still, I continued my prayer for deeper understanding.

Eventually—as always—God answered.

About a year later, something happened.

For weeks on end, I'd been noticing Mother reading a certain book. Usually when she read, you could tell she was enjoying it deeply; she would either curl up in the armchair in our living room, or maybe sit out on our front porch, basking in the sunlight, completely transported to some foreign and exotic world by the words within her book.

But not with *this* book.

Whenever she'd read this particular book, her facial expression took on a serious, sometimes pained expression. Worry wrinkled the space between her eyebrows. And when she read this book, she never curled up, but sat ramrod straight, at either the kitchen table or the card table where she did all of her writing. I'd even watch as she highlighted certain sections, shaking her head in disgust or disappointment. It was also clear that she didn't want me to come anywhere near her while she read—the first time Mother had *ever* spurned my presence.

So I took to sneaking. I took to peeking. I took to snatching quick glances at the words whenever I passed by, trying to appear completely disinterested.

One afternoon, though, Mother got careless—and I made my move.

The moment she placed her book down to get a glass of water from the kitchen, I pounced upon it like a caged tiger. I knew I didn't have much time, so I worked quickly. Most of the words were difficult to decipher, so quick as lightning, I snatched up the nearest pencil and a piece of scrap paper. I wrote down some of the words she'd already highlighted, knowing that I could look them up later in our dog-eared Webster's Dictionary or our wonderful set of Encyclopedia Britannica—the *complete* set, I might add, or maybe even out of one of our World Books. (Our household was filled to the brim with excellent reference books, thanks to Mother.)

Even as I wrote down the words, I could feel the hairs at the nape of my neck begin to stand at full attention. My stomach rumbled. My hands were perspiring so heavily I could barely hold the pencil; my fingers were shaking so badly I could barely read my own writing. But I didn't have time to feel guilty about the intrusion. I somehow felt something larger was at stake.

As I wrote down the words, my heart and hands seemed to freeze. Time slowed. And worse yet, I could hear Mother placing her drinking glass back into the sink, preparing to head back into the living room. Quickly but ever so carefully, I returned the book to the precise position in which she'd left it.

I barely made it out of the room in time.

As I peered through the living room doors, I could actually see tears sparkling in my mother's eyes. I decided I hated this book, and I hated what it was doing to the most important person in my entire life.

It was time to get to work.

Later that evening, when everyone else was occupied with their own projects and activities, I made my way to the television room, where we kept most of our books in these beautiful, built-in bookshelves that Mother had had constructed just for us, which still exist in that house to this very day. These wonderful books opened up worlds we'd never see and brought us face to face with facts and figures we never could have imagined. As I looked up each entry, my nervousness increased. It might have been the first time I'd ever experienced, on a personal level, the definition of the word *dread*.

I knew no one in the family would think it unusual that I was looking up specific words. Mother and Daddy constantly encouraged all us kids to seek knowledge from reference books as often as possible—but I knew I had to be careful to conceal my reactions, if there were any.

Slowly, but surely, using every reference book we had in the house, I looked up each word.

Auschwitz.

My breathing slowed until it was just about stopped.

Concentration camps.

Bitter bile began to rise up in my throat.

Hitler, Adolf.

Holocaust.

Gas chambers.

Gestapo.

Although I had trouble understanding some of the concepts, I was beginning to understand. And the more I understood, the less I wanted to read. But I was having trouble reading anyway for my vision was blurred by my tears, making it virtually impossible for me to see.

I ran to my bedroom and cried myself to sleep.

❧

I AWOKE the next morning to Mother's soft kisses covering my cheeks and eyelids and nose.

"Morning, Beauty," she whispered. But something caught in her voice. I could hear it the second she spoke. *Something was off-balance.*

I sat up and noticed right off that she was holding something in her hands. Rubbing my eyes, I peered closer. *Jesus-MaryandJoseph.*

It was the list of words I'd looked up the night before. I must have dropped it on the floor before I fell asleep.

The jig was up.

"Sweetheart, you know I love you and I would never intentionally mean to harm you, right?"

Even that she would ask such a question set my soul on fire. I didn't know whether to stand up or throw up. I didn't say a word.

She took me into her warm embrace, rocking me gently. Suddenly, the words exploded forth.

"I'm sorry, Mama. I just wanted to know what you were reading that was upsetting you so much. I didn't mean to spy and I didn't mean to snoop, but I was worried because it was making you so sad. That's why I did it, Mama. That's why I looked those words up."

She regarded me momentarily, her eyebrows knitted, either out of intense love for her child or because she was just so filled with anger and disgust that she couldn't speak.

Fortunately for me, it was the former.

"Sweetheart, I never ever want to hurt you. But there are certain things that you're just not ready to *know*—not just yet."

She shook her head sadly.

"For heaven's sake . . . *I'm* just now getting up the courage to really teach *myself*, in full detail, about what happened during that horrible time. For all these years, I've just been too much of a coward to read anything more detailed than a newspaper article or a short magazine piece. Even today, sweetheart, I still can't get my mind around what happened . . . It's called the Holocaust, if you want to know.

"This book I'm reading is the first full account I've read about that nightmarish time, honey—and you know how much I love to read. I just couldn't bring my heart or my mind to open that part of history back up again. It hurt too much— and I didn't want it to hurt you."

We looked at each other, silent. I'd never heard her speak that way—so open, so vulnerable, so emotionally honest.

She continued, "You know your father and I have always taught you children that knowledge is power. We still believe that, and we always will. But I don't want to lay something so heavy on your young, little heart that it breaks into a million pieces . . . and what happened during the Holocaust could break anyone's spirit. I was going to wait until you were a little older . . . but looks like you beat me to the punch."

Holocaust.

The very mention of that word brought us together in a closer, much more urgent embrace. My spirit felt raw. Hers probably felt raw *and* betrayed that I had snuck behind her back to get a look at the very thing that she was trying to protect me from. But I had something I needed to say.

"Remember about a year ago, when I spent the night with Mama Lilly and she gave me that pretty purse from Egypt?"

Mother nodded, her gaze never leaving mine.

"Well, she told me on that very same night that she thought that it was time I learned about some of the awful things that have happened in the world . . . She said that it's kind of my *responsibility* to know—for everyone to know—so that we won't make the same stupid mistakes twice."

I was sputtering now. Tears were pooling up, threatening to overflow. Still, I rambled on.

"I know that you and Daddy asked her advice about when to tell me about slavery—and I know that she believes I should *not* be so sheltered from the bad stuff that has happened in the world."

And then, a few last lines before I broke into tears: "I'm *not* a baby. I deserve to know—not just about slavery but about everything. Things like slavery and the Holocaust *happened*, Ma. It happened right in this very world we live in. I've read about some of this in the school library. I *love* it when we read books like *Black Beauty* together, Ma, but there are real-life books that explain history and how things happen in the world. I want to know, too! So tell me once again: Why is it fair for *you* to know—*and not me*?"

We both sat on the bed, shocked into silence. Finally she spoke.

"Part of what you say is right, Beauty. You *should* know the history of the world you live in. It's your right and your privilege. But as your mother, I reserve the right to tell you the things you need to know when I think you're ready for them. However, because you beat me to the punch this time, we might as well talk now."

I could tell she was a little mad about my spying on her, and about meddling in her and Daddy's parental decisions and child-rearing philosophies. But I was more interested in the notion that she was actually about to share with me a part of history that not only changed the lives of all those millions of innocent people who were killed (as well as the lives of their surviving loved ones), but redefined the very notion of good and bad, and right and wrong.

We spoke well into the morning. I cried, and she cried. I could tell she was still holding back a lot of information, but I knew it was out of love, and I knew that one day, when I was older, she'd let me find out for myself.

After that, Mother read her book openly. She still cried as she read (keeping a handkerchief tucked in her fist), but she read nonetheless—no matter how painful. Today, her book sits not in my Forever Box, but in my home library. It sits as a stark reminder—and a sorrowful tribute—to the millions of innocent men, women, and children who were so mercilessly led to their deaths during one of the darkest periods in history. And whenever I open its pages, I think of Mother—of her tears, her rage, and her driving desire to shield me from the truth until she thought my heart was ready to withstand its raw and ravaging ugliness.

The book: *While Six Million Died*.

The lesson: People hate. People kill. People can be unspeakably cruel to each other.

But out of darkness, comes the light. Out of pain, comes power and perseverance. Out of struggle—whether it's the sinful nature of slavery, the horrors of the Holocaust, or something as pure and innocent as a child's fear of the dark—comes gradual awakening.

In a very real way, it was that afternoon spent with Mama Lilly that spurred me on to spy on Mother and to recognize the importance of being aware of what's happening around us.

Decades later, when my own children were right around the same age as I was then—about seven or eight—they were exposed, in a very general sense, to parts of our history that can never be erased. Yes, the knowledge was initially unsettling to them, but it is infinitely better to know than not.

Ignorance is *never* bliss. It's tragic.

❧

EVEN through my tears—on that magical yet emotionally draining evening as I sat with my grandmother—I knew that my life had been changed forever. And it was Mama Lilly who'd opened the door of my heart to include people of all colors, cultures, and backgrounds. She was a trailblazer, that woman.

A woman ahead of her time.

❧

DEEPLY committed to her church, St. Philips Lutheran Church, Mama Lilly loved the Lord with passion and power. She was also a generous, compassionate woman who gave of herself freely and without hesitation—particularly to those who were in need. Whenever she encountered a hungry person, she provided a warm, home-cooked meal. If a neighbor or friend fell down on their luck, she'd offer up whatever financial relief she could afford. She cherished her family with a fierce, fiery pride. The memory of her warm smile and twinkling eyes will always burn brightly in my mind.

Without a doubt, my grandmother Mary Elizabeth Sorsby was a maverick.

She was also a capable, compassionate businesswoman and entrepreneur.

Many years earlier, before I was born, she started her own successful business. Quite early in her adult life, she'd worked for an elderly, scholarly doctor, and before he died, he passed along to her a secret formula that would change her life forever—and enhance the lives of countless others. It was a formula that he'd developed after many years of hard research—and he'd passed it along to no one but Mama Lilly. It was a formula that, when followed with the utmost precision, created a medicine that warded off the common cold, helped reduce arthritic pain, and successfully fought off many other commonplace maladies.

My grandmother's working laboratory was located in a downstairs room in her basement—actually, a second kitchen—which I always remember as being shockingly clean, neat, and organized. Empty, sterilized bottles stood in tidy rows, waiting to be filled to the brim with the magical elixir—a clear liquid with a very powerful, pungent smell. Labels were stacked in neat piles on the countertop, waiting to be affixed to the medicine bottles before they were shipped out to drugstores throughout the city. Friends and family members from near and far swore by her medicine, which she had named "Relief." (I remember clearly, as a child, making a quick stop with my father into the Davis Cut Rate store in downtown Detroit, seeing the familiar bottles of Relief lined neatly on the store's shelves, and how my little heart filled up with pride.)

Mama Lilly relied heavily on her children and grandchildren to assist in the medicine-making process. To this very day, every one of my older siblings holds clear, concise memories of assisting Mama Lilly in her laboratory—but she would never *ever* permit any of us to tamper with the actual formula or the liquid itself. She was meticulous almost to a fault, and she took her job as medicine-maker very seriously. On a regular basis, she'd ship boxes upon boxes of Relief to drugstores and to faithful, long-standing customers, who clamored for the miracle elixir from points near and far. Needless to say, every one of her family members (children, grandchildren, great-grandchildren) kept at *least* one bottle of Relief close at hand, either in the medicine cabinets or on their kitchen shelves. Admittedly, it *tasted* like dirty bathwater with cayenne pepper sprinkled on top, but it healed and helped like nobody's business.

Hers was not a fly-by-night, under-the-table enterprise by any means. For years, she interfaced with the Food and Drug Administration, who monitored the medicine quite closely. One important requirement from the FDA, as I remember it, was that her medicine be referred to as a "home remedy"— rather than the established, factory-tested brands from the major pharmaceutical companies. This technical requirement prevented stores from placing the actual bottles alongside the other, better-known cold remedies, but Mama Lilly pressed ahead nonetheless.

On a regular basis, Mama Lilly would descend into her basement to create fresh batches of the medicine. She had the secret formula memorized by heart, of course, but she was always extremely careful and precise with her measurements.

For her, it was an exact science. Human health was at stake. She also prayed over every bottle before it went out, blessing each one individually.

Every so often, she'd allow me to join her in her laboratory. I remember not only the laboratory, but the entire process itself feeling very scientific—and extremely somber. From time to time, my grandmother would even allow me to adhere the labels onto the bottles—but her standards were exacting and extremely strict. If I incorrectly adhered even one label—whether it was crooked or, heaven forbid, upside down—she'd stop me dead in my tracks and promptly send me back upstairs to watch cartoons or play in the backyard.

She was a wizard and a wonder, my grandmother. As I mentioned before, most definitely a woman well ahead of her time. How bountifully blessed I am to have shared with her the same familial blood.

It was Mama Lilly who taught me that women and business can and do mix together quite beautifully. She was frugal, fearless, and as forward-looking as any woman I've ever known.

Neither her gender nor the color of her skin were impediments; if anything, they spurred her into action with a ferocity that was rare even then, in the mid 1960s. Like my mother, she strongly believed in the notion that women everywhere, black and white, young and old, should be treated with the same amount of deference and respect as men. She believed that once you put your mind to it, anything was possible—and that no barriers existed that could not be overcome. ("With

God," she'd often recite from Matthew 19:26, "all things are possible.")

Mama Lilly "lived in the moment" long before "living in the moment" became trendy and politically correct. Utterly unwilling to worry about the troubles and travails that may be facing us down the road, this wonderful woman always welcomed each new day as a glorious gift, and she embraced the *promise* of tomorrow like a long-awaited friend. It was Mama Lilly who taught me to surrender my fear, give over my anxiety, and release all the uncertainties about the future to a Power far, far greater than ourselves. Her motto as it concerned life and living: "Don't ever worry about tomorrow—because God has been there since yesterday." It is a motto I live by today. I carry it wrapped in and around my spirit at all times.

Too many women, far too often, get caught up and forced down by the prospect of failure, of freedom, and of striking out in a world that is at times unwelcoming and unfair. It was Mama Lilly who first taught me, at the tender age of seven, that we cannot afford to mire ourselves in the mud and muck of negative thinking.

Without a doubt, Mary Elizabeth Sorsby blazed exciting new trails and set higher standards of excellence not only for her family, but for every person her life touched. To her, the prospect of "tomorrow" was a beacon—*not* a burden. Until the end of her life, she remained undaunted by challenge. And when the going became particularly rough, she would never *ever* slip into the shadows or wring her hands helplessly in fear or frustration (Another one of her favorite passages comes from Matthew 6:27: "Who of you, by worrying, can add a single hour to your life?")

Yes, indeed, my grandmother cherished all of her yester-days, lived fully and without apology within every minute of every day, and welcomed the arrival of tomorrow with emotional spunk and spiritual vigor. Positive thinking was built into her character; it abided deep, deep down in her soul. And, perhaps without even knowing it, she passed this positivity on down to the generations who came after her, to every one of her children, grandchildren, great-grands. Like a steaming locomotive, her path was straight and true: She passed the best and brightest parts of herself directly down to every one of my siblings, to each of my sibling's children, and to the new generations after that.

Her spirit will live forever among us—long after we have sung our last song and cried our last tear. I uplift and honor this miraculous woman with all my heart and soul—and I know that, without her, there would be no Mother, and with-out Mother, there would be no me. And certainly, as it stands to reason, I could not have brought my own precious progeny into this world had it not been for those wondrous women who came before me.

So it is these women I thank. It is these women who have entrusted me with their mementos and their memories. The mere fact that these miraculous women existed at all is a gift of such great magnitude that it takes my breath away. And being breathless—in this context, anyway—is a wonderful, wonderful feeling.

A child's Egyptian purse and a mother's sad-but-true book

on an ugly part of our history are two more of the precious treasures in my home that will live forever. And when I reach into my Forever Box to pull out the Egyptian purse my grandmother brought me from Cairo so many decades ago, I remember not only the true meaning of "victorious," but the life lessons my grandmother taught me. Lessons about the importance of familiarizing ourselves with the history of the world; with our civic and moral responsibility to do whatever we can to stop the vicious, repetitive cycle of man's inhumanity to man, and to celebrate the fact that women can be equally as competitive and entrepreneurial in business and finance as their male counterparts.

And to think that the stories and the life lessons attached to them are kept alive by, among other things, a child's small leather purse.

એજ

SINGLEHANDEDLY, during our special overnight visit that weekend, but also in the years that followed, my grandmother had drawn me a picture of what "forever" looks like. She'd taught me that forever has depth, breadth, and specific dimensions. Forever is not some vague, vacuous notion at all, but rather a touchable, tangible thing that directly connects us to our larger selves and celebrates the fact that our lives and the things we carry with us through life are not random at all, but intimately interconnected. Forever is made up of real people and real things.

Throughout her life, she taught me that history is real and can oftentimes be ugly, but that we have a larger responsibility, to ourselves and each other, not only to educate ourselves about the universe around us—whether it's by expanding our own horizons and trying to see as much of the world as possible with our own eyes—but also to do our part to actively halt cruelty and evil whenever and wherever we see it.

A quick glance at my Egyptian purse catapults me back to that evening on the porch with my grandmother, reminding me of the lessons she taught me about compassion toward others and the limitless potential that every woman should enjoy—whether they chair a board in bustling Manhattan or work the night shift at the local factory.

Whatever our personal circumstance, we must always embrace the individual and collective belief that we are, all of us, one and the same. And although our circumstances may differ, we should not only recognize but celebrate the fact that we are not traveling on our journeys alone. We are, all of us, inextricably bound together by faith and by friendship. We are the sum of our own positive, collective totality.

There are other life lessons as well, lessons about the importance of and sheer joy that comes with *throwing open* the doors and windows of opportunity, and pushing forward into uncharted territory, where no man (or woman) has ever gone before. To think new thoughts. Embrace new beliefs. Anchor ourselves and our spirits with the collective knowledge that, no, we do not walk in this world alone and lonely. We are *bound*. Bound together in a wide, loving embrace that can *always* be widened to include others.

And if I never ever make it to that ancient, bustling city of Cairo in my lifetime, that's okay with me. Why? Because it already exists within the dimly lit corners of my own memory. This knowledge lifts me up, strengthens my spirit, and makes me feel—for lack of a better word—simply *victorious*.

Yes indeed. A piece of Egypt lives right there in the darkened recesses of my Forever Box.

And so does Mama Lilly.

TOUCHING FOREVER

I HAVE FIGURED OUT many different ways of touching forever.
Some methods are simple; others require a bit more effort.

The concept of forever can exist within the elegant simplicity of a family name. From the moment they were born, for example, my two children—now responsible, respectful adults—have carried with them the mantle of "memory-maker." How? Simply by their given names.

My son, Lonnie Paul, is named after his paternal great-grandfather (whose name was Lonnie), his great-uncle (whose name was Paul), and his father (whose name is also Lonnie Paul). Similarly, my daughter's name, Mary Elizabeth (or some close variation) has survived within my family bloodline for many generations. My great-grandmother's name was Mary, my grandmother's name was Mary Elizabeth, and my mother was also Mary Elizabeth. It is my daughter, yet another Mary Elizabeth, who now proudly carries the familial torch. And it brings me untold joy, pride, and a sense of generational continuity to already know (because she's told me) that, when it's time, my daughter will name *her* daughter the same name as well. As a budding memory-maker herself, it has long been a solid part of her familial plan.

A relatively simple but lasting decision such as child-naming, then, can create historical connectivity and can assure the continuation of family lineage. I am certain that both of my children are happy and very proud to bask in the bright light of those who came before them—and not in their shadows, either, but toe to toe. Head to head.

Sadly, Mother left this earth before she could reach out and touch Mary Elizabeth's soft brown hair or play patty-cake with her in the warm afternoon sun. But my grown girl is intimately aware of her grandmother's existence. Both of their spirits are inexorably intertwined. One could even make the figurative claim that these two wondrous women have met before, on a spiritual level.

Similarly, Lonnie Paul was just six months old when Mother died, and not that much older when my father passed away a few years later.

The beauty here, however, is that although my own progeny never had the opportunity to know my parents in any tangible or intimate sense, there still exists between them a very comfortable familiarity nonetheless.

Keeping a Forever Box helps nurture this all-important process of preservation and continuity. Being a memory-maker

◦◦

binds us to something infinitely larger than ourselves and our own individual circumstance. When we can purposefully dust off the cobwebbed memories of the loved ones who came long before us, we play an important role in fitting the disparate pieces of our familial puzzle together to create a clearer, more concise picture of our collective pasts.

Every time my children open the Forever Box, they can reach in and pull out tiny treasures and beautiful baubles that represent, in a very real way, the most positive pieces of their *own* past—a past, I should add, that they would simply be unable to see or touch or feel had it not been so purposefully preserved. It connects them to something larger than themselves, and it helps them make sense of the swirling, turbulent daily world around them.

For my children, then—and for yours, if you decide to make the life-changing decision to become a memory-maker in your own right—the past is not only prologue; it's the promise of being able to reach back into yesterday to hear the stories, learn the life lessons, and preserve the principles of our ancestors who are now long gone. We have it in our individual and collective power, then, to ever so tenderly coax our special memories out of their darkened corners, allowing them to come bursting forth like bright, brilliant rays of sunshine. Doing so helps us know who we are, and where we're going. It helps those generations who'll come after us to center themselves and walk in that bright light of illumination that comes with increased self-awareness and deepened historical understanding.

Nurturing such self-awareness and connectivity helps my

children weave together—into one, whole cloth—their past, their present, *and* their future by reminding them that the fast-moving world around them is not a random world at all, but solidly, meaningfully rooted in personal history and familial pride.

Not only this, but I make the sustained and deliberate effort to steep into their spirits the abiding awareness that, if they are truly to become memory-makers in their own right, they must arm themselves with a sense of personal responsibility and commitment.

"Take good care of your things," I often whispered to them throughout their childhood—precisely the same six simple words my Mother whispered to me throughout so much of my own youth.

Take good care of your things.

Nothing less will do.

ᔕᔓ

ON any given afternoon or quiet evening (unfortunately, not often enough), my family comes together and gathers around our solid, beautiful Forever Box. If we want to pull from the past, we carefully open the hinged lid, bring out a bauble, and invite the magic to begin. If, on the other hand, my children want to make personal "deposits" of their own, we've had to create new, additional space, if only out of sheer physical necessity. And as both of them have evolved over the years into conscientious keepers of their own keepsakes, so, too, have their instincts to select the treasures they intend on preserving in a careful, purposeful manner.

My children are now memory-makers in their own right. What joy! What blessed assurance! The knowledge that yet another successive generation can now pull the past around its shoulders—and wear it like a protective cloak—brings me untold happiness and spiritual relief.

And if my life ended tomorrow, or even at this very moment, I know that I'll leave *this* earth armed with the comforting knowledge that life doesn't stop when we die. If anything, from a religious, spiritual, and symbolic perspective, it's really only just begun.

Such knowledge presents a study in contrasts:

My ability to successfully preserve the past showers me with feelings of calm, often when I'm in the midst of chaos.

It instills in my spirit an abiding sense of comfort, often when I'm in the throes of emotional pain.

It covers me with a sense of continued spiritual connectivity, often when I feel overwhelmed, isolated, alienated, or hopeless.

***

My daughter is not at all daunted by the prospect of stepping into the role of becoming the family's keeper of keepsakes once I've gone on away from here. My son, on the other hand, tends to shake such sentimentality right off his shoulders—which is neither good nor bad; but it does mean that his own personal "deposits" into our box are far less frequent. (Not surprisingly, it's been the females in my family, far more often than the males, who have historically carried the memories through generations. It is my belief that women, traditionally and habitually, instinctively embrace their historical role as memory-keepers within a family. More often than not, we are the lamplight that leads the way when the pages of our collective family histories grow dim and difficult to decipher.)

As for me, I will always remember the magic and mystery that crackles in the air around us whenever we open the lid and bring to the light of day the treasured trinkets of our past. And it is my fervent prayer that my children will remember these moments as well, with equal amounts of clarity and conviction.

To be sure, stepping into the role of memory-maker requires emotional energy. Assuming such a role also requires a certain degree of spiritual commitment. And the ability to preserve and protect our long-lost familial memories requires daily dedication and a heightened sense of self, place, and purpose.

છ૭

ONE gray winter afternoon many years ago, when my Mary Elizabeth was in the first or second grade, she and I sat down together to pluck memories. School was closed because of a sudden and severe snowstorm the night before, so our moments together that afternoon seemed leisurely and languid. My intention on that snowy afternoon was to show her pieces of her past that she'd never laid eyes on—and I realized, even then, that this would be her first experience with the symbolism and significance of being transported back through time.

This would be the first time mother and daughter would deliberately open the hinged lid, reach down inside, and pluck the precious baubles from the box. It would be her maiden voyage, her first journey into the faraway but real-life world of yesterday, to that magical place where time, place, smell, touch, and sight all looped over onto themselves and generations long gone stepped quietly into the bright light of *today*.

I was preparing my baby girl to reach out and touch forever.

She's old enough now, Beauty, I could hear my mother whisper as her maternal spirit moved in beside me, lingering close. I could almost feel the softness of Mother's hands guiding mine as I prepared to escort my daughter back to a time that actually predated her own existence. Mary Elizabeth sat quietly, patiently, an expression of mild curiosity flashing across her face.

The time had come.

Mother's spiritual urgings had been right on target: my gorgeous little girl was, indeed, ready to reach out and pull in her past. She was about seven years old at the time, and as she looked up at me expectantly, my heart pounded and my breathing became shallow.

The moment upon us was both significant and symbolic: It would represent one of the first times in her young life that she would be introduced to the physical memory of Mother.

"There's something very important I want to show you, baby," I said quietly, trying valiantly not to let the tremor in my voice betray my emotionalism.

Mother's presence became even more powerful at that moment, lingering so closely now that I could almost feel the freshly starched cotton of her dress—that very same polka-dot sundress she'd worn decades earlier, when she and I had reminisced together during that long-ago summer thunderstorm. Time was folding over onto itself. My breathing continued to come in short, shallow bursts.

Show her, Beauty. Tell her. Make sure she listens carefully as you speak, and let her hold it in her own little hands. I'm right here with you, sweetheart. In fact, I never really left.

By then, my tears were pooling, threatening to overflow into tiny rivulets down my cheeks. I blinked them away. I didn't want Mary Elizabeth to become worried at the sight of her mother in tears. (As we sat together on that wintry afternoon, with the snow outside blanketing everything around us in a thick, comfortable cushion, I knew that my tears would worry her mind rather than warm her heart. So I forced myself to pull it together.)

Still, I was nervous. My hands were shaking ever so slightly. A faint sheen of perspiration formed on my forehead and in the hollow above my upper lip. Willing myself to calm down, I reached for the box, talking softly the whole while.

"I want you to see this, sweetheart."

Carefully removing the object from its protective covering, I leaned toward my daughter and placed it gently into her hands.

"Whose is this, Mom?" she asked through a slight lisp, since two of her front teeth were missing.

I closed my eyes momentarily, praying fervently. *Thank You, Lord, for guiding us toward this shining moment. Thank You for leading us to this place that is our past. Thank You for letting us touch forever.*

At that very moment, I fully understood and absorbed the rationale behind my keeping a Forever Box at all: Not only did I painstakingly preserve the baubles and trinkets for sentimental reasons, but also for a shining moment such as this—when generational spans converge, and when we are finally able to witness the rare and wonderful coming together of past, present, and future.

Suddenly, and for the first time, I'd come face-to-face with that moment: the magic moment, when everything converges. I was no longer the receiver of treasured trinkets and beautiful old baubles—but the *giver.* Just as Miss Miriam had passed along to me her dainty perfume bottle, and in the same way that Mrs. Simpson had given to me her precious teacups, it was my turn to pass along the past. I smiled at the memory of Miss Miriam digging through her steamer trunk and pulling out an evening bag for me that, to this very day, lies safely tucked away in the cedar. My heart leaps with pride when I pull out my Egyptian purse, and I remember that magical afternoon when my grandmother gave it to me. Now, suddenly, the tables had turned. Yes, indeed. I was the giver, and my daughter was the recipient.

The changing of the guards.

And the peaceful, personal realization that, while my time on this earth is finite and limited, my loving legacy is not.

I cleared my throat, quickly swiping away a tear. I wanted to answer my daughter's question, clearly and directly.

"It was my mother's," I whispered, placing it into her hands with tender care. Pride and passion pushed itself into the air around us.

Mary Elizabeth turned the precious piece around and around in her hands, a lazy smile dancing a little samba across her face.

I leaned down to plant a sweet, brown Hershey-chocolate mother-kiss smack in the middle of her forehead. Time stood still, pulled us backward into the past, and catapulted us into the future—all at the same time.

Placing the flats of my palms on either side of her warm, lovely cheeks, I peered down into her eyes and began the story.

"It was your grandmother's," I said, pride dripping from my voice.

I paused, tears stinging my eyes. "It was her favorite church hat."

૯૭

As we sat together on the sofa that afternoon, snowflakes began to fall again. Mary Elizabeth readjusted her small body so that she was nestled comfortably in my arms.

"Tell me more about the church hat," she demanded demurely, clearly intrigued and appropriately reverent (as reverent as a seven-year-old can be, anyway).

Immediately and automatically, my mind skittered sideways, straight back to that rainy afternoon with Mother, when I'd begged her to tell me the church hat story just *one more time*! While I absently stroked my daughter's arm, I smiled at the memory of me and Mother sitting together in our living room on that gray, rainy day, thunder rolling in the distance. I even remembered Kaboodle, our family cat, and how he'd slithered around the table that afternoon, sitting sphinx-like and genuinely interested in Mother's story, too.

On that special day, literally a lifetime ago, my mother's voice rang out as clear as a bell. Her church hat story, to my little ears, filled my soul and my imagination with the vivid, visual details of her rich experience.

Sitting there that afternoon with my own daughter, I pulled the parallels in around me, smiling to myself: I'd been seven-going-on-eight when my mother shared with me her church hat story, just as my daughter was precisely the same age as I was now sharing the story with her.

And like my daughter, I, too, had been so thirsty for my mother's touch and for the soft lilt of her voice that it literally took my breath away.

On that snowy afternoon, I knew that my baby wanted—needed—to be pulled back into the past, and I knew that I was the one to do the pulling.

We sat together, mother and child, talking into the afternoon, as the snow outside fell in big, fat flakes. As I spoke, I watched closely as her gaze brushed past me and reached up to the window above us, so that she could watch the falling snow—much the same way I'd gazed at the heavy gray sky on that rainy afternoon with Mother.

And as we sat together, I wondered if she could feel my heart rhythms, in the same way I'd felt Mother's. *Please, God, let her feel my rhythm at this very moment. Let my mother's church hat story nestle deeply in her heart. Let the power of her grandmother's story heighten her sense of direct connection to the world around her. Please—let my baby girl reach out and touch forever.*

Mary Elizabeth held the navy blue hat in her hands the entire time I told the story. When we were finished, I showed her how to wrap the hat all by herself and return it carefully to its rounded, floral box.

On that day, Mother came to visit us both.

On that day, two beautiful people named Mary Elizabeth reached across time and finally introduced themselves, spirit to spirit.

How blessed we are when we are lucky enough to witness the time continuum fold over onto itself and link together, one generation with the next! The process is almost mathematical in its precision, and it sets into motion a divine and mysterious life principle: *As people die, others are born, and thus what was shifting remains constant.*

And if that's not about the best definition of "forever," then I simply don't know what is.

༽

SEVERAL weeks after that magical afternoon with my daughter, Mother's spirit stepped in quietly yet again. Mary Elizabeth and I were sitting by the Forever Box, laughing quietly at a joke she'd just told.

Knock knock.

Who's there?

Anita.

Anita who?

Anita borrow your pencil, please! I have a poem I want to write!

As we laughed together, I admired her crooked little snaggletoothed smile, wondering idly when her new front teeth would come in. When she laughed, everyone around her laughed, because the sound was so pure. So uninhibited. So deliciously heartfelt, like bubbles chasing one another.

There we were, mother and daughter, sitting shoulder to shoulder next to the Forever Box. Magic swirled in the air around us. Kinetic energy bounced and zinged this way and that. Mary Elizabeth had just finished placing her own newly acquired "First Place" blue ribbon into the box (for being the fastest runner at school), and our mood was jovial.

It was at about that moment I felt Mother's spiritual presence brush against my body, light as a feather.

You've taught her well, Beauty. Now she's ready to see more. Reach in and show her more pieces of her past. She gets it! Tell another of our special stories. Help her make sense of the world around her. It's time.

I listened to Mother's spiritual urging, vitally aware of the magnitude of the moment. Again, Mother was right on target. It was the perfect time to pluck another piece of our past from the darkened depths of our box and share it, mother to daughter. My ears tingled. Beads of perspiration formed on my forearms. I wiggled my toes.

"Remember your grandmother's church hat?" I asked, gently prodding, watching to see if her facial expression shifted even slightly—from amusement about her recent joke to genuine curiosity about what was to come.

"Yep, I do, Mom. It's wrapped up in the hatbox right here,"

she answered, pointing toward the floral box. "I remember the story—about how the store wouldn't even let her try that first hat on, so she made one for herself."

Although I might have been wrong (but I don't think so), I was fairly certain that I'd heard the slightest pull of pride in my daughter's voice as she recounted how her grandmother, all those many years ago, had been treated so coldly by the saleslady in the department store, simply because of the color of her skin.

How relieved and comforted I felt to know that she'd remembered the hat story to its finest detail. And in a flash of fresh awareness, I realized at that moment that the church hat story would burn as brightly as the North Star for generations to come. That is the power that comes from preserving pieces of our familial past.

"*She gets it*"—precisely what Mother's spirit had told me moments before. Thank the Lord. She gets it.

She continued gazing at me expectantly, waiting to be shown yet another artifact from the box. Her innate curiosity pleased me to no end. It made my soul smile. I could feel the time continuum looping over onto itself again and again; that circular, universal rhythm that reminds us that we are— all of us—a vital, visible part of something infinitely larger than our own solitary existence, and that our life here on this earth is not linear at all—but cyclical and predictable and perpetual.

Once again, I prayed: *Please let my daughter begin to feel the power and pull of these reassuring, repetitive cycles. Let this outwardly confusing world around her begin to make sense, and show* her, Lord, that the absolute surest way to move forward is by first reaching back. Whisper Your divine wisdom into her little soul, and guide her toward the realization that her ancestor's belongings are far more than mere accessories—they are, in fact, tangible, touchable family heirlooms rooted in history and steeped in symbolism.

It was time to lift the heavy lid and lay yet another family artifact into her small, awaiting hands.

"Well, here's another little something I want to share with you. This belonged to your grandmother, too."

Slowly, carefully, I lifted the lid.

The smell of cedar circled around us, its sooty, smoky fragrance permeating the air in the room.

Leaning forward, Mary Elizabeth peered in. I wondered to myself whether the smell of cedar was filling her little heart with feelings and memories as intensely as I'd felt them an entire lifetime ago.

Instantly, upon smelling the fragrance, I visualized myself again as an infant, comfortably swaddled by my beautiful mother in my Cinderella pink baby blanket. My mind painted the picture—for perhaps the thousandth time—of Mother bending down to lay her baby girl lovingly, tenderly, into the safe confines of the large cedar drawer which had been placed on the floor just beside her writing table. I visualized Daddy carrying the drawer down the stairs—from their bedroom to our living room—then arranging the drawer "just so" in order for Mother and I to remain as close as possible while she wrote. The familiar but faraway sounds of her Underwood typewriter—*tap, tap, tap, ding!*—still fill me with inexplicable joy, and I can *still* re-create not only the *tap* but the *ding*, too!

Why? Because today, Mother's typewriter sits proudly in the library of my home. The keys still hop from one to the next to create actual words on a printed page. The original bell still dings brightly when it's time to hit the carriage return and begin a new sentence. Even the space bar and the individual keys, which are worn and a bit blurry due to Mother's constant use, seem to leap with life. Looking at her typewriter transports me directly back to yesterday. I am an infant again, lying comfortably swaddled in my cedar drawer, lulled to sleep by the sounds of my mother *tap-tap-tapping* away.

With each passing minute, Mother's closeness became more palpable. I had the feeling that if I'd reached out and swiped my hand through the air around me, I would have brushed against her soft skin. My heart seemed to skip a few beats, but I settled my spirit down, determined to devote the pivotal moment completely to my little girl who sat beside me, waiting and expectant.

Reaching into our box yet again, I carefully removed a few of the items on the top layer so that I could more easily get to the layer beneath. Slowly, surely, I found what I needed, bringing it up into the brilliant light of day.

"What's that, Mom?" Mary Elizabeth asked quietly, leaning forward for closer inspection.

I unwrapped the package and carefully placed it directly into her awaiting hands.

"My mom wore this beautiful blouse on the day she was married. Hold it, honey. Feel the fabric. Try to imagine your grandmother all dressed up on her wedding day, maybe carrying a pretty bouquet of irises or lilies. What do you think?"

I watched as she lightly fingered the delicate material and I prayed that her imagination was transporting her back to that wonderful wedding day. Again, gentle, generational links were being created. Again, time lurched and tripped and galloped all over itself.

She cocked her head slightly in measured concentration, her eyes never leaving the garment that she held in her hands. I couldn't resist reaching over to brush her cheek with my fingertips.

"It's really pretty," she said quietly, still fingering the semi-sheer material lightly in her hands. "But I kind of don't get it."

The nature of her confusion confirmed for me, beyond the shadow of a doubt, that my young daughter would one day evolve into a fine, respectable memory-maker in her own right. Her questions were straightforward and completely logical.

"Why'd she wear a *blouse* on her wedding day? What'd she wear with the blouse—a skirt or something? And do you have that skirt stored away? I thought ladies wore long white gowns on their wedding day. If anybody in our family has your mom's wedding gown, it's got to be you, Mom—'cause you save just about everything you get your hands on! Why didn't you store her gown? And if you did, can I take a peek at it, just for a minute?"

I paused momentarily, slightly knocked off my center. The self-doubt began almost immediately: *Had Mother actually been married in a formal wedding gown—and if she was, where was it now? Wouldn't she have stored it away for safekeeping and passed it along to one of her six daughters? What in the Sam Hill*

kind of serious preservationist was I, anyway—not even knowing
where my own mother's wedding gown could be found? For crying
out loud!

I knew for a fact that none of my siblings were storing
the gown—but what I didn't know was whether there'd ever
really been a gown at all.

Maybe Mother hadn't worn one.

Maybe she and her handsome, soon-to-be husband simply
couldn't afford one.

Or, perhaps she had worn one to the ceremony, but had
changed into her beautiful, puckered lavender wedding
blouse immediately afterward (with a long, flowing skirt, perhaps?), for the reception.

These were riddles I couldn't solve, which momentarily top-
pled my spiritual equilibrium, but nudged me gently toward
a critically important realization: the process of memory-
making is, by no means, an exact science. It is not precise or
perfect. It is not premeasured, predetermined, or formulaic.
Somewhere along the way, as we pluck the memories we want
to preserve, there are bound to be memory gaps and unan-
swerable questions. But we, as preservers of our own pasts,
shouldn't allow this imprecision to frustrate us.

To the contrary. All the while—and as often as we can—
we should keep digging, prodding, preserving, and packing
away select pieces of our past so that the generational chains
remain unbroken. Pieces will go missing. Certain stories will
crisscross at illogical points. Ghosts of our past will rearrange
the facts every now and then, leaving us feeling somewhat
confused and disconnected. An inevitable and invariable fact:

The childhood memories and recollections that we choose to pass along will occasionally fall a tiny bit short of reality. Details can become muddled and murky. Why? Because our minds are not computers; our memories are not digitized. Such gaps and omissions are unintentional.

I, myself, as a memory-maker, struggle on occasion to bat away the cobwebs and shadows that can cloud my recollections. The passage of time, combined with the porous nature of our own childhood recollections, can at times create composites of memories, creating the sensation of peering through the fragmented field of a kaleidoscope rather than the razor-sharp focus of a microscope. To a degree, it makes perfect sense that our recollections are sometimes covered in silky cobwebs that can obscure our vision and stretch our imaginations out of shape. The memories we choose to preserve and retrieve—as frustrating as they may be—often resemble a string of last year's Christmas tree lights: difficult to untangle, but beautifully illuminating nonetheless.

Even as I recall some of the details within the shared stories of this book, I know that my memory bank is not airtight and ironclad. No one's is. But as memory-makers, we must not despair. The past still calls, and we must still answer.

In that same vein, I am careful not to position myself among my beautiful siblings as the sole keeper of the flame (but I am the primary "keeper," they'd all agree). I don't possess every last bauble. As memory-makers, my siblings and I are responsible like that; each of us has within our possession precious items and heirlooms that link us to our collective past; things we can hold in our hands and remember our parents by, in our own special, unique ways. No, my Forever Box is by no means the official or sole repository for all this familial history.

That would be selfish.

I don't possess every single last piece of my grandmother's twelve-piece dinner setting (in fact, I don't have *any*). I believe there are only a few settings left—and even those are incomplete.

But they do exist.

❦

OTHER belongings of Mama Lilly's exist as well: a beautiful Tiffany lamp and an ornate china cabinet sit proudly in my sister Noelle's beautiful home. Also in Noelle's home: a very large, dark, and stunning oil portrait of Mother in her mid-twenties, her delicate hands resting comfortably in her lap and her eyes cast downward in contemplation. I am relieved and proud to know that, among us, we spread the memories around, and we share our pieces freely. There's no such thing as a greedy memory-maker. The very nature of the process itself begs for physical and spiritual collaboration.

Mary Elizabeth and I both gazed at the blouse again, letting our imaginations wander back to that glorious wedding day. The blouse is lavender in color, delicate as a piece of antique lace, with puckered rows of material carefully sewn across the front. At the right shoulder, there are five tiny silver eyehooks, which gently close the blouse at the neck. Two more silver hooks at the waist. (Unfortunately, the blouse is slightly torn at the upper right shoulder, but all else about the garment remains perfectly intact.)

It's clear that the garment had, indeed, been handmade, because the stitching along the neckline is slightly askew in some places, and the eyehooks are a tiny bit misaligned. I love to hold the garment in my hands, because every time I do, I visualize Mother in the quiet evenings just before her wedding, threading her needle by the soft and dimming lamplight, carefully creating the blouse that would escort her into an exciting, new life as Mrs. James W. Clark.

"She sure did sew well!" Mary Elizabeth observed, taking an important, figurative step closer to her maternal grandmother.

"She was an expert," I said proudly. "She even made some of our coats, dresses, and skirts. Your grandmother was as good a seamstress as I've ever seen."

The scenes of their wedding day were still dancing around in my mind. I could see Mother: perfect, petite, and infinitely proud to be standing beside my father, her dashing new husband. Maybe my father was holding her hand. When they were pronounced husband and wife, perhaps they came together, momentarily, for a tender kiss and gentle embrace. I could see from my daughter's facial expression that she'd been pulled in by the powerful images as well, mesmerized by the magic of the moment.

When it was time to return Mother's blouse to the box, it was Mary Elizabeth who folded it, wrapped it, and carefully placed it back into the shadowed confines.

❦

WHEN Mary Elizabeth was a mere toddler, dancing was one of her greatest joys. By age four, we'd enrolled her in her first dance class.

She was blissful, obviously very much in her element.

As soon as the curtain came down on her very first end-of-the-year dance recital, we started making memories and continuing family traditions. Another pivotal moment presented itself: It was Mary Elizabeth's first time depositing one of her own personal and prized possessions into the Forever Box.

Quite the ceremony.

What we were preserving were her first pair of tiny ballet slippers; the same ones she'd worn during that first recital. On the bottom of the tiny leather soles, in dark blue ink, I'd carefully inscribed the details: "Mary Elizabeth's First Ballet Slippers, September 1993." Guiding her tiny, toddler-size hands (she was about four), I instructed my daughter on how to properly wrap the slippers in tissue paper then insert them into the ever-reliable, airtight zippered pouch.

Since that magical afternoon and over the span of her lifetime—even throughout her college days—Mary Elizabeth evolved into a serious student of classical ballet and modern dance. To visually capture my daughter's steady and sure progression as a dancer, one simple preservation technique proved highly effective.

Every several years, usually right after a recital (which always signaled the end of yet another year of dancing), she'd enter the slippers into the darkened confines of the box. To visually emphasize the passage of time throughout her years as a dancer, we placed each successive pair of slippers into the same bag, alongside the tiny pair from her very first ballet recital as a four-year-old.

Today, when she reaches into the box to bring her slippers into the brilliant light of day, she can more fully appreciate the fact that dance has indeed played a vital role in her life over and throughout her lifetime, from toddler to adult. I am enormously grateful that we thought to save them. Why? Because, along with the shared verbal history surrounding those years, they tell her dancing story by providing tactile proof of the passage of time; the passage of a lifetime, in fact. Passages that she, eventually, will share with her own daughters, and eventually her granddaughters, and the story will continue long after I am gone.

So the cycle dances merrily along.

ↂ

It is no coincidence that I, too, loved dance with the same passion and fury as Mary Elizabeth, beginning at about the age of five or six. To this very day, my memories of dance, particularly as it concerned dance with Mother, remain crystal clear and miraculously distinct. I remember very well the hot, hazy afternoon that I witnessed, for the first time in my little life, the sight of professional dancers moving across a stage. They were perfect. Precise. Powerful. And they had bronzed-brown skin, just like me!

It was a defining moment in my young life.

There we were, mother and daughter, sitting together in

the darkened performance hall of Detroit's beautiful (and historic) Fisher Building. Mother had splurged on two tickets to see the Alvin Ailey American Dance Theater, and the seats were great.

I will never forget it.

I was short, so my feet didn't touch the floor as I pushed my little bottom all the way to the back of my seat. I was mesmerized. Involuntarily, as I watched those dancers leap and glide across the stage, my body jumped a tiny bit this way and jerked a tiny bit that way; I was moving right along with them as they flew through the air with such soul and grace that it took my breath away.

I remember the feel of the chair's soft velvet against the backs of my legs and the hush that quieted the entire audience as the house lights dimmed and the curtain lifted. By the time the company reached their final, signature piece, "Revelations," I was crying happy, wholesome tears. I'd never ever experienced anything so physically precise and emotionally evocative—and my youthful tears just wouldn't stop flowing.

Mother allowed me to cry.

To this day, I remain steeped in gratitude toward my mom for simply allowing me the luxury of sitting through my own tears. Somehow, she knew instinctively that any interruption—from her or anybody else—would have diluted the power and intensity of this deeply personal experience. So what did she do? She let me be. She allowed my tears to flow that afternoon as we sat in that darkened theater. Mother simply knew, deep within that secret place nestled in her maternal soul, that her baby girl was experiencing, for the very first time in her young life, the power of witnessing art in its purest forms. The movement, music, and choreography threatened to stop my little heart. And as I watched them fly—those miraculous dancers who looked just like me—I somehow knew I'd never be the same again.

A part of my soul had opened up.

It took me decades to realize this, but Mother realized and appreciated my need to absorb that powerful experience in its totality, without interruption. After a few minutes, though, and to my great relief, she did reach over and grasp my hand.

During intermission, we filed slowly out with the crowd. Mother bought me a box of Milk Duds. ("Eat that candy out here," she whispered urgently, "because you're certainly not bringing that melting chocolate back into the theater with you!") At the conclusion of the performance, we filed out again with the dispersing crowd, emerging from the darkened theater into the Fisher's grand lobby and the brilliant light of day. Mother gazed down at me with a soft smile, something very close to sympathy in her eyes. She leaned down close to my little cheeks and gently kissed away the tracks of my recent tears. (She never wiped; almost always kissed.)

As we were riding home that afternoon, I remember feeling like some new layer of awareness had just gently washed over my spirit. This was a paper-thin layer of deepened enlightenment; thin as the skin of an onion and light as a fleeing thought. Something fresh and wonderfully invigorating had begun dancing a little jig in my soul. I realize now that it might have been my first youthful experience with spiritual enlightenment. Watching those dancers had completely removed me from myself, lifting me far above the finite little details of my own personal circumstances. That afternoon, the power and glory of dance, as a pure and powerful art form, insinuated itself into my spirit—and here it remains to this day.

So thank you, sweet Mother. *Thank you for opening up my soul.*

How blessed I am to have passed this passion to yet another emerging generation. The memories and the mother-daughter traditions remain comfortably embedded in our lives.

And even though Mother is gone, her passionate soul and her spiritual generosity will live forever.

☙

TODAY, taking my place in the proud line of preservationists, it should come as no surprise that my daughter and I make it a point to see the Ailey dancers every year, thereby continuing the mother-daughter tradition that my own mother began with me, decades ago. It is a highlight of our mother-daughter experience.

Each time, just before the performance, the two of us, now adult women, enjoy dinner—during which we pray, laugh, love—and remember that miraculous woman who was my mother. I describe to my baby girl, on a consistent basis, those vivid childhood recollections with my mom during that magical afternoon at the Fisher. Of how I sat in that soft velvet chair, joyous tears streaming down my face.

So it is with a sense of historical knowledge and generational continuity that, during every Ailey performance, I manage to sneak several sidelong glances at my daughter as

she watches the dancers leap across the stage. Why? To witness, up close and personally, the myriad of emotions that
shadow her face as the company performs. Yes, she's already
promised that when (and if) she has a daughter of her own,
the Ailey dancers will become a regular part of their cultural
life as well. So the tradition continues, mother to daughter;
mother to daughter. That comfortably repetitive cycle of life
that defines the concept of forever.

❦

WHEN Lonnie Paul and Mary Elizabeth were in grade school,
my husband, Lonnie, and I took them on safari throughout
Kenya. We were led by a miracle of a man, himself a revered
Masai warrior, who'd come to the United States to further
his education. Fortunately for our family, Joseph began teaching social studies at my children's middle school, and a close
relationship was quickly forged. It was Joseph, who was well-
loved and well-respected in his native country, who led us on
a pilgrimage home. With Joseph at the helm, we traveled back
to our ancestral homeland. Traveling with a small group of
others, my family came to know firsthand the kind, beautiful
people of Kenya and the country's breathtakingly beautiful
physical terrain.

Our days were spent traveling deep into the bush, watching as God's creatures moved freely about in their natural
habitat. A pair of graceful giraffes bending down to nibble the
succulent leaves from the tops of an acacia tree. The lazy leop-
ard, napping on the branch of a tree only a few feet above us,
its tail dangling so close we could almost reach up and give

it a soft yank. During the evenings in particular, the Masai warriors came in close around us. They built great bonfires, giant red-orange embers popping and crackling into the thick dark of night. The warriors cooked us feasts every night, and laughed with us well into every evening.

On one of these magical evenings in Kenya, my mind traveled back to the childhood memory of me and my grandmother sitting together in her living room. I smiled as I remembered how excited she'd been to share with me the details of her own trip to Africa. I thought about the leather purse she'd brought back for me from Cairo, and the pride I could hear in her voice as she talked about the dawn of civilization beginning on the very continent where I happened to be standing at that moment. I invited the powerful pull of these intertwining moments to shower over me, feeling the gentle presence of generational continuity wrap itself around my shoulders, as well as a newly heightened sense of self-awareness and ancestral pride.

God's presence moved somewhere deep in my spirit.

Fighting tears, I moved closer in toward my family as we stood before that raging Kenyan bonfire. I relished their comforting presence and tried mightily to preserve the magic of that special moment. Together, our little group gazed up at the stars; tiny pricks of shining light painted in a black velvet sky. The low-hanging Kenyan moon illuminated my children's faces with light almost as bright as the sun. They, too, stood in quiet awe.

Leaning in close to my son, I whispered softly: "Try your hardest to remember this moment forever. Think about it every day, if only for a moment, so that your memory of *right now* remains fresh in your mind."

He nodded, silent.

"Promise me?" I implored, fighting the suddenly desperate desire to cover his face in kisses. (Such a maternal display of physical affection would have embarrassed him to no end—*especially* in the revered presence of the mighty Masai warriors who stood with us, robed and regal, under the stars.)

"I promise, Mom. I'll do my best," he answered, sounding doubtful but deliberate at the same time.

"That's all I can ask, beautiful boy . . . That you try."

It was important to me that my children exercised and challenged their minds on a constant basis, not only to enhance their mental acuity but to strengthen their spiritual condition as well. Something as simple as preserving a specific memory—if only by *reflecting on it* each day—was an easy exercise that would (and did) massage and strengthen their emotional clarity. It taught them, from an early age, how to catalog special moments. In short, it taught them how to *memorialize* memories.

ᕙᕗ

So the ever-widening patterns continue, like a stone dropped in the middle of a pond.

Let each and every one of us take up our role as memory-keepers, resolving individually and collectively to keep our "centers" intact and well-preserved.

And, no matter whether you believe in God or Jesus or a Higher Power or a Supreme Being—whatever your spiritual/

religious beliefs—let us grow stronger by pulling our pasts around our shoulders. Let us give powerful and profound thanks to whatever Power is greater than us, and ask that we be led and guided, as conscientious memory-keepers, so that our legacies will live on long, long after we take our leave of this earthly place.

BY MARY ELIZABETH TAYLOR

BY MARY ELIZABETH TAYLOR

SANKOFA

O UR TIME ON this earth is finite. Each lifetime has a defined measurement. No, there is no crystal ball that can predict the precise moment our individual lives will come to a close, but this much is certain: We move about the world subconsciously aware that ours is a mortal, momentary existence. Life is fleeting and mercurial. Slippery and exhaustible. Utterly impossible to hold on to forever, although many of us might very well want to (thankfully, not me).

This much is sure: None of us can escape the eventual and inevitable clutches of death, but what we can control is the quality and significance of those cherished belongings we purposefully choose to leave behind. As the old adage goes, "You can't take it with you." My response to that has always been, *Who would even want to?* No matter what your religious or spiritual convictions, I think it is safe to say that many, if not most, of us can agree that when our lives finally come to a close, the earthly things we so cherish—even covet—won't be coming along for our ride. (Hence, the rhetorical question, *Ever figure out why you never see a moving van at a funeral?*)

Put simply, by exercising care and deliberation while we're here on this earth, we can almost leapfrog over the snapping clutches of death by preserving vital pieces not only from our past, but from our present-day lives as well, pieces that can be mulled over and turned around and softly touched by the loved ones who live on long after we leave. When we leave behind for our children not only the ability but the desire to weave their past, present, and future into one whole cloth, we're leaving for them invaluable spiritual road maps that will lead them and guide them as they struggle to negotiate the turbulent, topsy-turvy world around them. We should teach them to cherish and care for the items that are special to them, with a keen eye trained always toward the permanence of preservation. They need to know how to draw strength and sustenance not only from the magnetic pull of the past, but also from the power of the present and the promise of the future. They need to know, in their mind and heart and spirit, that these three things—the past, the present, and the future—can, and do, comfortably coexist. This three-pronged approach will enrich their lives and add depth and meaning to their daily existence. I am totally convinced that the most lasting and loving gift we can leave our progeny is the clear understanding that, in order for them to move forward in the world, they must be rooted (but not stuck) in the past, grateful for and cognizant of the present, and warmly welcoming of the future.

The West African concept of Sankofa encapsulates this principle perfectly. One of the images of this ancient concept is the Sankofa Bird, symbolic in spirit and magically mythic, who flies forward while continually looking back (while holding an egg in its mouth, which symbolizes the future). By doing so, he reminds us that in order to truly achieve our fullest potential as we move forward in our lives, we must reach back to gather the best of what our past has to teach us. It's an enlightened, holistic concept to be sure, and certainly a principle that each and every one of us can put to practical use.

I love the Sankofa Bird because it speaks directly to my spirit. I love that as he flies across his own brilliant blue sky, he's reminding each of us that whatever we think we have lost, we can find again; that whatever we think we've long since forgotten can be deliberately reclaimed, and that our lives can be spiritually revived, emotionally enriched, and physically reenergized when we make the deliberate attempt to piece together our past and preserve the most positive parts of our present.

It is this concept that I invite you to embrace by putting it into effect in your own daily life.

As you begin your personal journey toward becoming a more conscientious memory-maker, here are a few tips on how best to preserve the brightest pieces (and wisest principles) in your own lives. I offer up these tips as little bits of love. I pray that you not only receive them as acts of spiritual kindness, but that you try mightily to incorporate them into your daily routine. And here I make a personal promise: When you put some (or all) of these suggestions into practice, you'll find that, over time, your life will simply *open itself up*, like a delicate red rose or a bright purple morning glory. You'll begin to feel more consciously connected to the universe around you as your life expands far beyond itself—far beyond the earthly time constraints that define us as mere mortals.

Over time, I've found that these suggestions have worked for me. Unfortunately, I don't follow every last recommendation as precisely as I should. I can be a bit careless sometimes, or irregular with my "entries." None of us are perfect. As we move forward with the intricacies of this preservation process, we must remember that memory-making is a highly personalized experience. There is no one right way to do it.

The process should not feel formulaic, but free-flowing and fun, never forced. As you begin your memory-making journey, know with certainty that there are no rigid, preexisting sets of rules or binding criteria you must follow to make this process work. Never take the process too seriously. Only *you* can determine which items are significant enough to preserve and insert into your Forever Box. The beauty of this process is that it's deeply personal. These memories are *yours*—no one else's. So how, when, and why you decide to pluck certain pieces of your past is strictly and solely up to you! Have fun!

Listen Closely. Teach yourself to listen *actively*. To do this, you must clear your mind of all else—namely, your own personal circumstances—so that you not only hear but *understand* the memories, ideas, and life lessons that your friends and loved ones share with you. Remember, they are entrusting you not only to preserve and pass along their sentiments and stories, but to validate the fact that they even existed on this earth at all and that their lives counted for something significant and pleasing.

To become a better memory-maker, seek out the senior family members and friends who've been important in your life. Ask them questions about their past, and mindfully visualize their answers so that you can fit them comfortably, consciously, into your own psyche. Weave their wisdom into the fabric of your own life. To more effectively preserve the clarity of their shared memories, consider taping your conversations. (I regret not having done this myself.) Video is the best way to preserve simultaneously both the physical image *and* the verbal account.

Another important tip as you sit down with your senior friends and family: Be prepared! Map out your questions beforehand, and jot them down. And when dealing with seniors, always treat them with the dignity and respect they deserve. (When asking questions of them, speak clearly, succinctly, and loudly enough for elderly people to comfortably hear you. Never yell or gesticulate wildly in the mistaken belief that they might understand you more clearly.)

Here are some questions to consider as you begin these crucial steps toward becoming a plucker of memories:

- In what year were you born?

- Where did you grow up?

- How many siblings/children/grandchildren did/do you have?

- What were the names of two or three of your closest childhood friends?

- What did you do for fun?

- Can you describe your childhood home and community?

- What are a few of the brightest, most brilliant memories from your youth?

- Would you show me, or consider passing along to me for safekeeping, any mementos/objects from your past, and describe their history and significance?

Keep It Simple. Both literally and figuratively, keep the process simple. My Forever Box happens to be cedar. Why cedar? Because I love its smoky smell as well as the childhood memories its mere aroma evokes. Because of the natural preservative quality of the wood itself. Most important, because cedar is a comfortable medium for *me*. To create your own repository, select something that's comfortable and manageable *for you*—whether it's a cardboard box, a wicker basket, or a more elaborate, durable hope chest. Remember that it's not the box itself, *but the memories inside the box that count.*

Your ability to keep the process simple assures that you will also, hopefully, keep the process filled with fun. Don't take it so seriously that it becomes a stressor in your life. Go with the flow. Trust your instincts. Avoid using complicated charts, graphs, and overly detailed chronologies. You're not looking to become a professional historian; you simply want to learn to become a comfortably conscientious memory-maker.

Select the items that you want to preserve with great care, and try to develop a heightened sense of discernment. By this I mean avoid placing any and every "first" item into your box (avoid that "first science fair project" and the "first laptop computer" as well as that "first house of toothpicks that little Bobby made in second grade"). The preservation process itself mandates that you work within a confined amount of space. Surprisingly, this physical limitation is actually a good thing. Why? Because working within a specific and predetermined amount of space will strengthen your selectivity skills.

A few questions to ask concerning simplicity as you begin to build your Forever Box:

- Am I being careful to include not only the old items (preserving history), but the items from my present-day life as well (creating new memories)?

- Am I becoming overly anxious about what, when, why, and how to collect?

- Is the entire process of my memory-making becoming too complicated and involved, to the point where it's distracting? *Am I having fun?*

Handle with Care. When storing fabric or material, wrap the item first in several layers of tissue paper, being careful to insert tissue paper between every layer of fabric. Fold the item carefully, then store in a plastic bag. (Zipper-sealing bags work fine. For larger items, the clear plastic covering from your dry cleaner works well, too.)

Avoid preserving bulky items such as heavy clothing and thick garments. Rather than packing away Aunt Matilda's entire mohair coat, for example, simply snip a few small pieces of the inner and outer lining instead. Take a photo of the coat, then insert the photo into the bag as well. This way you're able to preserve and pass along not only the feel of the actual material, but you'll be able to enjoy the visual image, too.

Any delicate ornaments such as glass or crystal should first be wrapped in tissue paper, then covered in bubble wrap. If you have the space, try to stack your delicate items in their own separate section, dividing each artifact with solid cardboard to create a safety buffer between each piece. Ideally, whichever repository you select should have a lid or protective cover of some kind (this is why baskets don't always work), not only to protect the contents from sunlight but also to minimize the risk of damage if the box is accidentally dropped or suddenly jarred.

Keep your Forever Box in a cool, shady location. Be aware that direct and sustained sunlight fades and even disintegrates photosensitive chemicals in fabrics, newsprint, and photographs. Also consider using acid-free sleeves and envelopes for these items, which should help retard the aging process considerably.

Once you've selected a location for your box, if at all possible, make it permanent. Constant rearrangement of your repository unsettles the contents inside and gets you out of the habit of retreating to one safe, predetermined location when it's time to make an entry.

Label and date each item. This doesn't have to be a complicated process: even using a sticky note will do—just as long as each item is somehow cataloged.

VERY IMPORTANT: When entering, removing, or sharing the items in your box, *make sure your hands are completely clean and dry.* Never *ever* use hand lotions or creams before handling pieces. (The perspiration and natural oils from your skin will create stains, smudges, and fingerprints, particularly on leather items or extremely aged and delicate fabrics.)

Finally, don't be afraid of mothballs! Many new brands have been developed that are without any scent at all. What wonderful news: Your Forever Box doesn't *have* to smell like your grandmother's closet after all!

Some questions to ask yourself as you prepare to focus on safe handling:

- Is my box in a location that is convenient and comfortable for me?

- Are the pieces inside strategically placed and carefully wrapped?

- Have I remembered to catalog and/or date each item so that its significance will not fade over time?

- Have I politely requested that everyone participating in the memory-making process keep their hands clean and lotion-free?

Create a Quiet Sanctuary. Whenever you open your Forever Box—whether it's to insert a new piece or retrieve an old one—try to create a peaceful, tranquil environment. It needn't be overly ceremonial. Remember, though, that you're not simply tossing your pieces into a junk drawer or random box; you're reflecting on the memories, stories, and principles *behind* these baubles, and this process requires a heightened sense of inner calm and serenity.

To create a peaceful buffer from the noisy, clanging world around you, disconnect all things electronic. Shut the door on anything that buzzes, beeps, or brings stress or angst into your spirit—at least for these brief but vital memory-making moments. More than anything, know that *true* inner peace comes to us more easily when our souls are still. In the silence of our words, our Higher Power will speak.

Some questions as you prepare to still your spirit and seek tranquility:

- Is my soul as calm as it can be? Can I actually *feel* my heart rate slowing and my pulse slowing to a more relaxed level?

- Have I quieted my mind and emptied it completely of the day's frenzied, frantic activity, so much so that my thoughts are no longer racing and my stress has slowed to a virtual standstill?

- Have I tried deep breathing, prayer, meditation, tai chi, yoga, or herbal tea to bring about a calmer, more contemplative aura?

- Have I made enough emotional/spiritual space in my mind so that I can now invite the memories to come flowing in?

Share Your Skills with Others. When capturing the pieces of your past, try not to do it alone. Bring others along for the ride! Enlist the help of the young people around you, and teach them what you've learned so far about the importance of handling items properly, in a respectful, non-chaotic environment. Invite the senior friends and family members in your life to participate in the process as well. Perhaps they can even add a few of their own prized possessions to the box, while sharing the stories behind their pieces. This is not only a warm and wonderful way to validate a senior's sense of importance and significance, but it's also facilitates and nurtures the long-lost art of multigenerational bonding and stimulates meaningful, intergenerational communication.

Also try to make contact with other memory-makers to compare notes on what works best and what doesn't. Pull together an informal group of friends who might be interested in starting the process *together*—much like the quilting bees of yesterday. Although I don't do this myself, consider reaching out to others (even strangers—they have good ideas, too!) by posting and comparing notes on the Internet or even beginning your own memory-making website so that others can become a collective part of this exciting, collaborative process. Don't operate in isolation. This process is much too precious *not* to share with others!

Questions that will encourage you to reach out to others for ideas, fellowship, and fun:

- Do I actively solicit ideas and advice from other memory-makers?

- Have I been patient with and kind to my relatives/friends as I enlist their assistance with my memory-making?

- If I were to die tomorrow, could I leave this earth confident in the knowledge that I've passed along the necessary memory-making skills to my loved ones so that my living legacy continues?

The next step: Simply sit back and enjoy. Invite your life to open up around you.

You are a collector now.

And it is your baubles, your beliefs, and the rewoven bits of the most pleasing parts of your past that will bring sustenance, spiritual depth, and emotional solidity to the rest of your living days . . . and beyond.

As you live your daily life, fly like the Sankofa Bird. Propel yourself forward while looking back. Live in the moment, but keep an eye trained toward the future. Pull your past around you and seek comfort in its solidity.

And when all of these converge, your soul can smile a wide, warm smile . . . because you will have finally learned how to create *forever*.

QUESTIONS FOR DISCUSSION

1. In order to re-create poignant childhood memories, the author relies on every one of her five senses—sight, hearing, smell, taste, and touch—to take the reader on a journey into her past. For example, she chooses a cedar chest for her Forever Box because the smell of cedar evokes such powerfully positive emotions within her. Digging deep into your memory, try to recall a particularly powerful scent, sight, or sound from your youth that can still—even today—transport you immediately back to your childhood. What is it? What feelings does it elicit?

2. Reflect on the people who influenced you most profoundly during your childhood. Why were they important? What did they leave behind that continues to live on through you?

3. A recurring theme in *The Forever Box* is the power and beauty of lasting, durable friendships among women. Do you make the conscientious effort to cherish and celebrate the close friends in your life, or does the "I'm too busy right now" syndrome get in the way of your efforts? What steps can you take to maintain and nurture the close friendships you enjoy in your life?

4. In passing down her precious church hat, the author's mother also passes along several important life lessons about maintaining dignity in the face of adversity and grace under pressure. What larger lessons do you hope to share with the young people in your life, in hopes that they, too, will one day pass along to future generations?

5. The three-pronged approach to leading a satisfying, meaningful life is a constant theme throughout *The Forever Box* (that is, fearlessly embracing the future, mindfully living in the present day, and preserving the most positive pieces of our past). Would adopting this three-pronged approach add more balance to your life? What steps do you need to take in your own life to achieve the three-pronged vision?

6. It's clear that the author is powerfully drawn to all things that are old—whether it's her close relationships with the four elderly women in her life, or with the actual treasures that they share with her. Reflect on your own relationships with the seniors in your life. Do you make the effort to glean their wisdom, listen to their stories, and celebrate their existence?

7. Mrs. Simpson shares with the young Kristin not only her teacups and scratch biscuits, but her heightened spiritual awareness as well, an awareness that is the centering force of the author's life today. Reflect on not just the baubles but the *beliefs and principles* that were passed down to you by earlier generations. What are they? Have you successfully incorporated these principles into your daily life? How will you pass these principles down to future generations?

8. Why was the author's visit with Miss Miriam so transformative and powerful? Why were Miss Miriam's progressive views on women so relevant?

9. Not every element of our collective, historical past is positive. How are the painful pieces of our past treated in this book? (For example, the ravages of slavery and the horrors of the Holocaust.) Do you agree or disagree with the author's assertion that it's vital to pass along historical knowledge to successive generations—even if the lessons are painful?

10. Are you ready to become a more conscientious memory-maker in your own right? What ideas come to mind as you consider starting your own Forever Box?

11. Reflect on the pieces of the past that you may already have. What are they, and who passed them along to you? What was—and is—their significance in your life?

12. Are you confident that your treasures and beliefs will remain alive long after you're gone? Have you decided on the people in your life who will be your memory-keepers?

13. Beyond creating lasting remnants of earlier times, what else does *The Forever Box* seek to preserve?

THE LOST COLONY

A North-Western Story

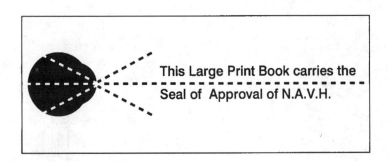

THE LOST COLONY

A North-Western Story

T. V. OLSEN

Thorndike Press • Thorndike, Maine

Published in 2000 by arrangement with
Golden West Literary Agency.

Thorndike Press Large Print Western Series.

The tree indicium is a trademark of Thorndike Press.

The text of this Large Print edition is unabridged.
Other aspects of the book may vary from the original edition.

Set in 16 pt. Plantin by Rick Gundberg.

Printed in the United States on permanent paper.

Library of Congress Cataloging-in-Publication Data

Olsen, Theodore V.
   The lost colony : a north-western story / T.V. Olsen.
     p. cm.
   ISBN 0-7862-1588-7 (lg. print : hc : alk. paper)
   1. Arctic Regions — Fiction. 2. Large type books. I. Title.
 PS3565.L8 L67   2000
 813´.54—dc21   00-034369

In Memory of a Gentle Woman
"Marceline Day"
eudæmon in locis ignotis

To this most remote ground of the Earth
are we come . . . an inviolate solitude.

Prometheus Bound by Æschylus

Prologue

January 7, 1934

The ice-breaker, *Sibiryakov*, although relatively new already had an illustrious record in Soviet naval history. In the winter of 1932 it had been commanded by the naval scientist and imaginative scholar, Professor Otto J. Schmidt, who was in charge of the Northern Sea Route Administration of the U.S.S.R. That year, under Professor Schmidt's guidance, the *Sibiryakov* had made the run through the Northeast Passage from Archangelsk to the Bering Strait in two months and four days. Now with the *Sibiryakov* ice-breaker in the lead, an entire flotilla of cargo ships was passing along an exactly charted course through the Kara Sea, the Vilkitski Straits, the Laptev Sea, the East Siberian Sea, the Chuckchi Sea, and down through the Bering Strait.

Four passengers had come on board the *Sibiryakov* at Cape Chelyuskin, a small port within the Arctic Circle in Siberia across the Vilkitski Straits from Bolshevik Island. All of

7

them had to share the same small cabin. It had two bunkbeds on either side of the entrance, a single overhead light, a table, and two chairs. The leader of the group was Nicolai Strehlnikov, familiarly called Lugu. He was a very tall man, with a skeleton-thin frame, and despite so much time spent in northern India and Afghanistan as a secret operative of the *Komintern* he had a very pale visage and dark, brooding, Slavic eyes. He was sitting in one of the two chairs, smoking a Russian cigarette and playing solitaire with a worn and smudged deck of cards. Kolia Kratsotkin, who was *Narodi Kommisariat Vnutrennikh Del,* an agent for the People's Commissariat for Internal Affairs, was of shorter stature, with a flat face and large, round cheeks, black, unruly hair, and eyes of a much lighter color than Strehlnikov's. He sat on the lower bunk on the left-hand side of the cabin and at the moment was cleaning and oiling a Mosin-Nagant bolt-action 1891/30g with a 3.5x PU sight mounted over the bolt mechanism that had been issued to him for this assignment.

"*Snayperskaya vintovka,*" Kratsotkin muttered to Strehlnikov.

"*Da,*" Lugu Strehlnikov answered indifferently in his hoarse, rasping voice.

The rifle was highly accurate, made to specifications for accuracy developed during the First Five Year Plan, and Kratsotkin had every right to be proud to have been issued it. The bolt handle turned downward to remain clear of the telescopic sight, and the side of the wooden stock was cut away for easy sighting.

Strehlnikov spoke and understood English, a necessity for his work in the merchant trade between the Soviet Republics and British and Indian commercial interests. It was in this capacity that he had made the acquaintance of Teh-Meh-Tayo, a man from the Far North beyond the North-West Territories of the Dominion of Canada. The small gold bars this man carried were convincing evidence that his distant and mysterious homeland did possess incredible gold resources as well as, Strehlnikov had been assured, petroleum deposits. Teh-Meh-Tayo, however, was a quiet and studious man who could pass hours reading in one or the other of the two thick books he carried. Both had texts in ancient Greek — one being Homer's ODYSSEY and the other an anthology of Greek fragments — and both had been printed in London. Teh-Meh-Tayo had come upon these books, he said, in Dehli. This Arctic islander was tall, almost as tall as Strehlnikov, with long, curly hair that was shot through with gray, classical features, quite handsome in his way. He claimed to be

9

— the *phylaxis* — for Nah-Loh-Tah, the woman with them. It meant, he said, guardian, but Nah-Loh-Tah referred to Teh-Meh-Tayo as merely her uncle.

Nah-Loh-Tah was unquestionably a woman of striking beauty, somewhere in her early thirties. In a way, although Lugu Strehlnikov knew very little of such things, she had the face he would have imagined as ideal for a medieval saint. Her forehead was very high with five horizontal wrinkles near the top if she would concentrate, and her very long hair seemed black but had a touch of gold in it when seen in the sunlight. Her eyes were neither blue nor brown, but a combination of the two with a light golden hue, surely the strangest eyes Strehlnikov could recall ever having seen. Her cheekbones were high but not pronounced, slanting downward to a graceful chin with only the slightest hint of a cleft. Her nose was narrow and straight, her upper lip somewhat thin but her bottom lip fuller. Had she worn lip rouge of some kind, which she did not, it might almost be called a sensuous mouth. There were two small parallel lines on either side of her mouth, which would appear when she smiled, but her expression was usually too demure and reserved to be called a smile. There was a wistfulness about Nah-Loh-Tah. Her figure was concealed by the heavy clothes she wore, but Strehlnikov imagined, based on what he had seen and what he could surmise, that she had very high and very small breasts and only slightly wide hips.

She was sitting on the top bunk on the right side of the room, and had been gently playing chords on her lyra, a guitar-like instrument. Nah-Loh-Tah composed songs that she sang in the purest, clearest of mezzo-soprano voices. Strehlnikov's greatest problem with this woman was that he detested music of all kinds, but especially songs. His dislike had only become increasingly exacerbated during the long journey he had already been on with Nah-Loh-Tah and her guardian, and it would certainly continue when they would be put ashore near Icy Cape in Alaska, perhaps two hundred miles from Point Barrow, and then head overland by dog sled. By the best calculations Strehlnikov could make, from that point they still would have over three thousand miles of the North American continent to cross before they reached the actual homeland of these people, an island in the Arctic Ocean that was claimed by no nation, but which would be accurately mapped and located by Strehlnikov and which, he had persuaded his superiors, could then be entered directly from the Arctic Ocean and all the gold seized and the petroleum pumped out and transported by tankers back to the Soviet Union. It would be an amazing achievement, once it happened, and it would be accomplished despite the American and Canadian presence in the North American Arctic.

It was all we had.
We were so in love.
But how much pain
can love sustain?

You would say
you were sorry,
if only I would not leave,
if only I would believe.

Until all hope was gone,
until we were both
so deep in debt.
Loving you, was this all I would ever
  get?

Now only the cold remains.
Memories of how I would forgive,
how you would forget.
Loving you, was this all I would ever
  get?

How much pain

can love sustain?
Only promises that would bring regret.
Loving you, this was all I would ever
    get.

Nah-Loh-Tah's voice with its haunting, dark tones and passion of expression, as she accompanied herself on the lyra, resonated in the cramped cabin that was very hot and stifling, although outside on the bridge the temperature was probably forty below zero. Strehlnikov had grown restless during this song — sung in English words he understood, but words he nevertheless detested as bourgeois sentimentality — while Kolia Kratsotkin, who knew virtually no English, seemed to enjoy its melodic timbre and rhythm. Strehlnikov gathered together the worn, smeared cards, put them in a stack, and, having extinguished his Russian cigarette in a tin ashtray, made his way alongside the narrow table, taking with him his parka from where he had thrown it atop the bunk above Kratsotkin. He put it on and then left the cabin.

It was the time of perpetual darkness now. When the sky was clear, it seemed a million stars could be seen in the heavens, and most clearly Ursa Minoris with Polaris at the tip of the tail, larger and brighter than all of the other stars in this constellation. To look into the heavens, of course, meant standing outside in the bitter cold at the guardrail, and tonight the wind was stronger than it had been during the day. Strehlnikov stood in his parka at the rail, gazing out over the vast expanse of ice and snow — a great expanse of ice, glittering dimly, with every now and then a giant ice ridge, sharp and jagged. The engines of the ice-breaker throbbed and strained in the darkness, and there was never silence on the *Sibiryakov*. Strehlnikov was coming to hate the throb of the engines as much as he did Nah-Loh-Tah's singing. Then he thought of how in 1930, by means of a Soviet ice-breaker under Comrade Ushakov's leadership, four government surveyors had headquartered on Bolshevik Island and, using dog sledges, had managed to map eighteen thousand square miles of formerly unknown land. The Northern Land, as it was called now, formerly Lenin Land, had been found to consist of four large islands within the Arctic Circle and had been newly named Young Communist Leaguer, Young Pioneer, October Revolution, and Bolshevik. In addition, many smaller islands had been discovered and mapped. More recently, since late 1933, the hut headquarters Comrade Ushakov had used was being utilized as a sub-station in conjunction with the Soviet contribution to the Second International Circumpolar Year. This work included continuous photographic registration of the electromagnetism of the Earth, study of the electrical currents flowing inside the Earth, measurement of atmospheric electrical pressure and conductivity, charting the height of the Kennelly-Heaviside layer (the so-called "radio roof" of the planet), the effect the Aurora Borealis had upon Arctic radio transmission, and tracking weather on an hourly basis. Surely, once Lugu Strehlnikov had attained his goal and led his nation to this obscure but incredibly rich Arctic island, he would be heralded as having made a contribution no less worthy of praise throughout the Soviet Union as the accomplishments in the past of Comrade Ushakov and Comrade Schmidt.

Chapter One

May 18, 1934

It was in the early afternoon of this sunny day that the former Marcelina O'Day — she now had been married to Christopher Fallon for eleven years — met the incoming train at the small, picturesque railroad station in San Fernando, California. Sir Wilbur Tennington smiled joyfully as he stepped down from a passenger car and embraced Marcelina who had been standing on the cement platform, waiting for him, and had rushed up to him. He had aged since the last time she had seen him, some eight years ago. His blond hair — what could be seen of it under the jaunty fedora with a snap brim that he wore — was shot through with grayish white, and he sported a mustache now of a somewhat sandy color. The lines in his face had deepened, especially the marks around the eyes from squinting, but his color was good, ruddy beneath the high-toned tan of his face and hands. He was wearing tweeds.

Marcelina, Sir Wilbur saw as he drew back

while still holding her hands, had also aged. They had first met in 1922 when she had accompanied him, Chris Fallon, and Luis Valera, a professor in archeology, in finding the lost city of Haucha, an ancient Incan stronghold long hidden in the upper Andes. She was dressed today in a bright plaid dress, a black sweater covering her hips, and a black belt over the sweater. She wore no hat. Her reddish-brown hair was parted on the right side and had been permed only along the bottom. Her face was more angular, less rounded, than Sir Wilbur remembered it. Her cheekbones were more pronounced, and there were three lines across the center of her very high forehead, but they could scarcely be seen except when she wrinkled her brow. Her teeth were perfect as she smiled — Sir Wilbur had always loved the way her smile lit up her whole face. What had once been a soft-toned delicacy of features, he decided, had become now more etched by character and, if anything, only enhanced her striking beauty. Marcelina's large blue-gray eyes glistened, drawing his attention, as they had viewers all over the world when a close-up of her in one of the films she had made was projected on the silver screen. Her eyes were not shielded by sunglasses when first Sir Wilbur saw her, but she carried a pair in her small handbag, and she put these on as she accompanied him to the baggage claim area inside the station's waiting room.

"You seem thinner, Marcelina," he said as they walked. "You haven't been ill, have you?"

"No," she laughed softly. "I'm just naturally thin . . . about a hundred pounds. I've probably gained a pound or two since you last saw me."

Sir Wilbur was certain she hadn't, but he said no more for now. He had two suitcases in baggage, and, as they were wheeled in from the train, the Englishman engaged a porter to carry them out to Marcelina's Packard V-12 LeBaron Speedster which was parked in a slot in the parking area adjacent to the station. Marcelina opened the trunk in the rear of the car, and the porter deposited the suitcases. With its elegant pontoon fenders, chromed windshield, radiator, headlamps, and bumpers, its wire wheels with white-walled tires, and single convertible seat, it was one of the most elegant automobiles Sir Wilbur had ever seen, although the red body paint was a trifle dusty from driving on dirt roads. The Englishman tipped the porter generously, who nodded at the gratuity and walked back toward the station.

"Don't worry, Sir Wilbur," Marcelina said,

smiling. "I shall drive very slowly, and you'll be quite safe."

The door handles were to the front of the doors, and Marcelina climbed in behind the wheel while Sir Wilbur climbed in on the passenger side.

Marcelina told him that Chris had been unable to meet the train because he had to go to an important business meeting at Paramount Pictures in Los Angeles. It was important because Chris's contract to produce documentary travelogues and travel stories for the Paramount News department was being extended, and there were certain contractual provisions he had insisted be included, the most salient of which was a three-month annual hiatus in each of the next two years that he could spend as he pleased.

"A lot has happened since we last saw you," Marcelina continued, as she pulled out into light traffic. "For one thing, I'm not acting in pictures any more."

"My word, why not?"

"Oh, it's a long story," she said as she braked the convertible for a stop at an intersection and then downshifted.

"Well, my dear, as you know, I've been mostly in India for the last four years where there wasn't much opportunity for me to go to the cinema. But I did see you years ago in

19

that film you made with John Barrymore as François Villon. Indeed, I once saw Barrymore in New York when he played in *Hamlet*. An excellent actor . . . and that's a lot for an Englishman to say about an American in a Shakespearean rôle."

Marcelina laughed gaily as she pulled ahead. "Well, I found him to be a terrible roué. He was constantly trying to kiss me when it wasn't called for in the script. My part was Charlotte de Vauxcelles, the ward of King Louis the Eleventh, and wardrobe insisted for my last scene in the picture that I be dressed in tights as a court page. I protested that a French noblewoman would never dress like that, but our director, Bill Menzies, said I must, since I was to marry a commoner and was surrendering my duchy to the king of France. I had to agree, but wearing those tights made Jack Barrymore all the more incorrigible. In the last scene of the film, we were supposed to walk away from my guardian, the king, stop at the great door, and then turn toward each other. Six times I made that walk with Jack, and six times the director had to call . . . 'Cut!' . . . because Jack would put his hand on my bottom and squeeze me. I wanted to slap him, I was so mad, but I couldn't because in the scene I was supposed to be starry-eyed and in love with him."

Sir Wilbur was laughing. "You know, I remember that scene. Of course, I don't remember Mister Barrymore's squeezing your behind, but I did think . . . if you'll pardon me? . . . that your backside had not looked quite so enticing when you were wearing those soiled white jodhpurs in the Peruvian jungle."

"There was almost nothing enticing about the way I looked on that trip . . . ever," Marcelina agreed, smiling, steering the convertible expertly on their way out of the small town toward the country road that would take them to the *Hacienda* de Ferrar.

"There, young lady, I beg to differ with you." Sir Wilbur was also smiling now. "Chris fell hopelessly in love with you . . . as we all did."

"You've seen the documentary Chris made about Haucha?" Marcelina asked, knowing he had.

"All right," the Englishman chuckled. "I shall grant . . . you looked a great deal better in that film."

"Not so muddy, anyway." Marcelina laughed. "And you know that travelogue was used as a screen test for me at Universal which is how I was offered the part of the heroine in a Hoot Gibson Western?"

"Yes, now that you mention it, I do believe

you once told me that. But you've quit? Why, may I ask?"

"Oh, it was kind of mutual," Marcelina said, her tone perhaps a trifle reserved. "It was great fun for the most part. I enjoyed working on a lot of the pictures I was in. I think my favorite still is the one I made with Buster Keaton during the three years I was under contract at M-G-M. I have the pressbook from it, and I still look at it once in a while."

"And with all that going for you . . . you just quit?" Sir Wilbur asked in a puzzled tone.

"Oh, believe me, Sir Wilbur, it wasn't caprice. I never studied to be a stage actress, you know, and I had no previous experience. It was just something that happened to me. I made that Western, and other rôles just came along. When talking pictures came in, I didn't know if I could make the transition. It was then that I did take some dramatic training, but the microphones made me seem awkward and nervous. In silent films, you know, it was very much your facial expression, your eyes, and your hands."

Sir Wilbur looked across at Marcelina's long, tapered fingers in gloves of thin brown leather wrapped around the steering wheel.

"Several directors told me that I had some of the most expressive eyes they had ever seen. But in a talking picture, and especially in the kind of low-budget pictures . . . small pictures . . . I found myself appearing in, there were very few close-ups. It is all in what you say, and what is said to you." Marcelina laughed suddenly. "In one of my last talking pictures . . . I even had a *nude* bathing scene."

"What film was that?"

"It was a low-budget South Seas story, which means the exteriors were shot in Santa Monica. I was billed third. Flash . . . a German shepherd . . . got top billing."

"Oh, no!"

"Oh, *yes!* I was playing the daughter of an island missionary, and there was a scene in which I was supposed to be swimming in a tropical pool when Flash comes to the edge of the water and starts barking at me."

"And you were actually naked in front of the camera?" Sir Wilbur seemed mildly shocked.

"Not completely," Marcelina assured him. "Oh, I would have been willing to do it, I guess, but it wasn't necessary. The scene was filmed in shadow. I wore nothing on top." She laughed again. "I'm so flat-chested, from that angle I look almost like a boy, anyway . . . but the camera never showed anything . . . except when I was coming out of the water. I had silk shorts on that fit as tightly as a body suit . . . and my hair was dyed blonde. The

23

scene was so filled with shadows, though, it did appear that I had nothing on at all. The magic of movies . . . !"

They were outside of San Fernando now, and on either side of the road there were pastures, a dull green in the brilliant sunlight, and occasionally orchards.

"I don't suppose there is anything inherently wrong with a scene like that," Sir Wilbur observed now in amusement, "provided only the dog really saw you."

"Oh, there were about a dozen people on the set when it was filmed," Marcelina said, smiling as she remembered. "I was game, as they say. I'd do what a rôle called for . . . but that picture was so bad. In fact, it was very, very bad."

"Not from anything you've told me," Sir Wilbur said supportively.

"That's because I haven't told you what happened at the sneak preview in Pasadena. There was so much laughing at the wrong times, and the audience was making so much fun of the lines we had to say in that picture, that the manager of the theater actually flashed a slide on the screen after the third reel begging the audience to be more considerate."

"I must confess, Marcelina, I've not seen any of your talking pictures, but I presume they weren't all that bad."

"Enough of them were that I didn't want to be in pictures at all any more. It wasn't just for the money, you know . . . I did enjoy working in some of them. The last Western I made was again with Hoot Gibson. My first picture had been with him, and . . . in those nine years . . . he had been married twice and divorced twice, I think . . . and I had a reputation on the set for being *very* married."

"It's the truth . . . isn't it?"

"Well, yes, but that's not quite what I mean . . . it was that I didn't fool around . . . didn't go to bed with my leading men, or the director, or some producer. In a Western that was so dreadfully awful I was on the verge of tears almost all the time . . . it starred another movie cowboy . . . Ken Maynard . . . I was supposed to enjoy kissing him . . . I had to kiss him four times in that one film. He would curse and beat his horse, and he would pester me . . . so, finally, I had to insist that he treat me like a professional and curb his ways, or I'd quit the picture altogether. The only good memory I have of that film is that I had a close-up. I remember it so clearly because a close-up of any kind not of the hero is so unusual in that kind of low-budget film."

"You say this Maynard person is a *movie* cowboy?"

Marcelina smiled merrily. "Movie cowboys make Westerns . . . and Ken Maynard is a movie cowboy."

"Like Hoot Gibson?"

"Yes."

"I've seen Hoot Gibson . . . I even think it was the picture you were in . . . the first one."

"And I had a lot of fun with him on our last picture together. At the fade, instead of kissing or hugging, which is what usually happens between the movie cowboy and the girl, I had the idea that we should look back over our shoulders at the camera . . . we were in a kind of church . . . in the congregation . . . and it was my idea that we should smile as if we were embarrassed, and then I took his hand as we smiled and looked again toward the front. It was a nice scene."

"What does Chris say about your quitting the movies?" Sir Wilbur asked, reaching into a pocket of his tweed jacket and bringing out a bulldog pipe. There was no tobacco in the bowl, but he clamped it between his teeth anyway.

"Chris said whatever I want to do . . . he's for it. He knows that it was all a lark . . . an accident, really. Back in Nineteen Twenty-Five we also needed the money. Chris and I didn't want to be separated, as we would have been had he continued his work as a field guide. I

26

was willing for him to continue, but he felt he had lost the hankering for that kind of life. But working on travel documentaries and writing articles about travel . . . many of them for magazines like *International Cosmopolitan* and *The Saturday Evening Post* . . . meant a different kind of travel, and I could go along, if I didn't have to work in a picture. It was always great fun when I did go. When we first met, you know, I was studying archeology."

"And you want to go back to it?"

"I *have* gone back to it. I started taking courses in anthropology, native American cultures and history, beginning the fall semester last year at the University of California, and in another month or so I shall be graduated with honors, finally earning a bachelor of science degree. A little late, maybe. I was thirty-three last month. But if you believe the studio biographies about me, I'm younger than that. Universal said I was born in Nineteen Oh Seven. Metro made me a little younger yet, claiming I was born in Nineteen Oh Eight, and my birth place was some place in Colorado, rather than in Lima."

"Good heavens, Marcelina, why would they lie about something like that?" Sir Wilbur asked, taking his pipe from his mouth.

"Ingénues . . . so they say . . . go over best with the public if they are barely out of their teens. As for being born in Peru! . . . well, they couldn't say that, or I would have been confined to rôles playing *señoritas* from below the border . . . which I actually did once, anyway, for a small, independent company, but I explained my blonde hair in that film and my light-colored eyes by saying that my mother was Irish."

"My goodness . . . Irish . . . your mother? Well, whatever your real age, my dear, you're still very, very young compared to an old duffer like me."

"You're not *that* old, Sir Wilbur."

"I was fifty on my last birthday."

"And Chris is forty-three." She smiled again and lowered her voice almost an octave. "OK . . . I guess we're all just . . . a lot older."

"You know," said Sir Wilbur by way of changing the subject, "before docking in San Diego, I had sailed from Calcutta to Sydney and from thence to Lima, and then I came up here."

"I know you've been to Lima," Marcelina affirmed. "Mama wrote that you had been to visit her and Papa. I suppose they told you how their only daughter continues to be just too busy to interrupt her career long enough to have children."

"As a matter of fact," Sir Wilbur chuckled, "your father did make such a remark to me."

He had meant the comment in a light-hearted way, but, now having uttered it, he became fearful Marcelina might misinterpret his meaning.

"It's not from want of trying, Sir Wilbur," she said earnestly. "Papa and Mama are wrong about that. I told them both that last summer when they came up for a visit . . . and, when I said I was finished with pictures and planned to return to complete my degree . . . well, they both seemed to make such big, sad sighs about it. The truth is Chris and I have tried and tried, and nothing has happened. Just about the last film I was in . . . the last one to be released, anyway . . . was financed by the Canadian Health Council . . . about the dangers of venereal disease."

"Marcelina . . . you don't mean?"

She had to laugh, seeing how dismayed he seemed. "No . . . I played a doctor's wife in that film . . . he slapped my fingers in one scene, when I was supposed to reach for a cigarette. You know, only *bad* girls smoke . . . in the movies, at least! But I wouldn't change anything about my life. I'm happy with all the choices I've made. Even quitting pictures. In a way, it was inevitable. Talking pictures just weren't right for me. The reality is that as a little girl in school in Lima the nuns made me feel humiliated whenever I would be asked to speak before the class. I was naturally shy then, and I had no confidence in myself. They tried to shame me out of my shyness. They thought I was being difficult. I wasn't. But the fear became so bad that I have never been able to feel comfortable in front of any group of people. All those faces looking at me . . . they make me self-conscious . . . unsure . . . so I only want to flee. When I was a school girl, that is exactly what I wanted to do. Then, when I was given a screen test for talking films at Metro, the same thing happened to me again. The microphones were turned on, and the sound technicians were there, and the director, and other people on the set, and the other actors . . . it was the same thing all over again. I was afraid. I would knot up inside and tremble. My hands would tremble, and so I tried holding them this way or that, or gesturing with them, or holding them clenched, or keeping them behind me, or in front of me . . . but I was so scared. There was simply nothing I could do to stop the fear. M-G-M dropped me. They said I couldn't make the transition from silent films to talkies. At first, I refused to accept that, but in the end they were right. It's not my medium. And don't think it's all that much easier for me in my college courses, although everyone has been very helpful and sympathetic."

"Marcelina, this is something about you I never knew. Granted, you were in some ways a shy girl when we were on our way to Haucha, but you proved a fine *compadre* in the field, and you saved young Ramón's life."

"Perhaps," she conceded, "but I didn't have any sound technicians there, trying to record me speaking my lines." She smiled, looking across at him. "Papa even says I've become too outspoken . . . living in this country." She looked back at the road ahead. "Maybe that was another difficulty I had in my movie rôles. I was always supposed to be the passive one, waiting for the hero to rescue me . . . the girl is always the reward the hero gets at the end."

Sir Wilbur chuckled. "Well, there's one person for whom you will always be a heroine . . . and not a cinema heroine."

"Ramón?"

"Yes. When I went back to Peru, I also went on to Tacho Alto."

"You did?" Marcelina's voice was excited now as she remembered. "I'm such an irresponsible person. It's like being in a movie. You get to be such good friends with everyone in the cast, and you promise each other you will stay in touch, and then you don't . . . because you've moved on to the next picture . . . and so have they."

"I don't want to embarrass you, Marcelina," Sir Wilbur said very diplomatically, "but Ramón remembers vividly the beautiful *señorita* whose life he feels *he* once saved. He has not married yet, don't you know, but he told me he has many girl friends."

"Did you also see Quinto? It's really terrible to admit it, but Chris and I haven't been back to Tacho Alto since Chris was producing that documentary about the journey to Haucha."

"Well, you wouldn't recognize those places . . . they've grown so . . . from tourism mostly. Ever since the Quivaris were pacified, they have been in the curio business, selling *genuine* Incan trinkets to visitors that come to Haucha from all over the world."

"No!" Marcelina said, somewhat in consternation, although the image brought a smile to her lips.

"But Quinto, I'm sorry to say, died last year."

"He wasn't that old," Marcelina protested, as a pang of guilt clutched at her because she had not known.

"Heart trouble, as I understand it," Sir Wilbur responded. "But Ramón runs the hostel now . . . and it has been very much expanded to accommodate all the people who stop at Tacho Alto . . . on the way to Haucha." He paused for a moment before continuing. "I said nothing the last time I saw you, but there has been something preying on my mind all these years."

"Something about Ramón?"

"No. It's something I did back in those days, and which I have since regretted often. I know I've already told you about your uncle and Abdullah Simbel taking Quinto and me with them into that cleft to the top of the plateau." Sir Wilbur's eyes searched Marcelina's face in profile.

Her brow was lined in perplexity now. "Yes," she said, very quietly.

"And you know that we had to cross quicksand. Thanks to Abdullah's felling a dead tree across that chasm, we had a bridge of sorts . . . and your uncle, Marcelina, you know he fell into the quicksand. He was the last one to go across. The tree trunk slipped a notch, and Don Esteban became rattled. He tried to jump to our side, but he didn't make it, and fell into the quicksand."

"Abdullah Simbel got him out all right," Marcelina interjected. "I saw *Tío* Don Esteban after that . . . and he was covered with mud, from head to toe, actually . . . but he was alive."

"I'm not quite sure how Abdullah managed it," Sir Wilbur responded, "but, somehow, he must have done it. At any rate, before that we were under attack by the Quivaris. Your uncle, Marcelina, was in the quicksand. Only Abdullah was armed at that point. It was then, while Abdullah was intent on driving back the Quivaris, that I did a most cowardly thing." Sir Wilbur's usually modulated voice fluttered. "I prodded Quinto to flee. He went willingly enough, and . . . so did I."

"But what you did wasn't the cause of my uncle's death," Marcelina argued. "And I did the same thing myself . . . when I fled . . . leaving him and Abdullah at the maw of that cleft to fight the Quivaris again . . . once the Quivaris had crossed over by that same dead tree and taken up the pursuit."

"You were a young woman, Marcelina, just a girl," Sir Wilbur insisted. "You couldn't be expected to stand your ground and fight."

"Possibly not," she replied. Her tone was suddenly stern. "But I feared at the time I might never see *Tío* Don Esteban again . . . that, in telling me and Ramón and *Tío* Luis to make a run for it, he was really saving my life and theirs. Having been a girl at the time doesn't excuse me, either, Sir Wilbur. If you feel you are guilty of cowardice, then so was I. Both of us did what we thought we had to do."

She used her right hand to go into her handbag on her lap and brought out a cigarette.

"Would you be so kind?" she asked.

Sir Wilbur drew out his pipe lighter and reached across with it, shielding the flame by cupping his hand, placing the flame at the tip of the cigarette.

"Thank you," Marcelina said, inhaling and then removing the cigarette with her right hand before returning the hand to the steering wheel. "You know that my uncle's body was retrieved from the Quivaris, but not Abdullah's. Apparently his was lost in the quicksand. *Tio* Don Esteban is now buried near Grandpapa and Grandmama on the de Ferrar family lands. My uncle's estate was finally settled in late Nineteen Twenty-Nine, about the same time M-G-M decided not to renew my contract."

"I suppose Chris told you something about the journey I have in mind?" the Englishman said, again changing the subject as he fetched his pipe pouch from his pocket. He was filling the bulldog pipe as he spoke.

"We're both excited about it," Marcelina said, her tone coloring the timbre of the words. "Chris has been to the Klondike before, the Barren Lands, and to parts of Alaska, but he's never been as far into the Arctic as this will likely be . . . and you surely know that I haven't."

"I was very much hoping you'd feel that

way," Sir Wilbur assured her, bending forward now to light his pipe. It was a strong flame, but, as he had done with Marcelina, he had to shield it with one hand as he puffed vigorously to get the top layer of tobacco lit. He smoked a black cavendish that had about it the suggestion of vanilla and gave off an aroma most people commented on favorably. "In many ways," he resumed, puffing on his pipe and returning the lighter to a coat pocket, "this will certainly be my last great quest . . . and probably the most important one I have ever undertaken."

"Chris said you really don't have a map this time," Marcelina said, drawing on her cigarette and then extinguishing it in the car ashtray, keeping her eyes on the road.

Sir Wilbur frowned. "Not any kind of parchment map, anyway," he replied. "Actually, Luis has been in touch with the Royal Astronomical Society, and he should have already the charts of the stars and constellations visible only from the Arctic Circle ordered according to the months of the year. Of course, I would rather expect that the relative positions of those stars and constellations have changed to some degree over the last three thousand years, but Shivapuri Baba assures me they are still within the northern latitudes and remain visible to the naked eye from only that perspective."

"Shivapuri Baba?" Marcelina asked, repeating the syllables of the name very precisely, as was her way.

"You would have to say he's a holy man. He now lives outside Darjeeling in Nepal, a part of the Indian Empire high in the Himalayan Mountains. He was born at the same time as his twin sister in Eighteen Twenty-Six in Kerala, India . . . that's down at the tip of the subcontinent, part of the state of Travencore-Cochin. Even though they lived that far southwest, his family is of Brahmin lineage. His grandfather, when he saw the twins, declared that the destiny of the family had been fulfilled and was, therefore, at an end. From infancy the twins were to forswear the world, taking a vow of poverty, and to live lives of seclusion as *sannyasins*. At the age of five, the boy who would become Shivapuri Baba began his formal training, learning Sanskrit, and by twelve he was able to recite the Vedas from memory, beginning to end. At eighteen he retired from all society and, upon the death of his grandfather, disappeared into the depths of the Narbada forest."

"Many native American Indian peoples have a similar practice," Marcelina interjected. "It is part of the male initiation ceremony during which they retreat into the wilderness and fast and pray . . . perhaps for several days . . . seeking a spirit vision. It is only after they have had a spirit vision that they can be named truly in the tribe."

"Well, in Shivapuri Baba's case it was more than a matter of days. His retreat lasted twenty-five years, during which time he did not see another human being . . . although his mission may have been similar . . . he was to follow the path of . . . to express it in English . . . the Absolute Realization of God Beyond All Forms and Images."

"The soul of God?" Marcelina asked.

"Yes . . . that is a very good way to say it. Once Shivapuri Baba had completed this spiritual exercise, he emerged from the Narbada forest. That was in Eighteen Seventy-Five."

"That would have made him nearly fifty then," Marcelina said, somewhat in astonishment.

"Yes," Sir Wilbur responded with a smile, and let his pipe go out. "It occurred to me recently . . . as I was making my way across Afghanistan by camel caravan . . . that we human beings tend to limit ourselves as we grow older. When we are young, we spend hours in happy speculation of what we will be when we grow up, of what we will do, and where we will travel . . . but, as we age, we tend to put such speculations away as merely childish things. But they're really not childish, Marcelina. Only death or incapacitating illness can ever truly prevent us, at any age, from venturing on a new road.

"At any rate, Shivapuri Baba had reached that age and that state of spiritual being where he was ready to begin his pilgrimage. Following the instructions of his grandfather, he dug up the treasure of diamonds that had been set aside for generations for precisely this purpose . . . to finance him on his pilgrimage. Usually such a pilgrimage is a journey to the holy places in India, but in this case it had been made clear to Shivapuri Baba by his grandfather that his pilgrimage would require him to travel on foot and, where that was impossible, by boat . . . all around the world."

"That must have taken a very long time," Marcelina commented, so interested that she had diminished the speed of the car.

"It did. He traveled from Eighteen Seventy-Five until he finally completed the journey in Nineteen Fifteen. He began by walking west through Persia, where he was admitted to Mecca. He passed through Jerusalem and through Constantinople, and Rome where he visited the Vatican. When Shivapuri Baba reached England, his fame had preceded him, and Queen Victoria summoned him to Buckingham Palace for a personal meeting. Although I have it on the best authority that Princess Beatrice later excised the dates from Queen Victoria's personal diaries, she met with him no less than eighteen times. Indeed, she requested . . . *requested*, Marcelina, she did not command . . . that he remain in England until after her death . . . and it was for this reason that he did not continue his passage around the world until Nineteen Oh One. He walked the entire continents of North and South America, from Ellesmere Island in the Far North all the way south to Tierra del Fuego, and went even as far as Mount Erebus in Antarctica. He saw the incredible Dry Valleys in Antarctica . . . which are deserts covered with sand looking just like the Sahara except that they are extremely cold . . . and he found a desert of sand as well in the Arctic . . . which is where I intend to go. Many are the times I have heard him tell of one or another of the wonders that he saw on this great journey, only to conclude how wondrous and great beyond all human understanding is the imagination of God."

"And Shivapuri Baba is still alive?" Marcelina asked, her tone reflecting the excitement this narrative had stirred in her.

"Very much so," Sir Wilbur replied. "In all,

his pilgrimage took him forty years, after which he retired to the Himalayas to live out his days in a bamboo hut on a small reserve provided for him by His Majesty's government in Nepal.

"I spent the better part of two years living in his vicinity in Nepal, continuing my study of Sanskrit, so I, too, could read the Vedas in the language in which they were recorded . . . rather like Chris who learned Greek so he could read the Homeric sagas . . . and it was during this time that Shivapuri Baba loaned me a very rare book from his library. It was written by a man named B. G. Tilak and titled THE ARCTIC HOMELAND IN THE VEDAS. Tilak had been imprisoned by the British Raj around the turn of the century, and he wrote this book while in his prison cell. It was published in Nineteen Oh Three. Oh, I took the most elaborate notes on it, but, you know, Marcelina, having searched and searched on several continents, I have never been able to find another copy of it outside the British Library."

"Did Shivapuri Baba ever meet B. G. Tilak?"

"As a matter of fact," Sir Wilbur replied, chuckling, "Shivapuri Baba told me that not only did he know B. G. Tilak, but that at one time B. G. Tilak after his release from prison

. . . he was convicted of political agitation against the British presence in India . . . had even taught him some astronomy."

"We're home, Sir Wilbur," Marcelina announced, turning the car from the road onto the long driveway of stamped red top that circled in front of the Andalusian architecture of the *Hacienda* de Ferrar, its red-tile roofs sparkling in the sunlight, the front lawn and elm trees very green, and with adobe outbuildings painted the same color of off-white as the main house. Sir Wilbur was struck at once by the tranquil beauty of it all.

Chapter Two

Rosa Caldero was the housekeeper at the *Hacienda* de Ferrar. She was descended from a Mexican family that traced its lineage back to the time when California was still a province of Mexico. Although Marcelina loved cooking and even regarded herself as something of a *cuisinière,* when her movie schedules or social activities — or now being a full-time university student — did not permit it, Rosa prepared the meals by herself. She also oversaw the daytime maid, Linda Ruiz, who cleaned the house and attended to the laundry. Santiago Cruz was a native Peruvian who had once worked for Don Esteban de Ferrar on the de Ferrar family estate in Peru. He had come to the United States at Marcelina's and Chris's suggestion, once Marcelina had inherited her uncle's property. They regarded him more as a close personal friend than as *amansador,* or overseer, of the livestock and the harvesting of the produce from the orchards, which constituted his main responsibilities at the ranch. Frequently, when there was no company for dinner, Santiago, who was not married, joined the Fallons.

Marcelina was comfortable being surrounded by people who spoke her native language, and Chris, over the years with her, had mastered conversational Spanish, but it was also true that English was the language he and Marcelina had spoken with each other from the beginning. Although in one of her talking pictures, as she had told Sir Wilbur, Marcelina had actually been cast in the rôle of a *señorita* in Spanish California, her dialogue had been in English which she spoke with such an unaccented precision that, however much she might "look" the part in such a rôle, she seemed to be more Anglo-Saxon than Peruvian. Her stage name of Marceline Day only furthered this impression, as did the carefully falsified studio biographies concerning her early life and background before she entered motion pictures. Thomas and Isabella O'Day had objected to these fabrications and could not understand why their daughter was not justifiably proud of her Peruvian ancestry. It was during the visit by her parents to the *Hacienda* de Ferrar in the summer of 1933 that Marcelina had finally succeeded in explaining to them — even though she was finished by then with motion pictures and it no longer mattered — that had it been known generally that she was Peruvian, and not Irish-American, she might have found no work at all in films except as an ethnic type. One of the benefits of her retirement, she had stressed to her parents, was putting an end forever to this biographical charade.

Upon the arrival of Marcelina and Sir Wilbur at the *Hacienda* de Ferrar, Santiago Cruz carried the Englishman's luggage to the guest room on the second floor that he would be occupying for the weeks of his planned stay. Then Marcelina and Santiago showed Sir Wilbur around the ranch compound, especially the fine Thoroughbred horses used exclusively for horseback riding. Day laborers were employed during the harvest time; otherwise, Santiago was able to see to the maintenance of the livestock, the outbuildings including the small, red-tiled adobe cabin where he lived, and the orchards. By the time they returned to the main house, having left Santiago at the great white barn that served as a stable, Chris Fallon had returned. He embraced Marcelina, leaning down to kiss her, and then cordially welcomed Sir Wilbur.

Chris was pleased with how things had gone in his negotiations and explained the details of his new agreement to Sir Wilbur while the three of them sat at a round table beneath a canvas awning on the back verandah. The new Paramount contract would allow Fallon to take off three months of each year, with the idea of scouting interesting places and locations for travel documentaries to be released as short subjects or integrated as features into the Paramount newsreels distributed to theaters by the Paramount film exchanges. W. S. Van Dyke's ESKIMO, called in the trades a "docu-drama," meaning it was partly fiction and partly fact, had been released with great success by M-G-M in January of 1934. A good part of it had been filmed in the Arctic with principally a native cast of Eskimos — and the fact that, following Marcelina's graduation in June, Chris would be going to the Arctic excited the Paramount executives who perhaps felt there might be the possibility of producing a straight documentary on this mysterious region that would garner as much interest with the movie-going public as ESKIMO had. At any rate, there would be no problem in his taking three months off to explore the possibilities, and Fallon said he hoped to take some photographs on this journey.

"Van Dyke had to use superscript titles much of the time," Chris explained, "so viewers would understand what the Eskimo characters were saying in American English.

It is sort of like a silent picture, except you can hear what they're saying, even if you have to read the superscript to understand it."

"The sound recording, though, was done in the Arctic?" Sir Wilbur asked.

"Some of it," Chris said, "but, for me, too much was done in the studio after they got back to Culver City. The whole company was in the Arctic for a year, and some of the footage they brought back of the thundering caribou herds, a whale hunt in the Arctic Ocean, and a walrus hunt was pretty terrific."

"Why did they have to come back to record conversations?" Sir Wilbur wondered.

"Because sound recording on location is often fraught with difficulties," Chris explained.

"A sound film is not like a silent film, Sir Wilbur," Marcelina put in, "such as when Jack Barrymore was squeezing my bottom, I could tell him . . . 'Keep your hand off my butt, you lecher!' . . . and the title card would say . . . 'I will love you forever.' Unless you could read my lips, you would never know *what* I was really telling him. If there had been a microphone turned on, recording what I was saying, the scene would have had to be cut. Beyond that, when you're outdoors, there's the wind, and other kinds of interference, that the microphones pick up, and so often you have to record the voices in a scene separately from the picture."

"Really, Marcelina, I've heard so much about that Barrymore film today," Sir Wilbur replied, rising, "I really feel I must see it again."

"But this is not the court of Louis the Eleventh, and I am no noblewoman for whom you must rise and bow," Marcelina assured him.

There was humor in her tone, and Sir Wilbur found himself grinning. "Believe me, my dear, I was not about to bow . . . although, perhaps, I really should . . . you have such natural grace . . . but I sha'n't say more for fear I would embarrass you."

Fallon instinctively got up, also.

"Please, Chris . . . ," Sir Wilbur said with a placating gesture, "I only rose because I have brought gifts for both of you and wished to go to my room to fetch them down."

"Gifts?" Marcelina asked, rising herself. "We have single malt Scotch. Wouldn't you like to have a drink."

"A spot of grog might go well," the Englishman conceded, "but I shall be back in a snap."

Chris and Marcelina had small goblets of chilled white California wine when Sir Wilbur returned, and there was an inch of Scotch whiskey in a glass on the table before the place where the Englishman had been sitting. Marcelina knew him well enough not to dilute fine whiskey with anything as barbaric as ice, although it probably would have seemed appropriate, in view of where they were going.

Sir Wilbur's gift to Chris Fallon was a specially bound two-volume edition in the original Greek of the collected plays and fragments of plays by Euripides, an author that, oddly perhaps, Chris had avoided. His gift to Marcelina was an ivory comb carved with the image of a human face, an early piece of Dorset art that, the Englishman stressed, while it had originated in the Arctic, he had come across in Nepal — somehow it had come that great distance in times past, and, of course, had made an even greater journey with him from Darjeeling to San Fernando.

Before her on the table Marcelina had a leather-bound eight-by-ten photograph of herself in a striped bathing suit with a beach jacket draped across her shoulders, standing on a riser in a swimming pool with the water about her ankles. She had inscribed it:

To Sir Wilbur
With Love,
Marcelina

The real surprise came when he removed

the photograph, marked in white ink on the lower right-hand side: MGMP - 4370 ★, from the leather case, for on the back there was a caption.

When it comes to decorating a coastline, Marceline Day, the winsome Metro-Goldwyn-Mayer star, could make an Arctic shore look genuinely inviting.

Sir Wilbur chuckled.

"I hope you won't think I'm just being vain," Marcelina said softly.

"Not at all," the Englishman replied, with a small smile, then he studied her bare thighs and calves in the photograph. "The only photograph I have of you is from your wedding. When was this taken?"

"Nineteen Twenty-Seven. That was the swimming pool where part of THE CAMERAMAN was filmed . . . the Buster Keaton film I was in. I really chose it for you because of the caption." Then, having noticed how he had studied her svelte form, she said: "I assure you, beginning today I shall surely start putting on the pounds."

"It is likely to be an arduous journey, Marcelina," the Englishman counseled, "and, no matter how fit any of us may be, there is going to be weight loss and privation."

"That's only the smallest part of the hard-ships, Tenny," Chris said. "I don't think you've ever been to the Arctic before."

"No, that's right, Chris, but I know you have, and that's one of the reasons it is so important that you be along on what surely will be the most important . . . and probably the last . . . quest of my lifetime. Later, I'll give you more precise details on the proposed route, but it will be above the eightieth parallel, although, certainly, not all the way to the North Pole."

"Well," returned Chris, "what's really amusing about that photograph is . . . were Marcie to be dressed like that on the shore of the Arctic Ocean . . . her death from exposure would be only a matter of a few minutes. The water, even in the summer, is seldom above zero, even if it is not frozen solid. There is usually some kind of wind, the way there is, say, in the State of Wyoming in this country, and that is another reason Van Dyke ran into sound recording problems. Out in that wind, no matter how warmly you're dressed, your eyes will water and your nose will run. You must always wear snow glasses, because otherwise the light of the Sun, reflected from the snow and the ice, will burn your retinas, and you might lose your eyesight altogether. The Arctic is not the coldest place in the world . . .

colder temperatures have been recorded in Siberia . . . but it is not uncommon for the temperature to drop to between thirty and forty below zero at night. We'll be there during the Arctic summer, so there will always be sunlight, although often you will see it as what filmmakers call back-lighting, since clouds will cover the sky, and the light will be behind them in a sort of diffused glow.

"Enough men have gone to the Arctic that, thank God, we have learned a good deal about surviving there. Snow houses, which are used by the Eskimos, are best when you are traveling across the barren snow regions and across glaciers and ice flows. Canvas tents, for example, can double in weight in a single night just from the condensation from breathing inside of them. If you bleed openly, your blood will freeze. What food you need must be packed with you. It is foolish to depend on game, because there may be none. A lot of nonsense has been written about wolves and wolf packs, beginning with Jack London, but the polar bear is truly catholic in his tastes and will eat *anything*. However, venturesome parties have tried it the other way around . . . tried supplementing their diet with polar bear meat . . . but, not having the proper scientific equipment, those who were unlucky and did not test the meat beforehand died from trichinosis. If a polar bear is in the vicinity, it must be shot, but the animal's flesh should be avoided, if at all possible, and, if cooked, it must be charred to the point where any young trichinæ eggs have been destroyed.

"Trichinosis is an insidious disease, because the cycle of gestation in a human intestinal canal can take three to six months, with early symptoms like nausea, loss of appetite, diarrhea, and fever giving way to muscular pain, swelling in the limbs, swelling of the eyelids, and finally delirium and death."

"You *know*, Chris," Sir Wilbur said. "That is the basic reason I would never even contemplate such a perilous journey alone." But he looked seriously at Marcelina with a dubious expression.

"*Déjà vu*," she said very quietly.

"Marcie gets no arguments from me this time," Chris put in. "I've told her all this, and more, because anyone heading to the Far North has to know these things."

"I hope we can fly very close to our ultimate destination," the Englishman said somewhat reassuringly, "using some kind of amphibian airplane."

"But part of the journey will most certainly be on the ground," Chris responded, "or, at least, on the ice . . . ?"

"Perhaps also by water," Sir Wilbur conceded. "Luis Valera and I will have the route charted as closely we can . . . but, as I was telling Marcelina, our map will not be topographical in the traditional sense, since our guideposts will be according to constellations visible primarily in the northern sky of the Arctic Circle."

"That's just as well . . . in view of the terrain," Chris said. "For the most part little is totally stationary in the Arctic, and much is illusory."

Marcelina lit a cigarette. "I was in a picture called ROOKIES in which some of my scenes were in a hot-air balloon. It was the strangest thing, Sir Wilbur, but, when you are moving with the wind, you seem not to be moving at all. There is no breeze in your face, no sound of air rushing past. It seems like you're just floating in a void."

"And that's the way the landscape is, Tenny," said Chris. "Much of the time it'll seem like you are in an endless expanse . . . a void . . . with nothing to distinguish the prospect before you from what is all around you." He paused to smile. "Marcie almost got to the North Pole once . . . when she appeared in THE BARRIER . . . it was based on Rex Beach's Alaskan novel."

"Oh, Chris . . . don't tease."

"Well, it *was* set in Alaska, and there were ice flows."

Marcelina looked imploringly at the Englishman. "You can perform wonders, Sir Wilbur, with modern methods of refrigeration."

"OK," Chris admitted. "It was just a movie."

"Science," said Sir Wilbur, "I imagine, is sometimes a more reliable guide to us than ever religion was."

"But not always," Marcelina interjected, "and certainly not in what counts most in life."

"Occasionally," Chris put in, "even bad religion has helped mankind take a step forward. When Columbus was intent on sailing west in the hope of eventually coming to the shore of Cathay or India, he consulted the Cardinal Pierre d'Ailly, chancellor of the University of Paris and regarded as the wisest man in the world. Columbus asked the cardinal how great was the distance, when sailing west, between Europe and Cathay. Now, two thousand years earlier Eratosthenes of Alexandria had devised a formula by which he thought the circumference of the Earth could be measured by using three hundred and sixty divided by seven multiplied by four hundred and eighty. He measured the distance in *sta-*

dia, not miles, but, if you substitute miles in this equation, you arrive at twenty-four thousand miles . . . very close to the actual circumference of twenty-four thousand, nine hundred, and eighty-nine miles. The cardinal, although he, also, believed the world to be round, did not consult mathematics, but scripture, and found in the Apocrypha that one-seventh of the Earth's surface is supposed to be covered by water. Therefore, extrapolating the known size of the Mediterranean, he computed the distance between Europe and Cathay at four thousand miles. Had Columbus known the truth . . . that the actual distance is closer to fifteen thousand miles . . . he would never have undertaken the voyage, since, had he not stumbled into the New World when he did, he and all his crew would have been dead of scurvy."

Sir Wilbur chuckled and looked significantly at Marcelina.

"It has never been . . . or never should have been the purpose of religion to ask or answer questions like that," she said quietly.

"My dear Marcelina," said the Englishman, "if religion cannot serve any practical purpose, of what good can it be?"

"It depends," she answered, "what questions you are asking. No religion I know of can explain what is . . . that is something left

56

for human beings to learn, if they are curious. What purpose religion has always had . . . perhaps, although I have not read it yet, even in the Rig Veda . . . has been to tell us not what is but what things mean and what our place is in the universe. And it is in this realm of meaning where similarities abound . . . be it the forbidden fruit in Paradise, or the legend of the fire-bird in ancient Russia, or the story of how Prometheus stole fire from the gods and gave it to human beings."

Sir Wilbur nodded his head, his expression now very grave. "I fear you shall get no argument from me on that score. In the Rig Veda the story is told of how the sun-bird . . . either transporting the god, Indra, or by himself . . . stole Soma . . . a substance like ambrosia among the ancient Greeks, believed to be a fiery liquid that engenders immortality, and later personified as Agni . . . how the sun-bird stole Soma from the demons and brought it to Manu . . . the first human being and progenitor of the human species . . . and how the sun-bird accomplished this with the loss of only a single feather."

"And what became of that single feather?" Chris asked.

"It fluttered down from the heavens where the Soma had been hidden by demons . . . as often the Sun was hidden from the gods and humans . . . and was turned into a plant that could be used as a substitute for the actual Soma plant."

"The seat of the passions?" Chris asked.

"Perhaps," nodded Sir Wilbur. He looked gently now at Marcelina but also with a little apparent embarrassment. "After all, one of the means for human immortality . . . according to the Rig Veda . . . is the male phallus brim full of seed being received by a beautiful woman . . . and so the cycle of life continues and continues . . . as when the Sun, once hidden, is restored to the heavens. We know one thing about the Sun in the Arctic. For approximately four months of the year, when the Earth in its spherical gyrations is most turned in the northern polar region away from the Sun, there is only darkness . . . there is no day . . . there is only night. And it is then, I understand, that Saturn in conjunction with Polaris in Ursa Minoris is most visible to human eyes and . . . I have every reason to believe, directly above the . . . if you will . . . lost colony."

"When," cautioned Chris, "the heavens are not covered by Arctic fogs or clouds."

"As I was telling Marcelina in the car on the way from the train dépôt, that is why for this trip a topographical map of the Arctic is of far less use to us than a map of the heavens and the constellations, for, when they are visible, we shall know what was meant in the Rig Veda by the reference to a horse with thirty-four ribs."

"But," said Marcelina, "horses have *thirty-six* ribs."

Sir Wilbur smiled. "You said it yourself earlier, Marcelina. We cannot ask of religion questions of fact, but only questions of meaning. Those who would converse with the gods must learn to love and thrive upon paradox and enigma. The horse with thirty-four ribs in the Rig Veda is a personification of the Sun, the Moon, the five planets visible to the naked eye, and the twenty-seven constellations that on Earth can only be seen above the eightieth parallel."

Their conversation continued through dinner, although it ranged to conditions as Sir Wilbur had found them during his recent visit to Peru, and Chris spoke of his work filming documentaries and Marcelina of her studies in anthropology. Once they had adjourned to the living room after dinner, somewhat to the surprise of the Fallons, the Englishman mentioned that on his visit with Ramón at Tacho Alto he had proposed to the young man that he would pay for him to travel to California in order to join them on this trek to the Arctic.

"Ramón?" Chris inquired. "But Tenny, you found him to be only troublesome on the way to Haucha . . . and, well, he is a native Peruvian who has never been beyond the Andes . . . certainly he could contribute little that would be helpful on this expedition."

The Englishman did not respond at once, and his tone, when he did, was intent. "I cannot tell you . . . either of you . . . perhaps in a way that you would understand . . . but let me put it this way. Although Ramón Aksut's joining us on the way to Haucha seemed accidental at the time. . . ."

"I had forgotten his last name," Marcelina interrupted.

"He was born," the Englishman said, "Aksut Rumi . . . that's his Quechuan name . . . *rumi* is the Quechuan word for rock . . . Aksut is his family name. The local *padre*, when he was baptized, changed his name from Rumi to Ramón . . . making it a Christian name. But what I was attempting to say comes to this . . . however our group came together, however much it may have appeared accidental, I would not wish to undertake the journey I have proposed without precisely that same combination . . . without all five members being together again."

"Did he accept your offer?" Chris asked.

"Yes, I am pleased to say he did." He

looked toward Marcelina who was sitting in a chair across from him while Chris sat in a chair beside her. Sir Wilbur occupied a sofa before which there was a coffee table, and there he had stacked some papers and a copy of the Rig Veda. "I left sufficient funds with your father, Marcelina, so Ramón could book passage. Your father said he would give him detailed instructions on how to find your home. I imagine he will be here before you leave to join me in San Francisco. Ramón was very excited when I spoke to him about this journey . . . he has become an experienced mountain climber since his days with us . . . throughout the Cordillera Real, including the Illimani which is over twenty-one thousand feet high. Incidentally, he has a photograph of you, Marcelina, one that he cut out of a magazine, and I think he said he has even seen one of your films."

"In Tacho Alto?" Marcelina asked in astonishment.

"That I cannot say," the Englishman said. "They do project films in the back countries, you know, although it may be they are shown against the wall of a building rather than in a theater. The whole world, it seems, is bowing before our mechanical civilization. Not everywhere, possibly . . . merchant caravans between the Soviet Union and India cross

Afghanistan by camel power even today, but you do know that the Soviet Union uses the Northeast Passage through the Arctic to conduct shipping from western Russia and Siberia to the Far East, Canada, and the United States. The world is becoming smaller and smaller all the time. I wouldn't be surprised in another few years to see motorized caravans cross Afghanistan and the deserts of the Near East. Such things are happening in Egypt and Palestine, perhaps as a result of British involvement. Certainly . . . and Chris, I am sure you know this . . . trains have united the Anglo-Egyptian Sudan and British East Africa for some time now . . . far more so than when we were in those places." He dropped his voice then, as if in embarrassment. "Or what has happened thanks to the Italian presence in Somaliland and what may happen in Libya."

"Yes," interjected Chris, "I have heard that Mussolini's greatest contribution to Italy is that the trains now run on time."

The Englishman laughed. "Yes, but he didn't do it by means of efficiency. He simply had the train schedules rewritten to accommodate the inevitable delays so that the trains *seem* to run on time."

Chris rose to get them drinks — white wine for Marcelina, Glenfiddich without water or ice for the Englishman, and Crown Royal for himself.

"The Rig Veda is probably the most worldly sacred book I have ever read," Sir Wilbur continued to Marcelina. "But like all sacred books . . . because, truly, the gods, if they speak at all, tend to speak paradoxically . . . it can seem to contradict itself. In one of the hymns the poet states that a man married to a beautiful woman should make love to her often . . . perhaps as often as three times a day . . . and so he will live a long time, and so will his wife."

Marcelina smiled impishly. "Does the Rig Veda also tell you how to find the time to do it that often?"

"Alas, no . . . but there are other passages, my dear," the Englishman said, smiling in return, "that call for a man to be chaste . . . to be a servant eagerly serving . . . and by this means and because of chastity such a man will become a limb of the gods. In another poem it is said that the twins . . . Sinvali and Sarasvati . . . the twin Asvíns who are lotus-garlanded gods . . . are the ones to place the embryo in a woman's womb . . . while with golden kindling wood they also churn out the fire so that the embryo will be brought forth in the tenth month. When I first read that, I thought of the bodies of those children we had found in the

63

Temple of the Sun at Haucha. Those bodies are now in a museum in Lima. Examination proved they were twins. Perhaps it was an irony, but more likely twins had a sacred significance to the Incas as they have in the Rig Veda. Yet, there is so much in that holy book that is uncertain . . . so much that is enigma . . . that you cannot always be sure exactly what is meant."

"But there are unmistakable traces in the Rig Veda that indicate the book was written in the Arctic?" Marcelina asked.

"The Rig Veda, I fear, is like the Homeric sagas . . . a redaction," Sir Wilbur replied. "By the time it was set down systematically for the first time . . . when written language was sufficiently developed for this to happen . . . the Sanskrit text reflected only to a degree the Arctic origins of these hymns and songs which had probably been in existence already for perhaps a thousand years. In general, it could be said that every prehistoric religious idea that managed to survive in these verbally transmitted texts and that emerged in what is known as the Rig Veda had been influenced by the Hindu culture that had grown up with it, so to speak, in northern India after the Indo-Aryan invasions of the Third Millennium before Christ and possibly later. The texts, as they exist today, can be dated at about the Sixteenth Century before Christ, certainly not too much earlier than that, and for some of them perhaps later than that. What had to be done was to study the texts for those indications of prehistoric images that could have been only conceived in the Arctic . . . especially the descriptions of constellations and the planets that can be perceived in such a fashion only within the Arctic Circle."

Chris brought the Englishman his drink, and set Marcelina's glass of wine before her. "There may be a more modern indication of an Aryan presence in the Arctic," Chris said, returning with his own drink. "Vilhjalmur Stefansson in his second Arctic expedition of Nineteen Oh Eight to Nineteen Twelve records that he lived among the natives of Coronation Gulf, and he reported a little-known tribe of so-called 'blond' Eskimos."

"Blond Eskimos?" Marcelina asked in astonishment.

"I do not think that Stefansson was using the word Eskimo the way you would, or as Marcie or I might," Chris clarified. "For him it was a generic term for those people who live in the Arctic."

"I have read his memoir . . . THE FRIENDLY ARCTIC," Sir Wilbur put in, "and I was most impressed with his view that a small party of white men with one or two sledges to haul scientific equipment, cooking gear, clothing, arms, ammunition, and the like could travel wherever it wanted over the polar regions, even during the winter across the frozen reaches of the Arctic Ocean . . . no matter what latitude . . . and remain indefinitely. I am pleased that the journey I have in mind shall be something we should be able to accomplish in a matter of weeks . . . and during the summer, where we will not have to contend with the terrible cold . . . although, where we will be going . . . north to the northern shore of Ellesmere Island, we will have to cross a small glacier . . . but nothing compared to the Greenland Ice Cap which Stefansson declared to be the only truly lifeless area in all of the Arctic."

"And you plan to undertake most of the journey by airplane?" Chris asked.

"Assuredly. I shall arrange for airplane petrol to be taken on at Seattle . . . at Juneau . . . and I have made preliminary arrangements at Point Barrow . . . there is a factor at a trading post there who also operates what passes for a landing strip . . . a chap by the name of Pierre LeBon . . . there is also an American physician up there . . . a fellow named Sean O'Meara. As I understand it, they are among the nine white persons who live at Point Barrow . . . the rest of the population being Eskimos. At any rate, we'll put in at Point Barrow . . . take on a shipment of petrol to Victoria Island. His Majesty's Government and the Dominion of Canada established a permanent station there . . . in Nineteen Thirty-Two . . . as part of forty-three permanent stations set up in the Arctic for the Second International Circumpolar Year . . . and we can store the extra petrol there . . . before flying on to set down on Ellesmere Island. Luis should have worked out our exact latitude where we are to land. I haven't made the final arrangements on the type of aircraft, but that should be done while I am in San Francisco. I know you have a pilot's license, Chris, but since you will be field guide, I shall also have to engage a pilot to handle the plane after we leave it . . . and, of course, to return for us once we have completed our journey."

"And you believe that there still are people . . . after all these centuries," Marcelina put in, "that belong to the original Indo-Aryans that invaded northern Europe so many millennia ago?"

"As was the case with Haucha," Sir Wilbur answered, "I cannot say if, where we are going, there will be people still living there . . . but, let me put it this way . . . I do truly believe that this . . . lost colony . . . not only exists but that there are people who live there still."

Both Chris and Marcelina were excited by this prospect — and Sir Wilbur had been so incontestably right in the past, when it had come to finding a lost Egyptian city in Ethiopia, on which journey Chris had joined him for the first time, and then when it had come to the discovery of Haucha in Peru where Chris and Marcelina had both accompanied him, as well as Luis Valera and Ramón Aksut.

"Just a minute, Tenny," Chris said. "There's a magazine I used to get that carried a lot of factual information in a section titled 'Northern Lights.' It's no longer being published, but I've kept the back issues."

"He's had them bound," Marcelina commented.

Chris went into the study and rummaged around on a book shelf where he kept the bound magazines. Presently he found the bound volume with the issue in it that he wanted and brought it back into the living room and over to where Sir Wilbur was sitting. He handed it to the Englishman, opened to the page titled "Northern Lights" in the issue of *North-West Stories* for January 8, 1926. Sir Wilbur read the editor's answer to the question about there supposedly being a tropical valley somewhere in the Arctic:

There has been considerable talk and news about this of recent date. The latest information is that received from an aviator, Colonel J. S. Williams, of Montreal who said that the section found was "the garden of the world" and gave promise of an amazing future. One American aviation company sent in a huge 450-horsepower plane to make further discoveries and even more interesting news is expected to be added to the list.

"This is it precisely, Chris!" Sir Wilbur exclaimed. "Do not ask me how it is possible for there to be a tropical valley in the Arctic . . . it is just that I have come upon so many indications that there is such a place . . . and that it is inhabited even at the present time. That is, indeed, where we're going."

"One thing, Tenny," Chris put in, "when you venture onto ice in the Arctic, as you intend in crossing the ice cap on northern Ellesmere, it lowers body temperature. For that reason I would suggest we all dress as if it were for the winter months. Even normal activity moving across ice will create sweat that will build up a layer of ice within your clothing . . . and it can break and cut the skin through movement."

The Englishman leaned forward and picked

up the Rig Veda. "I have marked a couple of passages I should like you both to hear, since they do give some indication of what we are likely to find." He had placed little strips of foolscap throughout the volume and had written brief notes upon them. He turned to a passage early on in the book. "Yes, here is the first one . . . 'With snow you warded off the red-hot fire . . . you brought him' . . . a reference to Atri, the Devourer, a Vedic priest . . . 'you brought him sustaining nourishment. When Atri was led down into the glowing oven, you Asvíns' . . . the Asvíns are horsemen, twin sons of the Sun, physicians and rescuers of men . . . 'you Asvíns led him and his followers back up again to safety.' " He looked up. "I believe we will find some volcanic connection in the Arctic that will account for this tropical garden." Then he flipped forward in the book until he found another passage. "This is from the Fifth Book . . . 'The Sun vanishes, struck down by a magical spell. Atri with the fourth incantation found the Sun hidden by the darkness.' "

"The fourth month . . . ?" Marcelina wondered.

"Precisely," agreed the Englishman. "The Sun throughout the Rig Veda is disappearing and being found again. But there is then this passage . . . perhaps the most important passage of all." He turned forward slightly to an earlier book in the text. "It is part of a poem about Agni . . . Agni, who understands the inner meaning of things. 'What in this is ours, what riches, what treasures? Tell us, for you understand, Agni, you who knows all creatures. Hidden is the farthest end of our road, where we shall have gone, while others who fail will have followed a false path.' "

Chapter Three

There was a small banquet set for Saturday night in Sir Wilbur's honor, and it was truly a very special occasion for Marcelina who, unlike her mother, took a personal interest in the preparation of elaborate dinners and in such matters regarded herself as something of an *artiste*, or at least a conjurer. Most of Saturday she was secluded in the kitchen with Rosa. No one else was allowed to enter. It was as if for this time Marcelina were a witch and Rosa her familiar spirit, and together they had taken possession of this region. Neither Chris nor Sir Wilbur could tell what fires were burning or what cauldrons were bubbling there.

Marcelina finally emerged long enough to dress for dinner with Chris in the master bedroom. She had chosen an evening gown of black velvet trimmed with large sleeves of rose tan flat crêpe and ecru lace. Chris had put on the trousers of a newly tailored suit, also dark in color, and was standing before the tall mirror. Marcelina came over and looked at the reflection of his face and the front of his body in the mirror.

"I like the way those trousers fit you in the seat," she said.

It irritated Chris, sometimes, the way she fussed about his appearance. "You're forgetting, aren't you, Marcie, that you're the one in this marriage with the beautiful backside."

She moved closer, so that her body was also reflected in the mirror. She cupped her hands over her small breasts under the black velvet and pushed them upward.

"You must always make the best of what you have, Chris," she said, an impish smile playing on her lips.

He smiled, too, then, as together they gazed into the mirror, no darkness here, seeing each other as they were seen.

Will Rogers was fifty-four, an almost avuncular figure, with a tan and weathered face, deep grooves at the side of each eye, prominent ears, and a shock of brownish hair now tinged with gray. Betty Rogers, whom Will lovingly referred to sometimes by her maiden name, Blake, had eyes almost as large as Marcelina's that could be arresting, a high forehead, and a smile that was instantly winning. Henry King was six feet tall, with brown hair and blue eyes. He was regarded generally as one of the finest film directors in Hollywood, but he had once acted before the camera, and he could just as easily have stepped before it successfully tonight. Gypsy King, like Betty Rogers, was not a "professional" as persons "in the business" were called, but she was a singularly attractive woman and could well have joined her husband in a *pas-de-deux* before the camera for a highly romantic scene.

Linda Ruiz had been engaged for the evening to answer the door and to help Rosa in serving dinner. Marcelina detested oblong or rectangular dining-room tables and had insisted on one that was large but circular in her home. She sat next to Chris. Next to Chris was Gypsy King, Henry King next to her, Betty Rogers, Will Rogers, and between Will Rogers and Marcelina was Sir Wilbur, the guest of honor. Usually at evening meals with the Fallons, Marcelina said grace in a simple prayer thanking the Lord for the bounties they were about to receive. This evening her grace was special.

> May my food my body maintain,
> May my body my soul sustain,
> May my soul in deed and word
> Give thanks for all things to the Lord.

The others had experienced Marcelina's

culinary arts before, but for Sir Wilbur they proved a most uncommon experience. The meal began with a dark-colored, tomato-based Peruvian soup with small cubes of avocado, little, submerged islands of melted cheese made from goat's milk, thin, soft strings of corn tortillas, and at the center a dollop of sour cream. The soup was served with the slimmer of the two wine glasses being filled with a fine Amontillado to compensate the pallet for the variety of hot chile peppers used to flavor the soup. A vintage Veuve Cliquot was served in the generous bell-shaped crystal goblets to accompany the entrées. There were two, the first *blinis Demidoff*, followed by *cailles en sarcophage*. Dessert was crystallized fruit over soft vanilla ice cream.

As they ate, Henry King commented that were he ever to make a film about a Christian saint, he would hope Marcelina would be willing to come out of retirement to play the rôle since no one he knew could so perfectly fill the part in life.

"Henry," Marcelina said, blushing shyly, "I'm too much of a sybarite really to be a saint, and as for pictures . . . I am *very* retired."

"Let her be, Henry," Will Rogers interjected. "Marcie's the only actress I know who came out of the movies with the same husband she had when she started in 'em." He looked over at Marcelina. "Besides, acting is jest like the measles, girl. Catch it when you're young . . . like you was . . . and you can get over it." He paused. "But . . . catch it when you're older . . . an' it can be fatal."

The seating arrangement did accommodate intimate conversations *tête-à-tête*. Sir Wilbur was very interested to learn from Will Rogers that his great-grandfather, Robert Rogers, had been the son of a British officer stationed in the American colonies, and that Robert had married Lucy, the daughter of an Irishman and a full-blooded Cherokee. Robert had upon his marriage been inducted into the Cherokee nation which was then situated in the Carolinas and had become what was known among the Anglo-Americans as a "white" Indian. When the Cherokee nation was removed west to the Indian Territory by the United States government in 1836, Will's grandfather and great-uncle John, the two sons of Robert and Lucy, joined in the great migration, which was how eventually Will Rogers came to be born in what had been the Indian Territory but now was the State of Oklahoma.

Sir Wilbur confided that what he found most amazing about the United States was that virtually everybody was from somewhere else and how everyone seemed to inter-marry without a second thought.

"It ain't really all that general," Will Rogers told him. "Now you take Lincoln Perry . . . he acts under the name Stepin Fetchit. He's a black man, an' he says it's more segregated out here in Hollywood than it is in Georgia. As a matter of fact, though, I'm gonna be with him in my next picture. I've just finished reading the screenplay. It's called JUDGE PRIEST right now, but they like to change titles out here like most folks do shirts. There are some powerful scenes in that story." He chuckled quietly. "In one scene Stepin Fetchit . . . well, he's convinced me that you can catch fish in this river where everyone believes there's no fish . . . but you gotta use a special kind of bait . . . beef liver. Well, we get to the river, and I've got my pole out . . . and Lincoln . . . he's forgot to bring the beef liver. So the judge . . . the fella I'm playin' . . . sends him back to town to get it. He buys it at the butcher shop, but some dogs attack him on the way back to the river, and fightin' with them dogs . . . why, he's hanging onto that liver so hard that there's blood all over his hand. A group of righteous citizens come on him once the dogs have run off. They're after a black man who is wanted for assaultin' a white man, and the blood on pore Lincoln's hands is enough proof for 'em.

They want to lynch him for murder. Anyway, he gets put in the jail, but there's a mob building up outside. They want to hang the poor fella. That's when I come to the jail and have to talk 'em out of it. There's a scene at the end where I end up defendin' another innocent man. It looks like it'll be a good picture."

"I loved Stepin Fetchit in DAVID HARUM," Henry King observed. "He's a genuine comic talent . . . with a touching human side to his acting."

"I'm not so sure how much of it's acting," Will Rogers returned. "You know, I was talkin' to him one time when we was workin' on a picture, and he told me what he put down as his chief hobby for the MOTION PICTURE ALMANAC. He told 'em his hobby was makin' folks happy . . . I believe him."

"I have trouble understanding what he's saying some of the time," commented Gypsy King.

Will Rogers laughed. "You're not the only one, Gypsy. Sometimes I've got to look again at the script when a scene's over just to figure out what was said."

It was during the *cailles en sarcophage* that the table conversation somehow had come to the subject of love. Perhaps it was something suggested by the cuisine. It did seem inevitable.

"Have you ever read what Aristophanes has to say about love in one of Plato's dialogues?" Henry King asked.

"Cain't say that I have, Henry," Will Rogers put in, smiling puckishly.

"Aristophanes," Henry King persisted, "tells of how in the beginning . . . but I imagine it goes on all the time, and this is how I prefer to treat it in the films I make . . . anyway, in the beginning human beings were androgynous . . . two-sided . . . with one face sometimes looking away from the other face and sometimes one face looking at the back of the other's head. When human beings wanted to move quickly, they would do so by tumbling around and around . . . using all four arms and all four legs. Their strength and vigor made them very formidable, but their pride in themselves grew to be overweening. The gods disapproved of this pride, and Zeus had a solution that would make humans weaker but at the same time more numerous. He cut all the members of the human race in half, and Apollo turned the faces so that each human being could look down and see that the other half was missing. Physically, of course, these half-bodies flourished, but not their souls. Each of us, being bisected at birth in this way, is doomed to search the world over to find the complement that alone will complete us. We

. . . all of us . . . can remember when we were whole and, when we love, we are only pursuing that part of us which was once lost. Because we are human, we often make errors and mistakes, but sometimes it really happens . . . we do find our other part . . . and then finally our soul is complete."

"It might have been that way for Marcie and Chris," Will Rogers said, seeing how struck each of them had been at hearing of this notion, "but Blake, here, took an awful long time . . . as I remember . . . to make up her mind about her other half."

"Only because you seemed more interested in looking for your other half all over the world rather than in Benton County, Arkansas."

" 'Taint true," Will Rogers affirmed. "I knew you was the one the very first time I saw you. Any way you want to put it, though, Henry, we men are the lucky ones . . . that these beautiful creatures want to stay with us at all."

After dinner, they all adjourned to the spacious living room for after-dinner drinks and conversation. Sir Wilbur took out his pipe, filled it, and lighted it.

"You know," he said, as Rosa brought him a glass of his favorite single malt Scotch, "I'm certainly pleased that you people in this country have finally done away with Prohibition."

"You haven't been readin' the papers, Sir Wilbur," Will Rogers said, who was now sitting in an armchair close to the Englishman. "Prohibition may come back ag'in. Right now we got us a President that drinks and smokes and, for all I know, even chews gum, but you don't understand politicians if you think anythin' like this is goin' to last. A politician ain't happy 'less he's interferin' with folks. The reasons for Prohibition, they say, had to do with religion, an', I guess, religion wasn't strong enough to make Prohibition last longer than it did. But religion these days isn't nowheres as popular in this country as science. Right now doctors are tellin' folks to smoke Camels 'cause they're easy on the throat, or . . ." — here he pointed over toward the green package with a red circle in front of Marcelina on a coffee table — "they're tellin' folks how they should take one of those Luckies Marcie's got, instead of a sweet. But just let some of these same doctors get together and have a convention and decide that smokin' and drinkin' . . . even chewin' gum . . . is no good for folks and there oughta be a law against 'em, and Prohibition will be right back. 'Course, we may consider this freedom an' such our right because we're all really just plain folks in this country . . . but over in Germany, now . . . there's a fella over there that calls himself the New Man for the New Age. 'Case you didn't know, Sir Wilbur, this New Man . . . why, he don't smoke an' he don't drink an' . . . for all I know . . . he don't even chew gum, an' I read he only eats herbs and vegetables. Well, there's your New Man for the New Age. Should he ever get popular over here, he'll have all of us swearin' off everythin' . . . except herbs and vegetables."

"But, Will," Marcelina said, "you don't smoke, and I've never seen you take a drink."

"But he has," said Betty knowingly.

"So have you," Will said with a shy smile at his wife, "but that's not the point, Marcie. I chew so much gum, the company's still sendin' it to me for free advertisin'. It's just I don't want nobody in a uniform . . . no German and sure no American . . . tellin' me I can't if I want to. Every time Congress makes a joke, it's a law, and every time they make a law, it's a joke, but that don't stop 'em from makin' lots and lots of laws. Politicians can't really control big things . . . like passin' a law against the Depression or a law tellin' Japan to stay out of China . . . but, since they gotta pass laws . . . that bein' the way of a politician . . . why, they pass laws that aren't needed, like against buyin' a bottle of whiskey. The reason the politicians really got rid of Prohibition was 'cause the only ones makin' money on it was the bootleggers. Now with the politicians makin' money on every bottle sold to the public and the bootleggers out of business, the government is in the liquor business . . . an' everyone is s'posed to be happier all the way around."

"For me," Henry King put in, "all these things go far back . . . to the idea of us and the others . . . whether it's Jews and Gentiles, Greeks and barbarians, Romans and non-Romans . . . there's always had to be someone who belongs to *the others* or people can't feel good about themselves and that they're somehow special."

"Maybe you're right, Henry," Will agreed. "Like it's been so long in this country . . . it was the Americans and the Injuns . . . then the North an' the South, the East an' the West . . . the Americans and the UnAmericans . . . like the Mad Hatter's Unbirthday party for little Alice . . . but, if that's the split, then count me on the side of the UnAmericans when it comes to the next Unbirthday party . . . the company's better, an' I'd feel a whole lot more at home among 'em."

"Why do you think, Sir Wilbur," Gypsy King asked, "the British government isn't doing more to stop Japan in Asia . . . after all, the British have the most to lose?"

"So do the French in Indochina and the Dutch in the West Indies," Sir Wilbur clarified. "I haven't been back home for a long time, except in Nineteen Thirty, when His Majesty was gracious enough to include me in the lists for the Order of Merit of the British Empire . . . but no one in England, except maybe that chap, Winston Churchill, seemed the least concerned about the very real danger to our Far Eastern possessions. Now I get the impression England is more worried about the possibility of a war in Europe."

"The last time Great Britain had a war on two fronts, I recall," Chris Fallon said, "was when George the Third had to choose between winning against the French in India or against the colonists in this country, and he chose to put all his effort into fighting for possession of India."

"Kind of lucky for us he made that decision, wasn't it?" Will Rogers put in.

"But Chris is right," interjected Sir Wilbur. "If there's another war in Europe, I'm afraid Great Britain will be in no position to protect the Indian Empire, or the Malay States, Australia or New Zealand, or even Hong Kong."

"I don't suppose," Will Rogers said, "anyone has thought to ask the Chinese what they think about the Japanese in Manchukuo or the British in Hong Kong . . . and, 'course, Congress won't pass a law about *that* . . . I once said if Mussolini came over here to run this country, he'd run it just the way Congress *has been* runnin' it . . . with his eyes shut."

"Do you think there really will be another war?" Gypsy King asked at large.

"I honestly thought it would be different once women got the vote," Betty Rogers replied, "because it's always men who want to make war."

"Old men," said Marcelina, exhaling a ribbon of tobacco smoke as she spoke, "and they always expect the young men to fight and die."

"I'll just bet, Marcie," said Will Rogers, "that women'll be in the next one. Why they're out there fightin' right now . . . in China."

"I will fight, too . . . if I have to," Marcelina insisted.

"We can hope no one will have to die in a war again," said Chris Fallon.

"I've heard people sayin' that since Nineteen Nineteen," Will Rogers said. "But as long as one country after another is puttin' young people in uniforms an' sendin' them out where they don't belong, it's not likely that there'll be no more wars. Does anyone

85

here believe that the Pilgrims would have let the Indians land? . . . the way the Indians let the Pilgrims land?" He winked at Sir Wilbur. "Bein' a Cherokee does have its advantages. I can ask that kind of question . . . and all you hear, after I ask it . . . is silence."

That night, long after the other diners had left, the three of them, Sir Wilbur, Marcelina, and Chris, remained talking, out on the back verandah. Marcelina apprised Sir Wilbur, who had been very affected by Will Rogers, that this friend of theirs had a rather rigid view of what was and was not appropriate for women. Marcelina told the Englishman about how once her friend, Carole Lombard, had showed up to watch a polo match at the Rogers Ranch in Santa Monica wearing a pair of tight-fitting slacks and how Will had accused her of dressing the part of a "fast woman." Chris then mentioned how, just before departing this night, Will had taken him aside and reminded him that the North Pole was no place for a woman. Yet curiously, Marcelina added, Will Rogers counted among his closest friends the aviatrix, Amelia Earhart.

When, finally, Sir Wilbur announced it was time he be in bed and he rose from his chair, Marcelina rose, also, and came over to him. Taking his arms in her hands, she leaned up very high, pulling him down to her, and kissed him.

"What was that for?" he asked her, somewhat in embarrassment.

"Because I owe you so much," she said quietly.

"You owe me?" he asked in bewilderment.

"Were it not for you, Tenny," Marcelina told him, using for the first time the diminutive Chris had used so long, "I do not know if Chris and I would ever have found each other again. We were born so far away from each other . . . whole worlds apart, really, and a decade in time. What would have been the chance that ever we would have met in all that darkness . . . but for you?"

Sir Wilbur held her gently, then, by her shoulders. "A hare's breath," he whispered, and smiled.

Chapter Four

The next day was Sunday. Chris and Marcelina together with Santiago Cruz and Rosa Caldero drove off in the Cadillac V-16 Phaeton to attend Mass at the mission church in San Fernando. It was truly a handsome automobile painted dark green, with four doors and a white canvas roof that was retractable. There was a large luggage trunk at the back and space between it and the rear of the car that could be used for transportation of additional baggage. They would need all that space, surely, when the car was packed for the trip to San Francisco.

Although Sir Wilbur had been brought up in the Church of England, he hadn't attended a church service in years, and so remained behind. He went into Marcelina's music room where the Victrola was also kept. With a cup of tea, which he made himself in the kitchen, he took out an album of Beethoven's "Pastoral" Symphony performed by Serge Koussevitzky and the Boston Symphony Orchestra. With the windows open, a fresh breeze wafting through the spacious room, Sir Wilbur sat, spellbound by the magical rise and fall of the music. He found this all such a miracle — to hear a full orchestra play symphonic music in something other than a concert hall — that he did not mind the side breaks every five minutes or so, requiring him to turn a record over or to take out the next record in order to continue. His soul could bridge the gaps in the music, as if he were hearing nothing while the side changes were made, the last note from the previous side resonating somehow until, once again, the music could resume.

When the Fallons and the others returned from the mission, Chris went to the master bedroom to change into clothes he found more comfortable than the suit he had been wearing. Marcelina joined Sir Wilbur in the music room.

"Oh, Marcie," he said as she entered, having just put the Beethoven album away on its shelf, "if you wish to practice, I shall be happy to go. I was just listening to some music on your gramophone."

"No, no, don't leave, Tenny," Marcie said, smiling. "My best friend is coming over this afternoon after lunch. I've mentioned her . . . Carole Lombard. She loves horses as much as I do, and we plan to go for a ride. She's a movie star, and she'll be staying for dinner. You'll fall in love with her, I'm sure, and she so wants to meet you."

"It is wonderful that you can make music," Sir Wilbur mused.

"Oh, I don't make music," Marcelina corrected him. "I only play music others have made."

"Even that," he said, "is far more than I can do. I can only listen to it. I was just listening to Koussevitzky conduct Beethoven. You know, I saw him conduct Beethoven in London once. He's a splendid conductor. As for music, I fear I can't read a note of it."

"Oh, that isn't true," Marcelina said, walking over to the grand piano before the windows that looked out onto the side garden.

"It most surely is," Sir Wilbur insisted. "When I went to school, we sang, of course, but the kind of education I received had me mastering Latin and French. I didn't want to be a musician, so I didn't study music . . . but I do love it."

"Come here," Marcelina said, seated now on the long bench before the keyboard.

Sir Wilbur came over to her. She indicated a place on the bench beside her, and he sat down next to her. Fixing him with her blue-gray eyes, she depressed the index finger of her right hand on middle C.

"This," she said, "is do."

"Of course," replied Sir Wilbur, "I know

the scale . . . do, re, mi, fa, sol, la, si, do. Every English schoolboy knows that much."

"But," asked Marcelina, smiling gently, "do you know what those words mean?"

"What they mean? Why . . . they mean just what they mean . . . don't they?"

"Those words are abbreviations," she explained. "Here, let me play each note of the scale for you." Again she depressed middle C. Her very long but sturdy fingers had gracefully sculpted nails rather in the shape of tiny spades. "Do . . . is short for *Dominus* . . . the word for. . . ."

"The Lord . . . in Latin," Sir Wilbur supplied, surprised.

"Yes," agreed Marcelina. She depressed the next white key. "Re is for *Regina cælum* . . . the Queen of Heaven . . . the Moon." She depressed the next white key. "Mi is for *Microcosmos* . . . ancient Greek for the Microcosm . . . the Earth." She depressed the next white key. "Fa is for *Fatum* . . . Latin for Fate."

"*Daivam* in Sanskrit," added Sir Wilbur, "the word for that transcendent force in life that is antecedent to, and more powerful than, all mythical personifications of the gods and all events that may be wrought by the gods."

She depressed the next white key. "Sol is for *Sol*. . . ."

"The Sun . . . in Latin," said Sir Wilbur.

"And . . . in Spanish," clarified Marcelina. She depressed the next white key. "La is for *Via Lactea*."

"My God, Marcelina . . . Latin for the Milky Way."

She depressed the next white key. "Si is for *Sideralis*. . . ."

"Latin for the stars in the heavens including the planets," Sir Wilbur answered.

She depressed the next white key. "And so, you see, we come back to do . . . for *Dominus* . . . a return to the Absolute, Tenny . . . to God Who is above all the forms He has created. You really did know it all the time. Since first human beings tried to write down the sounds of music and devised the scale, they have known deeply in their souls that there is some kind of connection between the vibrations of sound we can hear in this lower sphere and our human ability to understand that there must be some kind of order in all things . . . although it is probably greater than any one of us could ever understand . . . could ever imagine it to be . . . but with little building blocks that begin and end with *Dominus* we have come to understand how music is made. By its means, sometimes, God can touch our souls . . . and, even when we cannot hear all of the melody, we may approach some understanding of what it means. Our souls in that way *do* resemble God . . . for He has made us conscious . . . so that we can feel and be aware of what He must feel . . . love . . . honor . . . sadness . . . and even what we consider bad things like anger and greed . . . but most of all . . . something which perhaps only we must feel because we are so inferior to Him . . . we can experience wonder."

Sir Wilbur had become very solemn as Marcelina spoke these words. "You know, what you have just showed me brings to mind nothing so much as something that Shivapuri Baba told me in Nepal. When he was walking around the world all those years from Eighteen Seventy-Five to Nineteen Fifteen, he studied two things especially . . . geophysics and astronomy. He told me gravity is like electricity . . . we know only what it does, not what it is. If you were to do a graph of gravity by degrees and divided that spectrum between zero and one hundred, you would find that the degree of gravity necessary in the universe to support life at all is very precise . . . that the matter of degree between cosmic junk and the amount of gravity needed to sustain life is very fragile, indeed . . . a thousandth of a degree to the right or to the left of where it now stands . . . and there would not be . . . there would have been no possibility at all . . . of life."

Marcelina smiled at him with her large blue-gray eyes.

"By a hare's breath," she said very quietly. The Englishman nodded, as the play on words he had said to her only the previous night to express a substance so thin it has no breadth at all came back to him again, as if in reflection but with quite the same meaning.

Marcelina told him, then, that actually she had only come into the music room to ask him if she could get him anything to drink. Sir Wilbur indicated he had already made himself tea. Marcie rose to leave so she could make herself a milk shake. She had a machine that made them from ice cream, milk, and powdered white chocolate. It was her desire now to gain weight, so he should not be concerned about her at all on their forthcoming journey. By the time June came around, she fully expected to have thighs the size of oak trees, and, when seen from the rear, she would be waddling like an elephant!

About two o'clock Carole Lombard drove up in a white LaSalle convertible. She was dressed in riding clothes and even wore a jockey hat over her reddish blonde hair. She loved horses and attended polo matches. Marcelina had changed to white jodhpurs, a shiny black-leather belt, a white blouse with a red neck scarf, and highly polished, black-leather riding boots. She met Carole at the front door, took her briefly into the study to meet Sir Wilbur who was there with Chris, and then the two women went out the rear of the house, down the terraced steps, and across to the stable. Santiago Cruz had saddled the horses for them. Marcelina would be riding her favorite, a sorrel mare she had named Regina, Carole a black gelding named Star. Cruz stood by, but he knew better than to offer either woman any help in mounting, even though Marcelina's petite height meant that the stirrups were raised high so the step up was a big one for her. She managed it easily, using her hands to place her left foot in the stirrup; then, grasping the saddle horn with her left hand, the cantle with her right, she sprang up with a thrust from her right foot, in mid-air quickly changing her right hand also to the saddle horn over which the reins were draped. She seemed completely at ease once she was in the saddle. Carole had starred in only two Western films, while Marcelina, of course, had been in many. Marcelina had often had to drive a buckboard and manage a two-horse team, and in one picture she had ridden astride, as she invariably did off screen, except in this film she had had to do it wearing a dress that had come below her knees. The result was that the dress had pulled up to expose her bare legs on either side. It had been hard on her inner thighs. Marcelina was now bare-headed, although she had put on her sunglasses, and her reddish-brown hair was in the customary marcel. This style matched her name, as she had reflected more than once. Her hair, in fact, was very finely textured, and this is the way she believed she looked her best.

Carole rose easily to the saddle, and then followed Marcelina as they rode out of the compound and onto the dirt road that extended back through the property. As they left, Carole raised her jockey cap jauntily toward Santiago Cruz who smiled quietly and gave them a short wave of his right hand.

The road led across the pasture where it continued onto another property and still another, eventually coming out onto a paved road. They crossed this and went along the shoulder for a distance until another dirt road veered off, and they followed this over more ranchland. They had been in the saddle for well over an hour when they came to a quiet grotto alongside a creek, where there was a somewhat large rock outcropping. It was here that they paused, dismounting and tying up the horses. There was a stretch of grassy bank beneath some maple trees with a long flat rock on which they could sit, enjoy a cigarette, and talk. Marcelina took off her sunglasses.

"My next picture is with Gary Cooper," Carole said flippantly, exhaling smoke, "but I don't get to ride a horse. There're no horses in it. Just Shirley Temple . . . who's our kid."

"I won't be riding horses, either, where we're going this summer."

"Where's that?"

"The Arctic."

"You mean up where the North Pole is?"

Marcelina nodded, smiling.

"Too cold for me." Carole gave a little shiver. "I had enough of the Arctic when I was growing up in the Midwest. No thanks."

"There are no snowstorms there in the summer, although there might be dense fogs, and sometimes it can be rather windy."

"How windy?"

"I'm not sure, but Chris says sometimes there can be an Arctic equivalent of a hurricane."

"And this is where you and Chris are going for a vacation!" Carole laughed. "You can't be serious. Why?"

"We're going again with Tenny . . . Sir Wilbur . . . but he doesn't want it noised around."

Marcelina's use of slang amused Carole. Usually her English was so precise.

"Top secret stuff, huh?"

"Not that. Nothing to do with the government or anything. But. . . ." She paused for a moment. "You know, if I could tell it the way Sir Wilbur can, I'd probably get you just as excited as I am. It's like the last time . . . in Peru."

"You mean an abandoned city . . . up there with all that ice and snow?"

"Sir Wilbur doesn't believe it's abandoned. It may be a city . . . or, more likely, a village, but very ancient."

"A village of Eskimos?"

"No, not Eskimos," Marcelina said, laughing in spite of herself. "They're really Innuits."

"They're what?"

"Innuits. That what the Eskimos call themselves."

"OK. I'll ask it. If they're Innuits, why are they called Eskimos?"

"That's what Europeans called them . . . that's why."

"But I'm not European, and I've always thought those people in the heavy fur coats and all that snow were Eskimos."

"Well," said Marcelina with a light-hearted sigh of mock frustration, "it doesn't matter. We're not going to the Arctic to find Eskimos."

"I certainly hope not, Marcie," Carole said,

smiling broadly. "I think they've already been found."

"But this is serious. These people we're hoping to find have been there a long time, but no one has ever seen them."

Carole couldn't help laughing. "If no one has ever seen them, how do you know they've been there a long time?"

"Because of certain indications."

"What kind of indications?"

Marcelina broke out into laughter. "I know it must sound silly, but really it isn't. There is . . . well, there probably is . . . an ancient civilization there, maybe one from which all of our civilizations evolved."

"How?"

"Well, these people moved south . . . you know, into Europe . . . maybe all the way south to India."

"I'll bet the climate had a lot to do with it," Carole said. "With their going south, I mean."

"Possibly," Marcelina conceded.

"And what you're looking for are some of the hold-outs . . . right?"

"Yes," said Marcelina, and burst again into laughter.

"If these hold-outs have never been seen, and they're hiding out up there at the North Pole, do you really think they're going to be all that happy to see *you?*"

"Probably not," Marcelina admitted.

"Then I don't get it."

"Well, it's what we want to do," Marcelina said emphatically. "This is not a question of gold . . . or something like it was about Haucha. Maybe we can learn something."

"Learn something? . . . from people who have never been seen and don't want to be found? This has the sound of a fairy tale, Marcie." Carole paused to look very gravely at her friend. "You know, of course, who *else* is supposed to live up at the North Pole?"

"Carole . . . please . . . this *is* serious," Marcelina said, trying hard not to laugh again but not succeeding.

"How are you planning on traveling there?"

"By airplane at first, and then by dog sled."

"But you said there's no snow up there in the summer."

"There's some . . . and we'll be crossing the Agassiz Ice Cap. We'll need the sled for that . . . to transport our tents and supplies."

"Ice cap?"

"Yes . . . it's shaped like a huge bowl . . . all ice and snow on the surface . . . and ice islands . . . not icebergs . . . but large islands of ice . . . come from the Agassiz Ice Cap and float in the Arctic Ocean. Tenny and Chris are a lot more knowledgeable about where exactly we're going . . . but we have to cross this ice cap first, and beyond it may be the islands we're looking for."

Carole seemed struck by what Marcelina was saying. She flipped her cigarette stub into the flowing water of the creek and was silent for a moment. "It sounds dangerous."

"It will be . . . probably more dangerous than going to Haucha ever was."

"And this is something you want to do?"

"Yes."

"And you're not afraid?"

"I won't let it stop me, but I am afraid . . . a little. I had a disturbing, haunting dream last night . . . one I haven't told Chris about at all."

"Why's that?"

"Because he was nowhere in it. It was a dream about me, I suppose . . . not me as I am so much . . . but, well, it was odd . . . and you were in it with me . . . at the beginning."

"I was. What was I doing?"

"Well, it's absurd . . . I know . . . but you and I were singing in that big production number in THE SHOW OF SHOWS . . . 'Meet My Sister'. . . ."

"But you and Alice Day did that number."

"I know . . . in the movie . . . but in my dream *we* were doing it together . . . and it seemed we really were sisters . . . but then that

101

all faded, and I wasn't Peruvian, and I'd never met and married Chris . . . I was an American, just like you . . . and I did get married . . . to a man named Arthur Klein."

"Not Arthur Klein, the agent? I hope he got you better rôles in your dream than he got you while you were his client."

"In my dream he didn't get me any rôles at all . . . he was a New York furrier, and we just got married . . . and apparently it didn't work out because in the dream it seemed that I had married several more times . . . sometimes the marriages may have ended in divorce, but sometimes they ended in death . . . my husbands died on me . . . and by the time I was an old woman, I was living alone in an apartment complex . . . I think it was in Pasadena. My hair . . . I had lost most of my hair, which had turned white, anyway, and I always wore a wig, marceled, though, just the way I wear my hair now."

"And have for ages."

"OK, maybe I should change it."

"A little styling wouldn't hurt."

"In the dream that didn't matter. My hair was almost all gone, and as I aged, I had shrunk . . . I was shorter than I am now, and thinner. I was still living near Hollywood, but I refused to see anyone to talk about my life. I just wanted to be left alone . . . and in the dream I was alone, and my mind was beginning to go . . . I was forgetting everything . . . and . . . and so I made the decision. I would have to give up my little apartment and enter a nursing home. It seemed to me in the dream that my life had always been hard . . . very hard . . . and now the hardest part was before me. It was then that I woke up."

Marcelina fell silent, and then nervously reached for the little wrist bag she wore, took out a cigarette and her golden, monogrammed cigarette lighter. She lit her cigarette.

Carole said nothing, but looked at her in grave perplexity.

"I had nothing at the end . . . no children . . . nothing . . . and I was losing even my memory . . . I wasn't sure who I was any more." Marcelina paused for a moment, and then continued in a more intimate tone. "Both Chris and I have been to see several doctors, and they all say there is nothing more they can do. There's nothing wrong with Chris . . . and there's nothing wrong with me. We've tried doing it by the calendar . . . we've both taken vitamin supplements and other things . . . but nothing's seemed to work."

"I know," Carole said quietly, and there was a shadow in her blue eyes.

"Mama and Papa feel even more strongly about it than that. I'm their only child and their only hope for grandchildren . . . and now I'm thirty-three years old."

"Come on, Marcie, you haven't finished the story in your dream. What happened to me. Were we still friends when we were in our dotage?"

"That's another terrible part of the dream. I had become a Christian Scientist, and I didn't allow anyone near me who smoked or drank. You were still alive, I recall, with two children . . . both of them boys. Only . . . I guess one of them wasn't quite right . . . mentally . . . and you worried about him a lot."

"Who was the father of my two boys?"

"That wasn't in the dream. You were living alone . . . still here in California . . . but you had quit pictures, I think . . . if you had aged as much as I had, you would have been nearly eighty. I looked ninety. But I don't know what year it was supposed to be in the dream. I know that I couldn't drive a car . . . that I felt I was too unco-ordinated, or something. Which is true, Carole. I really didn't want to learn to drive . . . especially when you had to start a car by cranking it. But when the electric starters came in, and I was no longer working at Metro, but free-lancing, Chris insisted that I get a car and drive myself to the studio or out to location." She smiled and inhaled on her cigarette. "Chris said that driving a car was a lot easier than riding a horse . . . and, of course, he was right."

"And now," Carole interjected, "not satisfied with riding a horse or driving a car, you're going sledding across an ice cap!"

"I know. Only an ice cap isn't what you might think it is. It's not really made just of ice. There are all kinds of crevasses in the surface, covered by snow. Some go down only a few feet and are filled with water. Others seem to be so deep they have no bottom, and with walls of sheer ice, if you fall in, you probably won't be able to climb out again."

"And you're going?"

"I'm going."

"Don't you think that dream you had was telling you something? . . . like nix . . . stay home?"

"That's what I did in the dream. I stayed home. I didn't drive. I didn't go anywhere. I never dared anything. And I was old . . . I was losing my memory . . . I had lost everything . . . the men I had loved were dead or the marriages hadn't worked out. I had become a believer in Christian Science. Whatever happened to me was meant to happen, and I didn't have any part in it at all . . . except to cope with it, somehow . . . to survive. Then even that wasn't possible any more."

"Well," said Carole in a portentous tone,

"that may be how you look at that dream. Now, please, don't take this wrong, but you must live three times as hard as I do, since you put so much of yourself into every new shadow of emotion that flashes inside of you. But when it comes to that dream, I see it another way."

"How?"

"You ninny. The one thing that stays with me about your dream is that . . . if you don't change the way you wear your hair . . . which is the same way you've worn your hair forever and ever . . . well, Marcie, that dream's right. You're going to end up as bald as a goose egg, running around in a wig . . . and without being paid to do it. You need a change, and I'd say it was high time."

Marcelina crushed out her cigarette, her forehead wrinkled in perplexity. "You know," she said quietly, "I think you're right."

"Of course, I am. Come on. Those horses have had enough time to rest."

While the two women were out riding, Sir Wilbur and Chris remained in the study which housed on tall shelves all of Chris's books and all of Marcelina's. Chris had begun reading and was absorbed in Euripides's last play, THE BACCHE. He kept his Greek LEXICON near at hand, because this was a new author to him. It was over the titles in Marcelina's part of the library that Sir Wilbur quietly ran his eyes, for he, too, wanted a book to read. The Greek and Roman historians were all there, and Gibbon, Mommsen, Prescott, Bury, the many volumes of Maspero's HISTORY OF EGYPT, and a history of the Roman Empire by a Russian named Rostovtzeff. In fiction there were Jane Austen, the Brontë sisters, some Dickens, Balzac and Flaubert in French, Cervantes and Lope de Vega and Vincente Blasco Ibáñez in Spanish, and a rather recent novel, THE NARROW CORNER by W. Somerset Maugham. There were many books on anthropology and native American civilizations and on myths and legends of various American Indian peoples, and a substantial volume that he took from the shelf published in 1916 and titled PSYCHOLOGY OF THE UNCONSCIOUS by C. G. Jung. As he opened it and flipped through its pages, he came upon a passage which, obviously, Marcelina had marked when she had read it.

For the act of fertilization is the climax — the true festival of life, and well worthy to become the nucleus of a religious mystery.

At first, he thought that perhaps this book

would be too privately hers for him to dare to read it, but, when he asked Chris, he was told Marcie loved that book and certainly he should read it, because he might well find as much in it as she had. And so, like two gentlemen sitting in the reading room of an English club at Lahore in Punjab, that was how they passed the afternoon, quietly reading, interrupting their solitude only around four o'clock for Sir Wilbur to have tea and Chris a cup of coffee.

In this brief respite, as they sat now in the study, their cups on little tables alongside them, Chris was smoking a cigarette, the Englishman his bulldog pipe.

"I believe, Tenny, I have something else for which I am profoundly grateful to you," Fallon said.

"Euripides?"

"Yes. You know, in all the Greek literature I have read over the years, I deliberately avoided him. I'm no classical scholar, and my reading is strictly for pleasure. There was a fragment attributed to Euripides that I once came across that struck me . . . 'when God desires to cast a man into the void he first drives him out of his mind.' Supposedly this fragment was rendered in Latin by Plutarch, and so eventually became widely known. It was only sometime later, when I came upon a fragment of Æschylus . . . from the lost play, NIOBE . . . that I found the notion was his . . . it wasn't said by Euripides at all . . . or, if it had been, he had only borrowed the idea from Æschylus. I was so struck by it that I memorized it. Æschylus has Niobe say . . . *'Theos mén aìtían phýei botoîs ótan kakôsai dôma pampèhdehn phélehi'* . . . when God would bring a man's estate to total ruin, first he has him fall prey to a fault in his nature. That's how I would say it in English, of course, but the older I become, the more I am convinced that you really cannot translate anything from one language into another and retain the full integrity of its meaning. The way I translated it, I used the English word *fault*. The Greek word Æschylus used was *phýei* . . . it has the same stem and is very closely related to *phyma* . . . the Greek word for tumor or cancer . . . and *phýro* . . . the Greek word when active for mixing up something so as to confuse or destroy it . . . and when passive to befoul something. In a way all of those ideas are in *phýei*. Fault is simply the best I can do in English . . . like *culpa* in Latin . . . as in *mea culpa* in the Roman liturgy . . . which means through my *fault*."

"Well, however it is said, I can readily believe the truth of it," the Englishman affirmed. "I've seen it happen. So have you.

109

There is a dementia that seems to take possession of the soul of such a person when he is pushed to the extreme. Indeed, to go back to Haucha . . . because I was with him, you know . . . that is what happened to Marcelina's uncle. I don't think Don Esteban was in his right mind the whole time he was in the valley. There was something insane about everything that he did . . . and, I suppose, his death . . . which was so needless, when you think about it . . . was also inevitable . . . given his state of mind."

"Oh, I agree . . . to the extent that human beings dare attribute any motive to God. That is probably the best way to explain what sometimes happens. But my problem with Euripides . . . why I avoided reading him . . . was my understanding that he believed the universe at base to be irrational, and so I wanted no part of him. But after reading THE BACCHE today . . . the play Euripides wrote just before he died . . . I realized for the first time what he must ultimately have meant. It is not that the universe is basically irrational, but rather that it cannot ever be understood by reason . . . a very different thing . . . that reason has little to do with it, but rather imagination. When King Pentheus wants to go in disguise among the Dionysians, it is not that he dresses like a woman because he wishes to be a woman, but because how one clothes himself, like all of the culture we accrue during our lives from our environment, is ultimately meaningless when it comes to being who we are and to recognize, before we die, what is our true place in the universe. It is, after a fashion, the way it was for Marcelina when we were on that journey to Haucha."

"How's that?"

"We were all worried about her. I know that I was. Thomas O'Day even had second thoughts. Remember what Quinto told us? . . . how it was criminal to take an innocent *señorita* to certain death?"

"Yes," agreed Sir Wilbur, smiling and sipping tea, "I recall him saying that to us all . . . quite vividly, as a matter of fact."

"But, you know, Tenny, Marcelina is what the Greeks described as *eudaimon*."

"*Eudæmon*? . . . in Latin I believe that is what the Romans called south Arabia. I seem to remember that it is related to the Latin word . . . *felix* . . . for happy or lucky."

"Only as the Greeks meant it, *eudaimon* is not a place . . . rather a state of being. It is not something you can pray for . . . it is not something you can acquire by living a certain way, or behaving according to a certain code . . . it is just something that *is* . . . the way the Moon

111

reflects the light of the Sun. To be *eudaimon* is to be beloved by the gods . . . and so they watch over you. Who was the only one among us . . . the *only* one . . . whose life was never threatened . . . not really threatened? . . . Marcelina."

"As I recall, Chris," the Englishman said, shaking his head ever so slightly, "Don Esteban did threaten to whip her for what she had done . . . whip her as she had never been whipped in her life."

"Yes," Chris agreed, "but, when he made that threat, he was scarcely in a position to make good on it, and in the end it was just empty air . . . because a moment later he turned back and lost his life . . . but not before he counseled her to save herself . . . before . . . as Marcie insists to this day . . . he saved *her* life. It was as if he had that one flash of sanity amid all the madness which had taken possession of him."

The Englishman thought for a moment, then nodded. "You know, old boy, I think you're right. She was the only one of us who never really came close to dying in that dreadful place. *Eudaimon* . . . ," he repeated softly.

"Beloved of the gods . . . *felix* . . . lucky . . . happy . . . all the days of her life. Perhaps that's why I'm so happy just being with her

. . . perhaps more than a little of it rubs off onto me. Oh, not that she hasn't had her ups and downs . . . movies got to be so bad. . . . When she made THE POCATELLO KID . . . she always talks about it as that Western with the close-up of her . . . why, Tenny, production on that film took almost six days . . . two days on location . . . and I think there wasn't a moment she wasn't in tears when she wasn't before the camera . . . the dialogue she had . . . the ridiculous rôle she had . . . but she came out of it, finally turned her back on all of it, and went off in another direction."

Sir Wilbur smiled ever so gently.

"Understand, Tenny, I mean it when I say Marcie is *eudaimon*. Don't believe for a moment I don't realize how precious she is, because I do. A human soul is infinitely fragile . . . incredibly complex to create, I am sure, but easy . . . oh, so very easy to break. We . . . each one of us . . . Marcie and I . . . we're both finding our way through life . . . which is never easy. When I gave up being a field guide and went into producing films . . . and if ever I should want to give up films and do something else . . . like write fiction . . . which, I know, someday I want very much to do . . . Marcie will be there beside me. Who am I to say to my other half that it must be otherwise with her? It's like Marcie's ears. I love her ears. She believes her lobes are too big. She usually wears her hair in such a way as to cover them . . . and, even when you can see a little of her ears, she almost never will wear earrings . . . because they call attention to her lobes . . . only in one picture that I recall . . . VIA PONY EXPRESS . . . one of her very last . . . and she had to have her hair dyed blonde for the part . . . only that once did she agree to wear earrings on camera, but she also made sure that the small gold crucifix on the gold chain I had given her on our tenth wedding anniversary was visible around her neck in the same scene . . . probably to attract eyes away from her ear lobes. Well, however much I may love her ears, Tenny, I would never ask her to change the way she thinks about them. Will had it right last night, you know, when he said that we men are truly the lucky ones . . . that these beautiful creatures stay with us at all."

"I must say," the Englishman observed thoughtfully, "Marcelina has you going to church. I don't remember your being all that religious in the old days."

"I came into the Church so we could marry, Tenny, and I find I do love the Latin Mass. It is a beautiful work of art in its way . . . one that echoes back almost to antiquity." He suppressed a grin, but some of it showed.

"Of course, I was raised Lutheran, and I once chided Marcie that she has never experienced the Lord's Supper as I did when I was young . . . where real wine is part of the sacrifice . . . it's not like that in the Roman Church . . . just a wafer, no wine. But as a youth I had to fast before receiving the Lord's Supper, and, once that wine hit you on an empty stomach, it was really something."

Sir Wilbur smiled but rejoined seriously: "I have come to the conclusion, Chris, that the two greatest creations of civilization, East or West, are cities and theology. Cities . . . because their lights dim out the stars so we cannot see them and be reminded of the infinite loneliness and coldness of space . . . and theology . . . because it makes God somehow comprehensible to us, even within our control, if we learn the proper rituals through which to propitiate Him. Yet, in the end, although we may successfully dim them, the stars are still there . . . countless stars we can see . . . and more we may someday be able to see with greater telescopes . . . and so, too, beyond theology, there is God. Cities and theology offer humankind the same thing . . . security . . . only, it is a false security . . . unreal, man-made. The one may be bombed to rubble, and the other . . . the other is something in which we may lose our faith."

"Not completely . . . not where we'll be going, Tenny."

"How's that?"

"The heavens are sometimes filled with stars . . . and shooting lights . . . and we'll be so close to the eternal mystery of electromagnetism . . . and beyond them all, but even closer to us, somehow. . . ."

"Yes," agreed Sir Wilbur, his eyes now suddenly bright and his voice hushed. "Perhaps . . . very close."

"However it may appear from the outside, I do not really believe wholly in the Christian idea of God. He is still too human . . . human in the sense that human beings believe they can somehow barter or perform certain rituals to placate Him, or to have their prayers answered . . . absurd, when you think about it, because often people pray for very contrary things . . . as happens in wars . . . and probably most of the time. My debt to the Greeks is very great . . . and it has influenced the way I have chosen to live my life. At any moment there might come a catastrophe that will engulf us. In this country, and nowhere more so than in Hollywood, the existence of death has been moved to the periphery . . . as if it did not exist . . . as if it was not something inevitable and something that each of us must encounter at some point. It is so easy in the modern world to become entirely consumed with yourself, what you are doing, and what you want and demand of life, that it becomes possible for many to forget entirely about mortality . . . or, conversely, to dream, as some already dream, that science now may promise us immortality . . . which, formerly, was the province of religion. There are visionaries who say that medicine will conquer disease and perhaps extend human life indefinitely . . . which, of course, does not take into account at all what is regarded as accidents . . . the unexpected . . . the catastrophic. Yet, it does each human being well to remember that every day we are granted to enjoy what life has to offer is actually an unexpected gift . . . for which, above all, we ought to be grateful.

"So much about us is conditioned by what we have become accustomed to in our lives. Take sunlight . . . the idea of a day beginning with the dawn of the Sun and its ending with dusk and twilight as the Sun seems to set beyond the western horizon. Yet, where we are going, for four months of the year there really is never any such thing as sunrise or sunset. However small it may appear in the heavens, the Sun is always there, even if it is masked by clouds or fogs. And then, for four months of the year, there is no sunlight at all . . . just the glitter of the stars and planets in the sky and the reflection of moonlight on a world of tundra, snow, and ice. For nearly four months there is no dawn . . . the Sun seems to be hidden."

"Yes, yes," Sir Wilbur agreed. "And that is what is so remarkable in several of the hymns in the Rig Veda. The Sun has disappeared from the sky, and the hymns tell of the incantations and the rituals by which means it is summoned to return again to the sky, restored to its rightful place in the heavens. Even now, so many centuries after the Rig Veda was committed to a written text, every orthodox Hindu in India recites daily a stanza from this holy book, addressed to the god of the rising and setting Sun . . . 'that lovely glory of Savitar, the heavenly god we contemplate, our pious thoughts he shall promote.' In another hymn Savitar is praised as the generator of all life, as he approaches on the dark blue sky, sustaining mortals and immortals alike, coming in his golden chariot, beholding all worlds."

"Æschylus has Prometheus say much the same thing . . . *panoptehn* . . . *Hehliou* . . . all-seeing Helios . . . the Sun . . . and so even Homer described the Sun centuries before. What I remember most vividly from my first trip to the Arctic . . . where I went as far as the

Barren Grounds . . . what most stayed with me is how different life becomes in the Far North . . . the trees get smaller and smaller, so they can remain closer to the earth and absorb heat and light from a more distant Sun . . . just as life in the temperate zones has adapted itself to a life cycle of days and nights . . . life in the Arctic has had to adapt to a way of life in which sometimes days continue on and on, one into the other without change, only for there to come a long period when there is no light or warmth at all . . . except that from the distant stars . . . various sources of light in the heavens that offer no warmth. According to our perspective, we come to have certain expectations . . . and, if we stay always in one place, change seems to be very little. But in an extremity like the Arctic change is powerful and perpetual . . . and nothing is to be expected . . . or, rather . . . anything."

Sir Wilbur leaned back in his chair and nodded, as he mused. "No oblations . . . as propitiation of the gods is termed in the Rig Veda . . . may be said to pertain in the Arctic. That's why I think you're right . . . the further we get from what is to be expected, the closer we come to realizing that human ambition and human desire have nothing at all to do with cosmic order. Shivapuri Baba told me as much . . . but he also said he did not experience the Arctic the way a person would who has spent part or all of his life living there. Yet, there is another . . . one who believes very much as you . . . someone I met in Nepal."

"Why did you ever leave Nepal?" Chris asked gently.

The Englishman thumped his chest. "The altitude . . . the elevation, don't you know . . . it began to affect me. I would become enormously thirsty and even light-headed. We English seem to have gone everywhere in the world and tried to live there . . . perhaps because we are less than totally happy living in England . . . but we also tend not to acclimate all that well." He smiled, and there was definite humor in his light-blue eyes. "I fear the beastly heat in Bengal is no better than the rarefied atmosphere in Nepal . . . in fact, the heat becomes so stupefying in Bengal that I understood and even sympathized with the pervasive pessimism in the Upanishads . . . to be released from the Wheel of Life as it must be lived in Bengal really does seem like the only true path to redemption."

As he finished speaking, Sir Wilbur's imagination summoned into his soul images he had encountered in the Rig Veda — of how the woman who was weaving (she had luminous dark hair and the most shining of golden eyes) stopped what she was doing to roll up what was stretched out before her; of how the skilled craftsman paused in the work he had only half completed; of how all this had occurred because the god Savitar had stirred and stood up, and because he had set apart the different times. It is once his thoughts are gathered that Savitar comes. Then Sir Wilbur saw portals shaped by mammoth rocks, as they must have appeared when Stonehenge in England was new, only according to his vision the apertures created by some of those portals were dark . . . because the light was hidden . . . as hidden to him now as the furthest end of his road.

After the ride, Carole and Marcelina came back to the house. Since Carole was staying for dinner, the two repaired to the kitchen to smoke, enjoy an apéritif, and oversee Rosa who was preparing the evening meal. At dinner Carole was delighted with the Englishman and listened in fascination as he told something of the many places he had been in his life.

After dinner, Sir Wilbur suggested to Carole that it might be pleasant to take a stroll together. Marcelina, perceiving that they perhaps might not wish company, went to the music room to practice. Chris went with her, because he always loved listening to her play, and especially now that Marcelina was practicing Mozart's K. 331, one of his favorite sonatas.

The Sun was sinking into the west, burnishing the landscape with reddish and golden hues. There was a stream beyond the gardens and orchard, and it was in this direction the two walked.

"I made light of it, when Marcie was telling me about your trip, but there'll be danger, won't there? Where you're going?" she asked.

"Some, I expect," Sir Wilbur conceded, "but nothing compared to what we ran into twelve years ago in the Andes of Peru."

"Marcie's got guts . . . more than I'd have."

"Now, I'm not quite sure if I believe that," he responded gently, smiling over at her. She was not wearing the jockey cap now but a blue scarf of a shade that matched her eyes tied around her reddish-blonde hair. There was a soft breeze whispering. "From what I've heard from Marcelina it takes a good deal of guts to be an actress."

"Guts?"

"You must understand I know very little about what goes on in making pictures for the cinema, but I found John Barrymore's attitude toward Marcelina deplorable . . . when she told me about it."

"Oh, Jack's all right. You just have to know

how to handle his kind."

"And how do you handle such a rogue, when you're in front of a camera, and he begins cutting up?"

She laughed. "Did Marcie or Chris tell you I was just in a picture with Jack?"

"No."

"Well, it was directed by Howard Hawks over at Columbia. I was on loan-out from Paramount. Howard's a second cousin. We grew up together in Neenah, Wisconsin, when we were kids. There was this scene where Jack wants to turn me into an actress, and, to make me scream the right way, he pokes me in the ass with a stick pin! Later on in the picture, I'm supposed to carry that pin around with me like a keepsake . . . a little treasure from the days back when. Well, Jack got a little too realistic."

"What did you do?"

"I turned around and kicked him in the balls!"

"My word . . . did you get in trouble?"

"Not for doing that. Howard said it's just what my character was supposed to do . . . take nothing off Barrymore. Jack tried later . . . once . . . to get fresh with me . . . not in the picture . . . and I told him to fuck off. That was an end to it. He stayed docile enough. Later in the picture, when I was *supposed* to be

123

mad at him, I enjoyed hitting and kicking him. It wasn't hard to do at all."

"This is the first time in almost eight years that I've seen Marcelina. I was surprised, in a way, that she had quit working in films."

"It's not something for everyone. And let me tell you she made one picture I really love. THE MAD PARADE . . . about nurses in France during the World War. There were no men in the film at all. I'd love to play a rôle like that. But I can also tell you this. Marcie's a whole lot happier since she went back to school. She's got brains."

"But don't you think . . . somewhere . . . deeply inside of herself . . . that she misses it?"

"Why? She did it while she was enjoying it. Then it got bad for her. Almost all those pictures she made on Poverty Row after leaving Metro weren't good for her."

"Poverty Row?"

"The low-budget, nickel-and-dime studios. You have to do your own make-up. A lot of times what you're asked to do is just humiliating. Not that I haven't made bad pictures. I have. When I was a kid, Mary Pickford fired me off one of her pictures. She said it was because I was too young . . . I doubt it."

"Jealousy?"

"It's part of the business."

"Well, then, you should know what I mean

124

by saying it takes guts to do what you do."

They had followed the path now until it entered the orchard. The setting sunlight was filtered, forming dappled shadows, but the air remained balmy.

"Actors aren't real, Sir Wilbur. That's one thing you should know about us. Everything about an actor is make-believe. People don't come to movies to see real people. They come to see a dream . . . a fantasy. Hours are spent on make-up and the right gowns. How does her ass look in this gown? What about her tits? Her face? How should it be lighted for this scene? Where do you stand? Where do you move? How do you move? How is this line to be said? There's nothing real about it."

"I understand Marcelina had trouble playing characters that were so different from the way she is."

"She's not the only one who's felt that way. I was working with Georgie Raft on a picture called BOLERO . . . we played a couple of dancers . . . and he didn't like the way the part made him care only about his career and that all the women he met were just there to be fucked and forgotten. He got so mean he even socked the producer over it, but with Georgie . . . that's really the way he is. I was getting divorced at the time, and we started going out together . . . but Georgie just wanted to fuck me. The guy's married, but separated, and I doubt he'll ever divorce his wife, because then he might end up marrying one of the girls he fucks. I remember he was in my dressing room between calls one day. We were sitting there and talking. I had a little bowl of peroxide I'd mixed up. I stripped in front of him and, with a piece of cotton, began to touch up the hair around my honeypot. Georgie stares at me . . . all amazement. I told him to relax. I was just making my collar and cuffs to match." She laughed gaily. "But in Marcie's case, I think it's something else. She's real, and she knows she's real. That's one of the things I love most about her." She flashed a questioning glance at him, but there was a smile in it. "Do you know what actresses get for all the work they do?"

"Success . . . fame, I suppose. And money."

"That's what all the fan magazines say. And the glamour. But do you know what you really get for being up there on the screen, giving the public all those answers . . . answers to the questions they ask . . . the public asks . . . and the answers we give them that somebody else has written . . . fine and clear and sometimes wonderful answers . . . no self-doubt . . . no being baffled . . . do you know what we get?"

"What you get?" repeated Sir Wilbur in confusion.

"Yes," Carole said earnestly, "what do you think we get in return?"

Sir Wilbur looked back over what they had been saying, and then he looked even further back, over the many years that he had lived, and in all those years he could not find an answer to give her.

"In return, Sir Wilbur," Carole said, her voice in an altogether changed tone, "we get the world's distrust . . . and our dire loneliness. And nothing else."

"Nothing?"

"Oh, one thing . . . perhaps . . . if you're a woman . . . and meet a man you love and want him to love you. Then you have a chance to play the rôle he has made for you in his heart . . . the rôle of the one woman he most wants in all the world. At least, then, the physical loneliness goes away. At least that."

She looked at him, and her face was illumined by a mischievous smile.

"Even if you're a comedienne, you act out of loneliness. Marcie doesn't have that loneliness any more. She hasn't had it for years. From what I know of her, she lost it . . . out there . . . long ago . . . on the pampas near that ancient city all of you found in the mountains of Peru."

Chapter Five

On Monday, Chris took Sir Wilbur with him to Paramount Pictures where he maintained an office. With the help of Henry King at Fox, he had arranged to have theatrical prints sent over to a Paramount screening room so Sir Wilbur could see DAVID HARUM and STATE FAIR with Will Rogers. From Columbia Pictures in Gower Gulch he was able to borrow a print of TWENTIETH CENTURY with Carole Lombard, and he got hold of one of her Paramount films, NO MAN OF HER OWN, for Sir Wilbur to see.

On Tuesday, Sir Wilbur again drove in with Chris and had the opportunity to screen several of Marcelina's films in the same screening room. Chris explained they weren't perhaps her best films, but he personally liked them. Sir Wilbur saw two silent films, THE CAMERAMAN, from which had come the still photograph of Marcelina in a bathing suit that she had given the Englishman, and TRENT'S LAST CASE, a Fox film that Henry King had had sent over that had been directed by Howard Hawks who had directed Carole Lombard in TWENTIETH CENTURY, and among Marcelina's talking films THE MAD PARADE, which was released by Paramount, PARADISE ISLAND in which she sang a song, and THE TELEGRAPH TRAIL made by Warner Bros. and borrowed from the Burbank studio. That evening Marcelina was going to a beauty salon with Carole after her classes were over, then they were going to dinner (and, if Chris knew Carole, partying). Fallon drove the Englishman down into Hollywood where they went to dinner at the Oriental Gardens restaurant. They had a private booth.

Chris hadn't commented about Marcelina's films until after the meal when they were both drinking oolong tea, relaxed and smoking.

"What I like about THE TELEGRAPH TRAIL," he told Sir Wilbur, "are the close-ups of Marcie's left eye when she's peeking through that hole in the trunk. Once you've seen her eyes, I don't think it's possible ever to forget them."

Sir Wilbur chuckled. "Whoever made that picture, Chris, couldn't have known anything about fighting Indians."

"It's just a movie," Chris admitted. "I was at the wrap party with Marcie for that one over in Burbank. John Wayne, who played the lead, came over to where we were standing and told me I didn't know how lucky I was to have a girl like that to come home to every night. I told him I sure did."

Sir Wilbur smiled. "He reminded me a bit of you, Chris . . . not his looks, but he's tall and lanky like you, and in one scene he swings Marcie around just as I've seen you do, with her hanging onto him, kissing him and laughing. Doesn't it make . . . or, I should say . . . didn't you get a trifle jealous?"

"Tenny . . . it's just a. . . ."

"I know," the Englishman put in, smiling, "just a movie." Then he became very sober as he declared emphatically: "Chris, Marcelina, I am sure, does not realize it. Perhaps not even you do, but it also occurred to me as I was able to see those films of hers you had screened for me. I know she insists she will never make another one. And perhaps Miss Lombard is right. It may be for the best . . . but in a sense what is most important are the films she *has* made. They have captured forever her movements, that remarkably erect carriage of hers, her expressions, the way those long lines across her forehead come out when she frowns or concentrates, her beautiful, triangular face, and, as you say, those remarkable eyes of hers. Were I a poet, I could not capture so indelibly as a moving picture the unco-ordinated yet graceful way she moves, the innocence of her enthusiasm, the beauty, the depth of feeling inside of her, the magical brightness of her soul, the star shine that is in her eyes. I admit I've seen little of the cinema, but it was a bloody riveting experience for me when Marcelina died at the front in THE MAD PARADE, the way her voice faded away to a whisper and then nothing, and how in death her eyes were wide open. And the thought came to me as the last film finished . . . that Western" — he hissed the word — "the one with the close-ups, as you call them, of her left eye . . . there will come a time . . . soon or late . . . when those who have known her and loved her will no longer be here to remember her. What if someone, for whatever reason, fifty years from now, or a hundred . . . should wish to meet Marcelina O'Day . . . to talk with her? Nothing might otherwise be left . . . as so seldom anything is left but the fragments in what we have uncovered of the past. But there she'll be, Chris . . . ever alive . . . moving, breathing, being . . . transfixed for all eternity by a memory that is sharper and more accurate than that of any human being's."

"Please don't tell her that, Tenny," Fallon said, his voice now very low. "It might only bring tears to her eyes . . . if it didn't outright embarrass her."

"On the contrary, Chris, I would rather imagine her response would be to the effect that . . . if such were the case . . . it is unfortunate they weren't better pictures."

"Probably so," Fallon conceded, laughing in spite of himself.

"Only, you see, I wasn't watching those films as films . . . but to see Marcelina . . . so, don't you know, my view is rather more narrow . . . and it does not diminish one jot what I have said."

"Certainly not. But let it be between us . . . for her sake."

"And there I shall keep it," the Englishman promised. "For now . . . but, then, Chris, I wasn't speaking about now . . . or . . . even about us."

"I should tell you, Tenny, when for some of those Westerns Marcie made she had to dye her hair blonde for the rôle . . . like in THE TELEGRAPH TRAIL . . . I was not all that pleased. It's very odd, and I did not really think about it again until the other night when Henry told us that story of Aristophanes's that caused Marcie to thank you. . . . Do you know . . . if I were a sculptor, which I am not . . . but if I were, from the earliest time had I been able to shape in marble or stone the body of my ideal of a woman it would be exactly the same as Marcelina . . . her face, her eyes, her hair the color that it is . . . and something that can only be suggested in such a form . . . her soul. When the dawn was coming . . . that morning on the pampas beyond Haucha . . . it was like I saw Marcelina's face for the first time . . . and I so loved that face, and those blue-gray eyes . . . her very soul." His voice had become hoarse, so deep was his emotion. "It was . . . Tenny . . . it was like she said to you . . . as if I had found her again for the first time since we had parted before ever I was born."

"Please . . . Chris," said the Englishman softly. "Confidence for confidence. Something I haven't told anyone." His light-blue eyes now were bleak, and he laid his bulldog pipe down on the table. "It was while I was in Nepal with Shivapuri Baba . . . that man is truly a saint, Chris, anyway the closest I have ever come to knowing one in my lifetime . . . it was while I was with Shivapuri Baba that I met another of his pupils who had come there to see him . . . oh, she had come a very great distance . . . but it was no surprise that he should have attracted even one from so far away as Nah-Loh-Tah. Her very name reminded *me* of home. You know, I grew up near Exeter, on the sea, and there comes only very rarely a magical time when there is no low tide and, if the light is just right, the sea itself seems to be infused with a presence that is . . . that seems truly miraculous. In the accents of sea-faring men of my homeland it is the time of *na lo' tahd*. If you say it fast and accent the first syllable, it comes out like her name . . . *Nah*-Loh-Tah. I asked her where she came from, but she replied that the name of the place in the language of her people would mean nothing to me. It was not on any map I might see. She did tell me, however, that there was a name for her home that I might recognize . . . she did not write it down, but I did ask her to repeat it, so I could mimic the sounds. She came from a place called Makaron Nyesoeessee . . . something very like that."

"What did you say?" Fallon asked, his attention alert.

"Makaron Nyesoeessee . . . that's exactly how it sounded."

"Tenny, do you know what that means?"

The Englishman became cross. "You know, Chris, I find it bloody frustrating the way both you and Marcelina insist on treating me like a dull schoolboy! You with *eudaimon* and her with that business about the music scale. And now this!"

"What did Marcie tell you about the music

134

scale?" Fallon wondered.

"It's not important, Chris. It's certainly not what I'm talking about here."

"Sorry, Tenny. This woman you met . . . she said she was from some place you might recognize as Makaron Nyesoeessee . . . ?"

"It was more than just *some* woman, Chris," Sir Wilbur said, his tone now lower, more intimate somehow. "We fell profoundly in love. It had never happened to me before . . . no, not in all the years I've been knocking 'round the world. Of course, I was attracted to women before . . . I have not been celibate, you know. But never anything like this. And it happened to both of us . . . the way it happened with you and Marcelina, I imagine. It was something beyond words. Just something both of us knew. The Sun rose for me in the Himalayas of Nepal . . . at Darjeeling . . . the way you say it rose for you and Marcelina outside the lost city of Haucha . . . my God, Chris, even Miss Lombard knows that story . . . about you and Marcelina on the pampas when you two were supposed to be sleeping chastely in camp."

"Was it such a bad thing to have happened?" Fallon asked.

"No, it was not such a bad thing. I'm just thinking about the lack of privacy" — he pronounced the word in the English manner —

"or . . . should I say? . . . the lack of discretion with which you and Marcelina apparently now talk about it, even to your friends. Am I to presume you've told that scandalous story to Thomas and Isabella O'Day?"

"Why not? It was then that we knew, Tenny . . . that we both knew. It was strange up to that time. We knew we were in love before that . . . but something happened after the first time we kissed . . . it was on a promontory overlooking the valley jungle where the Quivaris lived . . . and I had been thinking about the Eumenides. It was as if we were entering the Underworld, and I knew that our only hope of coming out of it together was if I didn't look back at her . . . not once, Tenny, while it was dark. And I didn't . . . not until that morning on the pampas, and that's when we saw each other for the first time."

"Sometimes I think the two of you believe you really are living in another time altogether . . . another century . . . back there some place in Greek antiquity. This is the Twentieth Century, Chris. People don't believe in things like that any more."

"Pardon me, Tenny. I didn't mean to interrupt you."

"Perhaps it's just as well . . . because I *am* sorry, Chris. I actually do have a dim sense that there is something else in this world . . .

something that we cannot see but can only feel . . . and, when we feel it, the effect is really the same as if we know it. To a degree that is what that psychology book of Marcelina's is about that I have been reading since Sunday afternoon . . . that what we feel, what we sense, is quite possibly as real as anything we see or touch. And that is how it was for me and for Nah-Loh-Tah. We sensed ourselves . . . like you say it happened for you and Marcelina . . . as if we had suddenly, inexplicably found each other after having wandered alone for so long."

"What happened?"

"I . . . we wanted to be married . . . to be man and woman together."

"Tenny . . . ! You're married?"

"Yes," the Englishman admitted, smiling shyly. "I took Nah-Loh-Tah down with me from out of the mountains, down onto the plains and over to Peshawar . . . which is near the Khyber Pass, and an Anglican missionary married us there. I had friends in Peshawar in the Anglo-Indian army, and I bought us a bungalow where I hoped we might be able to live together. But . . . well, you know how it is, Chris . . . Nah-Loh-Tah is rather unusual . . . not an East Indian . . . and certainly not English, although her features are actually very English . . . she is just very different than other women . . . deeper . . . and she sings the most beautiful songs . . . she composes them herself." He paused to beat a hand on the table. "Oh, what does it matter what she is! I am in love with her . . . I love everything about her. But I could tell that she was ill at ease . . . miserable. She's like Marcelina, when it comes to her eyes . . . they're not the same color, golden . . . you might say blue-green, or perhaps hazel, but really they are flecked with the color of burnished gold . . . and they came to be sad so much of the time. It almost brings tears when I think about it now. It was probably inevitable . . . as you might say . . . that I should lose her."

"Did she die?" Chris asked in a hushed voice.

"She vanished." The Englishman spoke so quietly Fallon could scarcely hear him. "We had gone on an afternoon picnic with some friends. It came to be dusk. We were on a hill outside that frontier town, and we had decided to watch the Moon rise. Oh, we were a gay crowd, I thought. It was Nah-Loh-Tah who proposed that we play a game of hide-and-seek before riding back to Peshawar. I thought nothing of it, Chris . . . a harmless amusement. But that game was never finished. Nah-Loh-Tah disappeared, and I have not found her since. I searched frantically all that night until dawn, almost, and could not find her. Eventually I enlisted all British India in the search . . . in the jungles and the bazaars, in the walled cities and the teak forests. I searched everywhere for her . . . through all the subterranean channels of that no-white-man's land of Indian native life and even contacted the British Secret Service. I became convinced that she might have been taken captive by an Afghan merchant caravan, moving by camel through the Khyber Pass, and I actually pursued her through all of Afghanistan to the border of Tajikstan, which now is part of the Soviet Union, and where, as a British subject, I could not enter. What was especially trying was, it appears, she had actually passed that way. I found a trader at Feyzabad who had seen her. He was certain of it. A beautiful woman with golden eyes . . . he had seen her, and I could not follow!

"I had once asked Shivapuri Baba about Nah-Loh-Tah . . . when he and I were alone and after I had first met her. Her so-called guardian, Teh-Meh-Tayo, had not wanted to accompany us initially to Peshawar, which I felt was just as well, so he stayed behind. But they had come to Nepal together, Teh-Meh-Tayo and Nah-Loh-Tah. I also know Teh-Meh-Tayo was no longer in Nepal once Nah-Loh-Tah disappeared, so maybe he joined her. I cannot say. At any rate, I had asked Shivapuri Baba early on if he knew where Nah-Loh-Tah was from. His only reply was to ask me where had she said she was from? I told him where she said she was from. I knew it wasn't Latin or Hindi or Sanskrit. I had already taken the time to learn the rudiments of Sanskrit while I was in India. Shivapuri Baba said the origin of those words did not matter . . . that Nah-Loh-Tah had only used those words because where she came from was a place truly without a name I would understand. He said all he could tell me that I would understand is that from whence Nah-Loh-Tah came lightning occurs not in zigzags but in spheres and can be ten thousands of amperes, as we British measure electricity . . . or even more.

" 'How can anyone live in such a place?' I asked him.

" 'Very easily . . . if, when the lightning comes, you keep your eyes tightly closed,' he told me.

" 'Is this place on the Earth?' I asked him.

" 'Yes,' he said, 'but for one such as you impossible to find if you keep your eyes only on the ground, which will appear to be most desolate, or straight ahead, where sometimes everything is only white . . . you must look above . . . to the stars . . . as when one reads the Rig Veda truly.' "

Sir Wilbur shook his head in perplexity, and his light-blue eyes were tormented.

"He said no more?" Fallon prompted gently.

"No. He said what he had told me must be sufficient . . . even for an Englishman. But, damn it all, Chris, I couldn't make it out . . . not completely . . . and she wouldn't tell me a whole lot more herself."

"But you do have the answer, Tenny."

"Don't talk nonsense."

"It's not nonsense. I'm in earnest. Nah-Loh-Tah told you as best she could where she came from. So did Shivapuri Baba."

"Where is it?"

"Makaron Nyesoeessee is ancient Greek, Tenny."

"It is?" He seemed perplexed.

"Those words occur in Hesiod's WORKS AND DAYS. Pindar uses another expression in one of the OLYMPIAN ODES . . . *vasos okeanides* . . . but it means the same thing."

"And you know where this place is?"

"No. The ancient Greeks believed that there were two great bodies of water on the Earth. One is in the center . . . they called it *thalassa* . . . the Romans called it *mare nostrum*."

"The Mediterranean," Sir Wilbur interjected.

"The other is the *okeanides* . . . a river that flows in a circle about the Earth. The *vasos okeanides* . . . the *makaron nyesoeessee* . . . mean literally the Isles of the Blessed. So you see, Tenny, Shivapuri Baba spoke truly. He told you to go in precisely the direction in which . . . come June . . . we will be going . . . to that inviolate, untrodden solitude . . . as Æschylus called it . . . to that barren ground where the air is filled with magnetic electricity greater than any we have ever experienced . . . to the Land of the Midnight Sun . . . and, from the way it sounds, to what are most probably frozen islands in the midst of the perpetual concentric motion of the Arctic Ocean."

"My God, Chris!" Sir Wilbur's voice was trembling. It was the first time Fallon had ever seen the man so moved.

"In what direction was Nah-Loh-Tah going when you followed her?"

The Englishman only nodded.

"And it is best that, indeed, we do wait," Chris continued, "for it may well be a very good thing for *all* of us . . . on *this* particular journey . . . to have Marcelina with us . . . one who is *eudaimon*."

Sir Wilbur remained silent, but there were now tears in his eyes. Chris Fallon fell silent, also, except to summon the Chinese waiter for their check.

That night when Marcelina returned to the *Hacienda* de Ferrar, she wasn't the least shy about it. Her marcel was gone. No severe parts, either down the center of her head or on the side. There was no part at all. Her hair was very thin, so it had not been forced into tight curls, but rather had long waves, falling across her forehead in bangs and, of course, around her ears. Chris and Sir Wilbur were both delighted with the new style.

After Chris and Marcelina went to bed, Chris had a dream from which he started, awake. In it he found himself trekking across a tundra ridge when he came upon the ground nest of a snow bunting, a nest that was woven from musk-ox wool. He tried to stop himself, but he couldn't, and his foot inadvertently crushed a side of the nest and smashed an egg. He looked around desperately to find the mother, but all he could see, off to the side in an easterly direction, was the mouth of a cave toward which he hurried, as if in great fear. Inside the cave it was very dark, and it seemed to go on for miles, the passage opening up inside the ground until the vault of the chamber was not only beyond his touch but seemed of immense proportions. He did not have any source of illumination near at hand, and yet he was able to make his way, and at a very great distance ahead of him he could see, about the same size as the snow bunting egg he had broken, a tiny, oval-shaped window of light. It was toward this that he directed his steps, moving as quickly as he could across the rough floor of the cave. When finally he reached the maw at the other end, he had to pause. There was a remote pool of water on the floor of a valley, surrounded by spires of rock, and near the edge of this pool, as if she had been wading, was Marcelina. She was completely naked. He could see that, and even see her face, although her eyes seemed closed. Suddenly, then, she was closer to him, although he had not moved. Her eyes opened, but she did not say anything. Yet he did hear a voice from somewhere speak words to him. The name Abraxas seemed to resound in his soul, and perhaps it was he who spoke.

Weakness and negation here, eternal
    imagination there.
Here total darkness and damp coolness,
    There only Sun.

It was a warm night. Chris and Marcelina were sleeping naked in their bed, their bodies covered halfway by only a sheet. The windows were open, so the gentle breeze could flow into their bedroom. When Chris awoke from this dream, he rolled toward Marcelina. His hand reached out and lay upon her right hip through the sheet. At his touch, she stirred but did not awake, yet in sleep moving her body ever so slightly closer to him. Reassured by the feel of her body and its nearness, the way the blood seemed to pulse in her and throb when he would touch her, knowing that she still lived and breathed beside him, Chris allowed himself to drift back downward into sleep.

In the two weeks or so that followed, Sir Wilbur was kept busy visiting with people who wanted to meet him, or see him again. He was even interviewed by a reporter from the Los Angeles *Times* who drove out to the valley to meet with him at the *Hacienda* de Ferrar. No, he had no plans of finding yet another lost city, he told this reporter, but would be going to San Francisco presently to visit his old friend, Luis Valera, who was now professor emeritus in archeology. (The details of their present journey Sir Wilbur very much wished to be kept as quiet as possible, and so Carole Lombard, Will and Betty Rogers, and everyone else who had been let in on it had already been asked to keep their knowledge confidential.) No, he had not first come to know Marceline Day as a result of having seen her in a motion picture. He had known her before she ever was Marceline Day. No, he did not plan to appear in a Paramount travelogue produced by Chris Fallon. No, he hoped Will Rogers would not write about him in his regular newspaper column and actually would prefer that he did not, and that this reporter wouldn't. No, he did not regard Carole Lombard as the funniest comedienne he had ever met but, to be sure, one of the most profoundly honest human beings he had encountered in all of his world travels, and surely one of the most beautiful of all God's creatures. He did pass on his impression that, although the British government appeared rather hesitant about the matter, in his opinion the Empire of Japan had designs on all of Asia and, once Japan had conquered it, country by country, it would be looking across the Pacific to the United States.

Sometimes during the day Sir Wilbur stayed alone at the *Hacienda* de Ferrar while Marcelina and Chris were gone about their business. Rosa Caldero and Linda Ruiz might be elsewhere in the house, and Santiago Cruz out somewhere on the grounds, but the Englishman pretty much kept to himself in the music room or the study. He had time to read, and almost all of the books he did read came from Marcelina's shelves. Once he

finished PSYCHOLOGY OF THE UNCON-
SCIOUS, he read *La Recherche de l'Absolu*
and *La Peau de chagrin* by Balzac, THE
NARROW CORNER by Maugham (which
he admitted to having particularly enjoyed for
the way it portrayed how precious freedom
can be for a woman, or for that matter for
anyone). From Chris's shelves he read NEW
LANDS by Otto Sverdrup and FOUR
YEARS IN THE WHITE NORTH by Donald MacMillan. When it was time for him to
depart, he had not quite finished this last,
concerned with an expedition in 1913–1919
to reach, map the coastline, and explore the
interior of what Commander Peary had called
Crocker Land, the mountains of which he
had sighted in 1906 as being to the northwest
of Ellesmere Island. Although MacMillan
had no doubt that Crocker Land existed, his
expedition had been unable to locate it during
all the time they had searched for it. However,
in the entry for April 21, 1913 MacMillan had
noted in his diary how Green, one of the crew,
was no sooner out of the igloo than he had
come running back, calling in through the
opening:

"We have it!" Following Green, we ran
to the top of the highest mound. There
could be no doubt about it. Great

heavens! what a land! Hills, valleys, snow-capped peaks extending through at least one hundred and twenty degrees of the horizon. I turned to Pee-Ah-Wah-To anxiously and asked him toward which point we had better lay our course. After critically examining the supposed landfall for a few minutes, he astounded me by replying that he thought it was *poo-jok* (mist). E-Took-A-Shoo offered no encouragement, saying: "Perhaps it is." Green was still convinced that it must be land. . . .

Yet, as the MacMillan party had proceeded, they had found that the landscape before them gradually changed in its appearance and that it actually varied as the Sun swung around on its Arctic course, only for the vision to disappear altogether. Sir Wilbur was convinced that this time it would be found. Chris urged him to take the book along, which finally he agreed to do, promising to send it back by post from San Francisco. He would again be staying at the St. Francis, as he always did when in that city.

It was also during the days of solitude at the *Hacienda* de Ferrar that Sir Wilbur found an absurd thing was happening to him. He found himself worrying about his immortal soul. On the face of it, there was no reason at all for him to have such a worry. He was, on the whole, a moral person, loyal to his king and his nation (although he no longer liked going back to England even to visit), and many regarded his life as exemplary of a modern explorer. Yet in these moments of worry in his solitude, Sir Wilbur realized that he had increasingly come to regard the world not so much according to a moral frame of reference but as a mystical realm. He found himself wondering if the sum of a row of victories over many years and in many countries might ultimately be a defeat? The middle-aged Sir Wilbur Tennington wondered just how much he had fulfilled the young Wilbur Tennington's wishes and ambitions? It could well be, he admitted, that he had gained the whole world. Yet, here was a stately knight of the British crown, a holder of the Order of Merit of the British Empire, one who was a lord in his native land, and this worldly wise older man now found himself confronted by the naïve younger man who had first come of age on the family estate near Exeter, and this younger man seemed to be asking him gravely, perhaps even with a touch of bitterness, what in all this had he really profited? Had not something somewhere become lost to him? Nah-Loh-Tah, to be sure. But were he to find her again? What then? And what, oh, what, had become of Wilbur Tennington?

The day Sir Wilbur was to leave — Henry King would be flying him from Los Angeles to San Francisco in his personal airplane — Marcelina could not accompany him and Chris to the airport. She had classes to attend that were very important since it was now near the end of the term. She did have time, however, to drink a milk shake with them at breakfast. She had with her a small package which she put on the table near the Englishman, and instructed him very precisely that he was not to open it until he was alone in his hotel room that night.

Before Marcelina left, Chris accompanied her out to the foyer where, as he embraced her, he bent over so his hands could creep sensuously down her very straight back until they cupped the exquisitely rounded globes of her backside through the white, pleated skirt she wore. Then, holding her bottom where it met her thighs, he lifted her up about six inches into the air, and her hands with those long, tapered, strong fingers were then around Chris's neck and her head was pulled back so she could still see him.

"I have the whole world in my hands," he told her.

Marcelina laughed. "And as of this morning it weighs a hundred and five pounds."

They kissed while he was still holding her like that and she was clinging to him, and then he kissed her neck and nestled his face in the beauty of her.

Sir Wilbur, who prided himself on being somewhat distant from sentiment, except when he thought of Nah-Loh-Tah, having witnessed this embrace, having seen over all of these days how deeply and inexhaustibly these two were in love with each other, suddenly felt very alone, even after Marcelina gave him a huge kiss and hug before she gathered her school books and notebooks and, saluting Sir Wilbur in proper military fashion until they should meet again, went merrily out the front door.

Chapter Six

The night following Sir Wilbur's departure from the *Hacienda* de Ferrar was for Marcelina one of protracted concentration. She was intent on completing her major term paper for the semester, a comparative study of the religious, metaphysical, and ceremonial practices of the ancient Incas of her native land and the Hopi Indians of the North American Southwest. Chris had been working at the studio, preparing the release version of a travelogue on spring in the Mojave Desert, a project that had involved him earlier in supervising the location photography and which was now in the final editing stage before voice narration. Pleased to free his mind from what he had been doing during the day, he joined Marcelina in the study and read again the collected fragments of Herakleitos which she had been consulting while working on her term paper.

They took a break about ten in the evening. Marcelina brewed coffee in the kitchen and brought two mugs of it back to the study, stirred with honey as they both liked it.

"Just typing out the footnotes . . . that's all that's left, Chris," she said. She seemed happy and relieved. She had been working at the flat-top desk before the windows, but now sat in an armchair near to Chris. "There is one thing, though, that I have been thinking about. You know, in that forty-fifth fragment in which Herakleitos says that you cannot ever find the boundaries of the human soul? . . . he concludes by saying that the boundaries cannot be found because the *logon* is so deep. I know *logon* is in the accusative declined from *logos,* and in this context *logos* must be Herakleitos's way of saying meaning, or sense. Don't you think so?"

"As far as I know of ancient Greek, I take *logos* to be . . . depending on the context . . . either the word by which an inward thought is expressed, or the inward thought itself . . . or better, Marcie, the meaning of the inward thought . . . or in the broadest sense . . . yes, *meaning.*"

"Then," said Marcelina very intensely, "wasn't Saint Jerome less than correct when at the beginning of the Gospel According to Saint John he translated *logos* into Latin as *verbum?*"

"I've always thought so," Chris agreed. "I have always taken that opening verse to be . . . 'In the beginning was meaning, and meaning was with God, and meaning was God.' "

She collapsed backward into her chair, smiling hugely. "I'm so glad we agree. I was a little worried about it . . . in my term paper."

"Did you really find a great many parallels between Herakleitos and what the Incas believed and the Hopis?"

"Especially when it comes to the Underworld," she replied. "You know that the Incas believed that it was during the three days of the winter solstice . . . during the festival of Capac Raimi . . . that the souls of the dead returned to this middle world. Well, the Hopis believe the same thing. On the earthen floor of the kiva a small fire burns that gives light only for ceremonies, and near it is the *sipapu*, a deep aperture in the ground that leads to the Underworld. Usually the *sipapu* is closed off by a stone, but the dancers will occasionally stamp on it, so that the shades in the Underworld can hear them. But there is a time . . . an awesome time during the occasion of the winter solstice . . . when the rock is thrown back from the *sipapu*. At that time the shades of the departed are allowed to rise up out of the depths and mingle with those still living . . . and it is during that time the Hopis hold an initiation ceremony for young male tribal members . . . just as the Incas did during Capac Raimi."

"My God, Marcie, the parallels are that close?"

"In many ways . . . yes, they are."

"How do you account for it? You don't think . . . well, maybe, that . . . ?"

"Contact?"

"Well . . . yes."

"No."

Marcelina reached for a cigarette from the package she had put on the small table beside her chair. Chris reached for his lighter, rose, and lit it for her. It was something she often liked — having someone light her cigarette. Chris took a cigarette from her package and joined her.

"But where does Herakleitos fit into all this?" he asked, expelling smoke and lifting his coffee cup.

"I was reading him to learn what he teaches of the Underworld. It is pretty much the same place for the Greeks, the Incas, and the Hopis . . . maybe for everyone. But . . . mostly . . . I was puzzling over that passage where Herakleitos says that Hades, the ruler of the Underworld and the brother of Zeus, is the same as Dionysos, the god of fertility . . . *oytos de Aides kai Dionysos.* How can they be the same? I wondered. Then it came to me. Dionysos moves among the living and for him the *phallos* is the living representation of fertility because of what comes from it . . . while, for Hades, because his eyes are always deflected and because he is a shade, having no substance, fertility means the creation of more spirituality. In that way, they really are reflections of each other . . . the one physical, corporeal, *thymos* . . . the other spiritual, incorporeal, *psyche* . . . they are the same, only one exists in the world of the daylight, and the other exists in the world of the night . . . drinking deeply of the one creates new physical life . . . drinking deeply of the other creates more soul . . . more *imagination*."

"I hope you aren't making any kind of explicit sexual reference in your term paper."

"And why not?"

"Because you might offend your professor."

"I don't think so, Chris. She was once a witness in a kiva to the ceremony during which the seed corn is blessed. Each of the four corn collectors, as he mounts the ladder to leave the kiva, pauses four times and simulates sexual intercourse. My professor says she happened to be there at the same time as an official from the Bureau of Indian Affairs. That official said the ceremony was indecent and should not be something done with children present . . . that it must be stopped. The Hopi priest who was present overheard this remark and said to this official that, if he felt this way, how would he wish for children to be taught about the beginnings of new life? Those corn collectors are sacred messengers, and the act is being performed in a sacred place. How better for children to understand that the creation of life is a *sacred* act? That priest had also heard about white children . . . about how, when they talk about sexuality, they laugh. He told the official that children who first learn of it in the kiva do not laugh about it."

"OK . . . you know what you're doing. But twenty years ago, when I was in college, I doubt if I could have gotten away with so much as a single sexual reference . . . unless I said what I had to say in Latin." He laughed. "You know, for the longest time it was believed that no matter how nonsensical . . . if you said it in Latin . . . it was supposed to be regarded with solemn respect. And never, under any circumstances, did a girl ever so much as mention procreation or anything connected with it . . . not out loud . . . and certainly not in class."

"All the girls you went to school with must have been pussy-wussies."

"I was probably regarded as one, too . . . being so interested in zoology and field work to find specimens."

"Probably," she said, smiling very broadly and exhaling tobacco smoke.

"I don't suppose Tenny said anything to you about the woman he married in India."

"Tenny is old-fashioned, Chris. That's not the kind of thing he would discuss with me . . . perhaps not with any woman. I wonder if he'll mention it to *Tío* Luis?"

"He'll be in San Francisco a couple of weeks. That's a lot of time. He might." Chris paused a moment to reflect. "But possibly not. In a way, I'm surprised Tenny even told me about it. And the whole business is so strange. I don't doubt for a moment that he's sincere when he talks about how much they were in love with each other . . . but, maybe, it was more one-sided than he realized."

"Why do you say that?"

"Well, if this Nah-Loh-Tah really was as much in love with him, as he obviously was with her, she wouldn't have vanished like that, would she? Propose a game of hide-and-seek and use it to disappear? Every time I think about it, I can't help but reflect that, if she were in love with him, her disappearance could not have been voluntary. Maybe Tenny was right, when he thought there was something more behind it."

"Like what?"

"She might have been kidnapped."

"Don't you think that's a little melodramatic?"

"Perhaps . . . but remember that character you played in THE MYSTERY TRAIN? Look what happened to her?"

"She was going to prison. She saw a chance to escape . . . lose her identity . . . and she took it."

"It could've been something like that with Nah-Loh-Tah."

Marcelina laughed softly. "Chris, you've got to stop going to movies. That plot was pretty dumb . . . at least, that's what you said at the time, when you saw the picture."

"I don't remember saying that."

"Well, you did. I remember I tried to defend what happened to me in that picture . . . until I couldn't any more . . . because by that time I was laughing about it, too."

"You're missing the point of the whole thing, Marcie. If Nah-Loh-Tah really was in love with Tenny, why would she just disappear?"

"I can think of a couple of good reasons."

"You can? I'd like to hear just one."

"All I know about it is what you've told me."

"You know everything I know."

"Well, I know you said Tenny thought she was miserable . . . when they were living in Peshawar."

"Yes, and that's another thing that doesn't

make any sense. If she was so much in love with him, as he was with her, why would she be so miserable?"

"From what you've told me, Nah-Loh-Tah is not an Englishwoman . . . and not an East Indian."

Chris nodded his head.

"But . . . don't you see? . . . she was being made to live as if she *were* an Englishwoman?"

"If she loved him, would that matter?"

"It might . . . it might matter a lot. Did she feel she was loved for who she was? Or was she being made to live a kind of life that could only make her miserable? We can't know what was going through her mind. But she wouldn't be the first person who found herself in an impossible place and . . . and did the only thing she felt she could do."

"Going back to her home?" Chris asked in a mildly sarcastic tone.

The lines came out across Marcelina's forehead, and her blue-gray eyes seemed to flash in the lamplight. "Do you remember how miserable I was when we were on the *Sea Queen* . . . because *Tío* Don Esteban wanted me to get him a copy of the map to Haucha? . . . how I told you at the time I wasn't any longer certain I wanted to go at all? . . . when I asked you about betrayal? . . . and you told me that in life we understand only half the story

160

. . . and that understanding only that much, or less of it . . . is not really such a bad thing?"

"Yes," he said very softly.

"Well, you do not know very much at all about what happened in India . . . and I know even less. But I know what it is to be miserable. I have been that. And sometimes flight is the only thing you can think to do. But that is wrong. It's like some people who, when they want to go to sleep at night, try to think of a long row of llamas . . . or, in this country . . . a long row of sheep, passing through a gate . . . and how they all go in one direction, and you should allow your thoughts to go along with them. That, too, is wrong. You should, instead, think of a very deep well . . . one as deep as Herakleitos says the soul is deep . . . so deep that it has no boundaries. In the bottom of that well . . . probably just in the middle of it . . . there arcs up a spring of water, running out in every direction, like the rays of a star. Now, if you can make your thoughts run out with that water, not in one direction, but equally on all sides, you will fall asleep.

"There seems . . . in this world . . . there are only two roads before a person. The one is that which Tenny has followed for so long . . . certainly all the years I have known him . . . the road on which you ask . . . what am I to do the next moment? . . . or tonight? . . . or tomorrow? But the other road . . . that is the one on which you ask . . . what did God mean by creating the Earth, the sea, the desert, the wind? . . . and, if you are a man, what did He mean by creating woman? . . . and if you are a woman, what did He mean by creating man? . . . and what did He mean by creating music? . . . and what did He mean by creating life itself?"

"Are you saying that you believe Tenny is only dreaming?"

"Not at all," she said, smiling ever so slightly. "He does not know how to dream yet. I think he was beginning to learn how to dream when . . . as you say . . . he followed Nah-Loh-Tah through all of Afghanistan . . . but mostly . . . the man who has stayed with us so long this time . . . the world is still drinking him in. He has gone to its heart . . . and, as you say, when we ascended into the sky to find Haucha . . . because in the Underworld everything is *upside down* . . . he has even been down to the Underworld. But he is not dreaming yet. I believe he is praying to God. And it is only after you have finished praying to God . . . that is when, truly, you begin to dream. But the man who just left is still only praying . . . very loudly and very vigorously, Chris . . . and he is doing it with all the energy of an elephant copulating. But, once he concludes his prayer . . . then, I believe, he might be able to dream."

"But can you ever dream of the same person . . . or the same place . . . twice?" Chris asked.

"Yes, yes," said Marcelina. "That is the greatest favor of all that God grants to the souls of dreamers. He allows us to come back again . . . maybe only after a long time . . . but we are able to come back again to the same place as once we visited in an old dream . . . and, sometimes, to the same person. It is, then, that our hearts are truly full. And sometimes the places or the persons or the events of a dream are really a vision . . . a vision that isn't caused by anything in the world of the daylight, but which somehow actually corresponds to something that exists in the world of the daylight that wasn't known or suspected before. The way Johannes Kepler dreamed that the planets revolve in elliptical courses. For centuries . . . back to before recorded history, even . . . it was believed that celestial motion occurred in the most perfect of forms . . . in circles. Kepler dreamed otherwise . . . and, when he worked it out mathematically, he found that for the first time, ever, he could predict where a planet would be at a given time . . . once it was understood that their courses were not circles but ellipses

163

with the points of a curve and major and minor axes." She paused and looked at him somewhat quizzically for a moment. "You posed the right question to Tenny, Chris, when you asked him in what direction had Nah-Loh-Tah gone? Let us both hope . . . should he be granted the grace to dream the same dream, even if in a different place . . . that this time he shall be on the right road."

Sir Wilbur had flown many times in airplanes, but this time he was able to sit in the cockpit alongside Henry King on the flight to San Francisco. Visibility was excellent, and the route the film director had charted took them over the Sierra Madres and along the Coast Range. The plane landed at the Oakland Airport.

Sir Wilbur felt for the great first leg of this journey to the Arctic it would be necessary to fly, but it had to be a very special type of aircraft. In this regard, Henry King had proven most helpful. The film director knew Barry Kirk, a millionaire businessman in San Francisco, who owned an airplane that should be ideal. It was kept in a hangar at the Oakland Airport, and Kirk had suggested the two of them look it over upon their arrival. They could meet later at his bungalow office in the Kirk Building to discuss the details, should

Sir Wilbur wish to charter it. Through what might only be described as the most extreme good fortune, Mark Dworski, the pilot for the U.S. Geological Survey under the direction of Dr. Paul Ramsey, whom the Englishman had met in Peru at the time of the discovery of Haucha, was now a free-lance pilot working out of Oakland. In fact, it was Dworski who regularly flew Barry Kirk and his family back and forth to Hawaii where the businessman maintained a second home.

The pilot was at the hangar when the two men entered, having been given the approximate time of their arrival by Barry Kirk. Dworski was a man now in his late thirties, with a narrow mustache he had not had the last time Sir Wilbur had seen him. They all shook hands, and then Dworski began extolling the virtues of the Douglas Dolphin airplane owned by Barry Kirk. It was actually a high-wing cantilever monoplane amphibian flying-boat, developed originally from the Sinbad, and a model still being used extensively by the U.S. Coast Guard. In fact, President Franklin D. Roosevelt had owned one since June, 1933, using it as a five-passenger luxury transport for the First Family. Kirk's Douglas Dolphin, named *Janet* after his wife, who had formerly been a deputy district attorney for the City of San Francisco and was now the mother of two children, was powered by two three-hundred-and-fifty horsepower Wright R975-3 radial-piston engines and had been flown for the first time in April, 1931. The two radial engines, driving tractor propellers, were mounted on a complex strut arrangement atop the wing with a span of sixty feet and a total wing area of five hundred and sixty-two feet. In terms of performance, the plane had a maximum speed of one hundred and forty miles per hour and a cruising speed of one hundred and nineteen miles. The service ceiling was fourteen thousand, two hundred feet. Ordinarily, as manufactured, the *Janet* had had a range of five hundred and fifty miles, but Barry Kirk had had additional gasoline tanks installed to enable the plane to fly the distance from Oakland to Honolulu. Sir Wilbur described their intended itinerary in the Arctic. After refueling at Point Barrow in Alaska Territory and dropping off all their gear there, they would load additional fuel to be flown to Victoria Island to make a fuel dump at that point, then fly back to Point Barrow to retrieve all the gear including the dogs, and then fly to Victoria Island, again to refuel, before finally flying to Ellesmere Island. Both of these islands were possessions beyond the Barren Grounds within the territory of the Dominion of Canada and at the farthest point of their destination they would be within six degrees of the Geographical North Pole. Dworski said, based on the approximate mileage of these various flights and given the additional capacity of the *Janet* for transporting fuel, he could not foresee an operational problem.

The *Janet* had both wheel and flat landing gear. The flat landing gear was comprised of main units attached to the hull by hinged Vee-struts and to the undersurface of the wings by oleo legs. The *Janet* had a tail wheel, located at the rear of the second hull step. In flight or for operations from the water, Dworski explained, the main wheels could be retracted above the water line. The pilot, in this case Dworski who had expressed his enthusiasm to make the trip, and the co-pilot, Chris Fallon, would be seated side by side in a fully enclosed position just forward of the wing's leading edge, and the passenger cabin was located immediately behind them. There was room for six passengers, but Sir Wilbur stated that only four of the passenger seats would be occupied in transit. The various storage areas should also be sufficient for their needs. As Sir Wilbur pointed out, at Juneau they would be taking on a team of dogs, and Chris would presently be shipping up a sled of his own design for overland travel. Even more importantly, Chris had been to the Arctic before. Based on that previous experience and from a lesson he had derived from a careful study of Commander George Nares's expedition into the Arctic, in which Nares had ignored the advice of previous explorers to adopt the kind of snow house used by Eskimos during the winter and had met with disaster, Chris had designed two tents shaped in the form of small igloos, and he was having them custom-made. Although these canvas igloos would rise no more than four feet from the perpendicular when pitched and be held up by a single center pole and a series of curved spokes, they should withstand any high velocity winds with the same imperviousness as an igloo. The inner circumference of these tents, when spread on the ground, would comprise a circle of seventy-eight inches — after all, Chris was over six feet and Sir Wilbur six feet, while Marcelina, Luis, and Ramón were all shorter — so they should accommodate everyone for sleeping, although conditions would be somewhat cramped, with Chris and Marcelina sharing one tent, Sir Wilbur, Luis, and Ramón the other. In Sir Wilbur's tent, the three men would have to sleep in the form of a human triangle, whereas Chris and Marcelina could sleep one on either side of the center pole. Comfort wasn't really a primary consideration in the design, but rather ability to withstand adverse weather conditions — six eighteen-inch steel stakes would be used to anchor each of these tents to the ground or ice surface — and all in all they would be of light weight and easy to transport. There was only one significant problem the expedition might encounter for which they would not be prepared beforehand. Should there be a serious error in Sir Wilbur's geographical calculations and should the settlement they were seeking be separated by water from Ellesmere Island, they would be without a means for marine navigation. They would have no choice but to return to the base camp they were to establish where they landed on Ellesmere and try an aerial approach with the Douglas Dolphin. The fact that the *Janet* was capable of landing on either land or water would immensely facilitate such an eventuality.

Sir Wilbur thanked Dworski for his willingness to meet them so the *Janet* could be inspected, and the Englishman definitely engaged him for the expedition. Sir Wilbur estimated that the time required for the round trip would be three months, which is what Chris had told Paramount would be his time away from the travelogue production unit.

Henry King's airplane was a single prop and much smaller than the *Janet*. Conversation between the two on the flight to Oakland, while certainly not impossible, had still been difficult to maintain regularly above the roar of the engine. They would have ample time for talk, however, that evening at dinner. Since Barry Kirk was an acquaintance of Henry King's and King would be accompanying the Englishman into the city to meet with him, Sir Wilbur insisted that the film director stay overnight as his guest at the St. Francis. King accepted the offer provided Sir Wilbur allowed him to pay for their dinner at an excellent restaurant he knew in Chinatown called the Empress of China.

Henry King helped carry one of Sir Wilbur's two suitcases through the airport terminal, and outside they hailed a taxicab and were driven into San Francisco. At the St. Francis Hotel they checked into their respective rooms and, afterward, had a late lunch in the hotel dining room before going to the Kirk Building on California Street. The taxi they took passed from Geary Street to Market Street, where it followed the intricate streetcar tracks for a block before turning left into Montgomery. Presently they were in the San Francisco financial district, where the day was coming to an end. The huge buildings of trust companies, investment houses, and banks stood as solemn fortresses on either side, and some of the doorways had already shut their forbidding bronze gates. Sir Wilbur's eyes read window signs — THE YOKOHAMA BANK and THE SHANGHAI TRADING COMPANY — which made him acutely aware of the presence of the Orient here in the City by the Golden Gate. Their taxi drew up before a twenty-story office building, and the two alighted.

The Kirk Building was architecturally impressive. The pure white lobby was immaculate; the elevator girls were trim and pretty in neat uniforms; and the elevator starter was as resplendent in his uniform as an admiral.

"All the way," Henry King remarked to the operator as they entered an elevator car. When the door *whooshed* shut, he commented to the Englishman. "You'll find Barry Kirk a slightly older version of Tommy Beck."

"Tommy Beck?" Sir Wilbur inquired in some bewilderment. He had responded the same way at the airport as they were leaving the hangar when the film director had remarked that Mark Dworski reminded him of an older version of Bob Steele, an actor in low-budget Westerns.

"A promising young player on the Fox lot," King clarified about Tommy Beck.

As the Englishman nodded, he thought to himself that King's use of motion picture personalities as a key to physical identification was something a lot of people who worked in Hollywood seemed constantly to do, as if life were somehow like casting a motion picture and that, somehow, the cinema supplied one with a modern iconography that had as much meaning and substance as once had been attached to the Olympians. *Thank goodness*, he mused, *Chris and Marcelina don't do it.*

The meeting with Barry Kirk was held in his bungalow office which had massive windows overlooking the city. The millionaire explained that this office used to be part of his bachelor penthouse, but that, since the children were born, he had moved to a home on Nob Hill. Sir Wilbur was pleased to tell Kirk that the *Janet* would perfectly suit the needs of the expedition to the Arctic, provided there could be installed a better heating system. The Englishman wrote out a check for five thousand pounds and added that, if Kirk would approve, he would personally pay for the installation of the heating system.

Barry Kirk, who was about six feet tall and slender, with brown eyes and brown hair, graying only slightly at the temples, thought Sir Wilbur's offer for a three-month charter was splendid but insisted that he would see to the installation of a better heating system himself as his contribution. He was delighted to know that the Englishman remembered Mark Dworski and went on to assure Sir Wilbur that the man had proven an excellent pilot in all kinds of weather, including typhoon-like winds they had once encountered on a trip off the coast of Mexico. It was Sir Wilbur's intention to embark on Friday, June 22nd. By then all the arrangements along their line of travel should have been made. The meeting concluded amicably.

Henry King wanted to be at the airport early the next morning in order to fly back to Los Angeles where he had an important casting meeting in the afternoon. That night at dinner would be the last time they would have to talk and, not knowing what the future held for either of them, perhaps the last time they would see one another. The tall, debonair film director was a recent convert to Roman Catholicism and, probably as a result of having solved his own personal quest for a faith, evinced little interest in the Rig Veda, Hinduism, or Sir Wilbur's ultimate reasons for wishing to have the Fallons join him on this journey to the Arctic. The Englishman, on the other hand, had had quite a time meeting motion-picture personalities in southern California as well as having seen more films in two weeks than he had seen in the previous eight years.

"You know, Henry," Sir Wilbur remarked as they sat across from each other in a private booth at the Empress of China, "before I went to the Indian Empire, and more especially to Nepal in the Himalayas, some four years ago, films were still silent. Now that there are talking pictures, it struck me more than ever that the cinema is becoming the embodiment of the collective dreams for human beings everywhere. Even though Chris reminds me all the time that 'it's just a movie,' I imagine for a lot of people . . . perhaps more all the time . . . movies are more real than dreams and . . . if you'll forgive me for saying so . . . maybe more real than reality."

"Hardly that, Sir Wilbur," the director said, smiling gently. "I've been making movies since almost the beginning, and all they really are is a way of telling a story . . . but in a way that probably now reaches more people than any other form of storytelling. A principle I use when I am directing a film is to reveal for the camera only as much of the set where the action is to occur as necessary to provide a background to what the characters are doing or saying. The function of a set is to provide atmosphere. It must never distract from the actors and what is happening. The final test is that what is shown is convincing to a viewer."

"But my point," returned the Englishman,

"is that any film . . . taken as a whole . . . is basically an illusion . . . a dream . . . but one shared by many people who are experiencing it at the same time. Afterward, they even talk about it . . . as if it were somehow an experience they had shared with others. But it is an illusion. Miss Lombard assured me of that."

"She tends to have . . . to be perfectly frank, Sir Wilbur . . . rather a filthy mouth . . . even in mixed company."

"Perhaps." Sir Wilbur chuckled. "But I find her the most realistic person I've met in years."

"Realistic?"

"She knows the difference between appearances and reality . . . and she is uncanny in being able to see people for what they are. In fact, I found it curious that so great a realist should work in what basically is a business of creating illusions. I met Lincoln Perry when I visited Will Rogers at his ranch . . . he happened to be out there when I was . . . and that man does not talk in person at all the way he does in films . . . like DAVID HAREM . . . which you made it possible for me to see."

"Certainly not," Henry King agreed. "When he's playing a rôle in front of the camera, he's doing what the script and the director expect him to do . . . in order to be the character he is playing. On the screen he's generally a ne'erdo-well, while off screen he's quite a wealthy man."

"Were you serious the other night at dinner when you proposed to star Marcelina in one of your films?"

"Well," replied the director very slowly, even a bit cautiously, "part of that was true. Marcelina Fallon is one of the most inherently religious persons I know . . . outside the clergy. She has a profound and sometimes penetrating intelligence . . . besides being a rather attractive woman by Hollywood standards. However, when it comes to her film career, you must remember that Marceline Day began in silent pictures, where everything depended on facial expressions, the eyes especially, and emotion was conveyed largely by means of physical movement. Her first years in pictures she was an ingénue . . . and I know, as she says, it was just something that happened to her, and not something she had chosen to do. But, especially while she was at M-G-M, and later even, most of her best screen work was in light melodramas and comedies. By the time sound pictures came in, she was lacking in the one area that really was considered an asset . . . a good deal of experience on the legitimate stage . . . in the theater. At the same time, in terms of her chronological age, she was considered a little old to continue being an ingénue, and, I think, some thought she was not sufficiently talented to become a leading lady. I have a theory about that. Marcelina lacks that sense of the void, between the brain and the heart, if you will, that you find in the finest actresses on the screen. Her choices after sound were really smaller character rôles, or playing again in low-budget Westerns and melodramas."

Obviously, the director had become somewhat embarrassed speaking so bluntly about a woman he personally admired and regarded as a friend, but he also felt obliged to explain the inner workings of the American film industry system to the Englishman, something perhaps not actually all that comprehensible even to some who worked in it.

"Now, the rôle I had in mind," he continued, "and which I mentioned the night of the dinner the Fallons gave for you . . . would require primarily what are Marceline Day's strongest qualities . . . her strikingly beautiful eyes and her vivid, physical expressiveness . . . it would not be greatly dependent on dialogue . . . which would be, I believe, ideally at a minimum. The only other actress in my experience who has eyes to compare with Marcelina's is Vola Vale whom I directed in a film released in Nineteen Nineteen. Vola has dark eyes, but they are as large and expressive as

Marcelina's. But she's no longer working in pictures and would be too old, anyway. Understand, Sir Wilbur, I was not offended when Marcelina insisted she has definitely retired." His face took on a rather solemn expression. "I cannot begin to tell you what an extraordinary human being I believe Marcelina Fallon to be . . . in fact, both of the Fallons. Marcelina has a resilience, an inner fortitude, and . . . if you will . . . a spirit that can face personal adversity and overcome it. She might . . . as, God knows, a number of other actresses who found themselves in the same situation after sound came in . . . have turned to alcohol, or stronger means, as an escape from what they could only regard as an intolerable reversal in their lives. If that had happened, Chris might have been disillusioned with the marriage and sought an outlet in the company of other women."

"Not those two!" Sir Wilbur protested.

"Actually, a scenario like that is rather commonplace in Hollywood, I'm afraid. But in the Fallons you have two people who are secure in themselves, and in Marcelina especially a person who has perhaps too much soul . . . as she might put it . . . to languish in self-pity of that kind. Above all, they have each other, and, I imagine, if she were given the choice between living with a void inside of her, or the fulfillment she has obviously found in her marriage, she would have it no different, no matter what her career might have been. When it comes to Chris, I suspect he would make any personal sacrifice he felt necessary in order for Marcelina to be fulfilled in herself . . . yes, even if that would mean he might not be able to hold her to himself. To me that is the truest love." He paused and smiled. "That story I told by Aristophanes is pagan nonsense, of course, and rather pale when compared to what we know from the true faith, but in portraying some people . . . especially those in love stories in films . . . I do believe it *seems* true."

"Yes," admitted Sir Wilbur, "both Marcelina and Chris were quite taken with that notion. Indeed, although it may sound absurd to admit it . . . in their case I really do think it might be something very like that. I know the modern trend seems to be to treat love in a more cynical fashion . . . and everyone, I believe, is aware to some degree of the numerous marriages and divorces in Hollywood. Will Rogers did have a point saying how unusual it was for Marcelina to come out of pictures married to the same man she was married to when she started in them."

Henry King laughed. "Instability, I fear, is more the rule when it comes to lasting marriages. Yet, Sir Wilbur, maybe that's what it takes to be a great actor . . . to be more in love with yourself than you would dare to be with any other human being. But there is a price you have to pay for it. Marcelina wasn't willing to make that sacrifice . . . and, if she were, you realize, she wouldn't be the Marcelina we know."

He paused for a moment, and then regarded the Englishman with a surprising gentleness. "As a convert to Catholicism, I am in a somewhat different situation than someone who was born in the true faith . . . the way Marcelina was . . . and so she has never known what it is like to exist outside of the true faith. In fact, I've talked with her enough about the subject to say that it hasn't occurred to her how many of the things she believes are not really consistent with accepted Church doctrine. But, knowing her, such inconsistencies also don't seem to bother her greatly." He smiled softly before continuing. "But for me it has been somewhat different. I would never argue with her about any of it, but I find myself concerned sometimes about her spiritual welfare."

Sir Wilbur had been in India, and he had come to think long and hard about what is true and what may be only illusion. He was perhaps too much the gentleman, certainly too deeply steeped in Old World courtesy, to voice his innermost impression — that there might be more meaning in life and the universe than was imagined by the limited purview of the true faith. So . . . he said nothing more and changed the subject.

Once back at the hotel, having bid Henry King *adieu* and gone to his room, he decided the time had come to open the parcel Marcelina had given him that morning. He had known at the time that it must be a book because of its shape and the feel of it through the wrapping paper, but now to his astonishment he found the parcel contained the very book for which he had been searching so long without success — THE ARCTIC HOMELAND IN THE VEDAS by B. G. Tilak. There was a note inside, written on one of the small, pink sheets of Marcelina's monogrammed stationery.

Marcelina Fallon

May 31st, 1934

Dear "Tenny" —

I found this book, which you have so wanted, at the residence of a dealer in rare books. Chris agreed that it should be a surprise. So here it is!

Also, in doing research for my term paper on the Incas and the Hopis, I came across the following remark by Herakleitos that, somehow, seems prescient to this journey we are all about to undertake:

Those who are awake share a unified and common cosmos, but, when asleep and dreaming, each one of us is turned away from that cosmos and spirals downward into his own soul.

Love,
Marcelina

That night Wilbur Tennington had a dream which, for the first time in years, he was able to remember in detail the next morning. He found himself back in the valley of the Quivaris, the native tribe that had lived in caves along the bottom of the great plateau. On top, on the other side of that great plateau, there was a deep gorge. On the opposite side of that gorge, reaching upward into the sky, was the Inca city of Haucha, named by them for the planet Saturn. There seemed to be some sort of costume party going on among the Quivaris. They were all dressed in ceremonial garb once worn by the Incas, and everywhere in the firelight was the gleam of burnished gold. The odd thing about these Quivaris was that they were not dancing together. Each man and each woman among them seemed to be alone, dancing by themselves, as if they were all quite mad. Then he saw Nah-Loh-Tah. She, alone, was dancing with someone. He could tell because, although her partner was invisible, she was being whirled around so fast that she was clinging to a body that could not be seen. Her long, dark hair streamed about her head. Then, with a mighty leap, Nah-Loh-Tah and her invisible partner rose aloft to the top of the plateau, and Wilbur Tennington found that he was able to leap after them. They streaked across the plateau, and, suddenly, Nah-Loh-Tah was standing alone in the moonlight, looking down onto the ground. She stooped and picked up a blossom of henbane — enchanter's nightshadow — and then straightened stiffly as the gorge seemed to open below her feet. At first, she seemed fascinated, as was Wilbur Tennington, by the sound of mighty wheels crushing fragments of stone as a chariot raced along the floor of the gorge. Nah-Loh-Tah's partner of the dance had now cast aside the helmet of Hermes that had made him invisible. Wilbur Tennington could see this figure, with his eyes deflected, was really Hades, but now wearing the mask of Thanatos. It was at this moment Nah-Loh-Tah, truly fearful, turned to him, as if he were only a shade, and spoke:

Alone of the gods, Thanatos loves not
    gifts.
No, not by sacrifice or by libation
Canst thou in any way make him turn
    back.
He hath no altar, and no hymn of praise.
From him alone is all entreaty deflected,
As a wheel turns in endless rotation.

And then, before his eyes, Nah-Loh-Tah was turned into a pillar of stone, and in this form the right arm of Hades, still wearing the mask of Thanatos, reached up, entwined her body, and ripped the pillar from where it stood, as the chariot continued to thunder down the gorge. Helplessly, Wilbur Tennington watched as they vanished.

That same night, while asleep at the *Hacienda* de Ferrar, Marcelina had a dream that she also remembered upon awakening. It made sense to her in the world of the daylight, but she felt she should think about it for a time before she told anyone about it. The occasion for the dream, it seemed to her, must have been a remark that her mother, Isabella O'Day, had made the previous summer as a result of their looking over together some of Marcelina's press kits of stills from the films she had been in as well as pictures she had in a family album. One of the family photographs was of Marcelina at the age of three, and her mother was holding her hand. The photograph had been taken outdoors in the rear garden of the O'Day home in Lima. Marcelina smiled at the way in which Isabella was dressed. It was then that Isabella suggested that Marcelina should look at any photograph of herself once she had lived long enough — for thirty years, say — and regard then what she is wearing in that photograph closely. Whatever she is wearing that she would no longer wear would be merely a matter of fashion, but what she is wearing that she would still wear would be a matter of style.

In her dream Marcelina found herself standing before the tall mirror in the master bedroom. No one else was in the room. She was obviously dressed for warmth, since she had on a pair of slacks and over them a pair of thermal overalls. She also was wearing a parka with a fur-lined hood that covered her ears and buttoned under her chin. She had on heavy hiking boots and no less than five pairs of socks. Surely, she was well prepared this time for where they would be going. Yet, the strange thing was that, as she stood looking at herself in the tall mirror, she seemed to be remembering what her mother had told her. At this point it occurred to her that she should begin removing every piece of clothing she was wearing that would not be essential for her journey. Sitting down on the maple chest at the bottom of the king-size bed, she removed the hiking boots first, and then all the pairs of socks. There appeared to be a sense of urgency in what she was doing, because she kept relentlessly on, discarding the inessential. To her amazement in the dream she finally found herself standing before the tall mirror absolutely naked except for the small golden crucifix one inch in length and the gold chain on which it was suspended around her neck that Chris had given her for their tenth wedding anniversary and that she wore always, even when it was hidden under other clothing. That golden crucifix and her wedding ring — they were all she was wearing. And, somehow, those two images — the golden circle with her finger through it and the golden cross suspended from a ring of gold — seemed right, the way it had to be.

Ramón Aksut arrived at the *Hacienda* de

Ferrar early Saturday afternoon on June 9th, eight days after Sir Wilbur had departed for San Francisco. He was not quite what Marcelina had expected. After all, he had only been fifteen years old then. His hair was very long now, worn in the manner of a Quechuan Indian who had grown up in the Andes. He carried a large back pack and slung over one shoulder by a leather strap was a Spanish guitar. His dark face was clear, and his eyes black and lustrous. His clothing consisted of heavy cotton with a brightly colored shirt. On his feet he wore a pair of shiny black boots.

Marcelina was in her gardening clothes with a straw sombrero on her head, working in the rose garden beneath the windows of the music room at the front of the house when she saw the young man turn in from the road and walk up the stamped red top of the front drive. She was not exactly sure, of course, but had a strong premonition — her father had telephoned from Lima six days before to say he had seen Ramón on board a ship bound for San Diego. That was still far from San Fernando, and she had anticipated that Ramón, as Sir Wilbur before him, would take the train and let her know when he was scheduled to arrive at the station. Her father had insisted he had given the young man a map showing how to get to the *Hacienda* de Ferrar and the telephone number with instructions to call as soon as his ship docked. This he had not done, and Marcelina had been wondering if, somehow, he might have been delayed or become lost. Chris was of the opinion that, knowing Ramón from times past, he could be relied upon to find where they lived, provided his visitor's visa was in order — as Thomas O'Day had assured his daughter that it was, as well as his Peruvian passport, matters her father had overseen in Peru.

"Ramón?" Marcelina called, having walked out onto the front drive.

"*¡Sí, señora!*" he called, and quickened his pace.

When last she had seen him in Peru, Ramón had been an inch or two below her five feet, three inches, but now he seemed, with his straw sombrero, to be several inches taller than she was. As so often with people, she had to look up to see his face.

"You are the same," he said in Spanish, "*muy bonita* . . . just as I remember you."

"Ramón," she said, reaching out and taking his upper arms in her strong hands, and the lines came out across her high forehead beneath the sombrero, "I am . . . it is kind of you to say that." Then she gave him an affectionate squeeze. "It has been so long." She stood back. "You must forgive my appearance . . . I was working in the garden . . . and I had no idea when you were coming . . . you should have telephoned as Papa said you would." The planes of her face crinkled, though, in an impish, delighted smile, and her words betrayed only concern and not irritation.

"You do not have a servant to do the gardening?" he asked, smiling, ignoring the reminder of what he had been supposed to do.

"In this country, one does many things for herself . . . it is different here . . . and" — she laughed merrily — "I do like it better this way. These are my roses, and no one else would care for them as I do."

"Thees ees a wonderful contree," he said in English. "I do so weesh to espeak thees language . . . as a native."

"The language of the house here is English, but sometimes Spanish is spoken . . . even Chris likes speaking it upon occasion . . . and Rosa . . . and Santiago . . . he came here from my uncle's *rancho* in Peru . . . they speak more Spanish than English." She said this in English without thinking, and then smiled at the absurdity of it. "But it is good for you to speak English . . . and to practice it. Come, let's put your things inside . . . I'll show you your room. Are you hungry? Rosa could fix

189

you something to eat."

"Eet ees all right, *señora*. I eat on thee way here."

He noticed now that the planes of her face were thinner than he remembered them, less girlish, and she seemed somehow shorter than he remembered her as being, but her blue-gray eyes were still as large, deep and moist in a way that suggested an open sincerity without guile.

"You did not take the train?"

"No, *señora*. I preferred to com' by bus . . . to Los Angeles . . . and from there I walked . . . to see what I could of thees wonderful place they call thee vallee."

"But, Ramón, you might have been hit by an automobile . . . you should have telephoned. Chris or I would have come to get you at the bus dépôt in Los Angeles. That is a very long way to have walked."

"I started out yesterday een thee late afternoon . . . no, eet was not so ver' far. Eet ees moch farther from Tacho Alto to Lima, *señora*, and I walked that distance, also."

Ramón proved a fine house guest. He told stories of his experiences mountain climbing in the Andes. He had brought his crampons, ice-axes, pitons, and piton hammer with him. Chris drove him to a sporting goods store where Ramón could acquire what he felt he would need in terms of ropes while purchasing insulated clothing for the entire group. Although Chris doubted very much that any mountain climbing would be involved, he did agree to purchase crampons for everyone, ice-axes, hunting knives, and ropes. Marcelina had very tiny feet, and the smallest crampons Chris could get for her were still two sizes too big. He felt she could compensate for the extra room by wearing five pairs of woolen socks.

At Ramón's suggestion, Santiago Cruz built a wooden structure from a ten-foot square piece of plywood with a facing of one-by-fours at the sides and several on the back side for reinforcement. This "testing wall" was placed against the far side of the barn, and Chris and Marcelina found time to practice climbing up and down it using crampons and ice-axes for leverage. It might well be that they would encounter walls of ice, and it was best to be prepared. Marcelina perspired so much while engaging in this exercise that she quipped she might lose weight despite her regular quota of milk shakes. Chris patted her bottom and told her she shouldn't worry.

In his days at the *Hacienda* de Ferrar, Ramón formed a close relationship with Santiago Cruz, although with him Ramón also preferred to speak English. He helped Santiago with the work around the ranch, and as often as possible he loved to ride the horses. Cruz was an inveterate reader of magazine stories and subscribed to *Western Story Magazine* and *Dime Detective Magazine*. He drove Ramón into a cigar and magazine store in San Fernando where the Quechuan bought himself the July issues of *Star Western* and *Adventure*, obviously influenced by Cruz's preference for adventure fiction. In the evenings Cruz would regularly listen to the radio, and Ramón would generally visit with him in the living room of his two-room adobe cabin so he could listen as well. He especially loved *Amos 'n' Andy* on the NBC Blue Network weekdays at 7:00 P.M., but he also listened to, and laughed and laughed, at *The Jack Benny Program* on NBC on Fridays at 10:00 P.M. and the *Sal Hepatica Hour of Smiles* with Fred Allen and Portland Hoffa on NBC on Wednesdays at 9:30 P.M., and at 5:00 P.M. three days a week he listened to *The Tom Mix Ralston Straight Shooters* with Artells Dickson as Tom Mix. He had once seen a silent movie with Tom Mix in Peru and was tremendously excited when Santiago drove the two of them to the Valley Theatre in San Fernando that showed Westerns on weekends to see SMOKING GUNS with Ken Maynard, a new release, and RUSTLER'S ROUNDUP with Tom Mix, a reissue at the bottom of the double bill, plus a Universal newsreel, cartoon, short subject, and previews.

Seeing those movies, which he enjoyed (although the Tom Mix film more than the new one with Ken Maynard), led to all manner of questions to Marcelina. Why, if Tom Mix was in movies, didn't he play himself on his own radio program? When Marcelina told Ramón she had once been in a Western with Ken Maynard, there were even more questions. Marcelina explained to Ramón that she had turned her back on films. They had once been, she admitted, part of her life, and she would never forget them, but she had no desire to think about them any more. Chris was surprised to overhear this, but he felt he should respect her wishes. While Marcelina had been only momentarily displeased at Sir Wilbur's having seen some films of hers that she did not feel were her best work, given what she now said to Ramón, Chris thought it best not to avail the Quechuan of the opportunity the Englishman had had to see any of Marcelina's films. Yet, Ramón had seen her picture in a movie magazine in Peru, and he did want to look at her photo press kits, which Marcelina let him do. It was her belief, however, that in view of Ramón's sudden addiction to radio programs and pulp magazines, Chris should somehow encourage him to interest himself in things of more spiritual consequence.

As it turned out, Marcelina's desire for Ramón not to see any of her film work was frustrated by a happenstance she could not have foreseen. Hoot Gibson who had starred in her first Western and who had appeared opposite her in just about her last film stopped at the *Hacienda* de Ferrar one evening — after having telephoned first that he was coming, as was the local custom in Hollywood. He had been badly injured in the National Air Races in Los Angeles on July 3rd of the previous year and now had something of a limp that required him to swing his left leg around in a circular fashion when he walked. Running on foot was something he would never be able to do again. He was, he explained, still being kept off the screen by Allied Pictures with which he had signed a long-term contract and for which Marcelina had worked when she had played the heroine in THE FIGHTING PARSON. The movie cowboy chided Chris that while Chris had married Marceline Day only once, he had fallen in love with her and married her twice, first in THE TAMING OF THE WEST and, later, in THE FIGHTING PARSON. Prior to his contractual dispute with Allied because the company was no longer willing or able to finance films with him, he had been given a 16mm. print of THE FIGHTING PARSON, and it was this he had brought along as a sort of graduation gift for Marcelina. Apparently there was a growing 16mm. market for films to be shown in institutions such as hospitals, prisons, schools, and the like, and he thought it would be something Marcelina would want to show her children and grandchildren.

"Now that you're retired and have your degree, I imagine children are next," he said, amused by the thought.

"I haven't got my degree in my hand yet," Marcelina told him, "but at least I know it's coming."

Ramón as the Fallons' house guest was introduced, but he was very reticent and almost silent, fearful, he said later, because except for the *señora* he had never before been in the presence of a real movie star. He was even more awed when, a day later, Carole Lombard stopped in to visit Marcelina.

The Fallons had a Bell and Howell 16mm. film projector that would throw a picture against a wall in the living room painted an off-white. It was here that Chris projected THE FIGHTING PARSON, which Ramón thoroughly enjoyed and which even amused Marcelina when the scene came of painting spots on the babies to simulate measles so they couldn't be baptized by Gibson whose character in the film had been mistaken for a circuit preacher.

Chris had obtained a 16mm. reduction print from Pathé of Robert Flaherty's 1922 documentary, NANOOK OF THE NORTH, and this he was able to project next. He explained to Ramón that in his opinion this was, so far, still the finest documentary film that had ever been made and had set a standard for anything that had been filmed since. Although it was shot for the most part just above the sixtieth parallel and, therefore, not really within the Arctic Circle itself, it had captured indelibly the life of the Eskimo groups that lived throughout the Arctic and had for centuries. Above all, it showed the total focus their life had on just obtaining food year around, year after year. It was a silent film and the print was without a sound track, but this mattered little, so powerful and riveting were the images. Ramón wanted to know why the Eskimos were shown sleeping naked under animal skins, and Chris explained that to wear clothing of any kind while sleeping would cause perspiration and freezing. In the scene of building an igloo out of the snow pack, Ramón was amazed to see how a window was supplied by a piece of sea ice being cut out and inserted, and that the temperature within the igloo could not be allowed to rise above freezing or the shelter would melt. Chris explained the way an igloo is built was based on the way ring seals fashioned their igloos to protect themselves and their air holes in the ice as well as the manner in which female polar bears carve out their dens before giving birth to their cubs. The scenes of the vast wasteland of the frozen sea and snow pack during a windstorm reminded Ramón of a dust storm on the desert just beyond Tacho Alto in Peru which he had crossed with his uncle and the Tennington party years before — except, instead of being unbearably hot, in the Far North it was devastatingly cold.

Last to be shown was Marcelina's favorite of all the documentaries Chris had produced, a fifteen-minute film on the gathering of snow geese and numerous other birds in the autumn at Tule Lake and the Klamath Basin in northern California. Pintails, lesser scaup, Barrow's goldeneye, cinnamon teal, mallard, northern shoveler, redhead, canvasback ducks, Great Basin and Canada geese, white-fronted geese, Ross's geese, lesser snow geese, and tundra swans were among those identified by the narration. The microphones had been able to capture the sounds of the night flying of these birds, the hammering of the air by thousands upon thousands of wings, an eerie sound, yet, in its way, akin in Flaherty's film to the soundless yipping and howling of the savage sledge dogs of the Eskimos in the Far North after a seal is killed at an airhole in the ice. Most amazing of all were the images of nearly a quarter million of lesser snow geese floating on the water at Tule Lake, creating what appeared in human terms to be a raft almost a mile long and over five hundred yards wide. There was an oddly majestic sound, despite its resemblance to a howling wind storm at sea, when the birds in large groups would arrive, or take off into the air. The camera had been able to capture the dazzle of thousands upon thousands of wings, the flashing, opaque whiteness of their bodies, dappling the sunlight in contrast to the translucence of those wings and the tail feathers, a strange glow of light projecting in the shining, silver glitter of the black and white film a sustained brilliance that seemed somehow without shadows. There would appear to be forty or fifty thousand birds in the air at once, spreading out against the sky until they exceeded the boundaries of the camera's lens to capture them in their flight, causing a human eye to lose its spatial perspective of depth altogether, so it might be that you were at the bottom of the ocean and peering upward through fathoms of water with the sunlight beyond, and watching the passage of tens of thousands of shimmering bodies of fish.

While the reel of film was rewinding on the projector and with the lights on again, Chris remarked how wondering strange were the migrations of thousands of species, like the snow geese, that fly north to many points in the Arctic in the spring, molt and hatch their young, only to fly south again in the autumn. These birds had been doing this for many thousands of years, longer certainly than the histories of any of the countries who laid geographical claim to the land whence they fly or to the land to which they return. It was, he believed, as much a miracle and a mystery as electricity which, in sufficient quantity, can maim and kill any living creature, and yet in one form or another serves as the very nucleus of all that lives and is the most fundamental force in the solar system.

Marcelina may have been concerned, as she confided to Chris, about the effects of radio programs, movies, and the kind of stories Ramón was struggling to read in a language still so new to him, but for Ramón the experiences he had had since arriving in

America were disturbing in another way. There was so much magic here, so much that had seemed distant and even unimaginable in his life in Tacho Alto or venturing into the fastnesses of the Andes. One could see movies at home. One could go almost anywhere by automobile, and also by airplane, as he had done long ago in leaving Haucha and as he would do again in flying to the Arctic. There was music and news events and dramas and comedies transmitted somehow through the air here that were like nothing he had ever heard in Peru. There were magical people whose images were projected on screens and who could be seen everywhere in the world, moving and talking — heroes who were invincible against the evil in the human soul, heroines like the *señora* had been with whom you could fall so deeply in love.

Chris explained to Ramón that, even though they would be going farther north than had been the case in the documentary he had seen, at the time of year they would be there and where they would be landing there would be endless tundra which they would have to cross until they came to the ice cap. Chris would be acquiring ten Huskies as sled dogs at Juneau, and the dogs would have to be flown to where they would be landing near the center of Ellesmere Island. The dogs and sled would be necessary to cross the glacier in the north before reaching the Arctic Ocean. Getting across the tundra with a sled would be a daunting task, and so Chris had been asked by the Englishman to come up with a kind of runner for the sled that could glide somewhat more easily over tundra. Ramón had seen the struggles the Eskimos had had with dogs tugging a sled in snow and how water had to be poured on the runners to make for ready passage across snow pack and ice. The same kind of propulsion would be possible over dry or occasionally water-soaked tundra, Chris believed, by using runners made from spun glass, which were the kind of runners used in outdoor films shot on indoor sound stages that required dog teams to pull sledges over what photographed as snow pack but definitely was not. Later, once they were out on the glacier, they could use the water-freezing method of the Eskimos, but he suspected this might not be necessary. Spun glass also had the virtue of being lighter than a sled runner made out of metal or animal bone. The sled was being shipped on to San Francisco where Sir Wilbur would see that it was loaded aboard the airplane they would be using.

Marcelina had originally wanted her parents to come to Los Angeles to attend her graduation, but this, as it turned out, was not possible. Her father had pressing business in Lima, and her mother was unwilling to make the trip alone. When Thomas O'Day had telephoned concerning Ramón's passage to San Diego, Marcelina had even proposed that perhaps her mother might have come with Ramón so as to see her graduation. Her father, who had been so much in favor of her having a college education in the United States more than a decade before, seemed to her somewhat less than enthusiastic about her having returned to complete her degree so many years later. He told Marcelina that Isabella had thought of coming to the States with Ramón but had finally rejected the idea as impractical. Carole Lombard had very much wanted to attend the graduation ceremony only to decide that her presence might cause a distraction. So it was that Chris attended the ceremony in the company of Santiago, Rosa, and Ramón, and there was a quiet celebration that night at the *Hacienda* de Ferrar.

The night before their departure to San Francisco, Chris and Ramón went riding after the evening meal. It was dusk when they returned, their horses loping swiftly to return to the stable and their evening allotment of oats. Even though Santiago was on hand,

Chris insisted on unsaddling and rubbing down his horse, a zebra dun named Sandy, and he suggested to the Quechuan that he do the same with Regina, Marcelina's sorrel mare that Ramón had been riding. Santiago, seeing that everything was well in hand, left the stable area in the adobe barn and headed in the direction of his quarters.

After they had groomed and stalled the horses, Chris led the way out of the stable, pausing to slide closed the great wooden door. Twilight had fallen gently on the compound and already the buildings were in shadows.

"I have been wondering sometheeng, *Señor* Chris," Ramón began rather hesitantly.

Chris turned toward the younger man who was now beside him.

"You do not have to tell me, eef eet would offend you."

"I can't imagine anything you might ask would do that," Chris said, smiling in the dim light.

"Eet ees that I have seen so many beautiful *señoritas* since I have been in thees wonderful country. I know thee *señora* ees a most beautiful woman . . . and, believe me, *Señor* Chris, I would geeve my life to save her from danger. But . . . have you never been tempted?"

"By one of those beautiful *señoritas?*" Chris asked softly.

"*Sí* . . . tempted, *Señor* Chris . . . only tempted?"

Chris motioned to Ramón to follow him over to the near side of the corral where the rails were all painted white and glowed dully in the faded light. He paused, put one booted foot on the lowest rung, and leaned with an arm on the top rung.

"Had you asked me that question, Ramón, when we first met on the way to Haucha, I would have answered you differently. It may even sound absurd . . . what I would answer now. But, in all honesty, at forty-three years of age, I have even come to mark time itself as A.M. and P.M. Only for me those expressions stand for *ante* Marcelina and *post* Marcelina . . . before knowing her and after knowing her. I am aware that, when she was in pictures, many men would pursue her . . . even some of those who were in movies with her . . . or were producing the movies. I cannot blame them . . . because she is such an extraordinary woman. But I never doubted . . . even when she was gone on location for days and nights at a time . . . I never doubted her love for a moment . . . as I know she has never doubted mine for her. For me there is no sin more damning than betrayal. There was once an

Italian poet named Dante Alighieri who wrote a great poem in several volumes . . . he called it THE DIVINE COMEDY . . . and in the first part of this poem, another poet, Virgil, guides Dante through the Inferno . . . through hell . . . and there . . . on the lowest level . . . below the water, below the mud, below the fire . . . in the ninth circle . . . where everything is frozen in ice, and there is only utter coldness . . . that is the region called Judecca . . . so named after the one who is held there in highest honor . . . Judas Iscariot . . . and there is found Cain and even Lucifer himself."

Chris had been looking over the top rung of the corral as he was speaking, but now he turned and looked directly at Ramón.

"Were I ever to betray Marcelina, I would also be betraying myself. It is perhaps the greatest sin that one human being can commit against another . . . or tempt another to commit. Once, long ago, when Marcelina and I were talking on the deck of the *Sea Queen*, sailing to Lima . . . before we knew you . . . Marcelina was standing in shadow, for the time was very like it is now, and she asked me . . . 'And what of betrayal?' I answered that I wasn't sure I understood what she meant, and she told me she didn't completely understand it herself, but she said . . . it is like being torn apart, loving someone you should love but hating that person, too, because it is as if a part of yourself were an enemy. Not an enemy outside. When an enemy is outside, there are ways we can defend ourselves. But what happens when the enemy is within?"

Ramón felt suddenly very deeply ashamed, as if he had trespassed on what was sacred, but he also sensed vaguely what was meant. There had once been a time when Don Esteban de Ferrar had tempted his niece to betray *Señor* Chris and the others and provide him with a copy of the map to the lost city. Ramón's mouth was very dry, but he did manage to say: "And what deed you answer?"

"It is strange, Ramón, and I cannot tell you why it happened, but at that moment I had a vision from a play by Æschylus . . . an ancient Greek who wrote most truly about human beings . . . and I saw in my soul the image of the undefiled Artemis, a goddess driven to anger and pity at the fleet hounds of Zeus, her father, eating the unborn young in the shivering mother hare. And I was trembling when I did answer. It was the only thing I could say to her . . . the only thing that seemed true . . . that, when we betray another, we die a little, or, at least, a part of ourselves will surely die. Finding Marcelina has made me whole, Ramón, and I sha'n't ever betray her or leave her . . . until I die. But while I am alive, there is not a day . . . not a single day . . . whether she is physically around or not . . . that I do not thank God I found her." He paused. "Always . . . if you find the one . . . cling fast! . . . for it never . . . *never* comes again." As he spoke, he touched Ramón strongly on a shoulder, smiled, and, afterwards, turned toward the house where in the distance were the stone steps leading up to the back verandah. What he said then to the younger man as they walked side by side was in a language Ramón understood only in part, because it was medieval Italian, but enough of it was similar to Spanish that he could apprehend what was meant. " '*Attienti ben, ché per cotali scale,' disse 'l maestro . . . 'conviensi dipartir da tanto male.'* " And so they passed up such stairs as these, ascending into the light shining out through the rear windows of the *Hacienda* de Ferrar.

Chapter Seven

Early the next morning with everything loaded on and in the Cadillac Phaeton and Santiago Cruz coming along so he could drive the car back to the *Hacienda* de Ferrar, the first part of the journey was to begin with the drive to San Francisco to join up with Sir Wilbur and Luis Valera. The night before each of the travelers had to decide what books they wanted to take along. As always when on such a journey, Chris took with him the plays of Æschylus in two volumes, in this case the leather-bound edition given to him as a wedding gift by the Englishman. Marcelina was taking several books. The first was an English translation of THE HYMNS OF THE RIG VEDA by Ralph T. H. Griffith first published in London in 1889. She hoped that Sir Wilbur, who had the entire text of the Rig Veda in Sanskrit and who had studied Sanskrit in India, and Luis Valera, who had mastered both Sanskrit and Egyptian hieroglyphics in the course of his work, would be able to help her with any difficult passages she might encounter. Her other books were METAMORPHOSES by Ovid that she had already read several times and JANE EYRE by Charlotte Brontë that she hadn't read. Initially, neither Marcelina nor Chris was very enthusiastic about Ramón's choice for a book to take along. He wanted, doubtless because of his conversation with Chris earlier that evening, to read Dante's THE DIVINE COMEDY. Chris only had the work in Italian. Marcelina, in her section of the library in the study, had an English translation in one volume published two years before by The Modern Library. But it wasn't a good idea to read it even in English, Marcelina argued, since Ramón's grasp of this language was probably insufficient for such a daunting task, and also because this work was so extremely complex that despite the elaborate footnotes in her edition Ramón would still be hopelessly at sea. Ramón countered that, if the *señora* was taking several books on the journey, might he not take her small volume of THE DIVINE COMEDY and an English language dictionary? He was so insistent — for he believed that nothing worth accomplishing was ever really done easily and that only by trying very hard to ascend to a higher level of knowledge could one ever hope to increase his understanding of the world — that finally they gave in. So it was that Marcelina's edition of THE DIV-INE COMEDY and an English language dictionary (and so he would be on the safe side, Marcelina's Latin-Spanish dictionary from her school days in Peru) were loaned to him, and with obvious pride he placed these books in his personal pack.

Luis Valera and his wife, Francisca, still lived in the same bungalow in San Francisco on Laguna Street, between Vallejo and Post, that they had occupied in 1922 when Valera had joined Sir Wilbur to find the lost Incan city of Haucha. Although promoted to the status of professor emeritus at the University of California in Berkeley, he still lectured at the graduate level in archeology and the history and culture of native American societies. He was also still attached to the San Francisco Museum as curator of its Pre-Columbian and American Indian collections. In the early 1920s, when Marcelina was a student at the university, Valera and his wife had been charged with looking out for the young woman's welfare by Thomas and Isabella O'Day, with whom the Valeras had been friends in Lima before they came to the United States following Luis Valera's appointment to an assistant professorship.

Valera was almost sixty years old now, and

Francisca thought his age should preclude his leaving on this possibly dangerous and certainly arduous trek to the Arctic. Yet, Valera was adamant that he would go, that he must go, for it promised a potentially great discovery in the history and migration of civilization. Francisca finally reconciled herself that there was no preventing Luis's undertaking the journey. The Valeras were childless, and for a time both had come to regard Marcelina as the daughter they had never had. However, following Marcelina's marriage to Chris Fallon and Marcelina's film career, they had not been in close touch, visiting with each other only very occasionally in the summer months when the Valeras would drive down to southern California, and they had not seen each other in the last three years. Francisca had long been an avid film-goer, and she prided herself on having seen virtually all of Marcelina's films, and even kept clippings and articles and reviews from magazines and newspapers about Marcelina's career.

Chris drove into San Francisco and out to the Valera bungalow. Marcelina and Ramón would be staying there for dinner. Chris and Santiago did not stay longer than for the two of them to come in and visit briefly with Luis and Francisca before they left again, this time heading for the Oakland air field where Sir

Wilbur would be meeting them to help load all of the gear aboard the airplane. Chris had spoken on the telephone several times with the Englishman, and he was anxious to see the Douglas Dolphin he had heard so much about. He knew that Mark Dworski would be their pilot, and he was pleased about the happenstance that had made this possible.

The Valeras had a relatively new car, a 1931 Chevrolet two-door sedan, parked in the driveway, but they could not afford servants and had never had them. Luis Valera had aged. His curly hair, so long shot through with gray, was more gray than ever. Francisca's hair was now almost completely gray. The lines in her face had deepened, but the skin was still soft if a little pouched. She was preparing the evening meal herself. While Luis and Ramón brought each other up to date on what had happened in the twelve years since they had been together on the trek into the Andes, Marcelina volunteered to help Francisca in the kitchen. Marcelina could not help but detect a certain suppressed hostility in the woman she referred to as her aunt just as she still called Valera *Tío* Luis.

It wasn't until after dinner that Valera took Ramón with him up to the master bedroom he still used as a study to show him the topographical map and the astronomical transparencies of the heavens in the Arctic for the months of December and January by means of which Sir Wilbur had been able to fix with some accuracy where they would be going, even if the stars were not now visible in the heavens because of the extended sunlight and the frequent cloud layers. The two women went into the kitchen to do the dishes, something Marcelina insisted upon despite Francisca's initial objections that, rightfully, she should join the men.

Francisca did the washing and rinsing, Marcelina the drying.

"I know something is wrong, *Tía* Francisca," Marcelina said. "Won't you tell me what it is?"

"You say you have your degree . . . ?" Francisca said, scrubbing a plate.

"Yes . . . at last."

"And you think somehow that is better than being in the movies?"

"It's not the same thing. I just went back and finished what I should have done all those years ago."

"What I can't understand is why!" She had rinsed the plate and now handed it to Marcelina who stood ready with a dish towel. "You were a big star. You made pictures with just about every important leading man in Hollywood . . . John Barrymore, Lon Chaney,

213

Ramon Navarro, Raymond Griffith, Fredric March. . . ."

"And Clara Bow and Rex Bell," Marcelina interrupted, with an elfin smile, "only not in the same picture."

"I just don't understand you. You had all that, and you just threw it away!"

"That's not quite how it happened. Like Carole Lombard says, it's a tough business. I wasn't tough enough . . . or maybe talented enough to keep at it."

"Don't talk nonsense, Marcie." She handed over another dinner plate. "You have a lot of talent. I've seen your pictures. Don't forget that. How many girls get the chance you had? . . . to be on the screen in big picture after big picture? Tell me that?"

"Not many," Marcelina conceded in a quiet voice.

"What do you need a degree for?" Francisca pursued. "You're married. You have money. You don't have any children. What could possibly have made you throw it all away?"

"I didn't throw it away, *Tía* Francisca. My last couple of years I wasn't making those big pictures, as you call them. Toward the end I was getting supporting rôles."

"Have you no spine? You have money. Chris is working. You didn't have to take

214

those parts, if you didn't like them. You should have held out till you got offered the kind of parts that would be best for you." She handed Marcelina another scrubbed dinner plate. "That friend of yours . . . Carole Lombard . . . look at the kind of parts she once got? Did you see her in THE EAGLE AND THE HAWK?"

"Yes," Marcelina said very softly, and she was trembling slightly.

"It was some time ago that I saw it," Francisca went on relentlessly, "but I don't think she had much dialogue, if any. She just stood around and looked beautiful to all those flyers who were going to their deaths. Well, look where she is now! She's getting top billing . . . before even the male stars in her films. That's what you should have done."

"Insisted on top billing?"

"Yes."

"You mean . . . Marceline Day and Hoot Gibson in THE FIGHTING PARSON?" Marcelina gave a little laugh. "Nobody would go to see a Western with the girl billed over the hero."

"And why should you have been appearing in Westerns again? You did that when you were starting out. That's what I mean, Marcie. You just let things go from bad to worse, and then finally quit . . . to go back to get a degree. That was stupid. Do you think a degree is going to get you anywhere? Look at Luis. He has all kinds of degrees. We still live in the same house we've had almost since we came to this country. Don't you think he would trade it all for what you had . . . and threw away?"

"I don't know," Marcelina said, putting down the thoroughly dried plate on the kitchen table. "And, believe me or not, I didn't throw it away. I admit it wasn't something I set out to do. Not like Carole. It's her whole life . . . in a way. It was something she wanted, and she's earned every bit of success she's had. Maybe if I had wanted to be an actress . . . or a comedienne. . . ."

"You were! You made a lot of romantic comedies."

"All right. It didn't work out for me. Is that what you want me to say? In some of those Westerns I worked in, I didn't even show up on screen until the third reel."

"And whose fault was that?" Francisca demanded. "You shouldn't have been in those kinds of pictures any more . . . not after where you'd been and what you'd done!"

They both had stopped doing anything, and just stood looking at each other.

"I intend to finish helping you with the dishes," Marcelina said firmly. "But I don't want to talk about this any more. Can we let it drop?"

"All right," Francisca agreed, and returned to scrubbing a plate in the dish pan.

Sir Wilbur was at the airport when Chris and Santiago arrived. Santiago, Chris, and Sir Wilbur unloaded all the gear from the car and into the storage areas of the Douglas Dolphin. Then Santiago got behind the wheel, after shaking hands with Chris and the Englishman, and headed back to the *Hacienda* de Ferrar. It was nearly six. Santiago intended to drive straight through and expected to be back before morning.

Chris then checked the inventory to see that nothing had been forgotten. Sir Wilbur thought that perhaps they should have two sleds, instead of only the one Chris had had sent by express from Los Angeles, because they would be transporting so much gear, tents, stoves, and the like, as well as water and food for the humans and for the dogs. Chris insisted again that this one long sled should be enough. He declared it would be difficult enough getting just this one across the tundra and the desert with only dog power augmented by manpower, even with the special runners that had been manufactured for it to accommodate the varied terrain. The Englishman countered with his perplexity at how Marcelina would be able to ride on top of all their supplies, and Chris replied he had discussed this very thing with his wife, and she did not want to ride in the sled. She intended to walk, just as the men would be doing, or, if possible, she could take the gee pole. Only across the glacier did she believe she should ride the runners at the rear.

"But she's so tiny, Chris . . . does she have the stamina for it?"

"Marcie's roughed it before . . . lots of times . . . and she insists she doesn't want any exceptions made on her behalf. I don't argue about that with her any more . . . haven't since Peru."

They took a taxicab from the airport back to the St. Francis. Luis would be driving Marcelina and Ramón to the hotel for the night, and Sir Wilbur had arranged for rooms for all of them. Early in the morning, after a quick breakfast at the hotel, they would all take a taxi out to the hangar. Chris had hoped Mark Dworski would be on hand that night, but something had come up, the Englishman explained, although he would certainly be there bright and early the next morning.

It was after dinner that Sir Wilbur brought up his gratitude to Marcelina for finding him the book by B. G. Tilak. He also confided to

Chris the troubling dream he had had that first night in San Francisco, the memory of which had never left him.

"Tenny," Chris said, "if you want to understand more about dreams, you really have to talk to Marcie. I had a dream not so long ago that terrified me without making a whole lot of sense. Words that were spoken in my dream seemed associated with Abraxas, but I couldn't for the life of me . . . when I woke up the next morning . . . place that name. I asked Marcie about it, and she remembered at once. She had asked me years ago if I had ever encountered in Greek drama the name of a deity called Abraxas."

"And what did she know about this deity?" the Englishman asked in interest.

Chris shook his head. "These things . . . dreams . . . are never simple. The whole thing about Abraxas went back to when Marcelina and I were in London in Nineteen Twenty-Seven. Metro paid her way over to make a personal appearance at the London première of LONDON AFTER MIDNIGHT in which she was co-starred with Lon Chaney. She had encountered a British psychiatrist while we were there who had given her a little book . . . a pamphlet, really . . . that had been translated into English and privately published a couple of years before in England. It was titled THE

SEVEN SERMONS OF THE DEAD. Supposedly it had been originally written in German by C. G. Jung . . . the author of that book of Marcie's that you read while you were staying with us. In this pamphlet Abraxas is a figure identified as a being more indefinite than either a god or a devil . . . a being who is an improbable probability, an unreal reality."

"And did knowing where the name came from help you make sense of the dream?"

"Only in that I understood that my dream was about life and death . . . which, I admit, was obvious from the dream before I asked Marcie if she'd ever heard of Abraxas. You know, Tenny, the longer Marcie and I are together, the more invisible threads are formed that seem to bind our very souls together." He paused for a moment, and then continued. "Marcie did tell me . . . in fact, the night of the day you left for San Francisco . . . that she felt you were coming very close to the point where you would be able to dream."

"She said that?" Sir Wilbur asked in bemusement. "How could she possibly know?"

"She just does," Chris replied. "Call it a gift. But there is one thing I can tell you for sure about your dream. The words Nah-Loh-Tah says to you aren't her words."

"Do you know where they come from?"

Chris nodded. "I don't think I could say

them all of a piece, as you just have, but I remember vaguely when I read them to you. Good heavens, it was more than twenty years ago, when we were in Ethiopia together and had found the lost Egyptian city of Ka-Mor. We had a tent near the excavation work at the Temple of Kronos, and I was reading fragments . . . all we have of Æschylus's play, NIOBE. I remember translating that passage aloud for you at the time, and, for some reason, those words must have impressed themselves on some part of your mind, since they have stayed there . . . rendered perhaps exactly as I rendered them to you when I translated that passage to you all those years ago."

"Now that you mention it, I do recall it . . . quite well, in fact."

"And, perhaps, too, you remember from elsewhere that Niobe was punished for wanton pride . . . ?"

"By being turned into a pillar of stone!"

"Yes, but more than that I cannot say. Again, you have to talk to Marcie. For years now, when I've had a powerful dream, or one that recurred, I have always talked to her about it."

"And she can tell you what a dream means?"

Chris laughed softly. "No. She says a dream comes from the depths of the soul, and, once you interpret it in the world of the daylight, you change it . . . it's no longer a dream, but only what you think it means."

"Then what good would it do to tell her my dream?"

"You won't have that experience, Tenny, until you trust her with it."

"I don't know, Chris . . . I'm not sure."

Chris shrugged. "Do you remember when Marcie decided to change the way she wears her hair?"

"Yes. That was Miss Lombard's notion, I believe . . . that she needed . . . what you call . . . a *new* look?"

"Carole only suggested that to her after Marcie told her about a dream she'd had."

The Englishman smiled. "There does seem to be something of a difference, though, Chris. You say you had a dream about life and death. I can understand that. It was no doubt caused by anxiety concerning this journey we're going to make, and all of the dangers. Even my own dream, I suppose, has to do with life and death. But you say that Marcie dreamed that she had to change the way she wears her hair, and so that's why she did it?"

Chris smiled back at the Englishman. "Thank God, not every dream we have is like yours or mine. One thing I haven't told you

222

. . . but it occurred to me after we talked about Makaron Nyesoeessee. Nah-Loh-Tah may mean something to you in English, but it also means something in ancient Greek. It means . . . literally . . . 'yes, she loves bathing.' "

Sir Wilbur nodded and ran his hand inadvertently over his graying blond hair. Of course, he had not told Chris that he had heard those words from his dream a lot more recently than that evening they had been together so long ago near the diggings at Ka-Mor.

In some ways twelve years can seem a very long time. Marcelina had only a vague recollection of Mark Dworski, a pilot with the geological exploration party from the United States who had flown them from the pampas behind Haucha to Lima in a Blériot-SPAD S.33. Now the flat planes of his face, the sharp, rather large nose, and the thin lips (and the added narrow mustache) impressed themselves more strongly. Yet, Dworski seemed to remember her quite well. In fact, he had a very strong recollection of being with her on that occasion. Ramón, however, Dworski did not recognize at all. His added height, his sharp features, his black, coarse hair worn in a ponytail made the Quechuan seem altogether a stranger, and not at all the quiet boy who had sat in the rear of the SPAD S.33 with his Uncle Quinto who had himself been terrified making such a trip — even though Quinto and Ramón were only to fly as far as Tacho Alto. Chris Fallon struck Dworski as one of those men whose features change only slightly as they age, becoming sharper-edged perhaps, with deeper lines in their faces, but essentially the same person at any age. Chris was older, obviously, as was Sir Wilbur, but Marcelina apparently had aged less than either of them, and it struck Dworski that there was still a girlish quality about her when she was smiling, although less so when she was serious. Because of her height, she mostly had to look up at people, and she usually did so with a smile. Luis Valera, on the other hand, had quite definitely aged and had put on a little weight — or, maybe, he had just regained the weight he had lost as a result of the ordeal he had undergone in finding Haucha. Marcelina's regime of milk shakes may have brought her weight up to a hundred and seven pounds, but as far as Mark Dworski was concerned (and he didn't know about the milk shakes) she was a slim, highly attractive woman dressed in a light blue flight suit.

To Sir Wilbur, although he refrained from saying anything more on the subject, Marcelina, despite the padding of the flight suit, seemed still to be thin. Why, however, he now wondered, had he been so concerned about Marcelina's weight? She had always been rather petite. Perhaps because he had been unconsciously contrasting her with Nah-Loh-Tah who, while unmistakably feminine, was possessed of extraordinary physical vigor — as he had reason to know. Had Nah-Loh-Tah not come many thousands of miles, mostly on foot, to Nepal to begin with, and had she not later crossed Afghanistan, heading toward the north, across country of very rough terrain? Sir Wilbur couldn't imagine Marcelina's undertaking a similar ordeal, and he was even dubious about her desire to be one of the party this time. Before, in Peru, she had been younger, and Chris had been very concerned about her ability to withstand the journey. But then, the point couldn't be argued. If she wasn't protected by the gods, Lord knew she seemed somehow able to cope with adversity as well as any of them, and she was a vital member of what he had come to regard as an almost mystical quintet.

The last time Mark Dworski had seen Chris and Marcelina, they had obviously been in love but not yet married. Now they had been married for nearly twelve years and still no children. Perhaps Marcelina didn't want any.

He knew she was, or at least had been, an actress in moving pictures, and women in that profession did not stay in it if they wanted to have a family. At least, he had never heard of any who had. He had tried marriage himself and had even fathered a child, a girl named Elizabeth, but called Beth. She was eight years old now, while the marriage simply had not lasted because of his profession as a free-lance pilot. He loved flying, but could not afford his own airplane, and was not sure he actually wanted to own one. As a free-lance pilot he was frequently in the air, clocking thousands of air hours every year. He was always on call for Barry Kirk, but in between times he worked as a pilot on other commercial and private enterprises, such as the present trip which the Englishman estimated would require his availability for probably three months, to which absence Kirk had been agreeable. Dworski's marriage, however, had not been able to withstand such long absences, and so it had resulted in a divorce. Marge, Beth's mother, was remarried now to a man who worked in the financial district and who appeared to be a good enough step-father to Mark's daughter. Mark visited with Beth when he could and had even taken her flying with him. He was proud at how much she appeared to enjoy it, and he knew she wanted to learn how to fly, not exactly what the average eight-year-old girl would want, but then he was scarcely a conventional father who was able to come home every night to be with her. Mark had a girl friend who worked in a restaurant down on the waterfront, but she, too, seemed to dislike the prolonged absences his work entailed. In fact, he had been with her last night, which was why he had begged off the meeting the Englishman wanted him to have then with Chris Fallon. Her name was Lucile, and she felt Mark should at least be with her the night before he would be flying out for months.

The *Janet* certainly did have plenty of storage space for the transport of equipment. Most of the gear had been carefully packed in the tail and the lower hold. Sir Wilbur had brought his 6.5x54 Mannlicher-Schönauer which carried .375 Rimless Nitro Express cartridges in the magazine. Chris would carry his .30-30 Winchester and had lent Ramón his .45 caliber double-action Colt mounted on a .38 frame. Marcelina, once on the ground, would have her nickel-plated .32 Colt which she had had with her on the Peruvian expedition. Luis Valera alone would not be armed. With all this fire power, he remarked, he felt secure in relying on the others for his protection. Besides, where they were going, there was more likely to be no one at all, rather than fierce and savage natives such as the Quivaris had been. The hold below the cockpit now carried only ten large crates with wire mesh on three sides. These were for transport of the Huskies that would be taken aboard in Juneau. The accommodations in the passenger compartment were certainly ample for the four passengers. Chris loved the way the *Janet* handled in the air, and they were soon at cruising altitude, flying at a speed of a hundred and ten miles an hour. Thanks to the supplementary gasoline storage unit, they would be flying straight through to Seattle, where they would stop to refuel, and from there on to Juneau. The passengers would spend the night of June 24th, a Sunday, in a hotel in Juneau while Chris and Ramón bought and transported the sled dogs to the plane where they would be loaded on board before the flight was continued from Juneau to Point Barrow. Chris, in addition to spelling Mark at the controls, acted as navigator. This was a relatively straightforward job until they reached the Arctic and the series of waterways between land masses. Because of the problems with compass readings, the course to Ellesmere would be calculated according to the position of the Sun on a diagonal that originally would parallel the island until they reached the correct latitude, and then they would be turning to the right at an angle. To gauge latitude only a sextant was needed in order to measure the Sun's greatest height above the horizon, but to measure longitude by means of a chronometer it was necessary to record the height of the Sun according to local noon in a given time zone, and then this reading had to be compared with Greenwich time. Thus Chris carried a pocket watch set at Greenwich time, as well as his wrist watch which was to be reset as they crossed time zones. Because of the route they had chosen, there would not be a significant change in time zones until the horizontal flight almost due east from Point Barrow to Victoria Island.

To maintain the travel timetable that had been set meant night flying for which the *Janet* was equipped. The passengers would have to sleep in their armchairs in the main cabin. Chris and Mark would spell each other. It was understood by all that Sir Wilbur had delayed departure to allow Marcelina to be present at her graduation, but this also now meant that time was a matter of urgency. The leg of the flight from Juneau to Point Barrow would be continuous. However, once there, all the storage areas would have to be emptied to accommodate the fifty gallon cans of airplane fuel that would have to be flown from Point Barrow to the landing strip near the permanent Canadian military and scientific installation on Victoria Island. This was among the arrangements Sir Wilbur had been able to negotiate successfully from San Francisco. The flight to Ellesmere Island would begin in earnest, after the second refueling stop at Victoria Island. Mark Dworski, after leaving them off, would then fly back to Victoria Island where he would remain until the date scheduled for his return flight to Ellesmere Island to pick up the members of the expedition at the base camp they would establish upon landing, or, if it proved necessary, proceed to fly them over the Arctic Ocean above Ellesmere to try to locate their destination from the air, prepared for a marine landing.

Sir Wilbur and Luis Valera, however, were convinced that their calculations were accurate, and that the time allotted — almost four weeks in July and two in August — would be sufficient for them to travel overland, across the ice cap, and locate the lost colony Sir Wilbur so firmly believed still existed. Of course, a hundred different things could go wrong, causing delays in this schedule, from the weather to unforeseen problems on the way or trouble in locating the lost colony itself. This was Chris Fallon's third such excursion with the Englishman, and Sir Wilbur had been so invariably right in the past, first about Ka-Mor, the lost Egyptian city in Ethiopia which was found and excavated, and then about Haucha, the lost Incan city in the Andes, that this time should prove no less successful. Yet, there was one big difference, as far as Chris could see. There was no real map other than Luis's astral charts correlated mathematically with the geographical topography of the region in the Arctic toward which they were going, and even more significantly, perhaps, the validity of those calculations relying, as Sir Wilbur insisted, on the apparent obscurity of the source for them in the Rig Veda, admittedly a document widely open to a multitude of interpretations in all of its parts and totally speculative evidence at best for anything.

In the end, this attitude toward exact mapping probably constituted the essential difference between Chris Fallon and Sir Wilbur Tennington. Fallon had worked for years as a field guide, facilitating explorations and arriving at objectives set by others, not by himself, but according to a specific, mapped destination. Sir Wilbur was the true explorer, for he had been able to decipher clues from ancient sources and determine the whereabouts of places that had become largely forgotten in the course of time and change and that appeared on no known maps. Conversely, both Ka-Mor and Haucha had proved to be devoid of life once they had been found. In the present instance Sir Wilbur was convinced that the lost colony would not merely be remnants or ruins, but the site of an active, thriving society that had somehow survived since antiquity.

There were modern scientific theories advanced about the Arctic. It was believed that in times past and within recorded history there had been supposedly warming periods during which all the channels of the Arctic archipelagoes had remained free of the ice pack and open to travel by sea. Indeed, as recently as nine hundred to eleven hundred years ago this had presumably been the case, and it was at this time that what anthropologists called the Thule culture had flourished and expanded across the Arctic. The umiak, an open boat made of walrus or bearded seal skin, sometimes fitted with a square sail and a single stepped mast, still was in use among the Eskimo peoples in 1934. It had been a creation of the Thule culture — a culture named by historians after the Latin term for the farthest extent of the known world at the time of the Roman Empire: *ultima Thule*. It was believed that these Thule people had moved eastward across the Arctic in their time from what now was Point Barrow all the way to outposts in Greenland, and that one of their concentrations had been on Ellesmere Island.

What had changed all this was the Little Ice Age of 1650 to 1850. This change in climate altered the types and numbers of animals living in the Arctic on which the Thules had relied for sustenance. The Little Ice Age, in the event, had wiped out the Thules, and all that was left now were the small enclaves of Eskimos, or Innuit Indians, scattered across the upper Arctic lands from Alaska to Greenland, especially throughout the Canadian North-West Territories. It was said that the Norsemen, sailing west across the northern Atlantic, had made the first contacts with the Thules, and it was believed by those medieval adventurers that they had encountered a culture as developed as their own. The Norse had founded colonies on Iceland and Greenland, colonies that later withered and died, as had the Thule centers of population with the advent of the Little Ice Age. Centuries later, Europeans encountering the Eskimo descendants of the Thules regarded these people as brutish and primitive by comparison with themselves.

The Eskimos, however, had adapted to

their Arctic environment as it had become, and they knew how to survive the cold, the darkness, the ice and snow, and the scarcity of game far better than any of the Europeans who regarded them with such contempt and who had died by the scores and even by the hundreds battling the Arctic for whales and furs and valuable mineral deposits. The journey to Haucha had had a tremendous personal impact on Chris, and, whatever had been the Incas' religious beliefs, he had found himself admiring the Incan civilization that had come to control a land area as great as the British Empire. How ancient were these people of the lost colony supposed to be? If Sir Wilbur was to be believed, their culture extended back to the Third Millennium before Christ and perhaps further. At the very least, should the Englishman again be proven correct in his conviction, these ancient people might be able to shed decisive light not only on the growth of subsequent Indo-Aryan and European civilizations, but on the Thule culture as well and possibly even provide a coherent view of life and climate in the Arctic over the previous five thousand years.

The stopover at Seattle took several hours, while the entire party took their exercise. No matter how comfortable their passenger seats might be, sitting or sleeping, eating or reading, with movement in the cabin being largely confined to a trip to the chemical toilet the long flight did take its toll. Marcelina had been in charge of mess, but there were no cooking facilities that were not in storage (and their use was precluded anyway), so basically everyone had to make do with a variety of boxed lunches, something with which she was very familiar from her work in motion pictures, and she had tried her best, in buying food for the larder, to include as much variety as possible. Thermos bottles with coffee and tea had been taken along and by the time they had arrived in Seattle had been consumed. Bottled water had also been brought, and Ramón preferred this at meal time. There was no refrigeration, other than a single ice hamper in which some of the bottled water had been stored with large chunks of ice that had melted while they were in flight. These supplies also had to be replenished during the Seattle stopover. Because of problems of adequate ventilation, Sir Wilbur had proposed that no one should smoke tobacco, and this moratorium was observed while the airplane was in the air.

What was tremendously in their favor was the weather which had actually been clear all the way up the entire American coastline from San Francisco to Seattle, and not even

Seattle had any fog when they landed. The good weather held on the second leg of the journey from Seattle to Juneau, but Sir Wilbur, Chris, and Mark Dworski were all too familiar with how unpredictable weather patterns could be, and the distance between Juneau and Point Barrow might well make up in bad weather for all of the good fortune they had so far enjoyed. However, the good weather was holding, and everyone was pleased finally to be able to spend a night in a hotel and to sleep in beds with fresh linen.

The Tennington party, including Mark Dworski, had dinner together at the hotel, after which Chris and Ramón went to purchase the team of Huskies, while Mark returned to the *Janet* to supervise the loading and caging of the dogs. Chris would be taking care of their feeding and maintenance after being loaded and in flight to Point Barrow. For many, if not actually all, of the dogs, it would be a first experience at flight aboard an airplane, an experience that would be relished no more by them than their counterparts had enjoyed traveling by sea or river to upper Alaska or the Klondike in the past.

There was a broad verandah on the left side of the hotel. Restless despite air travel fatigue, after the group dinner Sir Wilbur returned to his room briefly and then went down to the lobby and out onto the verandah. He was pleased to find Marcelina there, sitting at a round table. She was drinking coffee and smoking a cigarette while reading a small book bound in red vellum. As the Englishman approached, she looked up and smiled.

"Chris is going to be a while, I fear," he said.

"I know," she answered. "He told me not to expect him until midnight."

"Luis is resting. I think all this flying has taken a toll on him already." Sir Wilbur pulled out a chair and sat down alongside of her.

"It is good for *Tío* Luis to take it easy when he can. He hasn't traveled at all the last several years."

The Englishman's face was illumined softly by the dim Sun. He had a quizzical expression as he glanced at the book Marcelina had been reading.

"Ovid," she explained. "METAMORPHOSES."

"I haven't read him in years. Not since I was taking Latin, in fact."

"I had six years of Latin in Peru. Church schools, you know. The nuns insisted on it. I suppose I know how to read it as well as Chris does ancient Greek . . . only. . . ." She paused to laugh. "Only I daren't pronounce Latin aloud to Chris. He says I Italianate everything, but that is the way we were taught, and so that's the way I say it . . . and that's the way it's pronounced in Church services."

"I'm not sure . . . from what I know of Ovid . . . that the nuns would approve of even a married woman reading him."

"Had I been caught reading him when I was a school girl, I'm sure I would have been thoroughly spanked and had to go to confession as well, but my father would approve of him now," Marcelina said lightly.

"Why so?"

"He would nod and say, oh, yes, when Daphne's father says to her . . . *'debes mihi, nata, nepotes. . . .'*"

" 'Daughter . . . you owe me grandsons' . . . or something like that."

"Yes, Tenny, something *very* like that."

Marcelina extinguished her cigarette while the Englishman leaned back in his chair. "I suppose love . . . family . . . are really what matters most in life," he said then, as Marcelina, who had closed the little volume, pushed it aside.

"Not always," Marcelina replied, "at least not in Daphne's case. Her mother was Diana, the huntress, and her father Peneus, the god of rivers. Her mother and Apollo were twins. Phœbus loved Daphne, but Cupid, because he was insulted by Apollo, played a cruel trick

238

against Daphne and, ultimately, against both Phœbus and Apollo. For Daphne did not want love. She preferred the freedom of the wilderness . . . to run through the forests and to exult in her flight. It was Cupid whose arrow smote Phœbus . . . and then, because Apollo insulted him, Cupid's arrow smote Apollo, too. It was Apollo who gave pursuit. Daphne, no matter how many pursued her, refused to surrender her freedom. She fled from Apollo. But flight could not save her. Apollo was consumed by the fire of his passion for her. It was almost as if, the faster Daphne ran, the more desirable she became to Apollo. Apollo marveled at all the parts of Daphne he could see . . . her fingers, her hands, her wrists, and her arms, bare to the shoulder, and he believed that what was hidden was lovelier still. Apollo called after her, begging her to listen, that she was no lamb, and he no wolf, that she was no creature fleeing from a foe, that he was only one who loved her. Yet she would not listen."

"I do not have to ask if Apollo found her," the Englishman said gravely, his voice tinted by sadness as his face was by the dim light. "I have seen Perugino's *Allegorical Combat between Chastity and Voluptuousness*."

"Daphne prayed to her father, Peneus, to save her. And he did save her . . . by turning her into a laurel tree . . . a numbness seizing her limbs as her soft sides became covered with a thin bark. Her hair, which had streamed behind her as she ran, was turned into leaves and her arms into branches and her feet, once so fleet, became fastened to the earth as roots. Apollo placed his hand against her trunk and could feel the beat of her heart. 'Since thou shalt not be my bride, thou shalt be my tree' . . . he told her . . . 'my hair, my lyre, my quiver shall always be entwined with thee, O laurel . . . with thee shalt Roman generals wreathe their heads when their long, triumphant processions shall climb the way to the Capitol.' " Marcelina paused and shook her head gently in the faded light. "It was not a battle between chastity and voluptuousness, Tenny. What most did Daphne desire? . . . her freedom. And what did she lose forever? And if Apollo became more impassioned as he pursued her, what did he lose? . . . the very object of his pursuit." Now her blue-gray eyes reflected the distant glint of the Sun. "The map we are following is only partially imprinted in the stars . . . isn't it? Aren't we really more like Apollo, following the fleeing Daphne through the wilderness?"

"I didn't think so in the beginning, Marcie." His face seemed hidden now by shadow. "It wasn't until Chris told me about Makaron

Nyesoeessee that I realized that the two places might, indeed, be the same. But I cannot be sure. Nah-Loh-Tah . . . I am certain Chris told you . . . ?"

Marcelina nodded.

"Well, she vanished into the Indian night."

"And you were given no indication by her . . . as to why she might wish to leave?"

"I have had a great deal of time to think about that . . . you know, in some ways she is like you . . . not in appearance, but her soul is filled with music . . . she composes songs and accompanies herself on an instrument like a guitar . . . Luis helped me identify it . . . it's a kind of lyra . . . as the Greeks called it long ago. There was one song in particular that she played often. I found myself dreaming about one of the verses . . . I talked to Chris about it . . . and, incredible as it may seem, he knew the source from which it probably came. . . ."

"He's a pretty incredible person about some things . . . but, then, you already know that."

"Well, one verse appeared in my dream. I remembered it well enough to quote it to Chris. But in spite of what you said to me that Sunday morning, I am not musical in the least, and there was no melody accompanying the words in my dream. Chris told me he believed you are *eudaimon*, and that you know about dreams." He paused, an ironical expression on his features. "You had one you interpreted as directing you to change the way you do your hair."

Marcelina laughed. "That was Carole's interpretation. I don't really know what to make of the dream I had. And I know Chris believes that about me . . . that I am somehow protected by the gods . . . but it just isn't so. I've just been lucky about a lot of things, I guess, but there is nothing so special about me. At least," she said, laughing again, "there have been an awful lot of times when I have felt anything but special . . . or one who has been especially favored."

" 'Debes mihi, nata, nepotes . . . ?' "

"Yes," she said, "to mention one *big* thing . . . but there have been many others, believe me. Movies are over for me, and, while I do have a degree now, *Tía* Francisca scolded me about that . . . she said I was a fool to retire from films . . . and asked what was I going to do with my college degree? She knows how it is for me . . . that I could never teach, just like I could never be a stage actress, really. I feel comfortable playing music alone or with just Chris there to hear me, or a friend. I can play, even sing, in a group, but I cannot perform alone before strangers . . . not without the terror setting in, and I begin to tremble. No,

Tenny, there are many, many ways in which this *eudaimon* has not been favored. But I have made a good marriage . . . and, for me, there is nothing more meaningful than that . . . nothing better could ever have happened to me."

"I believe, Marcelina, that Nah-Loh-Tah's leaving . . . as I've said, I've thought and thought about it . . . she would talk sometimes about Demeter and Persephone. And I saw her in that dream I had . . . Nah-Loh-Tah . . . being dragged into the Underworld by Hades. There was a time . . . believe me . . . when I would have felt such things to be utter nonsense, but less and less now. Nah-Loh-Tah told me over and over . . . if I am to be completely honest about it . . . that she would have to . . . that she would leave me if I persisted in what I most wanted to do. It didn't make sense to me when she said it, and she would say no more, and it makes as little sense now . . . except that I understand she meant it, and Chris seems to have found a connection I hadn't between . . . well, for whatever reason, Nah-Loh-Tah felt she had to leave. And unlike Apollo, I must accept her decision gracefully." He paused, and it seemed he had difficulty speaking, but he continued with effort. "Tell me, Marcelina . . . about Apollo and

Daphne? Why was it so hopeless?"

"In a way," Marcelina replied, "myths are like dreams. They have no answers to practical questions . . . their proper domain has to do with meaning . . . but, as when the gods speak to us, a myth as a dream may often seem to provide only a paradox. To understand this meaning is never easy. Take the myth of Psyche's love for Eros . . . her love for the god of love himself. Every night Psyche visits Eros, with whom she has fallen in love, coming to his beautiful home at the bottom of a high cliff. Psyche is asked by Eros to make only one promise to him . . . that she will never light a lamp at night, when they are together, so that she will never be able to see him in its glow. One of Psyche's sisters, who is jealous of her and her lover, tempts Psyche by saying that Eros is actually a horrible beast who uses darkness to conceal his bestiality from Psyche's eyes. This terrible lie works like a poison on Psyche until one night, when Eros is sleeping after they have made love, Psyche lights a lamp to prove to herself that it is a lie. In its glow she beholds the beautiful, winged creature who is her lover. But, alas for Psyche, she is clumsy, and a drop of oil from the lamp falls upon Eros, and he wakens. Seeing that Psyche has betrayed her promise, he flees into the night."

"My God, Marcelina, do you know there is a story just like that in the Rig Veda?" The Englishman leaned forward now in his intensity, out of the shadow that had been growing about him. "It is the same situation . . . only in reverse. A heavenly nymph . . . her name is Urvaçi . . . falls in love with and marries King Puruavas . . . but she compels him to make one promise to her . . . that she must not behold him naked at night when they make love. The promise is broken . . . but not through his fault . . . but instead because the Gandharvas, the trickster spirits, cause lightning to play in the nocturnal sky, and Urvaçi does see the king in his nudity, and she vanishes."

"And is she lost to him forever?"

"As a matter of fact, she isn't," the Englishman said in a stronger voice. "In her heart, Urvaçi feels regret for what has happened. She comes to the king in a vision . . . a dream, I suppose . . . and she tells him that one year hence he may come to her and spend one night with her. By that time the son they have conceived will have been born. A year later the king comes on that very night and finds himself in a golden palace. There are nymphs in the palace who send Urvaçi to him. Urvaçi tells King Puruavas that the next day the Gandharvas will approach him and offer to grant him a single wish. She says he

245

may wish for anything he might want, but he tells her to choose the wish for him. She advises her beloved to wish to become a Gandharva . . . which he does . . . and by this means he becomes a suitable mate for her . . . having undergone the necessary fire ceremony by which a mortal may become a demigod . . . and so they are united at last . . . and forever."

Marcelina's face brightened with amusement, and an elfin humor played in her blue-gray eyes. "Chris and Ramón are out fetching sled dogs, and here we sit . . . exchanging myths . . . about the search for happiness."

The Englishman sighed. "It has never been easy for me, Marcie. I haven't ever found the place where I could be happy for the rest of my life. I thought I had . . . with Nah-Loh-Tah . . . but then I was still restless. I had come upon an understanding of the possible Arctic homeland of the Rig Veda, and I was all fired up about someday finding that place."

"Was it the danger that worried Nah-Loh-Tah?"

"My goodness, no. That woman was through more than her share of danger in her life. That last afternoon I was with her . . . before going on the picnic into the hills where she disappeared . . . Nah-Loh-Tah and I did talk a little about our life together. As a matter of fact, it was after she had sung one of her songs . . . a very sad song. I asked her if she believed it possible to find joy in life. She told me that . . . for her . . . she has experienced perfect joy in three different ways . . . the cessation of pain . . . the feeling of having an excess of strength . . . and . . . to be convinced that by doing what you are doing you're fulfilling your destiny. I asked her . . . if that were so, then what of Nemesis? And she said something rather odd . . . Nah-Loh-Tah said she believed that Nemesis was not really a divine entity at all, but rather just the thread in the course of events in a person's life, a thread that is always determined by the assumptions you make in your own soul . . . but like the inexorability of the planets in their courses, the thread of Nemesis will be seen *never* to break . . . until, of course, the thread is finally severed by death. The game of hide-and-seek came later . . . at dusk."

She reached over and touched his hand affectionately for a moment. "Among the legends of American Indians of the Southwest there is also a Gandharva . . . a trickster . . . and he is called Coyote. There is a story told of a clever young Indian girl who declared that she would not be satisfied with any ordinary human marriage, even if the prospective grooms came dressed in the most splendid finery, had extraordinary talents, or brought rich gifts. Although this girl's parents were poor, she was able to weave the finest cloth on a simple loom, and her weavings were so beautiful that many of the young men of her village came as suitors. She only kept her eyes on her work and paid no attention to them. When Coyote saw her, he knew she must become his wife, but he swore he would offer her no gifts and no promises. Instead, he went off into the mountains and brought back with him some black currants. To disguise himself, Coyote put on the costume of a human being. Stamping four times with his foot, he put on a pair of white buckskin moccasins. Then, taking the black currants in his left hand, he went to the center of the village and danced. The girl watched him as he danced and was charmed. It is said she was so charmed that she took Coyote home with her, made love with him, and that presently there were little coyote children born to them. Then one day Coyote drew her and the little coyotes with him, away from the village, and brought them to a secluded place where there was a small hole in the ground. 'How can anyone go in?' she asked him. 'It is so small.' But he crawled in easily, and the little coyotes followed after him. The girl looked in and saw that inside the hole there was a home just like the one she had lived in all her life, and that it was filled with the kind of clothes she loved to weave. So she bent herself and went inside . . . where . . . it is said . . . she was happy to remain for the rest of her days."

When she stopped speaking, there was silence between them for a time. Then, perhaps a bit to his own surprise, Sir Wilbur nodded. "I could not put it into words before, but, you know, I think I really do understand my dream now . . . or, at least, a part of it. I think Nah-Loh-Tah knew I would follow . . . only there were things I had to do first . . . and I began, then, by going in the wrong direction . . . following her through Afghanistan. That was *her* way. It could not be mine."

"No," agreed Marcelina. "What is that line Chris is so fond of in Shakespeare? . . . by indirections we find directions out? . . . or something like that."

Now the Englishman chuckled — for the first time since he had joined her. "Yes, Marcie . . . dear Marcelina . . . something *very* like that."

A *playa* very close to Point Barrow was used as a landing strip for airplanes. It was an area that was experiencing the typical cold summer of the Arctic regions, where the temperature almost never rises above freezing.

Most plants could not grow here, except for some woody greenery and willows that seem to be more shrubs than trees since their twigs lie either flat on the ground or even under the surface. Yet, human engineering among some of the white inhabitants had succeeded in overcoming the obstacle of persistently cold temperatures through enclosed truck gardens constructed so as to resemble hothouses to the south. As a result of the temperature, however, what would be considered winter clothing in temperate climates remained the standard apparel when outdoors all year around, although clothing not quite so heavy in June, July, and August as it was the rest of the year. It would be about the same temperature on Ellesmere Island, after the group was debarked from the *Janet* to begin the final overland part of this journey, so Point Barrow would prove a good orientation to very different living conditions.

Marcelina, more accustomed to warmer temperatures, wore three pairs of woolen socks — she would increase the number of them when the time came for her to wear her crampons. Ramón lived at a somewhat elevated level in Tacho Alto, and, of course, he was familiar with bitter cold from his mountain-climbing experiences in the Andes. Chris had been to the Arctic before and so knew what to expect. Sir Wilbur was familiar with winter cold from his youth in England and to a degree in Nepal, but Luis Valera, except for his one foray into the Andes on the way to find Haucha, had managed to avoid freezing temperatures for most of his life. It was all a matter of acclimatation, Chris explained. Mark Dworski was a veteran of cold places — he had grown up in northern Wisconsin with its Arctic winters — but he would be in the cold and on the ground very little, for which good fortune he was grateful.

Pierre LeBon, a tall, dapper French-Canadian, operated the local trading post, had the only radio in the area, and carried on a commercial enterprise among the natives and visitors to the area for hunting or sea fishing. He was on hand to greet them as the *Janet* taxied to a stop. With him was Dr. Sean O'Meara, the only practicing physician within two hundred miles, a man nearly seventy with heavy, wavy white hair beneath his winter cap, a narrow but kindly face, and a ruddy Irish complexion. It was O'Meara who invited all the travelers to his home for refreshments — a rather impressively large, log structure compared to the other living quarters in the white sector. It had extremely well-insulated walls and roofs. Not even he had central heating, however, although every room had a stove, and there was a fireplace in the spacious living room.

The airplane fuel, that had been shipped in at great expense, was kept in LeBon's warehouse. Since it was midday according to the time schedule the travelers were still following, after an hour's rest and refueling the *Janet*, the men would begin the major job of unloading all the gear stowed in the plane and replacing it with the fuel that was to be transported to Victoria Island. LeBon had hired two Eskimo men from the village to help him and his assistant in transporting the fuel from the warehouse to the Douglas Dolphin. Even so, it required almost four hours to complete the job.

Sir Wilbur, Valera, and Ramón pitched the two tents near the warehouse and slept in their sleeping bags. Sir Wilbur had a tent to himself on this occasion, while Luis and Ramón shared the Fallons' tent. Chris and Marcelina accepted Dr. O'Meara's invitation to stay the night in the guest room in his home, while Mark Dworski was accommodated with a small room with its own stove within Pierre LeBon's trading post. Chris and Marcelina were pleased to accept the elderly physician's invitation for Marcelina to remain in the guest room while the men were gone.

Except for Chris and Marcelina, early

morning ablutions were made in a small shed near Pierre LeBon's outhouse. None of the men bothered to shave. Breakfast consisted of flapjacks and bacon with coffee served at the trading post by Pierre LeBon's Eskimo wife, An-Na-Do-Ah, whom he called Anna. By six o'clock in the morning according to watches and clocks, the *Janet* was in the air, on its way from Point Barrow to the circumpolar way station near Walker Bay on Victoria Island. Much of this flight would be over water, past Beechey Point and Herschel Island in the Beaufort Sea and up the sea corridor between Banks Island and the Prince Albert Sound. It was, all in all, a distance of about eight hundred miles, and Chris calculated, taking into account head winds, that they should make it in about ten hours. Sir Wilbur had acquired copies of the aerial survey maps made in 1930 by the British Arctic Air Route Expedition, and it was these that Chris used to chart the course for this flight, and they would also be used in the flight to be made to Ellesmere Island. In 1934 the North Geomagnetic Pole was located at just about the center of Prince of Wales Island, to the northeast of Victoria Island and across the M'Clintock Channel from it, approximately 77° North by 102° West.

Marcelina had been fascinated to learn that

the North Geographical Pole — that goal so many intrepid adventurers had set themselves to reach over the past two centuries — was not the same as the North Geomagnetic Pole. Although the principle of the magnetic compass had been in use for some time in maritime navigation, it was Arctic exploration that had first brought to the fore this variance between the two poles. Captain Edward Sabine, sailing westward in 1820 along the Lancaster Sound, had noted that the ship's compass pointed due south instead of due north. They were several degrees below 80° N, and the only way to explain this phenomenon was that the magnetic pole was not at the North Geographical Pole at 90° N but in a different place. Of course, it would be some years later before the movement of the North Geomagnetic Pole would begin being charted as it changed position up and down in degrees of latitude and longitude. It was pinpointed in 1831 as being just above King William Island, east of Victoria Island, but, since then, it had been ascending in latitude until its present position. Chris told Marcelina that like almost everything having to do with electromagnetism, just why the North Geomagnetic Pole moves, and what its movement might mean, could not be explained, certainly not by him. Perhaps more would be learned as a result of the studies being conducted on electro-magnetism that year in the Arctic.

Marcelina had joined the men at breakfast and saw them off. Of course, it was just after the summer solstice. On this day in the Arctic the Sun was making its flat 360° orbit at about 24° above the horizon. It did not rise, and it did not set. There was really no night as she had known it all the thirty-three years of her life. But were she a winged goddess and were she able to fly due south, she would be able to notice that the arc of the Sun would rise higher and higher in the southern sky as it sank lower and lower in the northern sky. It would be first when she encountered that point on the meridian between the poles where she crossed the line of latitude at about 66° N that she would begin to notice that the Sun had dropped low enough actually not to touch the northern horizon behind her for the first time.

Dr. O'Meara was also up to see the *Janet* take flight, and he witnessed the deep and passionate kiss Marcelina gave Chris before he boarded. O'Meara, like the travelers, regulated his life by the United States clock for this time zone. So did Pierre LeBon and the others, including the Methodist missionary and his wife, in the American segment of the village. However, the natives, Inupiat Eskimos, unlike even most Arctic wild life, did not synchronize themselves with the rhythm of day and night that guided all the peoples to the south. Eskimos generally in Alaska and the Dominion of Canada, Yakuts in the Soviet Union, and Laplanders in Scandinavia remained enclaves that refused to schedule and pattern their lives according to a solar chronology that was meaningless to them.

The medical man's passion remained painting Arctic landscapes, and this is how he would spend the morning hours, whether sunlight was present or not, in his studio. His late wife, Catherine, had been an English teacher in the Detroit school system for many years, before, their one son grown, they decided to homestead in the Arctic. O'Meara had taken several trips over the years into the Canadian North-West Territories and even to Greenland, where his object had been to pursue his desire to paint landscapes of the Far North. After years and years of Arctic winters in Michigan, nothing in the way of cold, ice, and snow in Alaska surprised either of them. It was Catherine who had begun conducting classes in English for the natives. She had felt that it was essential that the Inupiat Eskimos learn the language of their conquerors, or they would in all probability be faced in time with the same destructive fate that had befallen the four hundred Indian nations over the last four centuries in North America. In the beginning only a few of the native women had attended these classes, held during the winter months, but gradually some of the men had begun to attend as well, and sometimes native peoples had come from great distances to attend her classes. One of Catherine's most prestigious students had been Ahg-Gah-Guk, shaman of the Inupiats.

Since Catherine's death, Dr. O'Meara had not continued her classes in English, but like Catherine he had learned the Inupiat language sufficiently to understand it and even to speak it. In this way, for Catherine and for him, the teaching of the English language had really been an exchange of languages. Now the Reverend Mr. Davidson and his wife taught school for the Inupiat children during the winter months at the Methodist mission. They had about thirty students of various ages. It was not the same, however, as it had been when Catherine had been doing the teaching. The Davidsons included in their curriculum what they regarded as the spiritual truths of Christianity, which were intended to replace the primitive superstitions of the older generation of Eskimos, and they incorporated subjects that stressed the achievements of modern civilization. As far as Dr. O'Meara was concerned, this enterprise was not wholly successful, since the Davidsons complained that tribal customs and beliefs were particularly obstinate and almost as difficult to eradicate as a cancer. However, their efforts did have the financial and moral backing of the territorial authorities, and in the end they probably would succeed — at least to a degree — as had earlier generations of missionaries and educators among the various North American Indian nations.

That morning, after the *Janet* had become airborne, Marcelina returned with Dr. O'Meara to his home. The physician, showing her around the rest of the house, explained that, like Eskimo carving, their language is dynamic, and observations seem always to be from a variety of viewpoints. English, having its roots in Indo-European languages like Greek and Latin, is dependent on tense, which is to say time — the present, the imperfect, the perfect, and the future. Unlike Greek and Latin and modern romance languages like Marcelina's native Spanish, however, English has really lost the sense of the subjunctive mood. It tends to state only what is or was or will be, but cannot express save with great awkwardness what only may be or what might not but possibly could be. For the Eskimo, time or duration are not so important, but rather space. To Americans, there seems to be a linguistic consensus that the top of something is the top, the bottom of something is the bottom, and that north and south are meaningful directions. The Eskimo, on the other hand, in referring to some place that is very far away will ignore any land in between or bodies of water, but focus instead on certain geographical points, but not necessarily from the point of view of the person talking or of the person listening. Their language is also very seasonal, and certain words come out only in summer, and others only in winter, such as words for different varieties of snow. When hunting or fishing, Eskimos will travel sometimes incredible distances, but scarcely ever in a straight line, as if there were some definite goal ahead as is the case with Europeans and Americans.

"Ultimately, I suppose," O'Meara continued as he opened the door to his studio, "our language remains something we have imposed on reality, just as we have imposed ourselves on the land . . . any land . . . wherever we happen to be. For the Eskimo, the land itself is alive and is constantly changing. Nothing is truly permanent, and so they look at land and animals very differently. But . . . here is where my soul is."

He led the way into the room which was

like a small addition to the house, but with windows facing to the east, the north, and the west. There was a large, potbellied stove on the right-hand side of the southern wall in which the door was located. There was an easel, and a canvas was upon it, with its back to the entrance, and there was a long table with various tubes of oil paint and several jars with brushes in them against the far wall. On the southern wall on the left-hand side were two canvases that had been framed. Marcelina was immediately struck by the painting that was hung above the other. It was of snow geese in flight at dusk. The generating line of the painting had captured the unwavering intent of their passage. It reminded Marcelina vividly of Chris's film about the snow birds when they flocked to Tule Lake.

"I call it 'Night Voices,' " the artist said softly. "I have come to regard the migration of the snow birds and other creatures the same as breathing . . . as the breathing of the land itself. In the spring it is as if the land takes a deep inhalation . . . and with that inhalation comes the continuing light, the birds, and many of the animals. In the summer . . . as now . . . it is as if the breathing in and out becomes more moderate, more peaceful somehow. And then, in the fall . . . it is like a great exhalation . . . as if the breathing land itself were propelling them all to go south again."

Marcelina's blue-gray eyes were very large, like they, too, were breathing in the long sigh transfixed in transit in the picture, and then they dropped to the lower painting. In it were the waters of a lead, as dark as India ink with facing images of blue translucent ice being mirror images, one to the other, as two souls looking deeply into each other.

"I call this 'When the Whales Come,' " said the artist, "and, as often happens, you cannot see them except as dark shadows in a greater darkness. By the middle of May, here at Point Barrow, you can sometimes see the whales moving through the leads, after having come through the Bering Strait, and swimming north by northeast. Of course, you cannot really see the underside of the ice, but, if you could, you would notice where their backs have rubbed the undersides, and sometimes you will see where they have broken through seal holes in order to breathe, and how . . . look here . . ." — he pointed to the upper left of the picture — "and you will see how it appears that the ice has refrozen over an air hole that was once smashed by a whale in its passage. They are the most remarkable creatures, you know, able to find their way from one open lead to the next in heavy ice. Because they have white chins and bellies, you can sometimes spot them as they cruise just beneath the translucent ice . . . as there."

By having it called to her notice, the vague image suddenly became transparent to Marcelina, and she saw the suggestion of the white markings of the form through the ice, illumining the darkness of the water.

"I no longer have it . . . it was sold by a gallery in Toronto where I sent it . . . but there was a winter seascape to go with these other two . . . one I called '*Ivu*' . . . the Eskimo word for a phenomenon that happens here in the Arctic . . . when a huge island of sea ice suddenly comes surging hundreds of feet inland, as if propelled by some mysterious force you cannot see and can only imagine . . . as if, in that time, the ice itself were something alive. You can observe it, though . . . if you have what the Eskimos call *quinuituq* . . . deep patience. It is not the same as in the Bible . . . that everything comes to he who waits . . . because waiting is not to be confused with patience. *Ivu* is part of the rhythm of the Arctic, which is unlike the rhythm of life anywhere else I have ever been. To grasp *ivu* you have to understand that . . . despite our deep-seated desire to find invariance in nature . . . there is too much imagination, too much energy, too much life even in the seemingly inanimate to make invariance anything other than a human illusion. It is like the universe itself . . . because there seems to be invariance in the motion of the spheres . . . we believe it is invariance . . . but that is only because it takes thousands upon thousands of centuries to record that, even here, there is variance. Nothing is static." The physician smiled. "No, not even entropy . . . not even death. I am at work now on what I feel may be my finest Arctic landscape," he said, moving over toward the easel. On it was a canvas perhaps five feet wide and four feet high. "I know I should have made a larger canvas . . . because it is a bigger picture, as I am working on it, than really can be brought out in this canvas. But I am old, you know, and so I started small . . . and it probably means I shall have to start all over . . . on a canvas much, much larger."

Even though the canvas may have been small, Marcelina felt herself overwhelmed. She could only gaze in awe at the sheer wall of glacial ice rising up out of the dark water, a mighty, towering, implacable edifice, here blue-gray, there almost white, and above it and off to the right side a diffused, indistinct light. It was truly an Arctic landscape, a magnificent icescape reaching upwards, upwards into a panorama of sky filled with clouds, distinguished here and there by the varying intensity of the light, not direct light, but a glowing illumination, brighter here, shaded there, light that was white and gold and a grayish pink by degrees. There were no living creatures of any kind in the picture save for the snow birds, but it was as if the light itself were also alive, reflecting myriad hues from the gray, blue, and gold of the translucent wall of ice.

Here's a fence without an opening . . .
Up to heaven is the fence builded,
To the very clouds uprising.

As he uttered these words, Marcelina turned toward the physician, his patrician face illumined by the soft glow of light that filled this room.

"From the Kalevala, you know?" he prompted.

"I thought it might be," Marcelina said quietly, "but I wasn't sure."

"But," said the artist, "those are only words . . . while the emotions transmute into colors the pain, the loss, even death . . . transmute . . . allowing you to abandon common sense altogether, to laugh at experience." He reached out with his right hand and regarded the wall of ice. "My vision began here at the shallow edge of a vast, luminous sea . . . like

Henry More's ANIMA MUNDI . . . or Wordsworth's 'immortal sea which brought us hither,' and near whose edge at the great wall of ice the snow birds are seen to sport. In that sea there are some who swim and some who sail through the air . . . but explorers all . . . who perhaps alone know all of its shores. I think I shall call it . . . the 'Islands of the Blessed.' "

Makaron Nyesoeessee. Marcelina didn't dare to say it, even as the words rose in her soul. "Is this a landscape of a place you have ever been?" she asked instead.

"In a way," he said softly. "Not physically . . . no. But four . . . maybe almost five years ago now . . . two natives came here from far away . . . from a place such as this. They came in early winter and stayed until spring. They wanted very much to be taught the English language for they were going still farther away, and where they were going that language was spoken. Of course, it is also spoken throughout Canada and America, but that is not where they were going . . . or to England."

"Two natives?"

"Yes, a middle-aged man and a woman . . . perhaps then in her late twenties."

"Do you remember their names?"

"Certainly. Teh-Meh-Tayo was the man's name."

"And the woman's?"

"Nah-Loh-Tah . . . only both were pronounced differently than the usual Eskimo names, with the stress on the first syllable, the middle syllable aspirated quietly, and the last syllable with no emphasis at all. Catherine thought it very odd, but they dressed as Eskimos and lived in the village . . . a house made of skins fortified by snow. Nah-Loh-Tah was a fine musician. She often sang at the soirees we would give here. I play the 'cello, you know, although I am hardly a gifted musician, and Catherine played the piano. That upright you saw in the living room was hers. It hasn't been touched since she died."

"Was her death an accident?"

"Goodness, no. I'm a doctor, after all . . . have been for most of my life . . . probably most of all. She suffered from hypertension. I treated her as best I could over the years, but there really is no cure for it, and she died of an aortic aneurysm . . . burst a vessel, in layman's terms."

"It must have been very hard for you . . . having been together all those years."

"Yes . . . but we both knew she would probably die before I did. Everyone suffers from arteriosclerosis as they age, but combined with hypertension it finally became too much for her. She is buried near here in the community cemetery. It will be two years next December. But Catherine didn't die before her time. She had white hair . . . not like that woman W. B. Yeats talks about who did die before her time, and so, when her spirit was seen on All Souls' Day, as the years passed, her hair was observed to be turning increasingly gray.

"But you asked if this is a picture of something I've seen. The answer to that is, yes, I have . . . but not in the way most people today would understand it. Painting for me is the rendering of a vision, a dream, although because of my experience of the Arctic, landscapes and seascapes, the details are totally realistic. It is a sad thing, the way so many of us these days have forced from our souls the visions that are so vital to our spiritual welfare. Few of us draw or paint or imagine any more. We take photographs instead. But a photograph doesn't answer the same spiritual need within us. A painter recognizes that there are no limits to an impassioned vision, and often the vision is more real than physical reality. A painting has about it this greater dimension . . . which a photograph does not . . . that the painter imprints on it an expression of his own vision, his emotions, his individuality. You cannot separate the painting from what begins inside the painter. Satisfying ourselves with mere photographs is a two dimensional experience. Painting adds the third . . . like what timbre is to music." Dr. O'Meara smiled gently. "Do you play an instrument?"

The question was so sudden and so unexpected that Marcelina was embarrassed. "The piano . . . a little," she answered, very quietly. "But music is for me what painting, you say, is for you. It is something fantastic in which I can lose myself. It is then that I can dream openly, outwardly, freely."

"All of us need to dream," O'Meara observed softly, "and, if our soul is to thrive, if we are not to fall ill or into despair, we must attend very much to our dreams. And certainly our dreams stay the longer, the greater the passion with which they are created. So filled with life can they become that they can even grow into life with being. The most inconceivable thing about the Arctic . . . like perhaps the whole sidereal universe all around us . . . is that it should be conceivable at all. Those lines from the Kalevala struck me as I began this painting. They kept running through my mind. I've only read it in English, of course." He paused, and then continued somehow in a deeper tone of voice, more breathless. "Those words struck me as what this gigantic wall of ice *means* . . . to me, at least . . . a manifestation of a power more inexorable than the stars can ever seem . . . the apparent endlessness of creation . . . the infinitude of imagination."

"*Partes miserationis parcissimæ,*" Marcelina responded in almost a whisper.

O'Meara smiled. "The old Romans used to say that . . . quite aptly . . . 'most meager are our claims for sympathy.' "

Tears in Marcelina's eyes glistened in the gentle light of the studio.

"I recall a German philosopher who wrote that we have Art so that we may not perish from Truth," the physician said.

"Then he must have loved Wagner, and not understood Bach or Mozart," Marcelina affirmed.

"He came to hate Wagner later . . . and to love Bizet."

Marcelina laughed gently.

"You're mighty well read for an . . . ," he began.

"*Actrreess,*" she finished for him. "So I've heard . . . a lot, I'm afraid . . . but that was before . . . not any more."

"My son's an actor of sorts, you know. Not in films, of course. The legitimate stage . . . and, no, not in New York, but in Detroit."

"Is he married?"

"No-o . . . oh, he was at one time . . . to a . . . well, as Catherine used to put it . . . our only hope for a grandchild from that union would depend completely on the intervention of the Holy Ghost."

Marcelina nodded but did not speak. The certainty of divine intervention was extremely precious to her, and, when she seemed on the edge of losing it, as happened to her sometimes, she would feel especially helpless. In her innermost imagination, as when trying to portray a character on the screen or performing a piece of music on the piano, and most recently working on her study of Indian religious beliefs, she tried to arrive at a scheme of things that was so beautiful and so orderly that even the losses would have their place, like the spaces created by the apertures in a great colonnade. Ecstasy for her was never gratuitous. She had experienced it, as surely Sean O'Meara when painting his Arctic landscapes must, willingly and gaily, but knowing there is always a price attached, sometimes loss, sometimes death, and this very spirit for Marcelina was her definition of true heroism. One is forced by life, always, to pay a price even for existence, and that price is usually learning to live with pain and loss, even death, but in the process one is free to laugh at the price and even at oneself for caring about it. Perhaps this lightness, this seeming frivolity in her, might be mistaken for a perversity of the soul, but, if so, there could be nevertheless, she believed, a nobility about it. She realized on a level deeper than words could ever reach the freedom Sean O'Meara had finally achieved in his life, but also the great price he had had to pay for it.

"Would you like to see one of Nah-Loh-Tah's songs? She let me copy it down . . . for the 'cello, of course, and so it is all in the bass clef, but you could transpose it for two hands at the piano, if you wanted."

However, it was not to be, not then. An Eskimo from the village came to the front door. Hah-Nah-Nak had been injured while hunting. It was his arm. Perhaps it was broken. The physician asked Marcelina if she would be willing to come along as his nurse, as Catherine had when she was alive. Besides he had another call to make in the village. Nuh-Tung-Nuk, the young second wife of Ahg-Gah-Guk, shaman of the Inupiats, was expecting her first child, and the doctor had promised to look in on her. After reminding O'Meara that she was . . . well, she had been only a motion picture actress and really knew nothing of nursing — Marcelina said she was certainly willing to help in any way she could.

The previous night Marcelina had heard the frequent howling of the dogs in the Eskimo village which was just beyond the white settlement with the hothouses and truck gardens and Pierre LeBon's combination barn and warehouse. Today as she walked beside Dr. O'Meara, following the Eskimo who had come to fetch the physician, dogs were barking and growling everywhere, and increasingly she became aware of the penetrating stench of the village, a blend of decomposing terrene and marine and animal offal. The village consisted of many skin tents which would be fortified with snow during the cold time and a few wooden shacks or sheds. Some of the shacks had tin roofs. The largest of the shacks belonged to Ahg-Gah-Guk, the shaman, and they would be visiting it later that morning.

The medical man had brought his black bag with him and had given Marcelina some splints, rolls of gauze, tape, and a bag of plaster of paris to carry. These were to be used if Hah-Nah-Nak's arm were actually broken. The man lived in a skin tent at the far end of the village with his wife, children, and his mother, and it was here that he had gone after the fall he had experienced hunting. As it turned out, the arm was broken, fortunately a clean break so there might be no complications. Marcelina's assistance was careful — she did not wish to make any mistakes — but competent, and she proved especially adept at the bandaging.

It was actually to prove a busy morning. An old Eskimo woman with iron-gray hair and an incredibly wrinkled countenance had an abdominal complaint, and one of the middle-aged men of the village was suffering from a bad tooth. Notwithstanding having had no training as a dentist, Dr. O'Meara extracted the molar. Then there was a visit to the lodge of Ahg-Gah-Guk. Nuh-Tung-Nuk was approximately in her seventh month.

The lodge was spacious compared to the others Marcelina had visited with the physician, two rooms made of wood, a partition of skins separating the sleeping area from the living area. Marcelina was surprised to see among the furnishings of the living area a wind-up Victrola, and Ahg-Gah-Guk had three one-sided records of march music. Ahg-Gah-Guk's face was seamed by weather and perhaps age. He sat near an open stove on furs, and he invited Marcelina to join him in a cup of tea served by his first wife, a middle-aged woman who smiled pleasantly and was very solicitous but did not speak.

While O'Meara went behind the animal skin partition with Nuh-Tung-Nuk, Marcelina remained sitting opposite Ahg-Gah-Guk on the furs before the open stove in which burned a low fire that gave some illumination in the room's darkness.

"Before doctor man came, our women gave birth without such help," he said, "but perhaps this way is better. You are to help doctor man?"

"I helped Doctor O'Meara today when he went to see Hah-Nah-Nak. But soon the others who came with me will return with the airplane, and then we all shall leave. Our journey will take us to Ellesmere Island . . . and beyond."

"I know that place . . . I was there many years ago. It was near there . . . when we were hunting whales . . . that I died and so became shaman."

"You died there?"

"Yes. It was a terrible death. My harpoon had hit the whale, and the whale dove deep into the water, swimming under the ice. The rope on the harpoon pulled me from the umiak and into the water, and I followed that whale under the ice. That is where I died. I do not know how long I was dead there, under the ice. I must have been frozen, for they said I was frozen when they found me. I was not breathing. There was no life in my body. But then, after long time, I began to breathe again. I was born then as you see me now. I became shaman."

"Your people all believed that you had died?"

"We do not believe. We fear. Death is a part of life, and it is ever present. What we do believe . . . what makes us different from all the people from the south . . . is that we do not imagine ourselves as separate from the other animals . . . the whales . . . the bears . . . the foxes . . . the wolves . . . the seals . . . all living things. They are a part of us . . . and we are like them. We live until we die. But sometimes we die . . . and then we come back to live again. When that happens, it is very . . ." — he searched for the word — "very special. It does not happen often. But sometimes it happens."

"Did you remember anything from the time when you were dead?" Marcelina wondered.

Ahg-Gah-Guk smiled, the many lines of his wind-riven face crinkling, but his dark eyes never moved from Marcelina's. "When I was dead, I was like Tôr-Nârs-Suk . . . the polar bear. Tôr-Nârs-Suk once fell in love with a young married woman . . . a woman from the south . . . like you. And she fell in love with Tôr-Nârs-Suk. They would meet in a secret place, and they would make love together. Tôr-Nârs-Suk warned this woman he loved and who loved him that she must never tell her husband about him. If her husband should learn of Tôr-Nârs-Suk, he would kill him. This woman's husband was also from the south, and he had been hunting . . . hunting for days and days to find a polar bear to kill it. The husband only failed . . . over and over he failed . . . and he was so sad because he always failed to find a polar bear. Finally his wife took pity on him. She told her husband where Tôr-Nârs-Suk lived. Now Tôr-Nârs-Suk was far away from where these two were living in an igloo, but it was night, and on the night wind Tôr-Nârs-Suk heard her murmuring to her husband. Tôr-Nârs-Suk left his home where he and the woman had met so often to make love. He left, and, when the husband came, Tôr-Nârs-Suk was gone. While the husband had come to Tôr-Nârs-Suk's home to kill him, Tôr-Nârs-Suk had gone to the igloo where the woman he loved was living. He came quietly to the igloo, and he raised his paws to smash in a wall and to kill the woman who had betrayed him. But Tôr-Nârs-Suk could not do it. He could not smash in the snow wall. He could not kill the woman he loved. Tôr-Nârs-Suk was overcome with grief, and so he began wandering. It was a long and lonely journey that Tôr-Nârs-Suk made, and he wanders even now . . . he has never stopped wandering. When I died, I was like Tôr-Nârs-Suk. I wandered.

Only when I awoke, I stopped wandering. I was Ahg-Gah-Guk. I was shaman."

He motioned then with his right hand, urging Marcelina to drink her tea. She lifted her cup and drank.

"When the others come back, where on Ellesmere Island will you go?"

"I don't exactly know . . . but it will be beyond the glacier, beyond the island . . . perhaps out into the Arctic Ocean."

Ahg-Gah-Guk looked at her very severely, his eyes at once bright and deep. *"Unne-sinig-po . . . ooh-ah-tonie i-o-doria. Ooh ah-tonie i-o-doria."*

"Please . . . ?" Marcelina asked, and shook her head negatively to indicate that she did not understand.

Dr. O'Meara had come back from behind the curtain of skins, his examination evidently concluded, and he had heard what Ahg-Gah-Guk had just said. "It is well to die," he translated. "Beyond is impossible. Beyond is impossible."

Marcelina averted her blue-gray eyes to glance at the physician.

"I think doctor man say right," Ahg-Gah-Guk agreed. Then he repeated slowly: "Beyond . . . is impossible."

"To die is well?" Marcelina inquired softly, looking back at the shaman.

"Beyond is impossible," Ahg-Gah-Guk re-affirmed. "To go beyond is . . . to die. Beyond is impossible."

As they were walking back to the doctor's home, O'Meara confided more to Marcelina about that fateful whaling voyage on which Ahg-Gah-Guk had died and become shaman. The course he and his fellow whalers had followed was truly long and arduous. There were six umiaks involved, and Ahg-Gah-Guk was the leader. In their quest to find the whales, he was guided by dreams he'd had. Winter had been approaching, and the water was freezing over. Hunting had been very bad that year, and the men had been unable to find the food they needed. In pursuing the whales in the visions he'd had, men in two of the umiaks had begun to doubt him and his dreams, and they had turned back rather than perish following him. Only those men did perish, in trying to make their way back to Point Barrow, whereas those who stayed with Ahg-Gah-Guk did find whales, and they were able to stay alive, and they did, also, return safely to their homes.

O'Meara customarily did not have break-fast, coffee sufficing, but he did have lunch, and this Marcelina insisted on preparing. It was O'Meara's custom to spend his mornings in his studio painting, but that had not been possible this day, nor was it at all uncommon for him to be interrupted. He confessed that he supposed this made him an amateur, rather than a professional, since he lacked the tyrannical devotion to painting that he thought great artists had to have, but he enjoyed it, felt he was good at it — in which Marcelina wholeheartedly concurred — and he had even had some commercial success over the last ten years. In the warm months he would work regularly in his extensive truck garden, and he had taken to making his own preserves since Catherine had died. She had so enjoyed doing it.

After lunch, they went to the other side of the spacious main room, where Marcelina sat at the upright piano. O'Meara gave her the sheets on which he had transcribed Nah-Loh-Tah's song. Nah-Loh-Tah herself had translated the words as an exercise while she was learning the English language. Marcelina was able by sight-reading to transpose the octaves. After playing it through twice, the second time with O'Meara's accompaniment on the 'cello, she decided that she would like to try singing the words. Marcelina was not a professional singer, to be sure, but she had sung in several of her films, and her voice had a singular purity of intonation. The song was a ballad, to be played largetto, and there was about it almost a Celtic atmosphere of wistful melancholy.

> Thou dost not die from all the many
>   wounds
> That pierce your breast,
> Unless your life's end has kept pace
> With Thanatos.
> Nor by sitting at home before your
>   hearth
> Mayest thou escape the hour
> Thanatos hath decreed for your rest.
>
> Alone of the gods, Thanatos loves not
>   gifts.
> No, not by sacrifice or by libation
> Canst thou in any way make him turn
>   back.
> He hath no altar, and no hymn of praise.
> From him alone is all entreaty deflected,
> As a wheel turns in endless rotation.
>
> So dwell upon your happiness now
> And the happiness of your ways,
> And pray your time may be long and
>   darkness
> Remain a stranger.
> Blessed be your lot,
> And may you be beloved of the gods
> All of your days.

For we have crossed to the other side
Of the night.
Aurora, gleaming, hath prepared the
   way,
Delightful like the rhythm of a poem,
She smiles and shines.
Her beautiful face has awakened us
To the light.

Marcelina felt the strange, haunting spirit of the song, and, having sung it once, she sang and played it again, as O'Meara provided the 'cello obbligato.

There was other sheet music, from the days when Catherine was alive and the O'Mearas would put on their soirees. There were two musicians in the village, Ah-Wee-Lah who played a bone reed instrument and Etuk-Aih-Shook who played a sealskin tam-tam. O'Meara suggested that they should join them to prepare a musical soiree during this time that she was here, and it could be presented as an evening's entertainment when the travelers returned in the *Janet*. In fact, it could be quite a social event, with guests from the white settlement, including Pierre LeBon and his wife, the Methodist missionary and his wife — they had made some converts among the Eskimos after two years of proselytizing, and Etuk-Aih-Shook had been one of them. People should be invited from the village. Marcelina proposed Ahg-Gah-Guk should be included among them, if he would come. He would, O'Meara assured her. The shaman loved music, even if his personal taste did run rather exclusively to march music. So it was agreed between them, and the next afternoon they would have a rehearsal.

Chapter Eight

The return of the *Janet* was delayed almost two days beyond the schedule Sir Wilbur had set, due to heavy fog at Victoria Island. Pierre LeBon's radio receiver and transmitter, operated by means of a gasoline generator, kept him abreast of weather conditions in the Arctic, and he had received a radio report concerning this heavy fog cover in that area. He presumed it would likely cause some delay. O'Meara assured Marcelina once again that in the Arctic one must have patience, for much time was always to be spent waiting for the right weather, and only the foolish ignored weather conditions in any season. Not *quinuituq,* but just waiting, Marcelina affirmed, and the physician could only agree. Among her duties were feeding and attending to the dogs. She regretted she couldn't let them run free.

Dr. O'Meara had a combination operating-examining room and study in which he kept his medical books and supply of pharmaceuticals — mail was delivered by airplane, and he regularly received medical magazines and bulletins. His personal library was on shelves at the far side of the living room, across from the fireplace, and it was here Marcelina found a wealth of books of poetry. In her idle time, she read a thin chapbook of poetic meditations by W. B. Yeats titled PER AMICA SILENTIA LUNAE from 1917, and several of the poems from a collection of poetry by John Keats. She also finished reading Ovid's METAMORPHOSES which she had begun while they were in Juneau. But it was to lines she had encountered in the book by Yeats to which she returned again and again, as if, somehow, in their very depths they held a key to her life:

I call to the mysterious one who yet
Shall walk the wet sands by the edge of
    the stream
And look most like me, being indeed my
    double,
And prove of all imaginable things
The most unlike, being my anti-self,
And, standing by these characters,
    disclose
All that I seek; and whisper it as though
He were afraid the birds, who cry aloud
Their momentary cries before it is dawn,
Would carry it away to blasphemous
    men.

The physician was somewhat frail physically, and thin, but he conserved his energy well, being able to paint, work in the hot-house, practice on the 'cello, and discharge his medical duties. He was not a wealthy man by any means, but his needs in Point Barrow were modest, and he had a savings account in a Nome bank. Marcelina herself was pleased to spend some time at the upright piano, and her playing delighted the elderly physician who, as he once confessed to her, had been surrounded by too much silence since Catherine's death.

The *Janet* returned from the flight to Victoria Island on July 3rd. Not only had they been delayed by fog at Walker Bay, but they had encountered heavy fog again on the return flight off Beechey Point, and they had put down onto the water in the Beaufort Sea rather than change course completely and attempt to fly farther out to sea to bypass the fog. They were all tired and hungry, and Sir Wilbur insisted that they lay over at Point Barrow until the morning of July 5th. Somewhat appropriately the evening soiree was scheduled for July 4th, a national holiday in the United States and its Territories celebrating independence from Great Britain. Sir Wilbur accepted a little well-intended humor at the expense of the British Crown from

Mark Dworski and Dr. O'Meara. The medical man extended his remarks to encompass the possibility that someday, perhaps, Great Britain would finally get out of Ireland altogether.

Ah-Wee-Lah brought his family, including his three children. Etuk-Aih-Shook, who was middle-aged with streaks of gray in his straight hair and many wrinkles in the burnished skin of his countenance, brought his wife, his grown daughter, and her husband. The Reverend Davidson was a man of forty, still handsome with curly black hair and a red mouth. His wife, now the local schoolmistress, was perhaps two years older, her dark hair worn with a severe central part and gathered in a bun at the back of her head. They both dressed somewhat formally, as if living the year around in temperatures that never really rose above freezing were only another austerity that they must endure in the spirit of quiet sacrifice, for, after all, they seemed to agree, there is no human moral achievement possible without having to forebear with equanimity any adversity that may come. Ahg-Gah-Guk came with both his wives and was regarded with subtle but silent disapproval by the Davidsons who believed, as their religion instructed and as their nation had codified into law, that one man needs must have only

286

one wife. Mark Dworski obviously was influenced by no such reservation about the matter since he struck up a conversation at once with Nuh-Tung-Nuk, and, although shy, she seemed willing enough to converse with the pilot as well as she could in English highlighted by more than a few Inupiat words that then she would have to try to explain with difficulty, occasionally calling upon her husband for assistance. Ahg-Gah-Guk seemed flattered by Dworski's interest in his younger wife.

There were not enough chairs really to go around, so most of the auditors sat on the floor on blankets and furs. The room, due to the roaring fire and the number of massed people, was actually quite warm. The musical program was highly eclectic and lasted well over an hour, consisting of traditional Celtic songs like "Rose of Allendale," "Loving Hannah," "The Broom of the Cowdenknows" — this was the oldest of them, a ballad from the Scottish borderlands dating back to the middle of the 17th Century — and "Since Maggie Went Away" — the most recent with one exception, since the words were by Sean O'Casey. The exception was the song of Nah-Loh-Tah that appeared as the penultimate piece in the concert, following instrumental renderings of "Greensleeves" and

Handel's "Largo." The closing selection was the first movement of Beethoven's "Archduke" Trio with the bone flute playing the violin part, and the sealskin tam-tam adding bass emphasis in some of the 'cello passages. Marcelina sang the vocal parts for all of the songs. The ballad by Nah-Loh-Tah actually had no title, but Dr. O'Meara, before it was performed, introduced it as "A Song of the Morning." If Marcelina had had problems in the past performing or speaking before groups of people, she seemed this night to sing and play with what for her was extraordinary self-confidence. Chris, seeing how well it all went, was especially happy for her.

Marcelina had not been privy to the actual words that had been spoken in the dream about Hades that Sir Wilbur had had in San Francisco, and Chris had never discussed with her his subsequent elucidation of the probable origin of those words in NIOBE, but the effect, hearing the song whole and complete, the very words in Marcelina's pure tones reverberating back to the many times he had heard Nah-Loh-Tah sing it in Nepal and, later, in Peshawar, the musical accompaniment surrounding it with an incandescent aura, was both riveting and electrifying for the Englishman. Chris, too, recognized the stanza he had once translated for Sir Wilbur, and he looked with shocked perplexity at him, but the Englishman exchanged only the briefest of glances and remained silent, absorbed in the music.

It was after the concert that punch was served (despite Repeal, the Davidsons felt there was quite enough drinking among the Eskimos as it was, and so out of deference to them the physician and Marcelina had kept the punch non-alcoholic). Along with it were pastries Mrs. Davidson had prepared and brought. It was after the refreshments that Sir Wilbur was able to ask the elderly physician if they might have a word in private when the opportunity availed. To this Dr. O'Meara agreed, and, while some of the guests, including Chris and Marcelina, were smoking and talking, the two retired to the physician's little medical study and examining room. Neither said afterward what the conversation had been about, although Chris assumed that perhaps the Englishman had consulted the doctor about some personal medical problem. It wasn't until later that night, after the soiree was ended and the two had repaired to the guest room, that Chris and Marcelina were able to talk intimately with each other. Yet the austere furnishings of the guest room did not really accommodate comfort, there being but one chair of polished wood with arms and a high back, a small table beneath a very narrow window with a thick, double pane of glass to provide some insulation, and the bed. The only source of artificial illumination in the room was from a kerosene lamp on the small table, but given the season and the dim light from the ever-present Sun, this lamp was unnecessary, although shadows did shroud all of the corners. The others, except for Mark Dworski who was, again, staying in the spare bedroom at the trading post, were sleeping in the tents.

There was a wood stove directly across from the right side of the bed, and a fire was now blazing inside of it, keeping the chill off the room, at least in its immediate vicinity. Rather than sitting on either the chair or the bed, Chris invited Marcelina to join him on the heavy, shag, oval-shaped rug between the wood stove and the bed.

"I feel," he said, "as if I were dreaming while being awake, and wandering. It is as if I am no longer able to choose my own way . . . as if I'm only allowing the world to form itself around me . . . that, if I close my eyes and open them again, it will be only in that way I can really find out where I am . . . as if the waves of fate are washing all about me, and, I suppose, when once I open my eyes tomorrow, I will first learn where I am."

"While you were gone," Marcelina told him, sitting cross-legged across from him on the rug, "I went to the trading post, and I made a purchase."

"Something I missed?" Chris asked in amusement.

"In a way. Pierre LeBon had only two of them . . . and for some reason he had not been able to sell them. But I thought they would be the very thing." She smiled gaily. "They're in the corner over there." She indicated with her eyes the direction of the wall behind the door to the room. "They're folded up now, but I know I never saw anything like them. They're like a director's chair with very short legs, a canvas back rest, and a canvas seat, and in the very center of the canvas seat is a rubber bowl in the shape of a chamber pot. Once we're on Ellesmere Island and all sleeping in the tents, these potty chairs would give us some convenience, if not privacy. I also bought two bottles of ammonia-based disinfectant to keep the rubber bowls sanitary after use. The ammonia will also keep the liquid from freezing easily. I know we certainly never had anything like this when we were in the Andes."

Chris smiled. "The very thing . . . since from now on it probably will always be below freezing outside, despite the perpetual sunlight. Even making water can be awkward. In any event, the contents will have to be dumped very quickly."

Marcelina studied his face for a moment before asking: "Did you notice how deeply affected Tenny was by 'A Song of the Morning'?"

"How could I help it? I was going to ask you about that song . . . who wrote it . . . because part of the words I recognize as coming from Æschylus's NIOBE . . . a lost play . . . that part about Thanatos . . . and, strangely, those were the very lines I translated for Tenny long ago, when we were bivouacked at the buried city of Ka-Mor. Those lines came to him again in a dream he had while he was staying at the Saint Francis."

"I should have told you before, Chris . . . because it *is* so perplexing . . . Nah-Loh-Tah and her guardian . . . a man named Teh-Meh-Tayo . . . stayed here in the native village while Doctor O'Meara's wife taught them to speak and read English. They were on their way to Nepal . . . probably to see Shivapuri Baba . . . where Nah-Loh-Tah was first to meet Tenny. I was wrong before. I once thought there were several reasons why Nah-Loh-Tah might have chosen to disappear. But that song . . . what Tenny told me about her when we talked on the verandah at the hotel in Juneau . . . that perhaps she had dis-

292

appeared the way she had because she wanted the pain to cease . . . it could be that the lost colony which presumably gave birth to the Rig Veda may turn out to be something else entirely."

"I've the same feeling . . . that's why I said what I did about dreaming while being awake. Tenny, I fear, may not have been altogether straightforward with us . . . and that is a hard thing for me to admit . . . or maybe he hasn't even been completely honest with himself. In any event, it does begin to appear as if the lost colony and the place from which Nah-Loh-Tah came may be one and the same place."

"And if they are? What, really, would it change?"

Chris lowered his head and rubbed his face with his hands. "I don't know," he confessed, not quite daring to look at her as he spoke, for unaccountably he was afraid. "Maybe nothing . . . maybe everything. One thing is sure. Our destination may become as unexpected as the fog that plagued us at Victoria Island . . . or, again, the fog on the Beaufort Sea that we encountered when returning to Point Barrow." Then he did look at her, reached out, and took her right hand in his. "I love you, Marcie."

"I love you," she murmured.

★ ★ ★

Sir Wilbur was delighted with the potty chairs. In all his years of exploring in primitive places he had never come upon anything like them. Ramón was amused. Luis was indifferent. He was becoming more uncomfortable with the perpetual cold than any of the others.

The sky was clear and visibility good as the *Janet* began the flight that, following another landing on Victoria Island for refueling, would ultimately culminate with their debarking on Ellesmere Island. The Sun, although low on the horizon, shone brilliantly in the enveloping turquoise of the sky, and Marcelina, looking out the window at her right, could watch the whale-like shadow that the Douglas Dolphin cast across the sparkling water, or as it trailed them persistently across an occasional ice field. Only the Boothia Peninsula was a point more north on the North American continent than Point Barrow, and now their direction was east by northeast and, beyond Victoria Island, would be north by northeast. Once or twice Marcelina did make out polar bears below them, seemingly so tiny from this perspective, and once, surely, she was certain she could see whales moving majestically in the water. Intermittent light fogs would hide the water, or land, or ice from her view, as it all rolled below the airplane like a great, endless plain wisped by scattered fleece.

Good weather held through the landing on Victoria Island and, again, all the way to Ellesmere Island.

"Here we turn left," Chris told Mark as the Sun's image began to cover his sextant bubble.

After they had flown over a good part of Ellesmere Island, Mark dropped the *Janet* to within three hundred feet of the tundra. As the airplane was throttled and circled above the area where they would land and set up their base camp, there was probably not a soul aboard who was not lost in wonder at sight of this goal, the attainment of which had acted as such a motivating force on all of them. It was the afternoon of July 9th.

After he took off for the return flight to Victoria Island, Mark Dworski, who would sleep here at the base camp before rising early the next day, was not to return with the *Janet* until the date for the rendezvous which had been set for August 20th at approximately the same time of day. Of course, by that time they would have reached nearly the tail end of the continuous sunlight, and it would also be when more frequent fogs were likely to occur.

The dogs seemed happiest of all to be shut of the airplane, with their paws on *terra firma* again, the cold, sharp air an apparently welcome relief from the monotony of the pens in which they had had little choice but to recline and sleep most of the time. Koyuk, the magnificent black and white lead dog, growled viciously as Marcelina approached him, but she was determined that they would become friends. She had decided this despite Chris's warning that sled dogs are not by nature ever to be considered as pets, and to dare to make them something more than the essentially wild and savage beasts they are was to court disaster.

Even with the practice of having done it all before at Point Barrow, it took nearly two hours before all the gear was unloaded. Sir Wilbur sorted out what would be cached here and what would be taken onward. Chris found it curious that the Englishman had brought twenty pounds of smoking tobacco along, more than he might smoke in several years, but he didn't comment on it.

The meal they ate that evening was a festive one, and Sir Wilbur broke out a bottle of single malt Scotch to celebrate the occasion and the advent of their land journey. Everyone partook, including Ramón who had never been seen to drink before and who found himself made dizzy by the one small drink he did have. He was able, however, to play a few wordless Andean melodies on his guitar which, it was decided, was superfluous baggage and must be kept stowed on the *Janet* beyond this point.

It would be inaccurate to say that fog gathered unseen in the nocturnal sky, since, as the hours passed while they slept, there was always some kind of light, but a fog did begin to gather, and Mark became airborne in the *Janet* before it would become any more dense. As it was, the fog did have an effect on the landscape. They were surrounded by tundra, with more tundra before them. The word permafrost was sometimes used to describe this kind of ground that is always more or less frozen, but, as Chris observed, such a description was misleading at best, since this tundra did not exactly freeze and thaw and freeze again throughout successive seasons, nor was there necessarily water frozen in the tundra. In many cases it was, and long had been, completely dry. All of the Ellesmere Island tundra consisted of permafrost, yet by some miracle, in the summer months, certain species of protococcus flourished, such as that which they saw around them and off in the distance. Sometimes these rapidly multiplying unicellular plants were referred to as "red" snow because the chlorophyll in them in the form of green cytoplasm tended to change from green to a red color due to exposure to the atmosphere. The result was a continuous series of mosaics of varying colors, some gradient shades of green, some sprouts blanching to yellow and gold, and the predominant clumps of red protococcus that streaked the more rocky areas around and before them. Occasionally there were even ponds of grayish blue water, sort of like marshes, that, surprisingly given the temperature, were not completely frozen over. None of it really made any biological sense whatever to Marcelina who had been guided by practical horticulture in her flower gardens at the *Hacienda* de Ferrar, but she felt she must simply accept the way things were here without any need of further explanation.

The hard ground, the clumps of protococcus, the gradual undulation of the land, and having to avoid pools of water did, however, make travel with the long sled arduous even with the ten dogs, most of them harnessed in tandem and in line behind Koyuk. To lighten the load, Chris, Ramón, and Sir Wilbur carried as much as they could strapped to their backs, while Marcelina and Luis worked at the handles of the sled, helping the dogs to pull it as much as they could by a forward exertion of propulsive force. Given these conditions, progress was relatively slow, and more than once they had to pause to rest the exhausted dogs, and themselves.

A distant ridge became their objective for that first day, increasingly visible as the fog gradually lifted, stealing away as mysteriously as earlier it had seemed to descend. Little enough of the sky appeared, and that a grayish blue now, but there was continuous light as the Sun swung in its elliptical course around the horizon.

That evening, after supper, Chris proposed to Marcelina that they should undertake to scout the tundra ridge before them. According to his survey map it led up to an Arctic desert region. This reconnaissance would allow them to prospect what might be the best way to bring up the dog team and sled the next day. It was now after eight o'clock in the evening, and both of them were fatigued but scarcely exhausted by the ardors of that day. The fog was completely gone.

As they mounted the ridge, a moderate breeze seemed to be blowing over the cold desert beyond them, affected probably by the distant glacier. Certainly it had become perceptibly colder than it had been, although the Sun, appearing as a small, distant diamond in the sky, shone with an energy that burned now against their cheekbones. It was as they approached the crest of the sweeping ridge, even though still somewhat below it, that they discovered the first of the nests built by various tundra birds. Chris explained to Marcelina in a soft voice made almost inaudible by the very dry and coldly gusting breeze that most birds in the Arctic were known to locate their nests on the ground, and, under the conditions of a more temperate climate, this would make them extremely vulnerable. But here, on this sheltered expanse of ridge, they had little reason to expect to be disturbed.

The two of them had to step very carefully, indeed, and their passage did not go unnoticed. Marcelina observed a horned lark that was no larger than her clenched fist. The lark gazed up at her with a resolute wariness. A short distance beyond, Chris, who was in the lead, encountered golden plovers that abandoned their nests in what he interpreted to be a desperate ploy to distract him from the pale eggs with dark speckles, resting in tiny cups woven from Arctic grasses. Marcelina noticed how these eggs seemed to glow with a gentle, inner light, as through a window on an overcast day. They paused, then, and let their eyes range in all directions, struck by the fragile beauty all around them.

When Chris commenced climbing the incline once more, Marcelina stepping carefully behind him, they came upon nests of Lapland longspurs, sitting as mutely on their eggs as if they were large agates, their dark eyes gleaming as if in reflection of the distant Sun. It was when they found a nest of two owls whose feathers were as white as glacier snow that Chris paused. Marcelina stood motionlessly behind him. These were the most formidable birds they had yet seen here. It was only after several moments had passed that the fierce glare in the eyes of the owls began to dim. One of the owls settled back over three eggs, but with what was clearly a suspicious attitude. The other, that had not moved, sought to establish a bond with Marcelina's blue-gray eyes, should she have the temerity to move again.

It was then that, quite instinctively in her response, with her hands in the pockets of her coat, Marcelina made a delicate movement with her body, a combination of a modest curtsey and a gentle bow of her head. It was her way of communicating that she meant them no harm, that she acknowledged this unexpected vision of fecund luxuriance in so remote a region, and because, as she stood there, bathed in the serene light of the Arctic in the eventide, she felt somehow that the breeze tugging so tranquilly at her soul was the very breath of life itself.

Only after many more moments had

passed, this time with an incline of the head from Chris and another modest curtsey from Marcelina, did they pass beyond the owls and make it to the top of the ridge. There the diaphanous light pressed more intimately against their faces, the breeze, pacific perhaps but importunate, anointing their features as it coursed up from the glacier that they knew, without being able to see it, stretched vastly beyond the frigid sands on this far side of the ridge.

"Darkness will never come, will it?" Marcelina asked.

"Not for some time . . . and, by then, all of those birds' eggs shall have hatched, and the newly born will have learned to fly and wing their way south . . . before winter comes and with it what might seem to them perpetual darkness."

They were silent for a time, looking out into the horizon and what appeared to be distant clouds, refracting the pale sunlight. Marcelina smiled. She reached into her jacket pocket for her package of cigarettes, and Chris lighted one for her and for himself, not the easiest thing in so persistent a breeze. They smoked for a time, sitting close to each other on a flat section of the ridge.

"It's hard for me to know if you're aware of my hand when I pat you in those heavy clothes you're wearing," he said.

"If you think it's bad now, just wait until I have those thick snow pants on." She gave him an elfin smile.

When they had finished their cigarettes, they turned to make the descent, the light quite as it had been earlier, neither increased nor diminished, but they remained cautious about further disturbing the bird nests. How very different this was, Marcelina found herself reflecting, than when, on the way to Haucha, Chris had been attacked by giant condors as he descended a sheer cliff into the valley of the Quivaris. Here she was perhaps no less fearful, but this time the fear was only that she and Chris might again intrude on the nesting birds.

The ardors of the trek were felt by all of them as the expedition entered its second day. Getting the sled to the top of the ridge, avoiding coming within proximity of the nesting birds, required most of the morning hours. In the process, nearly half the gear had to be unloaded and carried up on their backs. Marcelina, however, remained with the sled and mastered handling the dog team, with Ramón pushing at the rear of the sled, Marcelina staying at the gee pole and occasionally snapping the whip in the air over the team. Koyuk pulled vigorously in the lead, and all of the other dogs labored with their breast bands invariably taut. The ascent, however, nearly exhausted the dogs as well as the humans. Having attained the top of the ridge at last, there was a long rest.

Beyond them, stretching out far into the distance, were the improbable sands of this Arctic desert. At the other side, still invisible, was the Agassiz Ice Cap. The only ice shelves known to exist in the northern hemisphere were to be found along the northern-most shore of Ellesmere Island. While the great ice cap, occupying virtually all of the central land space on Greenland, produces the many icebergs that then float out and down into the northern Atlantic, the bane of ships for centuries sailing in these waters, the ice shelves on Ellesmere Island create instead gigantic ice islands. Due to the great winds in the Arctic, blowing up over Ellesmere, sometimes patches of gravel, soil, sand, and even vegetation can occasionally be found on the surfaces of one or another of these huge ice islands.

Becoming detached through one of the many far northern fjords of Ellesmere, these ice islands float out into the Arctic Ocean and become part of the continuous circular motion of those icy waters, moving, constantly moving, at the rate of approximately one mile

an hour. In this case, too, as with the phenomenon Dr. O'Meara had sought to capture
in his painting of *"Ivu,"* ice itself, usually regarded by people from the south as something
brittle and inorganic, seems to be alive. Just as
the Greenland Ice Cap calves countless icebergs through its fjords, so these ice islands
emanating from Ellesmere Island might be
regarded as fledglings given birth by the glacier itself, the ice reproducing itself in these
magnificent, towering behemoths, finally set
off on their own, as would happen eventually
with the many newly born varieties of Arctic
birds Marcelina and Chris had encountered
on the leeward side of the great ridge.

Yet no less impressive was this frigid desert,
sand without water, without ice, without snow,
lifeless and barren and quite as imposing as
any southern desert. Despite the cold, they
had encountered a few insects at first on
Ellesmere Island, but there was none here, no
life of any kind really, however small, just
these billions upon billions of tiny granules of
sand, all that was left of mighty rocks and
crags from millions of years ago, over which at
one time surely a sea had surged. Queen Elizabeth, mindful of the *metæ* of the Colosseum
in Rome, had called London *meta cognita* and
by way of contrast had named Baffin Island in
the Arctic, when it was newly discovered,

meta incognita, but the notion applied no less to this part of Ellesmere Island.

Chris Fallon was proven right in his design of runners for the sled. It could pass as easily and as quickly across the wasteland as it would likely move across ice or crusted snow. The dogs actually seemed to be stimulated with the improved propulsion, and the pace of the expedition increased noticeably.

It was at the time that they halted for the day that they all became aware of an odd, whistling sound that seemed to be coming at them out of the east. It would begin on a very high note and then, gradually, would fade away, or metamorphose into a very low moan. Chris knew what it meant, and he urged everyone to work with alacrity in pitching and anchoring the igloo-shaped tents, while Marcelina was to feed the dogs and then hobble them as effectively as she could in what shelter would be provided by the tents and the sled. Food and water were allocated for each tent along with the usual one portable lamp and, of course, the innovative potty chairs. There was no way of telling how long they would be compelled to remain within the tents. The previous night Sir Wilbur and Ramón had opted to sleep outside of a tent, curled up in their sleeping bags. But during the torrential winds of an Arctic storm that could reach the level of a typhoon in the South Seas, even the dogs would be in need of shelter. It was even possible that, despite their being moored, the torrential wind would lift the dogs aloft bodily and in its fury transport their bodies miles away. Snow glasses were to be worn at all times, if one were to venture out into the storm, to protect the eyes from being blinded by sand and small rocks being blown at terrific speeds. In a place where one might expect a blizzard, it was ironic that it should be a dry wind that would be hitting them.

The tents were flapping and their clothes were being whipped by the increasing winds as the last of the preparations were made. The sky had become dark, and the Sun was almost invisible.

"We're so close . . . I can smell the glacier ice on the air!" Sir Wilbur shouted to Chris. It was the last words they would exchange for some time.

While the strong winds of the storm continued to beat at the igloo-shaped tents well into nearly two days and nights, their inhabitants could do little but remain sequestered. Of course, periodically, one or another of them had to go outside — cautiously and rather uncomfortably wearing snow glasses, black salve beneath their eyes, and scarves across their faces — to relieve the contents of the rubber bowl in a potty chair or to check on the dogs or to feed them. Marcelina quipped to Chris that under these conditions they had finally achieved a total lack of privacy in their marriage, to which Chris responded that it was no doubt even more awkward for the men in the other tent. Meals were eaten cold, out of cans, supplemented by beef jerky and water, while coffee or tea could be brewed on the Primus stoves. There was some air circulation in the tents, and much of the time light was generated by the portable lanterns. Some dust, however, did seep inside.

They all tried to pass the time by reading, and for a while Sir Wilbur, Luis, and Ramón played cards. Some of the time Ramón read in THE DIVINE COMEDY, although frequently he would ask Luis or the Englishman to explain the meaning of a reference or a passage to him. At one point Luis made the suggestion that, once he completed this book, Ramón should try Heinrich Heine's THE GODS IN EXILE. The premise of this satire was that the gods of Classical Antiquity, having found themselves made disconsolate by the apostasy of Europeans, had repaired to the Arctic where, ever since, they have worked their marvels and spells. It was intended as a witticism, but Ramón took it very literally and only needed an explanation of what the word apostasy meant before he could understand fully what that story was about.

Chris read *Prometheus desmôtes* — *Prometheus Bound* — by Æschylus, while Marcelina read JANE EYRE. It was after one of the times that Chris returned from tending to the dogs, finding them still buried in small hillocks of sand, sheltering themselves as they would have done instinctively in snow, that he accepted a cup of the coffee Marcelina had brewed for them. There was sand in it.

"I never realized what a change in perspective geography can make," he said, reclined across from her and leaning on one elbow. "I must have read *Prometheus Bound* twenty times over the years, and being here, where we are, is the first time I realized that the Greeks of Æschylus's time must have had a geographical knowledge of the Earth that is very similar to our own. How else could it be? . . . because in this play it is said of Io that she has ventured north to the uttermost extreme of Ocean . . . of Okeanides . . . and, in departing from the desolate crag where Prometheus is bound, she crosses a stream on her way to the mainland of Asia."

"Of Asia?" Marcelina asked, her voice raised so it could be heard above the

309

pounding of the wind.

"Yes. And you know . . . there is only one stream that separates the mainland of Asia from what we now call North America."

"The Bering Strait?"

"Yes. Just that one place . . . the only place where the continents almost touch . . . and sometime long, long ago it may not even have been a stream . . . but an isthmus connecting the two. By that means, as you know, it is believed the Asian peoples migrated to this continent, later to form the various American Indian nations."

"Let me read you something . . . ," Marcelina said, picking up her volume of JANE EYRE. It had a leather spine and marbled-paper covers. "It's right at the beginning . . . here it is . . . on the second page." Keeping her voice forceful so she could be heard, she read aloud.

I returned to my book — Bewick's HISTORY OF BRITISH BIRDS. The letterpress thereof I cared little for, generally speaking; and yet there were certain introductory pages that, child as I was, I could not pass quite as a blank. They were those which treat of the haunts of sea fowl; of "the solitary rocks and promontories" by them only inhabited; of the coast of Norway, studded with isles from its southern extremity, the Lindeness, or Naze, to the North Cape —

Where the Northern Ocean, in vast
  whirls,
Boils round the naked, melancholy isles
Of farthest Thule; and the Atlantic surge
Pours in among the stormy Hebrides.

Nor could I pass unnoticed the suggestions of the bleak shores of Lapland, Siberia, Spitzbergen, Nova Zembla, Iceland, Greenland, with "the vast sweep of the Arctic Zone, and those forlorn regions of dreary space — that reservoir of frost and snow, where firm fields of ice, the accumulation of centuries of winters, glazed in Alpine heights above heights, surround the pole, and concenter the multiplied rigors of extreme cold." Of these death-white realms I formed an idea of my own — shadowy, like the half-comprehended notions that float dim through children's brains but strangely impressive. The words in these introductory pages connected with the succeeding vignettes, and gave significance to the rock standing up alone in a sea of billow and spray — to the broken boat stranded on a desolate coast — to the cold and ghastly moon glancing through bars of cloud at a wreck just sinking.

She stopped reading, and put the book down in front of where she was lying on her stomach. "Do you think they'll be all right . . . I mean those birds we saw . . . with their eggs?"

"Possibly." Chris was looking across at her, the lamplight beyond their heads keeping his bearded face partially in shadow. "If this wind dissipates . . . before it reaches them . . . or blows out over the desert to the west and doesn't go toward the great ridge to the south . . . but then, too, I imagine the parents will do their best to protect their young, covering them with their wings. They've had centuries to learn how to survive here . . . and, so far, have done a better job of it . . . than many of the more recent human visitors."

Once the sandstorm died down, almost as abruptly as it had begun, the travelers dug themselves out of their tents, inevitably feeling dirty and stiff from their long constraint. Luis Valera climbed alone to the top of a serrated sand dune, now so silent in this cold desert. The landscape of polar sand stretched before him like the waves of a sea suddenly frozen in time. The distant Sun was now like a great red light just above the horizon, casting a purple hue across the sky above it, a layer of empurpled light running into dark red and then into a luminescent orange as it vaulted above, spanning the sky. It was withal an eerie light that seemed to create great shadows, only it didn't. It was more as if the shadows had become diffused throughout the light, dark refractions as haunting as the total silence. Only their watches told them that it was ten o'clock at night. He felt utterly exhausted. After all, sleep had been rather fitful for the past two days. Now, in another six hours, they must resume the trek. A watch — an instrument for measuring time passing — was meant for a world and life in which time regulated activity. But here, in the Arctic, time seemed meaningless, and the wafer circle on Valera's wrist counting time in this wasteland seemed the zenith of futility. In a real sense the five of them were living now in a timeless world. More and more it occurred to him how artificial was the effort to impose the co-ordinates of time when the living world they had all known had really ceased to exist.

He sat down, with some effort, on the sand. Looming ahead, distant and yet close, was the final ridge, the rise that would lead to the glacier. He drew from his pocket the two fossils he had found and collected. They were no great discoveries. Surely they could tell nothing about the entrance to the lost colony, if there was such an entrance. Yet, the fossils were amazing in themselves, had portent and meaning beyond any more tangible human discovery, for in their way they were about time — not time measured in days, or even centuries, but time so long past that it was dizzying to contemplate it. The first fossil was a petrified fragment of wood, probably of a ginkgo tree. Amazing that it should still be here on Ellesmere Island for one to find. Not forty centuries but four thousand centuries ago this land had been covered with ginkgo trees and giant sequoias. Here, well beyond the timberline now, where no trees grew at all, there had once been trees reaching far into the sky, mighty, somber, but surely in that time there was not this pervasive silence. There would have been the rustling of leaves in the wind, at least that, and probably also birds, and perhaps, if not warm-blooded, surely cold-blooded creatures moving across the terrain. Time? Could the modern human mind even grasp this kind of passage of time?

There were probably countless other relics of that age, caught in the clay and pumice, perhaps engulfed by the sea, or spewed out of volcanoes, forced through how many fissures from the molten center of the hot Earth, preserved then in the bottom ooze of a sea that had vanished or remained frozen in motion in the bowels of the Agassiz Ice Cap. A sea frozen in time, for that is how it was now. This period of the Midnight Sun was only a brief respite, without bone-cracking cold, without perpetual darkness. Life is movement, but not in the Arctic winter. The Arctic winter destroys movement, freezing water so that it is no longer free, all life stilled to the heart, so that the land is no longer pliant, but brittle, stationary, silent except for the distant crashing of frozen seas. The landscape rolled around him, drowned in this strange purple, red, and orange light, without animals, without any human trace at all, a silent, forbidding world seeming to stretch out to infinity.

But then Valera looked at the other fossil, part of an ear bone of a whale, covered with traces of coral and algæ that no longer lived in this region, probably hadn't lived here in centuries of centuries. A turbulent sea had once covered this barren plain, a sea warm and thriving enough to support coral and algæ. It appeared preposterous to contemplate, but it had to be true. The Arctic as it had been known by human beings for ages had at some time in the distant past not been cold at all, but a warm, flourishing world. Valera realized that in his time here he was sitting on top of a record of a sea and was just beyond the record of a forest in a region that had been named *Arctos* after the constellation of the Bear. The book of time had no boundaries. Valera's nearly sixty years would not comprise more than one letter on a single page.

"Pardon, *Señor* Luis."

It was Ramón's voice, and it startled Valera. He had not heard him approach even in this heavy, cold sand. He quickly put the precious fossils back into his coat pocket.

"I did not hear you, Ramón," he said, turning toward the young man. "What is it?"

"I wondered," said Ramón, "if you had seen it, also?"

"Seen what?"

"That flashing of sunlight off in the northeast? The kind of flash you see when light is reflected from a glass lens."

Luis Valera rose and cast his gaze intently in the direction Ramón indicated. He could see nothing, even though he stood there for some moments, concentrating his focus. The Quechuan now had raised his binoculars and was surveying with them the place from which he had seen the flashes of light.

"Are you sure you saw anything?" Valera asked, doubt in his tone.

"*Sí*, I am esure," Ramón said, taking his

binoculars from his eyes. "I saw it twice. Don Weelbur must be told."

Valera was inclined to dismiss Ramón's alarm as the result of an overly active imagination. Perhaps he was possessed of the illusion that they were in as much danger here from hostile natives as they had been long ago in that valley in Peru out of which rose the great plateau. There they had been hunted by the fierce Quivaris. But this was the Arctic, and there was very little, if any, wildlife at this latitude. Not since they had encountered the birds on the tundra ridge had they seen so much as a single other living creature.

Ramón, however, was unaffected by Valera's indifference. He made his way quickly down the broad dune of cold sand and back to camp. Marcelina was scooping away the mound of sand that had engulfed the Fallons' tent, while Sir Wilbur was separating from their gear the foodstuffs and water that were to be cached here. This was the best site to place the cache, since the next day they would venture out onto the glacier. The dogs, far from being restless for activity after nearly two days of enduring the sandstorm, were impatiently focused on Chris who was feeding them.

Approaching the Englishman, Ramón spoke in a quiet voice so as not to be heard by the others. He did not wish to cause the *señora* any unusual concern. "Don Weelbur," he said, "I am esure that we are being watched. Just now, from the top that dune where the *señor* professor ees keeping a look-out, I saw two flashes of light . . . reflections, perhaps, from binoculars. I saw the flash twice, but the *señor* professor deed not, and he believes eet was notheeng."

The Englishman had been rearranging tinned food in a wooden box, but he had paused when Ramón had come to him, and now he smiled briefly. "Luis is not really on watch. He probably just wanted an opportunity to escape confinement and be by himself for a while." He paused, his light-blue eyes glittering in the purple, red, and orange light. "But I fear you are right. I thought I saw something similar before the sandstorm stopped us here. From how far away would you say that flash of reflected light came?"

"Two . . . as you say . . . miles . . . perhaps three . . . but no more."

"That close, eh?"

"*Sí.*"

"You do realize that at this latitude, and above, the only life you are likely to find will be in the ocean . . . except, of course, for the minor possibilities of polar bears and Arctic foxes, but none of them will give off a flash of

318

light as would a telescopic glass. Might you have seen perhaps only the reflection from some crystalline mineral like mica or quartz?"

"I do not beelieve so, Don Weelbur."

"Frankly, Ramón, I do not believe so, either."

At this expression of confidence, the Quechuan stooped down before the Englishman. "I should like to go silently and weethout being seen myself een that direction and see eef I can find out who ees there."

"It could be very dangerous."

"I know that."

"You must not be seen. If there is someone else in this area, it is better that we find out what they are doing here before they know we're aware of them."

"Sí."

"Perhaps after we've eaten, you could. . . ."

"I would preefer to go now, señor. Eef they have already gone, perhaps I shall be able to read sign. Eef they are coming closer to where we are, eet would also be well to know that."

"Yes, indeed, it would. Perhaps Chris should go with you."

"No. Eet ees better there be only one person. There will be less chance of being seen."

The Englishman thought for a moment, then nodded briefly. "All right. Go now. It shouldn't take you very long."

"No more than an hour . . . perhaps two, *señor*. I can get sometheeng to eat when I return. Just say I have gone . . . like the *señor* professor . . . to be by myself for a time."

"You have your weapon with you?"

"*Sí* . . . and my hunting knife."

"Very good. I shall make an excuse for you. And . . . Ramón?"

"*¿Sí?*"

"*Vaya con Dios.*"

"*Gracias.*"

With that the Quechuan got again to his feet, and, veering off to his right, he headed across the sand to the northeast. Marcelina saw Ramón leave the camp, but she did not wonder about what he might be doing. Sir Wilbur went back to arranging cans of foodstuffs, while, mentally, he was trying to calculate time across an incredible distance.

Kolia Kratsotkin had once regarded the belief concerning the supposedly dark and depressed souls of Russians to be nothing more than bourgeois propaganda. In fact, even now he did not believe human beings had souls at all. But what had seemed a relatively simple assignment in Igarka, when he had been attached to Comrade Strehlnikov's expedition to locate a fabulous depository of gold and oil in the Arctic, had turned into what seemed now to be an endless nightmare of perpetual hardships. To have followed a straight line from Young Communist Island in the Northern Land directly across the North Pole to this mysterious island of fabulous natural resources would have gotten them where they were going in about a thousand miles. Of course, that would have meant crossing the ice pack and would have portended certain disaster. But to have come the way they had, overland across central Alaska during the winter, through the Yukon and the North-West Territories, had found them on the Boothia Peninsula in late April. Notwithstanding all the ardors of that journey, the route through the archipelagoes of Somerset Island and Devon Island and, by umiak, across the Lancaster Sound and the Jones Sound to the foot of Ellesmere Island had been even more fraught with difficulties.

Teh-Meh-Tayo had assured them that they were nearing their journey's end, but the push up Ellesmere had been extremely hard going, and now for two days without any source of wood and, therefore, no fire, they had endured a terrible sandstorm. It was following the storm that with his field glasses from behind a cold sand dune Kratsotkin had spotted the other party again, also with a dog team and sled, in the vicinity, and they even seemed now to be heading definitely in the same direction. He had gone back to the camp they had made in the mouth of an ice cave to take Lugu Strehlnikov aside and tell him what he had seen. Neither the man nor the woman who were leading them to this mysterious island understood Russian, and so at least they could talk without them knowing what they were saying. The tall, white-faced Strehlnikov concluded that there still might be no immediate danger. After all, they had managed to avoid contact with anyone except Eskimos in their villages over the last several months. But Kolia should return to his look-out post with his target rifle. If anyone from that foreign camp should approach the entrance to the ice cave, then, and only then, Kolia should fire a warning shot. It might be enough to scare off a curious and stupid intruder. Kolia was then to follow them into the ice cave — actually a crevasse that apparently extended right through the glacier — and take up a position some distance inside, preferably where sunlight penetrated the ice roof, so Kolia wouldn't freeze to death. If the intruders entered the ice cave, then they should be shot. If no one came after four hours, Kolia was to proceed to join up with them. Teh-Meh-Tayo had assured them it would be warm where they were going.

Kolia had begun to disbelieve anything that accursed Teh-Meh-Tayo said. They should have seized the small gold ingots those natives used for barter among the Eskimos as they had bartered, apparently, all along the route from northern India to the Soviet Union. Their gold should have been seized, and they both should have been sent to a labor camp. Instead, Lugu had believed them, and he had persuaded the N.K.V.D. to facilitate this folly of an expedition. If they didn't get soon to where they were going, Kolia would take matters into his own hands and execute the two natives. But . . . if he did that . . . how would he ever get back to the Soviet Union? When it came right down to it, how would either of them ever get back to the Soviet Union to report the location of this strange and fabulously rich island?

These thoughts were passing through Kolia's mind when he saw a stealthy figure moving across the sand in the direction of the ice cave. He followed Lugu's orders. He fixed the fugitive in the small telescopic sight, but his hands were cold and his fingers nearly frozen. He jacked a shell into the chamber, blew on the fingers of his right hand to warm them — it did little good, really, they had been cold for so long now — and then he fired.

Chapter Nine

Ramón made it back to the encampment about two hours after he had left. He had been very cautious, at first, in retreating from the point where he had been shot at by a rifle. The mounds of sand around the tents had been cleared, guns and utensils had been cleaned where they needed it, and the others were eating. They all had perceived to some degree the muffled sound of what might have been a shot, but when it had been followed by silence, they all had begun to doubt that it necessarily meant anything ominous.

The account that Ramón gave of his having actually seen a party of strangers where seeing another human being at all was extremely unlikely prompted Sir Wilbur and Chris to address the implications of this encounter at once. Despite the lateness of the hour and the lack of recent rest, it was decided that camp should be broken and that Sir Wilbur, Marcelina, and Luis would take the dogs and the sled and push on to the glacier and out onto it, while Chris, armed with his Winchester, and Ramón with the revolver he had been carrying but had not used to return the gun-fire, would proceed to reconnoiter the camp of the apparent enemies. Progress would be slow getting out onto the glacier, but to remain where they were might be only inviting another violent confrontation. Once on the glacier, visibility in all directions would be extremely good, given its relatively flat surface and the ever-present sunlight. Chris and Ramón would investigate but not attempt to engage in any exchange of hostilities with the alien group. They would try then to catch up with the three of them, which might happen before even they got out onto the glacier.

Marcelina was concerned for the safety of Chris and Ramón, but Chris assured her there would be little danger. It had been a long time ago, of course, but he had had his share of experience in the trenches during the Great War, and for all they knew the alien group may have only wanted to warn Ramón away from approaching any closer. The bullet burn across the left shoulder of his parka, however, was difficult to construe as simply a friendly warning to keep away.

Ramón took a few minutes to eat hurriedly and drink two tin cups of tea, and then he and Chris were on their way, while those who remained busied themselves in breaking camp. The wind had died down so much since the passing of the sandstorm that Ramón's tracks, both leaving the encampment and returning, had remained clearly imprinted in the sand. Because of what had happened, it was Chris's intention to make a wide circle to the south of those tracks before they turned in a northeasterly course. In that way, they might be able to approach the hostile group without being seen. Such a course took them about a mile away from the direct trail Ramón had originally blazed, and it proved uneventful. The dunes undulated dramatically here and there and, as a result, would afford them with some degree of concealment as they crept closer to the alien encampment.

It was perhaps the last thing Chris expected, but once they had come upon the site where probably the shot had been fired, the area was totally deserted. Pushing cautiously ahead, they found a depression in the sand that led downward into a barren half circle below the pressure ridge of the glacier. On the other side of this half circle was the most curious thing of all — what looked to be an ice cave. The way the ice had pushed out into the sand indicated that, perhaps in periods of freak melting, ice water might have trickled out of the ice cave. The cave was in the form of a lopsided oval, probably about fifty yards across at the base. The right-hand wall that slanted at an inverted angle to the top for a distance of perhaps a hundred and fifty yards in height was covered with a curtain of icicles, some of them near the top hanging down about twelve feet. Because of the scalene shape of the opening, there were no icicles at all on the left-hand side. The melting water from which they would be formed had simply dripped down the gentle slope of the left-hand ice wall.

According to the sign, it was apparent that it was here, near the mouth of the ice cave, that the other party had stayed during the sandstorm. It was obvious they had a sled and a team of dogs. So much was evident by the tracks left behind. It was also apparent that they had entered the ice cave with the sled and dogs and disappeared within its unknown depths.

"It looks to be a fault or ice-covered crevasse that runs straight into the glacier," Chris remarked to Ramón in a low tone.

"How far do you theenk thees cave goes?" asked the Quechuan.

"It's impossible to say. It does seem to angle toward the northwest. Since Tenny is heading northeast according to his star map, it might be that he will pass over the top of this crevasse . . . if it goes far enough out into the glacier."

"Could eet go all the way to the other side?"

"Couldn't say. It might."

"We should find out, no?"

Fallon studied the other for a moment. "It would be taking a chance, Ramón, and it could take us very far afield. If the direction holds inside the crevasse, there will come a point where we will have proceeded far beyond where Tenny, Marcie, and Luis will be on the surface. Then, if we have to come all the way back, it will put us far behind them . . . in fact, they might have crossed all the way over to the other side before we could rejoin them."

"I steel theenk we should try eet."

"Perhaps. For a mile or so, anyway. It might also give out before too long . . . or we might run right into these people . . . something we really don't want to do."

Even the ice that had spread out onto the bottom of the desert gully was very slippery, and so the two paused long enough to put on their crampons which they had brought in their back packs, knowing they would need them for crossing the surface of the glacier. Before leaving the encampment, Chris had reminded Marcelina that she must keep her ice-axes handy, one at either side of the rope belt she wore around her parka. He and Ramón carried theirs now in a similar fashion.

Since Chris had a waterproofed flashlight with him, this would occupy one hand and one of his ice-axes the other. Therefore, he proposed that Ramón should side him, carrying the Winchester in his left hand, which was covered by a glove inside the outer mitten, and take an ice-axe in his right. They should try to walk abreast as much as possible — the ice cave was certainly wide enough for this — and Chris would hold the light in his left hand far away from his body so as to diminish the target he made.

The crampons gave the two men extremely dependable traction, and, from what could be told from the tracks outside and leading into the ice cave, those they were following were not using crampons. This could provide the pursuers an advantage should it come to a confrontation. Chris had used his flashlight very little before this point, but wisely he carried two replacement batteries in his back pack. However far they might venture into the ice cave, it must not exceed that point when the flashlight began to dim from waning batteries. They could only be replaced once, and then they would be in darkness.

The temperature in the ice cave was several degrees colder than it had been outside and was probably at least ten degrees colder even than the temperature at the surface of the glacier. Their breaths came rawly and misted before them. The wolverine lining of their hoods offered them protection from ice build-up from just breathing, but it was still a painful process in this terrible cold.

They had proceeded about a half mile into the ice cave when Chris came to realize that his concern may have been unnecessary. It was his custom to flash the beam of light forward onto the floor ice and occasionally up either wall to the ceiling, but not far ahead light could be seen coming down from a barren place in the roof of the cave. Yet, were such breaks into this passage to continue, it might well mean that the others, passing over it from above, would in effect be crossing a treacherous ice bridge that could crumble beneath their weight and the weight of the sled. Also, off to the right side, the base of the passage had separated from the floor on which they were walking, making where they walked a kind of broad ledge of only about twenty-five yards wide, the other twenty-five yards to the right-hand wall increasingly dropping off. This fissure soon became so deep, in fact, that the bottom of it was not visible.

Chris was thinking it was about time for them to turn back, when a rifle shot resounded from within the depths of the cave ahead of them, from the expanse that was again claimed by darkness as the opening in the ceiling of the cave closed again away from the light. The shot missed Chris, but he dropped at once into a crouch and extinguished the flashlight. Ramón, who was now on Chris's left side between Fallon and the left wall of the cave and only slightly behind him, dropped onto to his stomach.

"Here," Ramón whispered, shoving the Winchester forward.

Chris sprawled on his stomach as he took off his right-hand mitten and the glove beneath it. He brought the rifle forward, released the safety, and levered a shell into the chamber. He kept the rifle aimed ahead of them and could only wait.

A moment later another shot came, passing over their heads. Chris saw the gunflame in the darkness, and it was directly at that he made his target. He levered the Winchester rapidly and fired again, and then once more waited.

It was a foolish strategy, if it was thought out at all, because their invisible antagonist was on his feet, and he came rushing at them now, out into the light, his rifle held at the ready. Chris had the heavily clad man in his sights, but he did not fire. The man, the moment he could make out that his human targets were down on the floor of the shelf of the crevasse, stopped, evidently intent on dropping to one knee and snapping off a more accurately aimed shot. But he was not wearing crampons, only fur-covered boots, and the abrupt halt in his rush caused him to begin sliding off to the right side of the cave from the perspective of Chris and Ramón, off toward the deep chasm. The man must have used the bolt action on his rifle to inject another bullet from the clip into the chamber because, even as he was skidding wildly toward the edge, he fired, although the shot went straight up into the air above him. It must have grazed the edge of the crevasse above the drop-off, since right after he plunged over the lip of the shelf into the deeper chasm fragments of ice came crashing down after him.

The climb up the last ridge of the cold desert was very difficult for the dogs, still harnessed mostly in tandem behind Koyuk, and Sir Wilbur drove the sled from the back board handles, pushing it before him, with Valera at the gee pole. Marcelina walked point, and so she reached the crest of the pressure dike before the others. For the last three hundred yards or so the sand had been covered by hard-packed snow that crunched beneath their boots, and the runners ran even more easily over it. As Marcelina paused on top of a snow-ice outcropping of the pressure dike, Koyuk and the two Huskies behind him stopped on an adjacent outcropping, and the other dogs paused as well, while Valera and the Englishman came forward to stand near the lead dog on the other side of where Marcelina stood.

Stretching out beyond them was a relatively flat surface of ice that seemed not to end, creating a blue line on the horizon, the sky above having become white, perhaps an extension of the bank of clouds that was above the glacier in the far distance. They all were wearing snow glasses in preparation for the encounter with the glacier. Studying the horizon more carefully, the flat ice surface of the glacier appeared to consist of bands of white with various hues of blue, although it turned to white again at the horizon.

There was a persistent cold wind that struck them from out across the glacier, and, despite their warm clothing, it had a penetrating presence, burning their faces. Yet, there was no flake of snow in this wind, and visibility was surprisingly clear.

"It was fortunate for us that we weren't out on the glacier when that storm hit us," Sir Wilbur said. "Now we must drive the sled down the other side of this snow ridge and then re-harness the dogs so they will all run parallel before the sled."

To himself, Sir Wilbur had to agree completely with Chris's planning. One sled would be hard enough to manage across that icy, cold surface for what surely were miles upon miles. There were these three at present, but even with the addition of Chris and Ramón, once they rejoined them, the crossing with just one sled would be sufficiently arduous. Sir Wilbur also realized that they could not proceed from this crest of the pressure dike with all the dogs harnessed to the sled. The drop was too jagged and steep, and to attempt such a descent would probably spell disaster. In the event, with the Englishman and Marcelina each using one of their ice-axes and with Valera wielding the shovel, it took over an hour to cut a trajectory slide down onto the surface of the glacier that the dogs could traverse, and then only with Sir Wilbur, acting as a constant brake at the rear of the sled. Their crampons were truly vital in allowing them to maintain their footing on the pressure dike as they cut out the pathway downward. Skis or snowshoes would have been useless for this kind of work, and for that reason they wisely had not been brought along for the journey.

Following the tense descent of the sled, Sir Wilbur called a brief rest period, and Marcelina was able to brew steaming cups of tea.

The vigors of preparing the descent and undertaking it had caused all of them to perspire, despite the sharp cold and the icy wind which actually seemed to diminish somewhat when they gained the flat surface of the glacier. This perspiration had begun to freeze on their bodies as they had worked, and this respite also allowed the perspiration to melt again and partially even to evaporate through aerification, although in the process Marcelina's nipples buried beneath the many layers of clothing became so erect they hurt, and the men felt similar discomfort. It had also become slightly painful for them to breathe through their noses, but they dared not breathe excessively through their mouths in order to avoid dehydration. Their eyes now constantly were tearing, and their noses ran. These emissions had to be wiped away regularly so they would not freeze on their faces. This was somewhat difficult to do since they wore gloves inside mittens, heavy woolen pull-over caps inside their wolverine-lined parka hoods, and wolverine-lined flaps across their mouths buttoned onto the outside of the parka hoods. Valera, in particular, felt fatigue in his lower extremities, but he did not complain of it to the others. Only his keen interest to get where they were going quieted his inner fear that perhaps he was not physically up to it at all.

Chris had stressed to all of them that it was on the glacier that they would be most apt to encounter polar bears. He had stressed that the polar bear was truly the king of beasts. They could travel easily across land, across ice, and swim in below-zero water surrounded by floating ice, onto which they could readily climb. They are always hungry, and they are accustomed to eat whatever they wish: seals, walrus, fish — and human beings would be regarded as a delicacy. *Nothing* frightens them. This image of these omnivorous predators jarred Marcelina's rather sympathetic response to Ahg-Gah-Guk's story about Tôr-Nârs-Suk.

After re-harnessing the dogs radially to form a crescent before the sled, Koyuk was still slightly in advance of the others. Marcelina, who appeared like a small walrus in her thermal snow pants, would be behind the sled, holding onto the handles but not riding the runners, while Valera would be walking behind her. They waited until Sir Wilbur was fully two hundred yards out in advance of them. He was carrying a wooden pole that was to be used for periodically testing the density of the ice in order to anticipate any hidden crevasse which might be bridged by frozen snow or possibly encountering an area where the surface ice had melted to form a pool of indeterminate depth. In either case, the Englishman was to guide the sled and dogs around such danger zones and keep the party on firm footing. The perpetual sunlight, not hidden by clouds or fog banks, was a potential enemy, since it could cause melting in the glacier's surface. On the other hand, the ground temperature, measuring about 20° below zero on the Fahrenheit scale, tended to work in favor of the crossing. According to the calculations Sir Wilbur and Valera had made, they were proceeding in a northeasterly direction that eventually was supposed to bring them to a point on the surface of the Earth that was directly below Epsilon, the third star from Polaris in the so-called tail of the constellation Ursa Minoris as seen in the heavens late in the month of January at approximately 84° N. Of course, this computation was based on having determined the sine of the obtuse triangle formed with Dubhe as the pointer in the constellation Ursa Maioris at the same time of the month and then calculated by means of an extension in solid geometry through the diminished inversion of the triangle corresponding to terrestrial co-ordinates. Even the most fractional miscalculation of the relative oppositions in these constellations with the correlations of the differential correspondences between them and the geographical surface points on the Earth would lead them astray. Sir Wilbur, although he had admitted it to no one, was proceeding entirely on faith — not faith in his and Luis's calculations, but in the referents that had once been given him by Nah-Loh-Tah outside Darjeeling in Nepal. Ursa Minoris to her had been Arcas — so named by the ancient Greeks after the son that Zeus had conceived with the beautiful nymph Callisto. Hera in her wrath had changed Callisto into a great bear that Arcas had tried to kill while hunting. Zeus had prevented this from happening only by also changing Arcas into the form of a bear, albeit a smaller one, and so they had become the Ursa Maioris and Ursa Minoris of modern astronomy. A fractional miscalculation could have been made on Sir Wilbur's part simply by having chosen the relative position of Epsilon in Ursa Minoris as he had at January 30th, instead of, for example, its position on January 7th — and if this should prove the case, it would mean, inevitably, that the place they sought might well prove to be as illusive to him as ultimately Nah-Loh-Tah herself had been.

When they were about twenty miles out onto the ice, Sir Wilbur called another halt for rest, warm tea and food, and an opportunity to feed the dogs. He could study the sky to the north through his snow glasses, but he removed them briefly and squinted. The sky in that direction had seemed to be changing as they had been moving, and it now appeared as if there were actual winds of light passing through dark and stormy air.

Marcelina went first to Koyuk with which she was developing a special friendship and, examining his paws, found the left front pads of his paw bleeding due to ice wedged between them. Removing her mittens but not the gloves beneath, she carefully cleared away the ice and then took off one glove to apply petroleum jelly to the injured pads. The fierce Koyuk trusted her in this and submitted to her ministrations. This was probably a good thing, she felt, because to a large extent their survival on this part of the trek had now become wholly dependent on the continued well-being of the dogs. The other sled dogs had also all settled down and were reclining on the ice, although they remained alert, as Marcelina passed among them.

The long sled was to be used during this rest stop as something of a shield for the humans from the frigid wind that was now sweeping across the vast expanse of the glacier. Were this winter, the temperature would have been closer to 50° below zero, and at such a temperature raw ice could not be consumed. While at the present temperature a piece of glacier ice placed in the mouth could melt and the water in it could be drunk — there is little trace of salt in ice — in winter this same ice, if consumed at the lower temperature, would instantly chill the mouth to such an extent that body temperature itself would be lowered, and to anyone on the brink of freezing inside consumption of ice as a precaution against dehydration would only accelerate the inner freezing process. Accordingly, a pot of frozen pork and beans and a quart tin pail of frozen water that would be melted for tea were placed on the Primus stoves by Valera, while Sir Wilbur took to chopping off steaks of frozen caribou meat that were to be warmed partially before being fed to the dogs. The primary reason for the dogs' continued alertness and frequent glances toward the sled was their anticipation of food. But they could not be fed too much at this point, only enough to maintain their vigor and energy which meant they worked best, if kept partially starved, and they were to be beaten with the testing pole or the whip should they become unduly vicious, especially at feeding time. This might seem harsh, but it was the law of the North and was only ignored at one's peril.

The Englishman next uncased his Mannlicher-Schönauer, which he would be carrying henceforth in addition to the wooden testing pole. He had to check the action and assure that none of the firing mechanism had been disabled by the cold. It would be after this point that he must watch especially for polar bears, not very easy to see against the persistent dazzling white of the ice and the pale-blue blankness of the sky above with only the faintest wisps of clouds, although the continuing heavier accumulation of dark clouds in the north by way of contrast did improve visibility somewhat in that direction. Valera then took out his binoculars and carefully began to essay their back trail for any possible movement that would indicate Chris and Ramón had completed their reconnaissance and were already on their way to rendezvous with them. He could see no movement at all. That he couldn't worried Marcelina, but she said nothing.

In truth, all three of them were becoming increasingly possessed by a mounting sense of consternation and awe. It was as if the power of their surroundings was creeping into them viscerally, its simple yet implacable character eclipsing their merely human motives. This land had taken on a life of its own, like some colossal leviathan that was humbling them in a way they could not express. Part of this enormous power, to be sure, was the increasing tension between all of this evident beauty and the incredible capacity of that beauty to take life, suddenly and indifferently. It almost made one wish to weep inside, as the eyes constantly were tearing, feeling as Niobe had once felt when gazing upon the cold, silent beauty of her dead children. These wayfarers, after their fashion, were akin to St. Brendan and his group of Irish monks who had sailed into the Arctic Ocean in the 6th Century and, seeing a huge iceberg, had had to row three days to reach it. Transfixed by its magnificence, St. Brendan had proposed they should row through a hole so as to be inside of it. There, in the dim light, it had appeared to them like they were within the eye of God. In a manner of speaking it was the same within the souls of these three, the merging of darkness and light to the north, making them feel that this apparently endless expanse of ice was somehow the very floor of all creation, and how insignificant was this minuscule warmth of heavily clad bodies in the face of such Arctic desolation, so utter and so final.

"I hope we can make it again as far," Sir Wilbur told Marcelina, who had just added tea to the hot water in the tin pail, "before noon. At noon, we'll have to stop and put up a temporary camp and bed down for the night."

"That should give Chris and Ramón time to catch up, shouldn't it?" she asked, her voice still slightly muffled, although she had unbuttoned her nose and mouth flap for the moment.

"Yes, it should . . . quite definitely," the Englishman agreed.

After the dogs had been fed and the human meal consumed, Marcelina smoked part of a cigarette as she finished her tea that had been laced with lemon juice. Then it was time to pack up what gear they had been using, after the tin plates were scrubbed with ice chips and a brush before being stowed. If anything, the darkness in the north had only continued to deepen and expand.

"Storm?" asked Valera.

"May be," the Englishman conceded. "Perhaps an electrical storm. I know they can be very dangerous. We'll push on as best we can."

Once all was in readiness, Sir Wilbur yanked at the gee pole, springing the runners from the slight set they had taken in the ice during this respite, and then, having pulled Koyuk's collar, yanking the lead dog to his feet, he proceeded to resume his position in advance of the sled. When he was far enough out, he waved his left arm, left hand holding his Mannlicher-Schönauer, at Marcelina, and she mushed the dogs forward. The dogs assumed their radial positions behind Koyuk, the lead dog's bells and the metal snaps of their harnesses jingling harshly on the frigid air, their breaths making little puffs of mist before them, many with their mouths open and some with their long, pink tongues showing. At those times when she rode the runners to rest her legs and feet, Marcelina had to be careful that the cleats of her crampons did not damage the fiber-glass surfaces. Unquestionably these runners slid across the ice even more smoothly than would runners made of ivory, and they seemed impervious to a build-up of ice caused by friction with the surface of the glacier.

᾿ Attached to either side of the belt she wore around her waist over her parka were her two ice-axes. Her most difficult task was occasionally having to slow the dogs so that they should not overtake Sir Wilbur, proceeding swiftly at point.

Despite Chris Fallon's warning about polar bears, they rarely range very far inland away from the pack ice, except for the mating season. It is then their custom for the female to find a suitable place inland or on the rim of glacier ice to dig out a deep hole, sometimes with the help of her mate, and to burrow inside of it to spend the winter. The layer of blubber that so easily causes a polar bear to overheat in sunlight is sufficient in this ice den to maintain the warmth needed for the survival of the cubs. The female also lives on this stored blubber while making use of it in nursing her young. Usually polar bears seek hibernation in October, but some already begin this quest in August. Ultimately, though, polar bears may not be any more predictable than human beings, and for whatever reason, when about ten miles farther out onto the glacier, still proceeding to the northeast, Sir Wilbur first had the vague impression that he could perceive some motion, coming from the direction of the north.

Marcelina had moved up to the gee pole, from which vantage point she could better control the dogs which were tiring somewhat. Luis Valera was about twenty yards behind her, his pace having slowed somewhat from increasing fatigue. Sir Wilbur raised his right hand to signal Marcelina to stop the dogs, which she did. Luis Valera paused behind her.

The two polar bears were now visible to them all, their coats a bright yellowish white in the sunlight. The Englishman was not here for big game hunting. He would rather leave the bears to go their way in peace, but it was not to be. The bigger bear began to quicken his approach, his front legs seeming to swing out to the side as his huge paws folded toward his body like wooden paddles until they would thrust forward, setting down securely on the surface ice. The rear legs were longer and so appeared almost to be kicking the front feet forward.

Sir Wilbur raised his high-powered rifle. The larger bear that was now so near to him stopped and gathered himself on his hind legs, his mighty front paws with their razor-sharp talons thrown out before him as he advanced, hissing angrily, his gray tongue visible in the pale, violet mouth, his teeth bared. The bear was probably twelve feet in height and easily weighed a couple of thousand pounds. As fierce and fearless as he was in his combative advance, the bullet Sir Wilbur fired hit him just above the heart. He staggered backward for a moment, and then the second bullet hit him.

At the very moment of the first detonation, no one realizing that the footing beneath here was but an ice bridge, the surface of the bridge broke beneath the weight of the sled and Luis Valera. As it gave out beneath him, Valera began plunging downward, his back actually colliding with the ice wall of the crevasse, and then he slid swiftly into oblivion. The bridge, as it collapsed under the rear of the sled, sucked Marcelina backward down into the crevasse. For a moment she dangled over emptiness, hanging onto a back runner of the sled. With an alacrity she would not later remember, her right hand darted to the right-hand ice-axe, and she smashed it forward into the ice wall of the crevasse that had been revealed with the collapse of the ice bridge. Using the momentary support the ice-axe gave her, she reached for the other ice-axe, and smashed it forward, also, into the ice wall. In the meantime, she swung her crampons toward the ice wall, and so found herself hanging precariously but away from the sled that was slowly sliding backward over the precipice while the dogs in front of it jerked frantically at their harnesses and scratched with their claws at the ice to retain traction.

Marcelina had been too desperate and too intently focused to scream when the bridge first broke, but she cried aloud now as she saw the sled sliding inexorably downward, until it pulled the scampering, struggling dogs down into the crevasse after it.

Sir Wilbur's rifle boomed again, and yet again. Marcelina could not see what was happening up there. Instead, she looked below where, about a hundred yards beneath her, the sled crashed onto the floor of the ice-covered crevasse, the dogs tumbling and screaming after it. Some of them surely were killed instantly, maybe all of them. She could not look far enough behind her and down to see what had happened to Luis, but his only chance, if he were alive after such a fall, would surely depend on her.

Not since those practice sessions on the great wooden plank leaning against the barn at her home had she had to climb anywhere using her crampons and ice-axes, but she did not think of that. She began, at once, to work her way down the face of the crevasse which, fortunately, was only abruptly curved inward at the very top and tended to bulge outward as it spanned down to the floor of the crevasse. This very curvature, however, would have made climbing upward and out extremely difficult, if not impossible, had she chosen to proceed in that direction. Her thermal clothing had kept her relatively warm to this point, but she noticed now that it did not completely repel the frightful, penetrating cold of the ice crevasse.

Cool-headed, with surprising self-mastery, even as she was drawn and shuddering from the cold, her arms and legs moved in obedience to her will. Very cautiously, fully aware of her imminent danger of pitching backward into the abyss and most probably breaking her neck or her legs in the fall, she continued to chop her axe-holds into the ice and thrust her widely spread legs and feet to maintain her support during her descent. Never letting her attention waver, she prayed at the same time to God. Mostly it was the icy chill of the glacier stealing through her that made her feel physically brittle, while from nervousness and incredible exertion she was perspiring freely. She was small, and she had become thinner, probably now not weighing more than a hundred pounds, but her arm muscles were strong and sure as she swung and fixed the ice-axes, and her feet housed in the crampons clung to the ice as tenaciously as she clung to life itself.

She dared not forget the need for accuracy in her swinging of the ice-axes, despite the numbing, biting frost that was getting to her fingers. With her teeth, she bit into her right-hand mitten, pulling it off and letting it drop from her, and then repeated the action with her left mitten. Her grip was improved on the ice-axes, but the cutting cold only attacked her hands more viciously, and she felt her fingers growing increasingly stiff. Her footholds, as she proceeded, were only nine inches apart, and it seemed to her at this rate she would never make it to the bottom. There was only silence above her on the glacier. For a fleeting moment, she wondered if the Englishman had been downed by the bears.

At this point she found it necessary to stop and spend a few precious moments in rest. Above all, she must not allow fatigue to dull her and take the cunning from her hands, but her legs were straining, and presently they began to tremble from the stationary exertion. She wanted in the worst way just to rub her hands together to restore the circulation, but she did not dare to attempt it. So she began edging her way downward again, too desperate for tears, while reverberating in her soul were the only words she was able to understand: *ego dominus tuus.*

She chanced a look downward. It had seemed that she had not been moving at all, but that swift glance told her that she was only twenty feet from the floor of the crevasse. She was too spent physically to move more quickly, and too innately cautious, but she also felt, suddenly, a wholly contradictory feeling of having an excess of strength. The fear she had experienced vanished, and in its place came a new intentness of purpose, even a feeling of physical triumph. She was still possessed of it when, at last, she reached the floor of the crevasse, and it was to stay with her for the rest of her life. Some of the dogs were whining and struggling, and some were obviously dead. But there was no time for them now. Her first purpose must be *Tio* Luis. The collapse of the ice bridge had allowed the distant sunlight to penetrate into the crevasse, and she hurried quickly to where this man who had once been her guardian in a new world was buried up to his neck in chunks and flakes of ice.

He was barely conscious. With one of the ice-axes she cut away at the mound of ice that was entrapping him. The cold was, if anything, more penetrating here at the bottom of the crevasse, but she did not think of it as she chopped and hacked away at the encrustation of ice.

Valera rolled his head slightly, which he was now able to do, and said: "Marcelina . . . you should not have come." Then his face twisted in painful agony. "I think my leg's broken," he gasped.

"*Por favor* . . . soon I shall have you free. Then we can see how bad it is."

Koyuk was one of the few dogs that had apparently survived the fall without serious injury, probably because, having been in the lead, he had fallen onto the bodies of other dogs when they had all crashed to the bottom with the sled. He began now a fierce growling, and Marcelina looked in the direction of the dark crevasse to the southeast. Two figures were emerging into the area lighted from above, and behind them was a dog team, pulling a sled.

As the figures before the sled moved closer, Marcelina could see that the man most in advance held some kind of strange petrol-based metal torch. The figure behind him, from the delicacy of what of her facial features could be discerned, was a woman. The man rushed forward, having seen there was an emergency. He moved with amazing sureness of foot in view of the fact that he was not wearing crampons, but he did have some kind of netting wrapped around boots made of animal hide with fur about the tops. The woman wore similar foot gear. A tall man with a ghastly white face reined in the dog team. Two other dogs that must have survived the fall had now joined Koyuk in a chorus of insistent barking and growling.

"My name is Teh-Meh-Tayo," the first man said as he came up to where Valera was still partially buried in the mound of ice. "Let me help."

Marcelina remembered that name. Dr. O'Meara had told her of Teh-Mey-Tayo. And the woman behind him with the golden eyes might be Nah-Loh-Tah. But, if true, it didn't make any sense. Why should they be here at all?

"I think his leg is broken," she told Tey-Mey-Tayo.

"Then we must be careful how we free him from the ice." He took a long, thick-bladed knife from where he carried it in his parka and began chipping away at the ice.

"Let me help," said the woman.

And together they all fell to work, clearing away the ice. Luis did not move, his breath coming in frosting gasps.

The tall man, having halted the dogs of their sled, walked around them now and over toward Koyuk and the other dogs, alive and dead, still harnessed to the wreckage of the alien sled. While the last of the ice was being cleared away from around Valera's body, Strehlnikov, still at somewhat of a distance from the fierce growling of the strange dogs, had taken out his Tula-Tokarev automatic with its eight rounds in the clip and red stars on the handles. Pausing for careful aim, he began shooting the dogs.

"My God! . . . what are you doing?" Marcelina cried in angry desperation. She made a rush toward the Russian, but the woman beside her was even quicker.

"Lugu! Stop that! Do you hear me?" she demanded, approaching him.

"I wass jusst killing the wounded ones," he explained.

"There has been enough shooting here . . . and before."

"You keep forgetting who's in charge," he told her bluntly. "I give the orders."

Marcelina had now come up beside the woman. "Please," she said very clearly. "Please, do not kill our dogs."

For the first time Strehlnikov could see something of Marcelina's face, and he seemed struck by its beauty. He must have been moved in a strange way, since he made what for him was a most uncharacteristic gesture. He put the automatic away. "I was only trying to help the dogs out of their misery. I am sorry . . . if it offended you."

"This man's right leg is broken . . . below the knee," Teh-Meh-Tayo called to them. "He will need to have it set in splints."

"I know a little about it," Marcelina said. She looked at the woman she felt was Nah-Loh-Tah. "I once assisted Doctor O'Meara."

The woman with the golden eyes looked back at her gently. "You are Mar-Sah-Lee-Nah?"

"How do you know? . . . we've never met."

"A man once showed me a picture of you from when you were married."

"All right," Strehlnikov interrupted them. "Do what you want to do with this fellow . . . or I'll shoot him like I did those dogs. I may

354

do it, anyway . . . once Kolia gets back."

The women said nothing. Marcelina abruptly went over to the smashed sled to see if she could find pieces of wood suitable for a splint. Nah-Loh-Tah joined her, retrieving one of the Primus stoves that had somehow been undamaged in the crash. At least, now, they would have a source of heat.

After the armed encounter with Kolia Kratsotkin in the crevasse, Chris and Ramón had approached the edge of the abyss that slanted deeper into the ice where he had disappeared and tried for several minutes to call to him without success. The beam from Chris's flashlight was not able to penetrate to the bottom of it, and they had to give up all hope of rescuing him — even if he were alive, they were not equipped with the ropes and the ice pitons, either screw-ins or drive-ins, that would be needed to make a successful descent. Perhaps the best course would now be to push farther on in the ice cave. The runners of the sled and the tracks of the dogs left enough of a trace to assure them that the other members of the hostile group were still somewhere ahead.

Since it was so bitterly cold in the crevasse, the pace the two set for themselves was a relatively swift one to keep up their circulation. At the very least, there was no wind, so while breathing the cold air remained moderately painful, their eyes watered but little and their noses ran almost not at all. Occasionally the crevasse was open at the top. The chasm in the floor of the ice cave also gradually lessened, and, after what must have been several miles, it disappeared altogether. Chris might have tried backtracking to see if they could find their assailant, but the distant sound of more shots ahead decided him against it.

They had gone several more miles before they reached the place in the crevasse where the ice bridge had collapsed. Chris did not know what to make of the seven dead dogs — two of them having been shot, following their injuries — or of the evidence that a Primus stove had been set to one side, had been lit, and then removed. Also two now empty boxes of heavy bandages had been discarded. Someone had been hurt . . . but who? The explosion of a shot from above them caused both Chris and Ramón to look upward. The light beyond the crevasse seemed much dimmer than it had at any time before, but they could hear Sir Wilbur's voice from afar, calling down to them.

With a rope retrieved from the smashed sled over his left shoulder as well as an ice hammer and a drive-in, it was Ramón who with his ice-axes and crampons scaled the wall of the ice cave upward. Given the concave curvature of the ice wall near the top, it was an extraordinary feat. Once there, Ramón hammered in the drive-in, looped the rope through it, allowing the Englishman to lower himself hand over hand into the crevasse. Ramón followed after him on the rope. It had been very difficult to communicate at that height with the Englishman, but Chris was able to learn that Marcelina and Luis were now prisoners of the alien group he and Ramón had been trailing through the ice cave, and that Luis had been injured in the fall.

Nah-Loh-Tah and Marcelina emerged first from the vault of a great cave. The heaviness of the extremely cold, dry air inside this rock cave was relieved somewhat now by the outside air, although the darkness of the sky overhead made it seem like an extension of the blackness in the cave. On either side were towering peaks, shadowed by clouds, illumined by shafts of brilliant, opaque, flashing light.

Nah-Loh-Tah paused for a moment to study the sky which was suddenly pierced by a flash of even more intense light behind the congealed clouds. She was only vaguely visible to Marcelina, as if she were a phantom, but they had been conversing almost without pause as they had passed through the remainder of the crevasse in the glacier, then across a broad strip consisting of a series of pressure ridges, before entering the great cave. Between the crevasse and the great cave, the sky outside had become so dark and menacing with congested clouds, illumined from within at times by rolling flashes of electricity, that it really had afforded little light by which to see. The gusts of wind had been such that the flame in the metal torch held aloft by Teh-Meh-Tayo flickered incessantly and almost had been extinguished.

"You must trust me, Mar-Sah-Lee-Nah," Nah-Loh-Tah said quickly now in a hushed voice, "and do exactly as I say. Our lives may totally depend on what we do."

"Yes," Marcelina responded in a voice no less hushed.

"Wait here. I shall be back. And . . . try to keep your eyes closed."

Nah-Loh-Tah turned and passed swiftly back down the slight incline to where the dogs pulling the sled driven by Strehlnikov were now emerging in this flickering, ghostly darkness. Teh-Meh-Tayo was calling to the Russian to stop the dogs. Nah-Loh-Tah walked back into the maw of the great cave, past Tey-

Mey-Tayo and past the dogs that had now halted and the injured Luis Valera who was in the sled but unable to see very well in all this darkness.

"Are we there?" Strehlnikov demanded gruffly from his position at the rear to the dark shape he could scarcely make out as Nah-Loh-Tah.

"Here we must make camp," Nah-Loh-Tah told him. "Build a fire. Rest the dogs."

"Why?"

"Because we are about to enter Makaron Nyesoeessee. Our belief requires that all who enter must first cleanse themselves at the Sacred Pool. Mar-Sah-Lee-Nah and I shall go first. Teh-Meh-Tayo will light the stove for warmth, and there is a quantity of coal kept here for building fires. You men will go in, once we return. It is required that all who enter must immerse themselves naked as an oblation to the gods."

"What would happen if I don't?"

As Strehlnikov asked this question, his pale, austere face was momentarily lit by an abrupt flash of lightning in the sky outside the cave.

"My people would kill you."

"Even the crippled man you insisted come along?"

"Everyone," Nah-Loh-Tah replied, and it

impressed Strehlnikov that there was fear in her voice.

"It is probably just as well," the Russian conceded. "Our stopping here will give Kolia a chance to catch up, and a fire may help him to find us."

For hundreds of miles there had been no sign of a tree. Yet here was a cache of coal near the maw of the cave and, above it, held by metal brackets to the right wall was a series of metal sheaths shaped like torches similar to the one Teh-Meh-Tayo had located at the opening of the crevasse ice cave. Teh-Meh-Tayo was, in fact, lighting the wick of another of them, having removed the torch from its bracket, and, putting it back in the bracket, it did increase the illumination.

Nah-Loh-Tah again passed the sled and the dogs and emerged from the cave, proceeding to where she had left Marcelina, who was still standing on the incline. She had kept her eyes turned toward the floor of rock and mostly shut.

"Follow me," Nah-Loh-Tah said, as she touched the sleeve of Marcelina's parka, "but keep you eyes downcast."

Marcelina said nothing but followed the other woman as she led the way up a rock passage to their right. It was very awkward to walk, although occasionally everything was cast into sharp relief by the flashes of light. Those sudden flashes, however, even with her glance downcast hurt Marcelina's eyes and left an after-image that burned.

Presently the inclined path they were following spread outward onto a flat table. There was a sizable pool of water in front of them, from which steam vapors arose into the air. The temperature around them no longer seemed to be below freezing.

Nah-Loh-Tah stopped on the hard rock shore of the steaming water.

"We must take off all our clothes and then go into the water of the Sacred Pool. Do not worry. The water is very warm . . . perhaps seventy degrees as the English measure temperature. You will not freeze."

"I might before I get into the water," Marcelina said. "Do I really have to take off all my clothes?"

"Yes."

"I have a gun beneath my parka."

"You may never need it."

"But what of the others . . . the men?"

"Their time will come . . . later . . . after we have finished."

It was truly strange, the way Marcelina felt now, as if Chris had been right, back at Point Barrow, when he had said he felt like he was dreaming while being awake, because, although she had nearly forgotten it, she suddenly could recall the dream she had once had — the dream in which she had been utterly naked except for the small gold crucifix she wore on a gold chain around her neck and the gold band of her wedding ring.

"I will not take off my crucifix and my wedding ring," Marcelina affirmed.

"No," Nah-Loh-Tah responded in a hushed tone. "Those things are really worn by your soul . . . not your body."

After removing her boots and several pairs of socks, Nah-Loh-Tah stood up again and began quickly shedding all of the heavy clothing she was wearing. Marcelina tried to keep pace.

"You must keep your eyes closed as you're undressing," Nah-Loh-Tah said so softly Marcelina could scarcely hear her. She paused for a moment as she stepped out of her fur-lined snow pants. "Do try not to look. I shall take your hand. You shall not fall."

Finally Marcelina stood beside Nah-Loh-Tah, both of them naked. She reached out with her right hand, and Nah-Loh-Tah clasped it with her left. It was curious to her, but Marcelina felt no shyness, no reserve, no need even for the silk panties she had worn during her nude bathing scene before the camera. She felt as if she were partaking in a ritual, and she was proud of her nakedness, of her slight breasts, of the curve of her hips and flatness of her stomach, of the sloping, full, womanly roundness of her posteriors, of her athletic thighs, of her dainty feet. Of course, she could not see the band of white skin that ran from her sternum to the tops of her thighs and from just above her shoulder blades down her straight back to encompass her callipygian globes, places that hadn't been tanned by the Sun because they had been concealed by her bathing suit. She was keeping her eyes closed all of the time now.

The water was, indeed, somehow heated — Marcelina could actually feel the steam rising from it all around her — while the air remained so chilled that she shivered involuntarily. This sudden warmth of the water was reassuring and inviting, and she walked forward with Nah-Loh-Tah, deeper into the pool. The rock floor beneath her bare feet was solid and not slippery, smooth and yet rough enough to provide ready traction. Marcelina blinked her eyes open for just a moment, long enough to see Nah-Loh-Tah alongside her, with her small breasts high up on her chest, her skin appearing darkly burnished, probably because of the poor light.

When they were immersed to their waists, Nah-Loh-Tah said: "Dip down, but do not let your head go under the water . . . and keep your eyes tightly closed."

Nah-Loh-Tah had let go of Marcelina's hand. Marcelina did keep the lids of her eyes tightly shut. They slowly lowered themselves into the pool. After all of the dirt and the sweat, it was good to feel the cleansing touch of the water. It was once Marcelina had raised her body, dripping, from the water, and was again standing at her full height that it happened. The light before her closed eyelids suddenly turned a bright red, then the most intense white. It caused pain to scream along her optic nerves, and about her neck Marcelina felt an icy touch so terribly, tortuously cold that the little gold crucifix and gold chain seemed to be burning themselves against her living flesh. She cried out.

"Don't look! It's lightning!" Nah-Loh-Tah commanded. "I can feel it!"

But Marcelina's brief cry had been nothing compared to the howling wail that now came from somewhere behind them, somewhere back on shore. It ululated, waned, and then increased in its dreadful anguish, before falling silent.

"Don't look! Don't look! . . . whatever you do!" Nah-Loh-Tah insisted, and again felt to clutch Marcelina's hand. "He was watching you . . . as you bathed."

"Who was?" Marcelina demanded, suddenly so frustrated that she wanted to throw off Nah-Loh-Tah's hand and rip open her eyes.

"It's all right," Nah-Loh-Tah said then. "You can open your eyes now briefly . . . but don't keep them open. It may come again."

"What?" Marcelina asked, abruptly opening her blue-gray eyes, but she had to blink them several times, because her focus seemed blurred. Then in the dim, vague illumination of the surrounding darkness she could see Nah-Loh-Tah's face in shadow, her golden eyes that seemed so bright as if from an inner light.

"God touched you," Nah-Loh-Tah said in a low, hushed tone.

Marcelina's right hand instinctively flashed to the gold crucifix at her neck. The skin beneath it and all around under the chain still hurt, so deeply had she been burned. Then she looked down at her left hand, at her wedding ring, and the band of skin beneath it on her finger also hurt. She dared not probe anywhere near those bands of pain.

"God touched you," Nah-Loh-Tah said. "I had my eyes closed, but I felt it . . . when it happened. The light was so bright."

Nah-Loh-Tah raised her own left hand, and, for the first time, Marcelina realized that she, also, wore a wedding ring.

"And you weren't touched?" Marcelina asked in fear.

"Yes, Mar-Sah-Lee-Nah," Nah-Loh-Tah replied, disbelief shattering her voice, "God . . . did . . . touch . . . me . . . too." And she began to weep, standing there naked, her small, high breasts trembling, waist deep in the water of the pool that was almost hot, with the steaming mist rising around her. She raised her hands to her face, and her great sobs made her sway ever so slightly.

Marcelina reached out and embraced her. They were together now in their beauty and their nakedness and their terror. Then, both remembering at the same time, they closed their eyes again, for the electricity in the sky was still alive and flashing all around them.

Chris had his flashlight and snapped it on as they entered a great cave. Sir Wilbur was directly behind him, with Ramón bringing up the rear. They proceeded cautiously. It was obvious that, once they were within, the cave vaulted upwards so high that the beam of the flashlight could no longer touch the ceiling, although there seemed to be a series of deep shelves carved into the rock at intervals, ascending as giant steps into the unfathomable darkness overhead. The air was dry and very,

very cold, and their breaths misted before them as they moved.

They had walked perhaps a mile, when dimly before them in the distance they could make out the flickering of a fire. The beam of the flashlight bobbed before the trio as they drew closer to that remote source of light. Then there was the sound of a shot, which resounded in the great vault, a dull sound as from a hand gun. Chris snapped off the flashlight, and the three of them waited, alert, breathing quietly.

"I don't think that shot was fired at us," Sir Wilbur said finally, but he removed his outer mitten and brought up his rifle. "Turn on the flashlight again, Chris, but hold it out and away from your body . . . as much as possible. I'll have us covered. If there is another shot, I'll fire at the powder flame."

Chris snapped on the flashlight, taking a firmer grasp on his Winchester, should he have to return enemy fire. But there was no further shooting from above or beyond them. As they cautiously made their way closer to the fire, they could discern the shape of a sled, of dogs reclining or standing, looking in their direction. There was someone sitting on the sled. It was Luis Valera.

Several dogs growled at their approach, and those that had been reclining rose to their haunches and were watchful of their coming.

"Luis . . . what the devil?" Sir Wilbur called out, moving out into the lead beside and then in front of Chris.

"Careful," Valera warned. "That Russian ran back into the cave. From the way he was staggering, he must have been blinded somehow. I think he fired that shot I heard."

Fallon said nothing, but he snapped off the flashlight, pushing it into the left-hand pocket of his parka. This allowed him to take up the Winchester in both hands, looking about him up the walls of the cave's vault which had been narrowing for some time as they were emerging on this side.

"Thank God you're alive, Luis," said the Englishman, very close now to the man in the sled. "I didn't know where you'd been taken. I was watching from the edge of the crevasse, but I didn't dare fire a shot, not knowing what would be done to you, if I did."

"That Russian wanted to shoot me. Teh-Meh-Tayo wouldn't let him. But he did shoot a couple of the dogs who hadn't been killed in the fall. My leg was broken. Marcelina climbed down to where I'd fallen, as you know. If it hadn't been for her, I probably would have smothered under all that ice."

"Where is Marcie now?" Chris asked, coming up to join them.

"She went off to bathe in some kind of volcanic pool. Teh-Meh-Tayo heard the Russian scream and went off after them . . . apparently."

"Koyuk is here," Ramón announced, "and two of our other dogs."

"They were the only ones that survived the fall," Luis said.

Chris asked: "What do you mean . . . Marcie went off to bathe? In this freezing cold? Is she crazy?" Adding to his terror was the memory of a dream he had once had.

A sudden flash of light in the heavens outside the maw of the cave hurt their eyes. It was so bright that it gave them the aspect of white phantoms in a photographic negative.

"There's some kind of electrical storm out there," Luis said. "Even in here the lightning hurts your eyes. Just before the Russian screamed, the whole sky was lit up . . . over there . . . where apparently the volcanic pool is. Teh-Meh-Tayo told me to keep my eyes shut as much as possible just before he ran out himself. I think that's what happened to the Russian. The lightning probably blinded him."

"And Marcie's out there somewhere?" Chris demanded.

"Yo!" called Teh-Meh-Tayo as he descended the steep incline on the right outside of the cave. "Yo!"

Chris levered a shell into the chamber of the Winchester. The sharp sound could be clearly heard in the hollowness of the cave.

"That's Teh-Meh-Tayo," Luis said insistently. "He hasn't a gun that I know of . . . and he means no harm."

The man, still heavily clad, now entered the cave and paused, looking at the newcomers from one to the other.

"Teh-Meh-Tayo," Sir Wilbur said. "Luis had the name right. If you're here, then . . . ?"

"Yes," Teh-Meh-Tayo replied. "The women are getting dressed. They should be along presently."

"Tenny . . . you know this man?" Chris asked.

"I told you about him," the Englishman said curtly. "He's the guardian of Nah-Loh-Tah."

"Damn it, Tenny! Then there is no such thing as a lost colony. We've really just been trailing your wife . . . who vanished in India?"

"Makaron Nyesoeessee is not a colony, and it isn't lost to those who live here and know how to find it . . . and Nah-Loh-Tah did not vanish," Teh-Meh-Tayo clarified.

"Did you force her to go with you?" Chris accused.

"I did not force Nah-Loh-Tah to do anything. I am her uncle. I watched out for her . . . as best I could." He looked at Luis Valera. "Did you see Lugu?"

"Yes. He staggered past the fire and went back into the cave. We heard a shot, but he seems not to have been shooting at my friends."

"He is blind," Teh-Meh-Tayo said. "I passed him on the way to the Sacred Pool, but he could not see me. It could be bad if he meets up with Kolia."

"A man who had been shooting at us died back there . . . in the crevasse," said Chris.

"You killed him?" Teh-Meh-Tayo asked.

"Not directly. But I believe he's dead. He fell deeper into the crevasse."

"I know where Lugu wanted him to wait. If Kolia fell there, he is surely dead."

"Chris!"

It was Marcelina's voice. She was fully dressed and came rushing into the cave. Chris leaned his Winchester against the sled and hurried to embrace her.

Sir Wilbur's light-blue eyes were fixed on the figure who entered the cave behind Marcelina. The lines on the sides of her mouth, formed from smiling, were creased now, but her golden eyes shone with tears. It was an expression that carried him back to a place that was not the Arctic, and to a time that was not cold, and his heart constricted with the memory. Silent, now, immobile, they stood apart from each other and beyond the reach of words, while the blood receded from Nah-Loh-Tah's cheeks and her high forehead, leaving her burnished skin a creamy white, like ivory.

Chapter Ten

The electrical storm passed without any onset of rain or snow, but the wind from the north became even stronger than it had been. Teh-Meh-Tayo claimed the lightning had been caused by cloud-gathering Zeus. It was the clearest sign human beings have of the terrible power and majesty of God. It would be an empty argument to attempt to explain lightning in the Arctic in terms of natural causes completely knowable to human beings, since, as Sir Wilbur recalled Shivapuri Baba having once phrased it, this only begs the question of how electro-magnetism had come to be created in the first place and ignored entirely what it means.

The Englishman had spent the time waiting for the electrical storm to recede, talking quietly with Nah-Loh-Tah, sitting somewhat removed from the fire, the stove, and the torch light. Chris was no physician, but he had found, upon examination, that as much as could be done for Luis Valera's broken leg had already been done by Teh-Meh-Tayo and Marcelina. He told of the confrontation with Kolia Kratsotkin in the ice cave, and Teh-Meh-Tayo explained how it had been that he and Nah-Loh-Tah had been joined by the two Soviet agents in making the return journey to Makaron Nyesoeessee. He did not address the reasons behind Nah-Loh-Tah's sudden departure from Peshawar, but Marcelina told Chris that she understood it as best it could be explained. Valera narrated the venture onto the glacier and the collapse of the ice bridge, while Ramón told of how he and Chris had come upon the section of the ice cave where the collapse had occurred, how they had managed to bring Sir Wilbur down, and the killing of the two polar bears. Marcelina was saddened by what had happened, because from her perspective they had been the intruders and the bears had every right to explore the glacier for a place to make a suitable den — if, indeed, that was what they had been doing. Most of all, though, they were all very tired, having been so long without sleep now and having undergone such extreme exertions. No one knew what had become of Strehlnikov, but it was likely that he would eventually make his way back to Makaron Nyesoeessee, and, Teh-Meh-Tayo assured them, he would surely be cared for.

When they started out again, Teh-Meh-

Tayo led, Sir Wilbur and Nah-Loh-Tah walking behind him, Chris and Marcelina behind them, with Ramón behind the dog sled in which Luis Valera was being transported. They mounted the long incline directly beyond the great cave until they reached an expansive ledge. There, before them, stretched the great valley of Makaron Nyesoeessee. Moss of various hues covered much of the ground, but there were also fields of stunted wheat, wooded areas of dwarf willows, saxifrage, and ranunculus. Although they could not be seen readily with the eye from this distance, there also lived here, Teh-Meh-Tayo told them, herds of deer, a large population of snow hares, ptarmigan and snow birds, even some musk-ox, and species of ducks and geese. The array of vivid and variegated colors nearly overwhelmed the eye — multiple shades of red, yellow, yellow-green, and green. In the distance a series of interconnected lakes could be seen, their waters sparkling.

In his travels Teh-Meh-Tayo had made a study of ocean currents, and he commented that what was known as the warm Spitzbergen current which flows fifteen hundred miles through the Arctic Ocean helped warm the climate in Makaron Nyesoeessee, complemented by the hot volcanic springs such as that at the Sacred Pool. The buildings were mostly made of stone, their walls whitened by a tincture of herbs and oil so they resembled nothing so much as the white buildings still so typically found in the Greek isles. Those who lived here felt that all good things were theirs, and it simply was accepted that for nearly four months of the year they lived in darkness, under the watchful benevolence of the planet Saturn — Teh-Meh-Tayo referred to it as Kronos. This life-giving ground bore its fruit freely and in abundance, and for many centuries its people had continued to live in what had seemed uninterrupted prosperity. Far off in the distance was a mountain — they called it Hyperborea — where gold was very near the surface and had been mined for as long as anyone could remember. In the spring, after Hyperborea became covered with ice and frost during the dark months, the rays of the Sun would glint and scintillate from its fastnesses. There was also a rich oil deposit in Makaron Nyesoeessee from which they made numerous useful things including their main source of light and fuel. There was also coal. The total population had remained somewhat stable over the years, numbering about four hundred persons at the time Teh-Meh-Tayo and Nah-Loh-Tah had left. Women were not especially encouraged to marry young, and child-bearing was not considered a woman's most important function, and somehow the population here had never exploded as it had in so many places to the south. Teh-Meh-Tayo contrasted population in China, which had continued to expand at a fantastic rate over the centuries, with the population in Egypt where civilization was certainly as old but had remained relatively small over the same period of time.

Many people came to welcome the return of Teh-Meh-Tayo and Nah-Loh-Tah, and the visitors were introduced to Epi-Tyg-Cha-Noh, a man with white hair and serene features who was the closest thing they had to a political leader. A common tent, consisting of animal hides with soft bedding of animal furs, was set up for the visitors. Teh-Meh-Tayo acted as interpreter during the festive meal that was served to them in a small municipal building, and by eight o'clock in the evening Canadian time for this zone these people from the south were finally allowed to retire in the common tent.

Chris and Marcelina occupied the same bed, while Sir Wilbur, Luis, and Ramón had their own beds placed variously around inside the tent. Chris reclined on his left side while Marcelina curled close, with her back to him. When they believed the others were asleep, they freed themselves from the clothing on their lower bodies. Always, since the first time these two had joined their souls together on the pampas in the shadow of the lost city of Haucha in the darkness before the dawn, they had experienced their orgasms of pleasure and fulfillment at the same time. The joy they experienced was always united with the ecstasy of having found each other. Only when they engaged in oral coition, after they were married, would this pattern alter, but this also depended on their position, and, when they did it together, Chris would caress Marcelina's beautiful cheeks in such a way as to tell her that he was close to coming, and she would slow down or pause altogether, until she would feel herself begin to come, and then she would respond vigorously so they could come together, so they could taste each other deeply inside of their bodies and their souls at the same time. But somehow now, perhaps because they were bound together as they once had been and so were unable to see each other's face and eyes, daring to say nothing, except for the abrupt, involuntary cry Marcelina uttered as she began her orgasm (which went unheard by blasphemous men), she started to come before Chris, and in her first spasm of intense pleasure grasped him deeply inside of herself just as he began to ejaculate. Somehow — whether it was their position, or the moment, their passion, or her clutching him like that — a channel opened deeply inside of her, and for the first time these two breathed life now, one into the other together, and inside of Marcelina the twins came to be. When they were born, after she knew they were fraternal twins, a boy and a girl — they would have large blue-gray eyes and reddish-brown hair and would grow to be taller than she was — Marcelina thought of twins she had known or knew about, of the two Quechuans in faraway Peru, Quinto and Pedro, now both gone, of the twins whose remains they had found in the Temple of the Sun at Haucha, of Castor and Pollux, the brightest stars in the constellation Gemini, and Marcelina O'Day y de Ferrar's twins with Christopher Fallon, whom she believed to be anointed and marked by God as she had been at the Sacred Pool, were named Christina and Marcus Fallon y O'Day.

The sky above began further to brighten around four o'clock in the morning, although there was now a heavy, enveloping cloud cover to the south. The Sun was a bright globe, low on the horizon, turning the clouds around it a bright yellow merging into gold, while clouds more distant from the light seemed awash with hues of pink and edges of dark blue. Nah-Loh-Tah came to the common tent, crept inside, and wakened Sir Wilbur, taking caution not to disturb the others. Although Ramón roused enough to be aware of their departure, he said nothing.

Nah-Loh-Tah led the Englishman up out of the valley and to the broad shelf on which had been raised, centuries in the past, the great, circular, stationary chronometer. The huge whale ribs which were paired in arches, touching each other at the intersection of their upper tips, were, in turn, united by strips of solid gold linking the tops of the ribs in a trilithon arrangement, and so formed a circle a little over three hundred feet in diameter. The whale rib arches created a total of fifty-six apertures. Inside the circumference of the arches was a circle of thirty-six menhirs that had been fashioned from the tusks of mastodons, and within this was a final circle of twenty-four slim rock pillars sculpted from stone. Nah-Loh-Tah showed where outside the circumference of the structure but between arches were located four small structures fashioned from pure gold in the shape of a *crux ansata* mounted in pillars of stone six inches above the ground. These crosses, she explained, represented the four stations, perhaps best understood by what the English call the four seasons, except they are very differ-

ent in the Arctic than they are to the south —
it was obvious to Sir Wilbur that Makaron
Nyesoeessee, being so far north, really meant
every other place on the planet was to the
south. The chronometer was still used by the
Makarons for a determination of calendar
time and had nothing at all to do with worship
of the Sun. In fact, for nearly four months of
the year all of the apertures were dark, so it
was the precession of the constellations and
visible planets that were used to calculate the
equinoctial points on the Earth's ecliptic from
east to west. It had been known by the earliest
colonists in Makaron Nyesoeessee that the
effects of what came to be called the electro-
magnetic attraction of the Sun, the Moon,
and the planets upon the equatorial protuber-
ance of the Earth had an impact on duration
in the precession of the equinoxes, and for the
full cycle to run its course had been projected
mathematically by early astronomers among
her people to be twenty-six thousand years.
This was known in the outside world as the
so-called Platonic Year. The oldest records
kept by her people were dated — according to
a chronology Sir Wilbur would understand —
at 405 B.C., but for her people this present
year was 2339. They computed smaller mea-
sures of time in increments of seven years, the
seasonal time between Persephone's disap-

pearance into the realm of Hades and her re-appearance upon the Earth, although their computation of a year had only ten months, not twelve. However, those ten months did encompass three hundred and sixty-five and one-quarter days each, completing two full cycles every eight years.

"Then," said the Englishman in a gentle tone, "this wasn't . . . Makaron Nyesoeessee wasn't where what has come to be called Indo-Aryan culture began . . . intimations of which are in the Rig Veda?"

"It may have been, Wil-bur . . . I don't think anyone knows for certain any more. We do know there were people living here when the first Greek colonists arrived. The Arctic was different then . . . as it would be later . . . for hundreds of our years at a time. When those Argive colonists sailed up the passage between what now you call Greenland and Ellesmere Island and into the Arctic Ocean until they penetrated here to Makaron Nyesoeessee, they found there were people already living here, but those people had no written records. All they had of their tribal history was what could be transmitted in narrative myths they memorized and passed on through generations . . . rather as was the case with the Rig Veda itself when it was in its purest form. These early people . . . so it is said . . . had golden skin . . . and our people . . . the Greeks, as you know them . . . may have been here before even that time because Makaron Nyesoeessee is already in the verbal tradition of Hesiod. Those original people, it is believed by our people now, lived like gods in a spirit free from all care, with little toil and no grief . . . much as we have lived here since . . . just as sunlight has continued to be refracted from the mountains of ice and gold, intensifying the growing season and allowing harvests possible nowhere else in the Arctic. Makaron Nyesoeessee owes its security to what I have learned is called a superior mirage."

"Yes," rejoined Sir Wilbur, "I remember your talking about superior and inferior mirages when we were in Darjeeling."

"Because light does not really travel in straight lines at all, but curves, the presence of the colder Arctic air all around Makaron Nyesoeessee and the colder temperature of the Arctic Ocean creates exactly the opposite effect from the illusion of water in a desert where the mirage is created by warmer air on the surface of the ground and colder air above. Here, the warmer air is also closer to the ground, but the colder, surrounding air so bends the light that an opposite image . . . that of water and not of land . . . appears above the horizon when viewed from northern Greenland or northern Ellesmere Island, or the image sometimes is such that the mountains appear inverted . . . as if they were clouds in the sky and not mountains at all. It must be that way even high up in the atmosphere. Had you come this far in an airplane, you probably would have still been able only to see the superior mirage."

"Chris showed me in a magazine where a tropical garden was, indeed, seen from an airplane somewhere in this vicinity."

"It is possible, then, I suppose, that Makaron Nyesoeessee will someday be discovered again and exploited as Lugu hoped to do for the Soviet Union." She looked very gravely at him with her deep, golden eyes while the wrinkles on either side of her mouth curved into a small smile. "Or perhaps you . . . as I fear . . . will claim Makaron Nyesoeessee for the British Empire on which the Sun now never sets."

Her words jarred him, and his expression became anguished. "I shall never tell another living soul about Makaron Nyesoeessee."

"I hope I can believe you," she said somewhat hesitantly. "But you did not talk that way when we were living together as man and wife in India."

"No," he admitted. "No. Only there are

two separate ideas at issue in that statement. The first has to do with the British Empire. I haven't said it before, but I believe the Empire is ultimately doomed in the modern world . . . not because of British arrogance toward colonial peoples, but because there was never enough arrogance. The average young man working in the Colonial Service has had to master Latin, but not the Roman idea that, truly, the mother country's culture and political institutions could have a civilizing effect throughout the colonies. After the Great War, India surely should have been granted Dominion status as had been done with Canada and Australia. Instead, all the British have continued to do there is hide in their army cantonments and all-white clubs. A truly enlightened Britain would have seized on the idea of a unified Empire made up of many different castes and races. The only way this ever could have happened is if the British really believed in their civilizing mission . . . but . . . sadly . . . they never really have." He paused, and then continued. "But to speak personally . . . it was after you vanished . . . after I could no longer pursue you . . . that I remembered what you had said to me close upon that last night . . . that before I could ever truly go northwest to find your homeland . . . I must first go southeast . . . back to Haucha."

"And did you go there again?"

"I did."

"And what did you find?"

"Oh, it's still there . . . the ancient city . . . but stripped of all its treasure and. . . ."

"And?"

"Do you remember Shivapuri Baba's telling us of the subterranean tombs he went to see on Malta when he was walking around the world?"

"Yes."

"Of how prehistoric people had excavated there a tomb for Hal Safieni . . . ? Do you remember what word Shivapuri Baba used to describe what had happened to that tomb and all the others carved deeply into the living rock?"

"Yes . . . desecrated."

"Well, that's the very word I would use to describe what has happened to Haucha."

She nodded but remained silent.

"You knew that would be true, didn't you?" he asked.

"Did you also go back to Ka-Mor?"

"No. When I saw what had happened to Haucha, there was no longer any need. I knew if, by the grace of God, I should ever find this place . . . you know, I didn't even understand the name you gave me for it, until Chris . . . he knows ancient Greek . . . told me its meaning

. . . but, long before that, I knew . . . should I find it . . . and I really wasn't certain until I saw you that your homeland . . . Makaron Nyesoeessee . . . and the place for which I was searching . . . a place Shivapuri Baba seemed to know something about that I did not . . . anyway I knew . . . should I ever find it . . . I would never reveal it to anyone."

"Shivapuri Baba is a holy man, Wil-bur . . . and he is also very wise. He knows of Makaron Nyesoeessee. He has been here."

"He was here?"

"Oh, yes. Our people remember him and speak of him to this day. I was too young to have more than a vague recollection of him when he was here, but Teh-Meh-Tayo . . . he is . . . was my father's brother as well as my guardian . . . he had talked with Shivapuri Baba. He agreed . . . because I wanted to go to Shivapuri Baba . . . to learn what I could from him . . . he agreed to make the journey with me . . . he stayed with me at Point Barrow where we studied English with the Irish schoolteacher from Detroit. . . ."

"Doctor O'Meara's wife?"

"Yes. Cath-Her-In."

"She is dead, now."

"Yes . . . so I have heard. I am sorry. She was a fine woman."

"Do you know that Doctor O'Meara transcribed one of your songs . . . that he taught it to Marcelina? . . . I heard Marcie sing it."

"Mar-Sah-Lee-Nah told me. I knew he had done it while we stayed there. Mar-Sah-Lee-Nah told me he had taught her to sing it and that she thought the song very beautiful. I told her it was an old song. I have written others since . . . I hope more beautiful."

"By the grace of God, Nah-Loh-Tah, I have found you again. That is all that really matters."

"Has it never occurred to you . . . even with all you have seen in your life and especially here in the Arctic . . . that all creation is eternally changing, even if that endless change sometimes is to be measured only in æons upon æons . . . just as what Ursa Minoris appears to be over the last four thousand years is not what shape it will have a hundred thousand years from now, any more than this is the shape it had a hundred thousand years ago . . . that even the *fixed* stars are only a convenient illusion that mortals of a day chose to believe in . . . as we know from the Rig Veda . . . how, when the Rig Veda was composed, Thuban in Alpha Draconis was then the North Star . . . which Polaris has only since become . . . and that the laws of creation are based only on hazard . . . that change is the only true constant in all of creation?"

"Was it just hazard . . . what happened to that Russian chap?"

"He is *Komintern*. For months and months he had been undressing me with his eyes, and then I saw him looking at Mar-Sah-Lee-Nah that same way . . . only with her it was even stronger. He was a man who had not had a woman for a very long time . . . not since before we boarded the *Sibiryakov* at Cape Chelyuskin. Was not what happened inevitable? Do you remember the story about the blind seer, Teiresias, who . . . Homer says . . . alone among mortals was allowed to retain his wits when he entered the House of Hades . . . do you remember how he became blind?"

Wilbur shook his head.

"One day in a forest Teiresias came upon a grotto where gray-eyed Athena was bathing . . . and so he alone of mortals beheld her divine nakedness. Athena punished Teiresias for his sin. She permitted him to retain his life . . . but not his eyesight. Her nakedness was the last thing he saw before he was plunged into darkness."

"But it was really an accident . . . for all of that . . . with that Russian . . . wasn't it?"

"Mar-Sah-Lee-Nah told me that Chris believes her to be *eudaimon*."

"Do you believe that?"

"She was naked. Lugu saw her naked. And

God touched her at that moment . . . marked her while our eyes were tightly closed . . . marked her with the sign of a small cross with a circle above it . . . marked her in the form of the *crux ansata* . . . the *ankh* . . . the Egyptian symbol for life . . . the cross with handles . . . the cross through the eye of which we believe it is possible to conceive eternity . . . the shape of our symbol for the four stations . . . and at the same time as He touched Mar-Sah-Lee-Nah . . . Lugu was blinded. What do *you* believe? Mar-Sah-Lee-Nah's body will carry that mark until she falls into dust. Even your very presence here in Makaron Nyesoeessee you owe to Mar-Sah-Lee-Nah. You were going to the northeast . . . not northwest."

"Our calculations were based on the position of Epsilon in Ursa Minoris on January Thirtieth . . . you were rather vague about *when* in January."

"Can you blame me? I did not want you to find Makaron Nyesoeessee until you were ready to find it. Where were you on January Seventh, Wil-bur?"

"I was on an ocean liner, bound for Peru."

"You cannot see Arcas or Callisto in the sky in the Andes." It was not a question.

"No . . . you know that. They only seem to move toward the equator from the direction of the north and then begin to retreat back to

390

the north. You cannot see them at all when you are south of the equator."

"And so you would not have found Makaron Nyesoeessee . . . ever . . . were it not for Mar-Sah-Lee-Nah."

"Chris is right about her. I know that now."

"I knew it when I first looked into her eyes . . . they are as I imagine Athena's eyes must be. Mar-Sah-Lee-Nah is *eudaimon*."

"You speak of gods and goddesses as if there were many . . . not just one."

"Did not Shivapuri Baba say the many gods and goddesses are but masks of the One whose name cannot be said . . . the One who cannot ever be known? God has no gender. God is above and beyond all genders." She chose not to tell him yet that she, too, had been touched by the hand of God. Instead, she said: "Come . . . we must go now to the vault of the great cave."

"We passed through the great cave when we were coming here," Sir Wilbur reminded her, profoundly moved in spite of himself.

"But you did not look upward."

"It was all darkness in the vault . . . and bitterly cold."

"Dark, perhaps, for eyes that cannot see, and cold . . . but it is there that all our people are buried . . . and have been for generations upon generations before even the ancient

Argives came here to Makaron Nyesoeessee for the last time at the end of one of the warm times in the Arctic and so found they could not return. It is where my father who was very old when I was born is buried. It is where I shall be buried."

There was a confidence in Nah-Loh-Tah that was different. She had seemed so vulnerable and easily intimidated when they had lived as man and wife in India. Yet, maybe it was more than confidence now — maybe that was the wrong idea altogether — maybe it was, instead, a quiet pride in herself, her home, and her people. It was also pressing down on Wilbur that, now he had found her again, nothing else in the world other than being with her seemed important. The terrible time of the pursuit of her through Afghanistan, the loneliness afterwards in Peshawar, in Delhi, and across the sub-continent on the British-Indian railway, boarding the ship in Calcutta and sailing to Sydney, and from Sydney to Lima, then into the hinterlands of Peru to Tacho Alto and even beyond to the ruins of Haucha, sailing from Lima to San Diego and from there by train to San Fernando. There were those days at the *Hacienda* de Ferrar — of which he had come to remember most of all Marcelina's music lesson and the walk at dusk with Carole Lombard.

But there was more — not so much a memory, as a consuming emotion — those times when he had been alone, and the younger Wilbur Tennington had come to him and had seemed to be asking him solemnly, perhaps even with a touch of bitterness, what in all this had he really profited? Had not something somewhere become lost to him? Nah-Loh-Tah. Were he to find her again? . . . and if not, what, oh, what, would become of him? He had found her again . . . — and the pain of it was tearing him so deeply asunder that his very soul trembled. His left hand crept toward her right hand, and she clasped it, silently, as she had so many times when they had walked together in India.

Near the entrance to the great cave from this side there were still the several tall metal torches that Nah-Loh-Tah called *puros*. They were hollow and filled with the refined petroleum used in Makaron Nyesoeessee for illumination during periods of darkness. Wilbur had matches with him, and he used two of them to light the *puros* they would carry into the interior. Among what was left of their supplies back at the common tent, Chris had a flashlight, but he had not thought to bring it, and actually it was not needed, since the *puros* gave off a sufficiently intense light. Tiers of deep parallel shelves beginning halfway up each of the walls had been carved from the living rock. Without a thermometer, it was impossible to tell the exact temperature in this vault, but it was certainly well below freezing, and their breathing created vapor in the cold air. Steps carved into the walls led up to each of the tiers that extended, it seemed, for thousands upon thousands of yards. She beckoned him to ascend behind her. As they rose into the vast inner reaches of the vault, Wilbur was able to distinguish the first row of fur-wrapped bodies.

"This is our Underworld," Nah-Loh-Tah explained. "The cold, dry air as it moves through the cave has mummified all of the bodies . . . and they have been so for centuries." She paused on the first landing. "Our people also have long had something like the caste system in India," she continued. "Those who have been our wisest men and women, our heroes and sages and noble women . . . even children who died young but had already made an impression on our people . . . they are buried according to the rank accorded them in leaving life. These catacombs go on and on . . . there are thousands and thousands buried here and on the other side . . . all along the walls. Not only our people but those who came to live here . . . occasional sailors or explorers who were lost in the Arctic during the winter time and managed to stumble into Makaron Nyesoeessee . . . or were found by one of our hunting parties . . . or by trading parties . . . for we do trade with certain Eskimo villages and by this means have acquired some of the implements created by the people to the south . . . but we never want to be a part of them or their way of life."

"What's that?" Wilbur asked suddenly. He had been holding his torch aloft and, in its flickering light, saw a strange, huddled shadow about a dozen yards down the first tier.

Nah-Loh-Tah did not answer but at once walked forward along the rock floor of the tier past several mummified bodies. Wilbur followed.

The form sprawled with legs and feet jutting outward whereas the mummified bodies were all sitting upright, with their backs to the wall of the cave, their legs drawn up close to their torsos.

"It's Lugu," Nah-Loh-Tah said, pausing before the body.

"This must be where he ran . . . after he came back into this cave," Wilbur said. "He didn't escape, after all."

"He was blinded . . . you know that," Nah-Loh-Tah said, stooping down and moving the stiff shoulder of the corpse with one hand, holding her *puros* in her other hand.

The body was stiff, probably not *rigor mortis* but from having frozen. The movement caused by Nah-Loh-Tah's touch, however slight, revealed the Tula-Tokarev in Strehlnikov's right hand. He had shot himself in the mouth, and there was frozen blood on the back wall of the cavern that had probably spurted out upon exit of the 7.62mm slug.

Nah-Loh-Tah raised her *puros* toward Wilbur. "Please hold this. I want to move the body."

"Let me do it."

As Nah-Loh-Tah rose from where she had been crouched, she took hold of his *puros*. Wilbur passed around her and, bending down, grasped the frozen corpse by the upper arms and leaned it back against the wall as best he could.

"He cannot remain here," Nah-Loh-Tah said. "He was not one of us."

Wilbur said nothing until the body was in more of an upright position. Then he stood erect, turning to her. "But he was of no little help to you. Without him, you could . . . you would never have gotten out of the Soviet Union. You might have faced a terrible fate . . . rape . . . prison . . . a labor camp. Those Bolsheviks are a scurvy lot."

"Some of them are brutish . . . Kolia was.

But not Lugu. He was greedy and lustful . . . yet you are right. Teh-Meh-Tayo and I could not have made it back without him. I do not know what should be done with his body. I shall have to ask Epi-Tyg-Cha-Noh."

"It was suicide . . . that's sure. He's still clutching the gun."

"It would have been worse . . . if he hadn't become . . . lost. I guess that is what happened. It would have been worse had he come out the other end . . . blind and all . . . and tried to cross the glacier, or wandered into the ice crevasse."

"With no food . . . no source of heat . . . blind . . . yes, I should say so. In a way it's a damned shame . . . but . . . perhaps he became terrified . . . finding himself among these frozen mummies. We'll never know . . . not for sure."

He stopped speaking as he thought of what should be done about the body. It would be difficult to transport it back to the rendezvous with the *Janet*, but it could be done.

"It is best that we leave him for now," she said, handing Wilbur his *puros*.

By the light, looking at Nah-Loh-Tah, Wilbur could see that there were tears in her eyes. Then she bowed her head, turned, and led the way slowly to the rock stairs.

Nah-Loh-Tah had traveled over ten thousand miles on land and sea with Nicolai Strehlnikov. He had been cold, it seemed, in every human way, and, had it been lust he had felt toward her, it had never gotten the best of him. It was the appearance of Mar-Sah-Lee-Nah that had changed him. She had seen it, as it was happening. She had used it, and she had enlisted Mar-Sah-Lee-Nah in what surely had been a conspiracy that would, she had hoped, conclude as it had — she had hoped Lugu would not shut his eyes as he watched them strip themselves naked and wade into the Sacred Pool as the electrical storm enveloped them. But never — never! — had she wished him dead.

They had descended the rock stairs leading down from the first tier of the burial vault before she spoke. "Wil-bur. I *am* sorry. I did not think he would flee. I did not think he would get lost . . . or that he would kill himself. I thought . . . if he were blind . . . he could live with our people . . . we could care for him."

Wilbur stopped walking, still holding his *puros* aloft. "Much has happened . . . to me . . . especially in this last year. I now believe in many things I once would have scoffed at. I do not know how or why it should be so, but I do believe that Marcelina is *eudaimon,* and I believe that what happened at the pool . . . that it was a . . . a terrifying manifestation of the power of God . . . this imagination beyond anything a mortal can ever hope to understand. But if that is so . . . if God left the imprint of the *crux ansata* on Marcelina's body for all of her life to come . . . then, truly, I also believe that, if God touched Marcelina, He also touched a tumor in the Russian's soul that began to grow madly and drove him finally out of his mind. I cannot tell you how exactly . . . much less why . . . but it's what must have happened to him. What was it you told me about Teiresias? . . . that he alone was allowed to enter Hades and keep his wits about him? Well . . . as harsh and cruel as it is to say it . . . Lugu, as you call him, was no Teiresias . . . he lost his sight . . . and then he lost his mind . . . and, in the end, he took his own life."

As they walked toward the ridge overlooking the valley ahead of them and the great, circular chronometer just below that ridge, it was Nah-Loh-Tah who paused. The golden light from the Sun seemed to diffuse all about them, as it shone and flashed in distant reflections from the mountains of ice and the mountain of gold. Wilbur paused beside her, looking off toward the Sacred Pool.

"Wil-bur . . . ," she said softly, "you were not to find Makaron Nyesoeessee . . . but you have. It has been a year since we parted, and you have found me again in . . . this golden palace."

Wilbur reached out to her, and tears came into his eyes. "If I could have but one wish . . . ?"

"Yes?" She was looking at him with her golden eyes, the contours of her beautiful face illumined more from within than by the light that surrounded them.

"I would want . . . ," — he began slowly, painfully — "please . . . Nah-Loh-Tah . . . I would have you choose my wish."

She smiled then, her eyes glistening. "I would wish that you become one of us . . . so we may remain together for as long as we live . . . so we may have a child together."

When, late in the afternoon, Chris and Marcelina returned to the common tent, they learned that Sir Wilbur was still absent and now so was Ramón. Luis Valera, of course, was there, chained to his bearskins, as he complained. He had been reading from the copy of the Rig Veda Marcelina had brought along.

"Epi-Tyg-Cha-Noh was here again," he told them. "He brought with him Apo-See-Kah-Kos, their man of medicine. He examined my leg . . . and it looks as if it's going to be all right, as long as I don't try to walk on it any time soon. That prognosis, however, isn't very good in one way. I wonder how the devil I'm ever going to get back to base camp in time to meet the *Janet*."

"By sled . . . at least across the glacier . . . or, rather, this time . . . probably through it," Chris assured him.

"And then?"

"And then, *Tío* Luis, you will be carried . . . if need be." Marcelina smiled.

"I really am sorry about all this," Valera said, regret in his tone.

"You're alive," Chris replied. "You probably wouldn't be . . . if help hadn't come."

"At the risk of Marcelina's life."

"It would have been no less difficult for me to have climbed to the top."

"But, my dear, a good deal the shorter distance."

"We have made wonderful discoveries," Marcelina said, changing the subject as she sat down on the edge of the bearskins on which Valera reclined. "They make a paper like parchment from the kind of willow trees that grow in the valley. Ink is made from resin and soot. They use ivory styli carved from narwhal tusks."

"Is that how they have copied all the papyri over the years?" Valera asked, his interest now keen.

"Not the most ancient of the documents," answered Chris, who made himself comfortable on the other side of Valera's bed, "like the literary works that were brought . . . apparently . . . by the original colonists. These have been etched by expert craftsmen onto thin pages of pure gold foil that are bound together by loops of thicker gold. They have some chemical solution they use to prevent tarnishing, or at least that corrects it, when it sets in. But vastly more important than any of this is what they have here . . . an absolute treasure."

"I imagined they might have some works that were lost in Europe after the fall of the Roman Empire in the west," Valera said.

"They do, indeed," Chris assured him. "Just let me tell you. It was a little difficult, at first, to acclimate myself to reading lines in Greek without any breaks between words, but, after a time, I grew accustomed to it. I didn't know, for example, that *Prometheus purkaios* . . . *Prometheus, the Fire-Bearer* . . . was a satyr play Æschylus wrote to follow his Prometheus trilogy of tragedies. Having read all three plays in the trilogy now and the satyr play, I found this to be a greater cycle than the *Orestia* . . . and for that trilogy we do not have the satyr play. Had I been more prescient . . . I just read *Prometheus Bound* again in our tent during the sandstorm . . . at any rate, even with just that one play at hand I should have been able to foresee" — he smiled quietly — "the argument in *Prometheus luomenos . . . The Unbinding of Prometheus . . .* because it is already anticipated in *Prometheus desmôtes . . . Prometheus Bound . . .* when the chorus affirms to Prometheus that never shall the plans of mortals be able to equal the harmony of order that alone belongs to *Diós . . .* to Zeus . . . to God. Time, the chorus sings in *The Unbinding of Prometheus*, alone will bring justice . . . but not time as measured by creatures of a day . . . but by ever-aging Kronos. Ever-aging time will vindicate *moira . . .* that due portion which belongs to every human being . . . so much, and no more. It does no good to expect any event before the fullness of time . . . time as measured by the immortal and the infinite, not by human beings. Zeus is the third king of the universe . . . after Ouranos . . . ."

"Varuna in the Rig Veda," Marcelina put in. Her blue-gray eyes shone from the excitement of the experiences of that day.

"And then after Ouranos . . . Kronos," Chris resumed, nodding. "But Zeus differs from those who went before because He can suffer, as Prometheus has suffered, and He can learn by experience . . . as Herakles says . . . a descendant in the thirteenth generation

403

from Io and the one who frees Prometheus from his bondage after destroying the mighty eagle, gnawing at the Titan's soul, by means of a single arrow. It is because *Diós* can suffer and learn by experience that He, alone, can save the world. It is injustice and unholiness that bring destruction . . . perhaps not quickly . . . but inevitably.

"In *Prometheus Bound* there seems to be an enmity on the part of Zeus toward mankind, and the play shows graphically the chaining of Prometheus to the crag as punishment for his friendship with mankind. The chorus illustrates the *sympatheia* . . . the fellow-suffering of all creation for the fallen Titan. Yet, this is clarified . . . given its true meaning . . . in *The Unbinding of Prometheus*. Although to the human mind . . . belonging, as it does, to such finite creatures . . . the natural order seems terribly imperfect, it is not something that can really be understood . . . much less measured by standards that have been set up by the very finite and narrow experiences of human beings. Prometheus learns that what Zeus feared about mankind was its terrible arrogance . . . its wanton *hybris* . . . its passion to be more than a creature who lives but a day . . . its passion to fashion its idea of God in its own image and at the same time to become god-like . . . to destroy the harmony of order that Zeus created . . . to exceed on every frontier and on every field of battle the limitations inherent in human beings . . . to use the tools of fire and knowledge that Prometheus had brought them to make themselves into gods who have absolute power and to become immortal themselves through the use of the knowledge that he gave them . . . to make the universe and even God subject to human self-will. Suffering was imposed on Prometheus and thirteen generations allowed to pass so he might learn through experience the evils his gifts made possible among human beings. But Prometheus's suffering is not for naught. It was meant to symbolize to all mankind that God's power is infinite and eternal . . . that all that exists does so because He created it . . . that, although Prometheus's name means foresight . . . his foresight was imperfect . . . just as, when he foresaw in *Prometheus, the Fire-Bringer* he would be punished for thirty thousand years, it did not come to pass . . . his bondage lasted only thirteen generations. In awesome fear before God, Prometheus is released from bondage, while the chorus in its pity for the self-will of Prometheus and for the self-will of mankind brings forward the divine reconciliation that transcends to pure contemplation of the harmony of order that belongs to Zeus. This is the message that

Prometheus, the great benefactor of mankind, brings to human beings at the end of the final play, and human beings express their gratitude by creating the Festival Prometheia to commemorate the enlightenment the Titan has made possible."

It was rare, indeed, for Chris to hold forth so long in conversation with anyone except, perhaps, with Marcelina, and, when he fell silent, long moments passed before Luis Valera spoke.

"And this trilogy is being presented tonight?" he asked finally.

"Yes . . . *Prometheus the Fire-Bringer*, *Prometheus Bound*, *The Unbinding of Prometheus*, and the satyr play, *Prometheus, the Fire-Bearer*," Chris responded, "how Prometheus first stole fire from the gods and his first encounter with Io. I never realized before how important Io is to so much that happens in these plays . . . and how she came, after all her suffering, to experience the purest joy."

"Because of the many parallels between the argument of the one play I have read . . . the only one that has survived on the outside . . . and the Book of Job," Valera suggested, "perhaps there is something to the belief that the author of that book in the Bible became familiar with Æschylus's Prometheus trilogy in Egypt."

"But it doesn't have to have been so, *Tío* Luis," Marcelina objected. "The Sanskrit word for the harmony of the divine order is *rta*. It is stated in the Rig Veda that the Sun is the wheel of *rta* with spokes for the months . . . as it courses across the sky in a year . . . only here . . . where the Sun hides for four months of our year . . . the perception of the *rta* would be otherwise, because the perspective is otherwise . . . here the wheel of the Sun has spokes for spaces that are dark. Human perspective everywhere is always limited. If there are similarities between what is written in the Book of Job and in *The Unbinding of Prometheus*, could it not be that they are the same because . . . in the end . . . the reality of God is the same? The more I think on it, the more I believe that all so-called mythologies only codify what was once seen in the heavens . . . that the great flood in the Bible and in the Rig Veda are so similar . . . not because of what may have once happened on Earth . . . but what was once seen in the heavens by people . . . in Peru by people more ancient than the Incas . . . in the Near East by the ancient Hebrews . . . by people in Persia and India . . . and this experience was codified in myths so that it would be remembered by descendants . . . never to be forgotten . . . since the recording of events for posterity is the only

real way human beings can hope to touch immortality."

"I recall Tenny saying once," Chris interjected, "that the two greatest creations of civilization are cities . . . because their lights shut
out the heavens . . . remove them from our
sight . . . and theology . . . which removes God
from our immediate experience."

"He never used to think like that," Valera
observed. "The time he spent in India certainly changed him."

"Perhaps not enough," Chris mused.

"He's made it this far," said Marcelina,
smiling. "Who's to say now?"

"It's just like a movie, Chris . . . what?" Sir
Wilbur asked, as he let down the skin flap that
hung over the entrance of the common tent.
"It is time for me to make my entrance. I
know where I should stand. I even know what
I must say."

All of them turned toward the Englishman.

"Only what I have to say isn't very dramatic
. . . nor, do I suppose, even very shocking. I've
come to gather my things. I shall be living
henceforth with Nah-Loh-Tah . . . and her
mother . . . Peri-See-Mos . . . whom I've just
had the pleasure of meeting today for the first
time . . . we had tea, no less." Then, noticing
the astonished expressions on Chris's and
Luis's faces, he asked: "Tell me, Chris, do you

408

know the Greek word . . . *othniotymbos . . . ?*"

"I believe I do, Tenny," Chris said, rising to his feet. "It has something to do with being buried in a foreign land, I think."

"It does, indeed," the Englishman agreed. Then he looked at Marcelina, who had not risen, but whose expression seemed at once radiant and knowing. "I suppose, Marcie, that you've known it all along."

"Not so very long, Tenny," she said softly. "But I am happy I gave you that photograph of me as I might look on an Arctic shore. I should never want you to forget me . . . or Chris . . . or *Tío* Luis. We shall never forget you."

"What is all this?" Chris demanded. "Have I missed something?"

"No," said Sir Wilbur, "should you have fallen off the *Sea Queen* when we were sailing to Peru all those many years ago . . . then, you would have missed everything that matters . . . but, as it is . . . as I am sure you very well know . . . you haven't missed what many never find at all."

"Wilbur," interrupted Valera, "what is all this about?"

"Tenny won't be going back with us," Marcelina said, and she touched Luis's right hand, resting at his side close to where she still sat with her legs pulled up beneath her.

409

"But you can't do that," Fallon insisted. "You're forgetting who you are . . . Sir Wilbur Tennington can't just disappear in the Arctic! Remember what happened when Sir John Franklin and his expedition disappeared? Why, search parties were mounted to find him for over a hundred years. Nobody can be told about Makaron Nyesoeessee. I can accept that. Marcie accepts it. Luis and Ramón accept it. None of us will say anything, ever, about Makaron Nyesoeessee. But *you* can't just disappear in the Arctic without leaving a sign and honestly think a search won't be made."

"You know we found the body of that Russian . . . Strehlnikov . . . Nah-Loh-Tah and I found it earlier today in the vault of the great cave. He shot himself."

"Oh!" Marcelina said in surprise, withdrawing her hand from Valera. "I had hoped they would find him alive somehow . . . that he might find some kind of life here. . . ."

"I was afraid the whole time he would kill us both," Valera insisted sharply.

"It was a waste . . . I'll admit," Sir Wilbur said, regarding her gently. "Nah-Loh-Tah said he had told her he had no living relatives any more in the Soviet Union . . . his whole family was killed during the Civil War . . . by the Whites. Lugu was an officer in the Red

Army under Trotsky, but, later, he made clear his preference for the Stalin faction. He was *Komintern*. The plan was to invade Makaron Nyesoeessee from the Arctic Ocean and loot it. That is the reason . . . the only reason he and that other chap had agreed to accompany Nah-Loh-Tah and Teh-Meh-Tayo all the way here. They were kind of an advance guard. They were to locate Makaron Nyesoeessee on the map. The rest would be done by the Red Navy." He looked at them gravely. "But in death, I believe, he shall have a monument . . . buried under another name and in a foreign land . . . at Point Barrow . . . but . . . sometimes . . . like Abdullah Simbel in the Andes . . . when you give your life for something . . . or someone . . . you have no monument at all."

"Tenny," Chris interrupted. He was hurt and disgusted. "You must be mad to think you'd ever get away with it! What if we do take that Russian's body out and bury it, as you say, at Point Barrow . . . a knight of the British Empire buried in an American territory. That's bad enough. But what if, for some reason, the body is ever exhumed? Then what?"

"Then, Chris, there will be just one more mystery of the Arctic to solve . . . ?"

"This is ridiculous. What if you tire of being

411

here, and want to come out and resume your old life? What'll you do, then? Be resurrected?"

"That won't happen."

"How can you be so sure?"

"I have made my one wish, Chris . . . to become a Gandharva . . . to remain forever with the woman I truly love . . . until the thread is finally severed. My God, of all people *you* should understand. From what I know of you . . . both of you . . . you and Marcelina found the same thing . . . out there . . . long ago . . . on the pampas near that ancient city in the mountains of Peru. Would it matter . . . did it matter one jot . . . what it might mean for the course of your lives forever afterward?"

Chris was no longer able to argue.

Marcelina's large blue-gray eyes shone in the light that emanated from the oil lamps in the common tent. She rose, approached the Englishman and, looking up at him, reached out and touched his arm.

Before she could speak, he cut in on her. "I once said it of you, Marcie, but now, by the grace of God . . . finally, I can say it of myself."

Ramón returned to the common tent after Sir Wilbur had already departed with the few things he had been carrying with him in his back pack and his high-powered rifle. The Quechuan had been able to find Koyuk and the two other dogs that had survived the collapse of the ice bridge and the fall into the crevasse. They had been placed in the dog compound with the dogs the Makarons used to pull their sleds when they ventured outside the valley. He had also met one of the musicians, a young woman about his own age, who played what she called a kithara and had even accompanied her to the musical rehearsal that had been held in preparation for the festival performance of the Prometheus plays that night. From the appearance of the sky, the Sun would be visible throughout, although so low on the horizon that only part of it could shine through clefts in the mountains of ice.

Chris had more or less reconciled himself to the Englishman's decision, although he was scarcely as optimistic about it as Marcelina and irritated as if it had been a personal betrayal of trust. Valera had been inclined to accede to this latest turn of events with a shrug of the shoulders. He had had, now that he looked back over the last several weeks, an increasing suspicion that this was no longer the same man he had known for so many years. He was more than before convinced that his time in India had produced some profound emotional alteration in the Englishman. He was no longer the intrepid explorer. In fact, he now seemed content to turn his back on almost everything he had been. But for this, Luis felt, they should be grateful, because no one could be sure, had Sir Wilbur not made this decision, that they would have been allowed to leave Makaron Nyesoeessee on their own recognizance, which now it appeared they would be permitted to do. After all, look at what had happened to the Russians . . . ?

Ramón was of an entirely different mind when he heard about Sir Wilbur's decision. He was openly delighted. Life here was not so very different from what it had been for his people for centuries in the Andes, and there was much to be said for it in preference to civilization to the south.

"There are no radio programs here," Marcelina teased him as she was preparing the evening meal with Chris, "and no movies. No wonderful automobiles, and not even any horses. No electric lights." She looked down at the flat carving stone on which she was kneading a kind of flour that would be used to make biscuits in an iron kettle very like a Dutch oven.

"As eef any of that really matters," Ramón returned, his tone far more serious than hers.

"Don Weelbur told me how he lived when he was een Nepal. Eet wasn't so deeferrent from the way he weel live here. There ees a ver' good family life here . . . and a knowledge that reaches ver' far . . . that ees . . . *intimo* . . . with what matters most . . . your . . . *patria*."

"Yes, but for how long?" Chris asked, as he was gutting a capelin that had been caught and frozen, one of several that had been brought to them earlier by Teh-Meh-Tayo. "Makaron Nyesoeessee will be discovered someday."

"But, *Señor* Chris . . . who weel tell? Eet has been a secret for soch a long time already. To deescover anytheeng beautiful from the past ees only to destroy eet."

Luis had picked up the Rig Veda while this discussion was going on and surprised even himself as he interrupted them. "I came across this passage earlier today . . . 'He lives a chaste student, a servant eagerly serving. He becomes a limb of the gods. In this way, Brhaspati won his wife back again. . . .' "

Neither Chris, for all the times he had read the surviving plays of Æschylus, nor anyone else on the outside had any idea what a public performance had been like when the poet had been alive. Chris knew that, like a modern film producer in Hollywood, Æschylus had

had total control of his productions. He wrote all of the text for the actors and the chorus, some of it recited and some of it sung. The poet wrote all the music for the production, orchestrated it, and guided the musicians, choreographed the dancers, and directed the players in their various rôles. Yet, more than two millennia had come and gone since the Greek colonists had come for the last time to Makaron Nyesoeessee, and surely the performance the Tennington party witnessed that evening of the Prometheus trilogy and the concluding satyr play had been transformed somewhat over the ensuing centuries. Instead of merely flutes, tympanons, and kymbalas, there were a plethora of exotic instruments, including kitharas, lyras, a large syrinx monokalamos, and, according to Marcelina who knew about such things, the music had abandoned the Dorian mode with its total reliance on minor harmonics. Chords, sometimes in major keys, had been added to the melodies, augmenting their resourcefulness as did the expanded instrumentation. One thing Chris did know was that the Greeks, as the Elizabethans, had excluded women from playing any of the female rôles in dramas or satyr plays, substituting male actors in those parts, their gender being conveyed by the masks they would wear. The Makarons still had all of the actors and the chorus wearing masks, but women played female parts, and the choruses were equally balanced with men and women, boys and girls.

A stretcher had been improvised so Chris and Ramón could transport Valera to the performance — which was held in an amphitheater about half the size of the ruins of the one that survives at Epidaurus. About three hundred Makarons attended the performance, Sir Wilbur sitting with Nah-Loh-Tah, her mother, and Teh-Meh-Tayo somewhere in the middle of the theater section, while Chris, Marcelina, Valera, and Ramón sat closer to the right-hand parodos away from the stage building but close to the circle of the orchestra. It came as rather a shock to Chris, who hadn't expected to see any women at all in the performance, that Io's *pas-de-deux* in the *Prometheus purkaios*, the satyr play, was danced by a comely young woman who was completely naked, as was the male dancer who was the satyrical gadfly sent by the jealous Hera. The male dancer had only one article of apparel other than his mask, a huge artificial penis with which once he slapped Io across the buttocks and which once she caressed and took deeply into her mouth during their ritualized dance, but then she appeared to bite it. The gadfly's penis was thrust out before him as he chased her across the orchestra and out through the left-hand parodos at the close of the *pas-de-deux*. When Io had the artificial penis in her mouth, Ramón had glanced briefly at the *señora* to see if she were embarrassed, but he found that she seemed only greatly amused.

"I'd forgotten," Marcelina leaned over and whispered to Chris following the *pas-de-deux*, "but Io came to be worshipped by the Egyptians as the incarnation of Isis. The *crux ansata* was a symbol associated with the worship of Isis. Zeus reached out and touched Io with his hand, and that is how she became pregnant."

Chris nodded but did not answer. He knew from Æschylus that Epaphos, the son of Zeus and Io, meant in Greek "he of the touch." Unlike Marcelina who, on this journey, had read the METAMORPHOSES, he did not know that Ovid had written:

Huic Epaphus magni genitus de semine tandem creditur esse Iovis perque urbes iuncta parenti templa tenet.

What Marcelina also knew, but did not tell Chris, was that Epaphos had been *eudaimon*, that he had found a companion of complementary mind and soul in Phaëton, who was a child of the Sun. Marcelina really didn't have to say anything. When Io appeared very briefly again, at the end of *Prometheus purkaios*, she stood alone and naked in the orchestra, her hair streaming down her back, her arms thrust widely apart to embrace life, her bovine mask replaced by one that gleamed about her beautiful human face canted toward the sky as, miraculously through adroit stage mechanics from the round altar behind her, ten snow birds were released into the sharp, clear air, their wings flapping majestically as they rose into the shafts of light from the Midnight Sun slanting across the stage from so low on the horizon.

Epilogue

The journey back from Makaron Nyeso-eessee was not easy, but it was fraught with fewer difficulties than had accompanied the passage there. Teh-Meh-Tayo, Nah-Loh-Tah, and Apo-See-Kah-Kos, who was both a priest in the temple of Apollo and a man of medicine, accompanied them. The body of Nicolai Strehlnikov had been carefully wrapped in sheets and placed in a wooden coffin transported in one of the dog sleds while Luis Valera was carried in a second along with a limited amount of provisions distributed in both. The three dogs brought originally from Juneau were to be left at the base camp. After removing the coffin from the one sled at the base camp and Luis from the other, the supplies, including the many cans of smoking tobacco Sir Wilbur had cached there, were packed onto the sleds for the return trip. As it turned out, tobacco had been a trade item for centuries between the people of Makaron Nyesoeessee and the Eskimo groups with whom they had limited commerce. This again irritated Chris, at least

420

momentarily, because it was only another indication to him that Sir Wilbur had probably intended to remain behind all the time, should they find the lost colony and should it reunite him with Nah-Loh-Tah, but this mood was quickly dissipated as the time came for parting. Sir Wilbur wanted to be well out of sight before the *Janet* should appear on the horizon.

It was, in fact, difficult for Chris to keep from tears for over the years he had come truly to love this persevering Englishman, and Marcelina did weep openly as she embraced Nah-Loh-Tah and reached up to kiss Sir Wilbur for the last time. Luis shook hands with Sir Wilbur, and the Englishman embraced Ramón. The Quechuan assured him his experience in the Arctic was something that would remain with him all of his life.

The first of their efforts at telling the lie about Sir Wilbur's death came with the arrival of Mark Dworski who was only an hour late from the appointed time. The news was imparted to the scientists and military men at Victoria Island, and so it actually preceded them south before the arrival at Point Barrow. Dr. O'Meara, somewhat to Chris's astonishment, was willing to sign the death certificate and arrange for the burial. It had so happened that he and Sir Wilbur had had a talk about

Nah-Loh-Tah and her homeland following the evening's entertainment when Marcelina had sung "A Song of the Morning." The Englishman had even prepared a hand-written will that had been witnessed by Pierre LeBon and Dr. O'Meara in which his capital estate was to be left in trust with Christopher and Marcelina Fallon as trustees who were to settle any and all accounts remaining behind him out of the principal and see to the dispersal of his lands in England to his two male cousins. As his gift to the Fallons, the physician presented them with his first effort at painting the "Isles of the Blessed" which he had completed in the time they had been away. Chris wanted to make him a payment of some kind, but this the artist refused, saying that some of the happiest hours he had spent since the death of his wife had been the time Marcelina had stayed with him at his home. The physician also did a strange thing. At one point he put a hand under Marcelina's chin, raised her blue-gray eyes to where he could look into them more closely, and then patted her shoulder, and smiled. He was a medical man who always could tell a whole lot about a person from the color of the sclera, the posture of the body, even the lines of the face and the color of the skin. All she knew — then — was that she had not had a period since leaving Point Barrow the first time, and she attributed this to the ardors of the journey and her age of thirty-three years. Even when she became nauseous on the return flight with stops again at Juneau and Seattle before reaching San Francisco, she tended to attribute this to motion sickness, something from which she had never suffered before; but it was too absurd to believe that a woman of her age who had had sexual intercourse but once in almost two months and who, for years, had been unable to become pregnant should so suddenly fly in the face of all that had been. However, when she would break out in perspiration, the ring of the *crux ansata* around her neck and the imprint of the crucifix on her chest would invariably tingle.

Although two of the dogs they had with them were sold again at Juneau, Koyuk was taken home by the Fallons. Ramón Aksut remained an additional month at the *Hacienda* de Ferrar after returning from the Arctic, until, in fact, the *señora*'s pregnancy was medically confirmed. In his fashion he had come to love Marcelina in a distant and unattainable way, as he believed Dante had come to love Beatrice, and, even after he had gone back to Tacho Alto, he remained in contact with the Fallons. Once he married, he introduced them to his Quechuan wife, whose baptismal name was María.

Luis Valera had his broken tibia attended further by Dr. O'Meara at Point Barrow before making the return flight to San Francisco. He retired from his academic duties in 1941 and was honored by his colleagues for his significant contributions to anthropology during his career.

Wiley Post was the first pilot to fly solo in an airplane around the globe. He had completed the trip in eight days. In the summer of 1935 Will Rogers with Wiley Post as the pilot announced he intended to fly to the Arctic. Rogers kept their ultimate destination a secret, although many believed his goal was the North Geographical Pole. Mae Post, Wiley's wife, wanted to accompany them, but Will Rogers told her: "Alaska is no place for a lady." The two men were alone in Post's airplane when it crashed fifteen miles outside of Point Barrow on August 15, 1935. Both were killed instantly upon impact. A simple funeral service was held for Will Rogers at the Wee Kirk O' the Heather on August 22nd and only a very few friends were invited to join the immediate family. Lincoln Perry, better known as Stepin Fetchit, was one of those very few friends.

Carole Lombard remained close friends with Marcelina even after her marriage to

Clark Gable in 1939. Born Jane Peters in Fort Wayne, Indiana, Carole Lombard died when the plane she was aboard crashed on Table Rock Mountain, near Las Vegas, Nevada, on January 16, 1942. She had been on a War Bond drive for the Hollywood Victory Committee. Gypsy King died in 1952. Henry King married again in 1959 and bought and lived in the North Hollywood home that had formerly belonged to aviatrix Amelia Earhart, who had been a friend of his as well as of Will and Betty Rogers.

During the Second World War, Chris Fallon served in the OSS, because by that time he was considered too old for combat duty and, besides, he was the father of two children. Marcelina donated her services to the American Red Cross and financially supported this organization throughout the war. It was in 1943 that Chris Fallon's father died on the family ranch in Skull Valley, Arizona. Chris's mother died near the time the war ended in the Far East. In 1946 Chris and Marcelina moved from the San Fernando Valley to live in Peru on the de Ferrar estate so the twins could be near Thomas and Isabella O'Day during their grandparents' final years. Occasionally Ramón and María Aksut would come to visit the Fallons once they were living in Peru. It was during one of these visits, in 1948, that the Aksuts encountered a strange couple also on a visit to the Fallons who had come from the Far North and who had with them a daughter of thirteen. Santiago Cruz and Rosa Caldero, who were married in 1938 in California, accompanied the Fallon family in the move to Peru. Chris Fallon found a new career after the Hollywood years writing action-adventure fiction that proved very popular among readers throughout the world, but especially in Italy and Greece, which pleased Marcelina because, as she said, his stories owed so much to those who had once lived in those places. If Marcelina had once been intimidated by sound microphones in motion pictures, and never was able to speak comfortably in front of any gathering of people, she did find her true voice in the written word and came to transcribe and compile several volumes of native American tales and legends from both North and South America.

In 1963 oil was discovered near Point Barrow. Some of the Eskimo population became among the wealthiest people in the world. A fully electrified city came to be there, with an annual budget funded by property taxes of more than $100,000,000.00. Over $20,000 a year was spent annually per student for education and related community activities. Yet, with all this wealth, there were also numerous families living below the poverty level, unable to afford the extremely high cost of living, and each spring, when the snow would melt, the casual litter everywhere was a source of civic embarrassment.

On April 30, 1934, shortly after Marcelina had celebrated her thirty-third birthday and only days before Sir Wilbur Tennington's arrival at the San Fernando railroad station, Ida Rubinstein's ballet company presented at the Paris Opera the first performance of Igor Stravinsky's opera-oratorio, *Perséphone*, with the text by André Gide. This work was not recorded by the composer until January 14, 1957 with the New York Philharmonic and Vera Zorina in the title rôle of Perséphone. Chris bought a copy of this recording, issued on the Columbia Masterworks label, while he and Marcelina were on a trip to the United States a year later. When they listened to it, the performance of this music sent shivers up their spines, for never had any composer in their purview come so close to capturing in words and music the poetic dramas by Æschylus they had witnessed in Makaron Nyesoeessee. In particular were they struck by two utterances of Perséphone: *"Qui m'apelle?"* — which the pinioned Prometheus also calls out in response to Herakles upon his arrival on that untrodden ground — and — *"Je t'écoute de tout mon cœur, chant du premier matin du monde."* — which words Prometheus speaks to the chorus of the daughters of Okeanides as they raise their voices in song upon his release from bondage. Of course, the miming could not be seen, but Marcelina was certain that, whether or not Stravinsky had intended it, in this work he had mastered enharmonic diesis, or the difference between progression by three major thirds rather than by the octaves of the chromatic scale. Whatever the case, the sound was diatonic in the same way as had been the modified music composed by Æschylus, and each number in *Perséphone* was given its own, and different, instrumentation, with the full orchestra being used only twice, as had also been the case in the performance of the Prometheus cycle.

Chris and Marcelina were actually buried beside each other in a mausoleum in the family cemetery plot on the de Ferrar estate where also were buried nearby Marcelina's grandparents, her father and her mother, and her uncle, Don Esteban de Ferrar. As it happened, Chris Fallon died only a few days before his beloved. Marcelina told the twins, who were with her at the end on April 24, 1990, which happened also to be her eighty-ninth birthday, that, although she had en-

428

tered life somewhat behind their father, it was not really such a bad thing for them to have finished it so close together.

About the Author

T. V. Olsen was born in Rhinelander, Wisconsin, where he continued to live all his life. "My childhood was unremarkable except for an inordinate preoccupation with Zane Grey and Edgar Rice Burroughs." Having read such accomplished Western authors as Les Savage, Jr., Luke Short, and Elmore Leonard, he began writing Western fiction and went on to become one of the most widely respected and widely read authors of Western fiction in the second half of the 20th Century. Even early works such as HIGH LAWLESS (1960) and GUNSWIFT (1960) are brilliantly plotted with involving characters and situations and a simple, powerfully evocative style. Olsen went on to write such important Western novels as THE STALKING MOON (1965) and ARROW IN THE SUN (1969) which were made into classic Western films as well, the former starring Gregory Peck and the latter under the title SOLDIER BLUE (Avco-Embassy, 1970), starring Candice Bergen. His novels have been translated into numerous European languages, including French, Spanish, Italian, Swedish, Serbo-Croatian, and Czech. His novel, THE GOLDEN CHANCE (1992), won the Spur Award from the Western Writers of America in 1993, and several of the characters in this story return in DEADLY PURSUIT (Five Star Westerns, 1995). His work will surely abide. Any Olsen novel is guaranteed to combine drama and memorable characters with an authentic background of historical fact and an accurate portrayal of the terrain.

The employees of Thorndike Press hope you have enjoyed this Large Print book. All our Large Print titles are designed for easy reading, and all our books are made to last. Other Thorndike Press Large Print books are available at your library, through selected bookstores, or directly from the publishers.

For more information about titles, please call:

(800) 223-1244
   or
(800) 223-6121

To share your comments, please write:

Publisher
Thorndike Press
P.O. Box 159
Thorndike, Maine 04986